LEVINAS AND THE ANCIENTS

LEVINAS AND THE ANCIENTS

Edited by Brian Schroeder and Silvia Benso

WITH A FOREWORD BY ADRIAAN PEPERZAK

INDIANA UNIVERSITY PRESS
BLOOMINGTON AND INDIANAPOLIS

This book is a publication of

Indiana University Press
601 North Morton Street
Bloomington, IN 47404-3797 USA

http://iupress.indiana.edu

Telephone orders   800-842-6796
Fax orders   812-855-7931
Orders by e-mail   iuporder@indiana.edu

© 2008 by Indiana University Press
All rights reserved

The paper used in this publication meets the minimum
requirements of American National Standard for Information Sciences—Permanence of Paper for Printed Library Materials, ANSI Z39.48-1984.

Manufactured in the United States of America

Library of Congress Cataloging-in-Publication Data

Levinas and the ancients / edited by Brian Schroeder
and Silvia Benso ; with a foreword by Adriaan Peperzak.
    p. cm. — (Studies in continental thought)
    Includes bibliographical references and index.
    ISBN 978-0-253-35180-7 (cloth : alk. paper) —
ISBN 978-0-253-21998-5 (pbk. : alk. paper) 1. Lévinas, Emmanuel. 2. Philosophy, Ancient—Influence.
I. Schroeder, Brian. II. Benso, Silvia.
    B2430.L484L475 2008
    194—dc22
                                    2008000606
        1 2 3 4 5 13 12 11 10 09 08

For Brad Schroeder, Julie Farinha,
Umberto Benso, Ulisse, Clio,
and all those we love
who have become a
part of the ages

The time to depart has come,
and we go our separate ways—I to die,
and you to live. Which is better
the god only knows.

—Socrates

CONTENTS

FOREWORD BY ADRIAAN PEPERZAK • xi

ACKNOWLEDGMENTS • xiii

ABBREVIATIONS OF WORKS BY EMMANUEL LEVINAS • xv

TO RETURN IN A NEW WAY:
INTRODUCTION • 1
Silvia Benso and Brian Schroeder

1. THE BREATHING OF THE AIR:
   PRESOCRATIC ECHOES IN LEVINAS • 9
   Silvia Benso

2. THE ETERNAL AND THE NEW: SOCRATES AND LEVINAS
   ON DESIRE AND NEED • 24
   Deborah Achtenberg

3. LEVINAS QUESTIONING PLATO ON
   EROS AND MAIEUTICS • 40
   Francisco J. Gonzalez

4. GETTING UNDER THE SKIN:
   PLATONIC MYTHS IN LEVINAS • 62
   Tanja Stähler

5. LENDING ASSISTANCE ALWAYS TO ITSELF:
   LEVINAS' INFINITE CONVERSATION
   WITH PLATONIC DIALOGUE • 79
   Michael Naas

6. ETHICS AS FIRST PHILOSOPHY:
   ARISTOTELIAN REFLECTIONS ON INTELLIGENCE,
   SENSIBILITY, AND TRANSCENDENCE • 103
   Claudia Baracchi

Contents

7. ARISTOTLE AND LEVINAS ON
   WAR AND PEACE: THE ONE
   AGAINST THE OTHER • 127
   Catriona Hanley

8. STOIC ETHICS AND TOTALITY IN
   LIGHT OF LEVINASIAN ALTERITY • 144
   Julie Piering

9. OF A NON-SAYING THAT SAYS
   NOTHING: LEVINAS AND PYRRHONISM • 165
   Pierre Lamarche

10. THE TIME AND LANGUAGE OF
    MESSIANISM: LEVINAS AND SAINT PAUL • 178
    Bettina Bergo

11. PROXIMITY IN DISTANCE:
    LEVINAS AND PLOTINUS • 196
    John Izzi

12. A TRACE OF THE ETERNAL RETURN?
    LEVINAS AND NEOPLATONISM • 210
    Brian Schroeder

13. ETHICS AND PREDESTINATION
    IN AUGUSTINE AND LEVINAS • 230
    Thomas J. J. Altizer

LIST OF CONTRIBUTORS • 243
INDEX • 247

"To show that the first signification emerges in morality—in the quasi-abstract epiphany of the destitute face stripped of all qualities—an absolute that absolves itself from all cultures—is to restrict the understanding of the reality on the basis of history; it is a return to Platonism."[1] Thus concludes the summary of *Totality and Infinity,* which Emmanuel Levinas, after its defense on June 6, 1961, handed to the University of Paris.

It is clear that his thesis about the independence of ethics vis-à-vis history and all cultures—a thesis carefully developed in his "Meaning and Sense"—appeals to the Platonism of all those who, like Plato, Aristotle, and Plotinus, look up to "the Good beyond essence" and the Beloved that moves all persons, events, arts, and things "by being loved." As Augustinus, Dionysus, Scotus, Bonaventura, Cusanus, Descartes, Hegel, Blondel, Bergson, and Levinas himself show, it is also the Platonism that, in many crises of the Western tradition, has played a leading role in various renaissances.

Greece is more, however—for example, speculation about the elements, all-encompassing cosmologies, gigantic battles about being, movement and difference, geometry and exemplary art, enchanting myths and sobering enlightenment, political experiments and theories—all of which have marked the thoughts and cultures of the next millennia. Even if the all-too-enthusiastic modes of humanism have faded, gratitude to Greece continues to accompany our search for new beginnings, despite the illusions and cruelties that taint that heritage. Therefore, all lovers of Levinas' philosophy who are interested in the Ancients, and all lovers of the latter who are interested in Levinas, will be grateful for this collection of studies on various links and contrasts that connect their works from a variety of perspectives.

Thanks to the initiative of Silvia Benso and Brian Schroeder, the authors of this volume not only explore the easily forgotten dimension of Levinas' debt to some early sources of European philosophy but also focus on the ways he has used these sources to show their relevance for us. Like most creative thinkers, Levinas does not remember any past without transforming it into a constitutive element of contemporary thought. Consequently, even if, from an archaeological perspective, one might disagree with some of his interpretations, these provide us with new possibilities of memory and inspiration.

Adriaan Peperzak

Renewed attention to the "Greek" elements in Levinas' thought might even assist us in a fruitful re-reading of his other, still older source and background. Can the "Greek" logos of philosophy also illuminate the collection of texts and commentaries that we call "the Bible"? Those—or some of those—who, after losing their first naïve understanding, continue to seek a more sophisticated but non-superstitious access to this other source, might discover that the Levinasian style of integration—more fascinated by the Good than by *phusis*, autonomy, or ousiology—favors their search for a lucid, neither arrogant nor ashamed, kind of enlightenment.

Adriaan Peperzak

Note

1. Translated by Adriaan Theodoor Peperzak and cited in his *Platonic Transformations: With and after Hegel, Heidegger, and Levinas* (Lanham, Md.: Rowman & Littlefield, 1997), 121.

Acknowledgments

We would like to thank, first of all, the contributors to this volume, without whose time, patience, and scholarship this work would not have come to be. We are grateful also to John Sallis for including this work in his series Studies in Continental Thought, and especially to Dee Mortensen, Laura MacLeod, Marvin Keenan, and the staff at Indiana University Press.

Abbreviations of Works by Emmanuel Levinas

(Unless stated otherwise in the endnotes, all references to Levinas' work refer to this list. All citations refer to the latest published edition.)

AT   *Alterity and Transcendence.* Translated by Michael B. Smith. New York: Columbia University Press, 1999.

BPW   *Emmanuel Levinas: Basic Philosophical Writings.* Edited by Adriaan Peperzak, Simon Critchley and Robert Bernasconi. Bloomington: Indiana University Press, 1996.

BV   *Beyond the Verse.* Translated by Gary D. Mole. Bloomington: Indiana University Press, 1994.

CPP   *Collected Philosophical Papers.* Translated by Alphonso Lingis. The Hague: Martinus Nijhoff, 1987.

DEH   *Discovering Existence with Husserl.* Translated and edited by Richard A. Cohen and Michael B. Smith. Evanston: Northwestern University Press, 1998.

DF   *Difficult Freedom: Essays on Judaism.* Translated by Séan Hand. Baltimore, Md.: Johns Hopkins University Press, 1990.

EE   *Existence and Existents.* Translated by Alphonso Lingis. Pittsburgh: Duquesne University Press, 2001 (originally published with Dordrecht: Kluwer, 1978, and reprinted with minor corrections in 1988).

EI   *Ethics and Infinity: Conversations with Philippe Nemo.* Translated by Richard A. Cohen. Pittsburgh: Duquesne University Press, 1985.

EN   *Entre Nous: On Thinking-of -the-Other.* Translated by Michael B. Smith and Barbara Harshav. New York: Columbia University Press, 1998.

GCM   *Of God Who Comes to Mind.* Translated by Bettina Bergo. Stanford, Calif.: Stanford University Press, 1998.

GDT   *God, Death, and Time.* Translated by Bettina Bergo. Stanford, Calif.: Stanford University Press, 2001.

HO   *Humanism and the Other.* Translated by Nidra Poller. Introduction by Richard A. Cohen. Champaign: University of Illinois Press, 2003.

IRB	*Is It Righteous to Be? Interviews with Emmanuel Levinas.* Edited by Jill Robbins. Stanford, Calif.: Stanford University Press, 2001.
LR	*The Levinas Reader.* Edited by Séan Hand. Oxford: Basil Blackwell, 1989.
NTR	*Nine Talmudic Readings.* Translated by Richard A. Cohen. Pittsburgh: Duquesne University Press, 1999; also translated by Annette Aronowicz. Bloomington: Indiana University Press, 1990.
OB	*Otherwise than Being or Beyond Essence.* Translated by Alphonso Lingis. The Hague: Martinus Nijhoff, 1981.
OE	*On Escape.* Translated by Bettina Bergo. Introduced and annotated by Jacques Rolland. Stanford, Calif.: Stanford University Press, 2003.
OS	*Outside the Subject.* Translated by Michael B. Smith. Stanford, Calif.: Stanford University Press, 1993.
PN	*Proper Names.* Translated by Michael B. Smith. Stanford, Calif.: Stanford University Press, 1996.
RH	"Reflections on the Philosophy of Hitlerism." Translated by Seán Hand. *Critical Inquiry* 17 (1990): 63–71.
TE	"Transcendence and Evil." Translated by Michael Kigel. In Philippe Nemo and Emmanuel Levinas, *Job and the Excess of Evil.* Pittsburgh: Duquesne University Press, 1998.
TI	*Totality and Infinity.* Translated by Alphonso Lingis. Pittsburgh: Duquesne University Press, 1969.
TIH	*The Theory of Intuition in Husserl's Phenomenology,* 2nd ed. Translated by André Orianne. Evanston, Ill.: Northwestern University Press, 1995.
TN	*In the Time of the Nations.* Translated by Michael B. Smith. Bloomington: Indiana University Press, 1994.
TO	*Time and the Other.* Translated by Richard A. Cohen. Pittsburgh: Duquesne University Press, 1987.
TrO	"The Trace of the Other." Translated by Alphonso Lingis. In *Deconstruction in Context.* Edited by Mark C. Taylor. Chicago: University of Chicago Press, 1986.
NTR	*New Talmudic Readings.* Translated by Richard A. Cohen. Pittsburgh: Duquesne University Press, 1999.
UH	*Unforeseen History.* Translated by Nidra Poller. Introduction by Richard A. Cohen. Champaign: University of Illinois Press, 2004.

LEVINAS AND THE ANCIENTS

TO RETURN IN A NEW WAY:

INTRODUCTION

Silvia Benso and Brian Schroeder

To the question "What is Europe?" Levinas replies, "It is the Bible and the Greeks" (*TN* 133; cf. *IRB* 182–83); however, he qualifies, "it is . . . the Bible which renders the Greeks necessary" (*IRB* 64), thereby establishing, if not the primacy, then at least the primordiality of the biblical experience. Nevertheless, he ardently claims, "I'm all for the Greek tradition!" only to clarify immediately that such a tradition "is not at the beginning of things, but everything must be able to be 'translated' into Greek" (*IRB* 224). And echoing this sentiment, he emphatically remarks, "Oh, welcome messages from Greece! To become educated among the Greeks, to learn their language and their wisdom. Greek is Europe's inevitable discourse, recommended by the Bible itself " (*TN* 134).

The question of the relation between the Greek and the Jewish (or at least Judeo-Christian) traditions within Europe—and by extension within the Western philosophical tradition as a whole, and by intension within Levinas' own thinking—is, by Levinas' own admission, "the great problem." "Is it," he asks quasi-rhetorically, "simply the convergence of two influences that constitute the European?" Though he does not provide a definitive answer to the question, he suggests that the notion of convergence is not sufficient, either phenomenologically or programmatically, that is, either descriptively or prescriptively, to define such an identity (*IRB* 64). Indeed, with respect to his own thought, he resists the idea that his philosophy might have "aimed explicitly to 'harmonize' or 'conciliate' both traditions" (*EI* 22). "Were they supposed to harmonize?" he asks (*EI* 23), thus emphasizing that it is not a matter of conciliation any more than of convergence.

1

Silvia Benso and Brian Schroeder

The two traditions are not, Levinas notices, "historical wholes" (*IRB* 182); that is, they are not self-contained, exclusive, and exclusionary totalities. At various places in his work, he identifies their specific contributions or "great directions" (*IRB* 182). At times, the Greek contribution seems to be equated with a formal structure of speech and reasoning capable of elevating the religious contents that sustain Judaism from the level of the idiosyncratic, localistic, nationalistic discourse (from *muthos*) to the "horizon of the universal" (to *logos*), as when Levinas writes, in an allusion to Heidegger, that "[Greek] is a language without prejudice, a way of speaking that bites reality without leaving any marks. . . . It is a language that is at once a metalanguage, careful and able to protect what is said from the structures of the language itself, which might lay claim to being the very categories of meaning" (*TN* 135). In this sense, Greek is the ability "of unsaying, of resaying" for which Penelope, a great Greek woman figure, stands as a model. Greek, in other words, is the formal ability to perform the ethical gesture of language as expressed in the closing pages of *Otherwise than Being*. At other times, however, Greek as metalanguage gives way to Greek as language, as "vocabulary, grammar and wisdom with which it originated in Hellas" (*TN* 134). The specific contributions of the two traditions take up, then, a more content-related character; they refer to thematic nodes such as, on the one hand, the biblical affirmation of "a primordial responsibility 'for the other,' such that, in an apparent paradox, concern for another may precede concern for oneself" (*IRB* 182), and on the other hand, the Greek "reflection upon the question of harmony and the order of being . . . the dimension of the State, justice, and the political" (*IRB* 183). In this sense, the specific contributions of the two traditions have to do, one could argue, with the opposition between ethics and politics, mercy (or charity) and justice, election and equality, particularity and universality, transcendence and immanence, infinity and totality, religion and philosophy, metaphysics and ontology, and, within Levinas' own thinking, confessional writings and philosophical essays.

Since the relation between the two traditions is neither convergence nor conciliation, a binary logic might be seen at work in these pairs of alleged opposites, which would then force the Levinasian reader/interpreter to decide for one or the other of the alternatives, with Levinas seen as siding mainly for the biblical horn of the dilemma, insofar as his thinking is an attempt to realize "ethics as first philosophy" in the Greek tradition. The Greek horn, on the other hand, would become "the problem" within Levinas' own thinking—the problem(s) of politics, being, immanence, history, memory, and so on—with Levinas himself seen as trying to retrieve and rehabilitate some "great moments," which remain exceptional, however, within a philosophical tradition that is in and of itself corrupt and destined to failure (that is, at least until Levinas) as far as metaphysical ethics is concerned. As Heidegger invokes a return to a Presocratic, premetaphysical understanding of being—another beginning—so does Levinas call, in this line of interpretation, for

2

a prephilosophical, that is, "religious" experience of reality. Such a straightforward opposition, however, is challenged by Levinas himself. Starting with the title of his first major work, *Totality and Infinity*, he compels us to rethink the nature of such an envisioned opposition, of such an "and," which, giving in to a great temptation, lends itself to being too readily misread and mistaken for an "or."

By Levinas' own admission, the two traditions do not harmonize or reconcile: is there then an opposition between them? And, if so, what is the nature of such an opposition? Is it within the language of relation—of which opposition (as well as conciliation) is a modality—that Levinas' discourse in fact moves? Relation is, for Levinas, a category through which representation synchronizes terms and places them in simultaneity within a system. But his discourse escapes such simultaneity insofar as it moves within the language of asynchrony, asymmetry, and diachrony. Its logical category is therefore not relation but *proximity*, as repeatedly indicated, especially in *Otherwise than Being*.

The category of proximity is ethical before being ontological or epistemological. It allows for a "relationship" (for lack of a better word) in which terms neither exclude nor reconcile each other because they are not part of the same synchronic system; rather, in its incommensurability, each term opens itself up to the other term through the other. This other is, however, an other who is (with a beautiful expression from the phenomenological tradition) "always already" beyond, always already passed, always already a trace, a face to which I can only say "after you" because it is always already before me, ahead of me, more essential than me. Proximity is therefore the I that nourishes itself by giving being—that is, consistency—to the other first; it is a hand that takes the bread away from the mouth to give it to the other; it is a being-for-oneself through being-for-the-other. It is language that says only by unsaying and resaying its own said, by undoing what has just been done.

It is not within the scope of this brief introduction to dwell on the notion of proximity, either in terms of its nature or in terms of its possible configuration as far as the proximity between the Jewish and Greek traditions goes. What is important is to reassert the fundamental significance of the notion of proximity so as to open up the path for a more sympathetic reading of the role played by the Greek philosophical tradition within Levinas' thinking. Such a reading is aimed at retracing, precisely in that very Greek tradition, themes that Levinas might initially seem to derive from the Jewish inspiration but that are not absent (and not as exceptional moments) from the Greek tradition either, if we simply bother to look in such a tradition with a "listening eye" (*OB* 30), that is, with an eye that has been awakened by and to the presence of a possibly Jewish other.

It is in the spirit of such proximity and with such a "listening eye" that the contributors to this volume have written on possible proximities (or distances) between Levinas and the ancient tradition, engaging epochs ranging chronologically from the Presocratic, classical Greek, and Hellenistic, to the late Roman and early Christian, and considering Levinas' thought in relation to that of such thinkers as Anaximenes, Heraclitus, Socrates, Plato, Aristotle, Sextus Empiricus, Epictetus, Seneca, Marcus Aurelius, Paul, Plotinus, and Augustine.

The collection opens with an essay that puts Levinas' thought in direct proximity with the origins of Greek philosophy. In "The Breathing of the Air: Presocratic Echoes in Levinas," Silvia Benso inquires whether, and to what extent, Levinas' thought is nourished by that of the Presocratics, and more specifically by the presence of a rather minor Presocratic thinker, Anaximenes, and his "theory" that air is the *arche* of all things. Benso explores how, within that psychism that Western philosophy has understood mainly as a spiritual and immaterial principle, Levinas retrieves the naturalistic, material element and thus situates himself, with Anaximenes, before—or rather, beyond—the split between materiality and immateriality, body and soul, nature and spirit that Anaximenes himself has contributed while remaining at its threshold.

A certain proximity between, or rather complementarity, of Levinas and another ancient thinker, Plato, is retraced in Deborah Achtenberg's essay, "The Eternal and the New: Socrates and Levinas on Desire and Need." Achtenberg argues for the lack of any fundamental difference in Plato's and Levinas' basic conceptions of desire insofar as they both invoke need in order to highlight human vulnerability or responsiveness. Levinas' and Plato's distinct understanding of the concept of the good beyond being, however, effects a difference in the sense that Socrates' construal of desire centers on responsiveness to form, while Levinas' focuses on an open responsiveness, a responsiveness beyond or before form. Achtenberg concludes by arguing for the need for each type of responsiveness in ethics, since each delineates a fundamental type of vulnerability.

Plato's conception of eros also constitutes the central theme of "Levinas Questioning Plato on Eros and Maieutics" by Francisco J. Gonzalez. Levinas' emphatic self-distancing from Plato is to be attributed to the Platonic conception of eros as a lack to be satisfied, of the object of eros as what once belonged to us, and of learning as the recollecting of what is already within us (maieutics). Yet, Gonzalez argues, this opposition is not as clear as it might at first appear. While both Levinas and Plato give primacy to ethics, it is possible to find in Plato a conception of metaphysical desire that in identifying it neither with a lack to be satisfied nor with absolute exteriority, neither with the *jouissance* of a self-sufficing separate being nor with a self-emptying in the absolutely Other, brings into question the Levinasian opposition between ethics and ontology.

Plato's figure is also at the center of Tanja Stähler's "Getting under the Skin: Platonic Myths in Levinas." For Stähler, Platonic myths play a significant role in

Levinas' work, with the myth of Gyges being the most conspicuous in *Totality and Infinity*, and the myth of the last judgment at the end of the *Gorgias* playing the more important role in *Otherwise than Being*. Both stories are based on the ambiguous relationship between visibility and invisibility, exposure and secrecy, according to Stähler. Tracing the connections between Levinas and Plato with regard to the two myths, Stähler illuminates several main concepts in Levinas' philosophy—interiority, exteriority, and infinite responsibility—through his reading of the two myths, and in turn sheds new light on these myths in Plato. Levinas brings those two myths back into our world, the world of the living, Stähler contends, since it is not after our death that we encounter the Other; rather, the very condition of our existence is the proximity of naked soul to naked soul.

The last essay to put Levinas' philosophy in proximity with Plato's thought is Michael Naas' "Lending Assistance Always to Itself: Levinas' Infinite Conversation with Platonic Dialogue." Naas examines Levinas' reading of Plato from the 1940s through the 1970s in order to account for what appears to be an unexpected rehabilitation of Platonic dialogues. In *Totality and Infinity* this rehabilitation goes so far as to reinterpret the Platonic critique of writing in the *Phaedrus* as an affirmation of the face-to-face relation in spoken dialogue—an interpretation that would appear to be diametrically opposed to those of Maurice Blanchot and Jacques Derrida. But, Naas asks, how is Levinas able to affirm Plato's emphasis on the spoken word without falling into what Blanchot calls Plato's "humanism" and Derrida his "phonocentrism"? Naas' position is that this question has profound implications for Levinas' reading of Plato but also for his understanding of speech and writing more generally and the "infinite conversation" he will or will not have had with Blanchot and Derrida.

A different philosophical figure, Aristotle, is introduced onto this scene of proximities by Claudia Baracchi's essay, "Ethics as First Philosophy: Aristotelian Reflections on Intelligence, Sensibility, and Transcendence." Levinas' key contribution to contemporary debates, his understanding of ethics as first philosophy, calls for a critique of the priority traditionally accorded to rational-scientific knowledge. In this perspective, theoretical knowledge is exposed as emerging out of practical involvements and, more broadly, out of the involvement in sensibility and phenomenality. By reference to the ethical treatises and the *Politics*, but also to other texts of the Aristotelian corpus (most notably, the *Metaphysics* and the treatises of the *Organon*), Baracchi proposes that in Aristotle theoretical knowledge is acknowledged as integrally involved in becoming, sensibility, experience—and hence, in action. Ultimately, encountering phenomena, the world, or nature in the broadest sense is always a matter of *ethos*. As Baracchi concludes, Levinas' apparently "modern" intimation is to be found at the heart of Greek thought.

Although on an entirely different topic, Catriona Hanley's "Aristotle and Levinas on War and Peace: The One against the Other" continues the line of proximity between Levinas and Aristotle initiated by the previous essay. In the *Politics,* Hanley observes, Aristotle argues that war must be only for the sake of peace. Peace, indeed, is the highest end of the state exactly because it makes possible the highest rational end of the human individual—contemplation. This teleological notion of peace seems at odds with Levinas' conception, Hanley contends, since for him, peace as non-war is itself a form of war: it is politics. True peace, in his view, precedes the political; it is eschatological. Hanley's essay shows how Levinas' call to justice through the recognition of a third, his way of reconciling the pre-political peace with the hope for peace among nations, relies on an Aristotelian notion of individual self-development.

The theme of the political constitutes the core of the following essay, which poses Levinas in proximity with the tradition of the Stoics. In "Stoic Ethics and Totality in Light of Levinasian Alterity," Julie Piering explores the way Levinas' ethical conception of totality would, at first glance, seem to offer a critique of the Stoic system. Nevertheless, the specifics of the Stoic system share important insights with Levinas. As Piering argues, the Stoic adoption of cosmopolitanism coincides beautifully with the opening insight of *Totality and Infinity,* that is, that morality is opposed to politics. The Stoics help to redefine the political by making sense of it via the *kosmos* rather than the *polis.* Moreover, the Stoics invented the conception of duty, and this notion looks much more Levinasian in its absolute character than Kantian. Thus, Piering concludes, in the end Levinas provides a foil for understanding both the compelling and problematic aspects of Stoicism.

A post-Socratic tradition parallel to Stoicism, namely, Skepticism in its Pyrrhonian variance, is taken up by Pierre Lamarche in "Of a Non-Saying That Says Nothing: Levinas and Pyrrhonism." In *Otherwise than Being,* Levinas argues that skepticism periodically returns in spite of its refutation as the dissatisfied, though "legitimate," child of philosophy. Lamarche focuses on the ways in which distinguishing between Pyrrhonian and modern skepticism, and particularly between skepticism as a therapy and way of life and skepticism as an epistemological position, may trouble Levinas' gesture toward skepticism, and our contemporary evaluation of the meaning of that gesture within Levinas' broader project.

An explicitly religious proximity is broached in Bettina Bergo's "The Time and Language of Messianism: Levinas and Saint Paul." After examining Levinas' "messianic texts," which define the two almost contradictory meanings Levinas adduces for legitimate messianism, Bergo examines which of the two Levinas takes up in his philosophical writing. Levinas' rethinking of the meaning and function of language and temporality in *Otherwise than Being or Beyond Essence* invites comparison with the letters of Saint Paul. Bergo follows the central arguments of

Giorgio Agamben's *The Time that Remains* and then shows thematic similarities between Levinas' conception of the time of responsibility (or "substitution") and the messianic "time within a time" that Agamben adumbrates, reading Paul's Letter to the Romans. Bergo concludes by turning to other definitions of messianism, notably as found in the work of Gershom Scholem and Walter Benjamin.

Levinas' relationship to Plotinus' thought is taken up by John Izzi in "Proximity in Distance: Levinas and Plotinus." Izzi's goal is to show that a close reading of the philosophies of Plotinus and Levinas helps us to understand how the same has a relation with the other that preserves both the identity of the same and the alterity of the other, where the other refers to what Vladimir Jankélévitch calls "the absolutely other, always-wholly-other." Izzi concludes by showing that the same's relation to the other consists of proximity in distance.

Levinas also has a decidedly ambiguous relation to Neoplatonist thought, observes Brian Schroeder in "A Trace of the Eternal Return? Levinas and Neoplatonism," retaining some of its fundamental insights while clearly rejecting its gnostic overtones and its totalizing, idealist objectives. A principal concern of Schroeder's is whether Levinas' Jewish-based philosophy truly marks a significant departure from the idealism of Plotinus and later variants of Neoplatonist theology, expressions of the very ontology that he claims is implicated in the originary violence of absolutely conceptualizing, that is to say, of totalizing the other. Schroeder asks whether, although taking recourse to a preoriginary difference that ostensibly frees thought itself from the "imperialism of the same," Levinas' thinking nevertheless signals a return to a primordial transcendent plenum, one that is barely distinguishable in the end from the primordial myth of the eternal return, the very myth that captivated preexilic Israel along with the rest of the ancient world, ultimately finding a full philosophical expression in Plotinian metaphysics and a theological one in orthodox Christianity and Islam. Schroeder addresses this question by focusing on three main points wherein Levinas and Plotinus are brought into proximity: the transcendence of the One, the status of the trace, and the problem of evil.

The volume concludes with Thomas J. J. Altizer's essay, "Ethics and Predestination in Augustine and Levinas," which seeks an understanding of Levinas' pre-primordial ethics by way of contrasting it with its polar counterpart in the subject-centered theological ethics of Augustine. Altizer argues that Levinas' most ultimate conflict is with the Augustinian tradition. The Levinas who refuses an actual pronunciation of the Name of God is, for Altizer, the Levinas who refuses every trace of the death of God; such a refusal is only possible by way of a dissolution or reversal of the subject of consciousness, a reversal opening the way to that absolutely pre-primordial whose domain is our only possibility of a real and actual ethics; yet this is a domain truly paralleling Augustine's absolute pre-destination.

The philosophical figures as well as the scholars brought into proximity in this volume come from various approaches and traditions. A number of the contributors would, in fact, not identify themselves as specialists in the philosophy of Levinas, whereas others would not qualify themselves as strictly ancient philosophy scholars. Indeed, the goal of the volume is neither to assess specifically the issue of Levinas' relation to ancient themes or figures nor to consider his reading of ancient thought in the light of past or present scholarship such as one finds in the recent work of Jean-Marc Narbonne, Jean-François Mattéi, Stella Sanford, and Christopher Long. Levinas' connection to certain central themes such as Plato's idea of the Good beyond being and Aristotle's concepts of *eudaimonia* and *sophrosune* has been taken up previously in a number of books and articles as well as in this volume, and while they are of paramount importance to understanding fundamental aspects of Levinas' thinking, the essays gathered here aim to broaden and deepen the numerous other dimensions of ancient thought that Levinas only marginally or tangentially, if at all, addresses. Rather than viewing this as a problem or deficiency, we editors take this approach to be one that enriches and enlivens the worlds of both Levinas and Continental ancient scholarship, thereby expanding new horizons of interpretation. In so doing, a genuine proximity emerges between these worlds, calling forth new openings and opportunities for reflection and exchange.

THE BREATHING OF THE AIR:
PRESOCRATIC ECHOES IN LEVINAS

Silvia Benso

1

> Are not we Westerners, from California to the Urals,
> nourished by the Bible as much as by the Presocratics?
>
> —Levinas, "No Identity"

PRESOCRATIC PRESENCES

Relinquishing the rhetorical interrogation in the above epigraph, let us restate it positively: "We Westerners. . . ." Others have already explored some of the ways in which Levinas' philosophy is sustained by the biblical inspiration. And Levinas himself is willing to recognize, at various points in his essays, the presence of the Socratic, Platonic, and even Aristotelian legacy (to stay with some major Greek, post-Socratic thinkers) within his own thought. Is Levinas also nourished by the Presocratics as his statement suggests? And what would a Levinasian reading of the Presocratics reveal? Would different possibilities of philosophical thinking open up, within the very origins of Greek philosophy, if one were to let the Levinasian inspiration breathe through such an originary thinking? These are the questions I would like to take up in the remainder of this essay. After a necessary, brief, and certainly unsystematic excursus on some Presocratic themes that might be said to echo in Levinas' philosophy, I will focus more specifically on the presence in Levinas of a rather minor, but thus even more significant, Presocratic thinker, Anaximenes, and his "theory" that air is the *arche* of all things.

Some ways in which Presocratic thinkers and themes resonate in Levinas' thought are more evident than others, insofar as such echoes are identified by Levinas himself. Indeed, there are moments when Levinas is highly critical of themes inaugurated by the Presocratic tradition. Thus, an equal criticism associates the two giants of Presocratic philosophy (which some, for example, Nietzsche,[1] see as representatives of two very different, distinct tendencies within Western philosophy): Parmenides, the philosopher of being and unity, and Heraclitus, the philosopher of becoming and *polemos*. Levinas' contention with Parmenides as being at the origin of a recurrent attempt, within the Western tradition, at reading being in terms of unity and, more specifically, in terms of a unity of being and thought—that is, in terms of a reassembling of differences within the circularity of thought—is well known, since it implicitly inspires much of the pages and themes unfolded in *Totality and Infinity* (see 33–52). In *Time and the Other,* Levinas declares his programmatic intention to distance himself philosophically from Parmenides, writing that "it is toward a pluralism that does not merge into unity that I should like to make my way, and, if this can be dared, break with Parmenides" (42). What is here rejected is Parmenides' *hen kai pan,* the monism of the logic of the One in which all possibilities for proximity with the Other are denied in favor of a mysticism of representation prescribing either unity in the object, as in religious mysticism (which Levinas constantly rejects), or unity in the subject, as in all theories of the conformation of the object to the subject whether configured in a Cartesian, Kantian, Hegelian, or even Husserlian and Heideggerian mode. Analogously evident is Levinas' condemnation, which once again inspires much of the opening pages of *Totality and Infinity,* of the Heraclitean motif of being as *polemos,* which ends up in an ontology of war where the other is seen as the enemy to be conquered, subsumed, annihilated. "We do not need obscure fragments of Heraclitus to prove that being reveals itself as war to philosophical thought, that war does not only affect it as the most patent fact, but as the very patency, or the truth, of the real" (*TI* 21), Levinas states.

Far from seeing Parmenides and Heraclitus as separate, like and yet unlike Heidegger, Levinas unites them as being the necessary counterparts in a project that aims at denying what he calls "the eschatology of messianic peace" inspired by the idea of the Infinite, "a relation with *a surplus always exterior to the totality*" (*TI* 22). Thus he writes, "The visage of being that shows itself in war is fixed in the concept of totality, which dominates Western philosophy" (*TI* 21). Heraclitean ontology of war (and annihilation) and Parmenidean logic of totality and unity are two explications, one practical and one theoretical, as it were, of the same attitude toward alterity and transcendence. True becoming, then, the true passage from the same to the other, is not that indicated by the Heraclitean movement of flux. Rather, in agreement with the appearance in Plato's *Theaetetus* (152a–e) of Protagoras, for whom "man [appears] as measure of all things, that is, [is] measured by nothing, comparing all things but incomparable," for Levinas, who rehabilitates the great sophist, "a multiplicity of sentients would be the very *mode* in which a becoming is possible" (*TI* 59–60).

Besides the ones just indicated, there are other places where a remainder of Presocratic inspirations is acknowledged as playing more positive roles in Levinas' thinking. Although the concept of *il y a* is not the final point in Levinas' project, nevertheless it cannot be denied that such a notion plays an essential part in enabling the constitution of a subjectivity capable of responding to the appeal of the Other, that is, capable of making itself ethical. Without the *il y a,* in fact, without this resurgence of being that never allows for escapes or exits into nothingness (and here the subscription to Parmenides' prohibition of the path of nonbeing should be evident), "the I" could easily find a way of contenting and thus quieting itself in a quasi-Buddhist notion of emptiness or nothingness, or in the death brought about by suicide. But the inability to rest upon itself, the impossibility to sleep, even in death, the wakefulness to which the *il y a* forces the I is also what prepares the I, in its exposure and vigilance, to the possibility of later being disrupted by the Other. And it is what provides the *I* with the elements that will enable the I to remedy the thirst, hunger, and nakedness of the Other, to welcome the Other not with empty hands.

The Heraclitean moment in the notion of the *il y a* is recalled by Levinas himself when, in a page of *Time and the Other,* he writes that "if it were necessary to compare the notion of the *there is* with a great theme of classical philosophy, I would think of Heraclitus. Not to the myth of the river in which one cannot bathe twice, but to Cratylus' version of the river in which one cannot bathe even once; where the very fixity of unity, the form of every existent, cannot be constituted" (*TO* 49). Still in the same context, Levinas dismisses possible Anaximandrian reminiscences of the *apeiron,* an indefinite infinite to which one might be tempted to assimilate the *il y a.* "The indeterminate ground spoken of in philosophy textbooks," Levinas writes, without citing any names, "is already a being—an entity—a something. It already falls under the category of the substantive. It already has that elementary personality characteristic of every existent" (*TO* 47–48), whereas what Levinas has in mind when speaking of the *il y a* is the "very work of being" (*TO* 48), verbal and not substantive or subjective, and therefore anonymous and impersonal (*EE* 57–64).

In *Time and the Other* as well as in *Existence and Existents,* such anonymity and impersonality is exemplified through expressions such as "it is raining" (*TO* 47; *EE* 58), "it is hot" (*TO* 47), "it is warm (*EE* 58), "it is night" (*EI* 48), "a heavy atmosphere" (*EE* 58), thus possibly suggesting an affinity with the general realm of what the Presocratic naturalist philosophers, namely, Thales and Anaximenes but also Empedocles (who, however, in this similarly to Anaximander, identified such a general realm with specific, particularized beings), might have called *phusis*—nature in its preobjective, prescientific meaning. Could Presocratic *phusis* resonate, then, in the *il y a*? To ask this question means to ask about the place of nature in Levinas' thought both with respect to being and in relation to the beyond being; that is, it means to ask, among other things, whether ethical subjectivity requires a breaking open and a relinquishing of the self's natural attitude, or whether ethical subjectivity is to an extent rooted in nature, although certainly it is not grounded there, since its reason of being comes from the transcendence of the alterity of the Other.

Presocratic *phusis,* or the natural elements to which many of the Presocratics refer, properly falls under what Levinas calls "the elemental" (*TI* 131). What is the relation between the elemental and the *il y a,* that is, between the Presocratic conception of elemental *phusis* and the *il y a* on which the I as hypostasis, as substance, raises (*EE*), but which it leaves behind in its move toward ethical subjectivity, toward subjectivity without autonomous substance or substantivity? Indeed, the elemental shares many features with the *il y a.* Like the *il y a,* the elemental is indeterminate, boundless, timeless, without origin: it is "a common fund or terrain, essentially non-possessable, 'nobody's,'" Levinas writes (*TI* 131); and he continues: "The depth of the element prolongs it till it is lost in the earth and in the heavens. 'Nothing ends, nothing begins'" (*TI* 131). Content without form (*TI* 131), the elemental is pure "qualit[y] without support . . . adjectiv[e] without substantive," quality "determining nothing" (*TI* 132), and thus anonymous like the *il y a:* it "presents us as it were the reverse of reality, without origin in being. . . . Hence we can say that the element comes to us from nowhere; the side it presents to us does not determine an object, remains entirely anonymous. *C'est du vent, de la terre, de la mer, du ciel, de l'air*" (*TI* 132). Self-sufficient, incapable of raising any questions regarding "what is the 'other side'" of it, the elemental calls for a "bathing," for an "immersion . . . not convertible into exteriority" (*TI* 132)—what Levinas names "enjoyment—an ultimate relation with the substantial plenitude of being, with its materiality" (*TI* 133).

Yet in Levinas, the elemental is not simply *phusis* (although *phusis* is elemental), and the elemental is not the *il y a,* which means also that *phusis* is not the *il y a.* First of all, the elemental is not simply *phusis* in the sense of the natural elements as understood by the Presocratics, insofar as Levinas certainly includes in it earth, sea, sky, air (*TI* 132), light (*TI* 130), but also, and in a sense surprisingly, city (*TI* 131). That is, the elemental escapes the distinction and separation between natural and artificial, between *phusis* and *techne,* perhaps allowing for an understanding of both as forms of *poiesis,* perhaps enabling a reading of technology as an inevitable component of nature, or perhaps opening up some other possibility of discourse that cannot be explored in the context of this essay. Second, for Levinas the elemental is not the *il y a*. Whereas in the *il y a* Levinas stresses the verbal aspect without a substantive to support such verbality, what is stressed in the elemental is the qualitative aspect without substantiality. Thus, the two forms of anonymity differ. The *il y a* refers to an impersonal anonymity, to the sheer event of being without form or content because prior and indifferent to both. The elemental instead refers to an anonymity that is already identified and identifiable, personalized or hypostasized, as it were, through a certain way (a certain quality) of its being, which thus becomes its content; it is an anonymity where what remains undetermined is not the content but the form, the face, the absence of which compels Levinas to talk about the gods of nature as pagan, mythical, faceless deities with whom no personal relation can be entertained.

This lack of complete coincidence between the elemental and the *il y a* also means that being and nature do not coincide in Levinas. Nature is already a way of being, an existent, a content, a mode of carving oneself a niche in the anonymity of the *il y a*. As we know from other places in Levinas' philosophy, there are other ways of being: the egology or egoism of the ontological subject (which thus is not necessarily natural), the being-for-the-other of ethical subjectivity, the beyond-being of transcendence (whether God or the Other), to name a few. This lack of coincidence between nature and the *il y a* allows for the possibility, I argue, that unlike the *il y a*, nature, for Levinas, may already be spiritual, that is, open to the ethical; or perhaps, which amounts to the same thing, spirit may already be natural because in fact nature is beyond the separation between materiality and spirituality, mind and body, matter and soul. It is at this point that Anaximenes' "theory" of air being the *arche* of all things becomes interesting.[2]

AER, PSUCHE, PNEUMA IN ANAXIMENES

We know very little, almost nothing certain, about Anaximenes' life and activities. Certainly in the eyes of the contemporary reader, often trained in the shadow of Nietzsche and Heidegger, among the three Milesians, Anaximander appears more prominent than his "associate" Anaximenes.[3] According to Diogenes Laertius, however, Theophrastus (Aristotle's pupil) wrote an entire monograph on Anaximenes,[4] which signals the recognition Anaximenes enjoyed in the ancient world and thus the possibly widespread influence of his thinking.[5] Although the theory of *pneuma*—pneumatology—occupies an important place in the theories of the medical schools as they developed in the fifth century BCE and received its most complete and significant form in the doctrines of the Stoics, it is in Anaximenes that its first philosophical mention occurs, according to a longstanding tradition in the West.[6] Therefore, it is to him that I turn, regardless of the only alleged authenticity of the fragment in which such a theory appears (for although some alterations and rewording might in fact have occurred, this would not radically change the general sense of the quotation).

As handed down to the tradition by Aetius, the words commonly accepted as a direct quotation from Anaximenes are: "'Just as,' he says, 'our soul [*psuche*], being air [*aer*], holds us together, so do breath [*pneuma*] and air [*aer*] encompass the whole world.'" And, Aetius adds, air (*aer*) and breath (*pneuma*) are synonymous here.[7] The *psuche* is *aer; aer* and *pneuma* are synonyms; therefore, the *psuche* is also *pneuma.*

First of all, a brief semantic observation. It is questionable what Anaximenes exactly meant by *aer,* whether atmospheric air (invisible) or, as in Homer, mist and vapor (visible). There is no doubt, however, that for Anaximenes air is something substantial, and indeed, the basic form of substance. Whether such substantiality retains material or spiritual features or neither is part of what I would like to address here. In the fragment reproduced above, even more radical than the association between air and breath (breath is, after all, in a merely physiological sense, warm air) is the suggestion that our soul—the *psuche*—is not only air but also, and at the same time, *pneuma.* In other words, the soul is indeed assimilated to a natural, physical principle (*aer*) that is seen at work in the entire universe (thus also suggesting, though not our interest here, an analogy, if not a structural coincidence, between microcosm and macrocosm). By itself, this move would amount to understanding the soul in terms of its physical makeup, of what was later called "matter," and would subject it to obedience to the deterministic, mechanistic laws that are seen at work in the universe of physicality. What would derive would be a philosophical vision in which the psychic dimension, otherwise known as spirituality, would be reduced to its natural, physical, material component. However, there is something else going on in Anaximenes' fragment.

Moreover, and more notably, through Aetius' clarification that air and breath are synonymous, the soul is also associated with another term, *pneuma,* a word indicating a component that, besides physically making it up, enlivens the soul, makes it mobile, pulsating, active, verbal, and not substantive, and in this sense subtracts it from immediate association with the pure materiality of air and renders it certainly forceful, vital, organic, and, with a terminology that will appear only later, almost spiritual, although perhaps of a peculiar spirit. In fact, there is no *pneuma,* no breath (substantive) except in breathing (verbal), and breathing is a pulmonary activity (and not a status) of taking in and letting out, of inspiration and expiration. It is breathing, not simple air, that individualizes the human being, that gives him or her subjectivity, and that ultimately constitutes his or her soul. Such an activity of breathing provides physiological as well as psychological, physical as well as spiritual life; and in this sense, more than a material element (as air is), *pneuma* is a force, a life-force. If it is a life-force, it is certainly natural, but is it still truly material? Is it even truly physical, or is it already also something else?[8]

Yet *pneuma*, we are told in Aetius' remark, is nothing else than air, a material, physical, natural element that, present at the cosmic level—that is to say, outside—is internalized and externalized by the soul so as to nourish, sustain, even make possible the life of the *psuche*, which itself, then, *is* air. This is why the soul is in fact air: because the soul is the air-breathing that by bringing the air from outside inside and back gives the soul its subsistence. The soul is itself this movement of the air, this inhaling and exhaling, this folding itself in and turning itself out, this pulsating lung in which the inside (properly, the soul) is always already the outside (the air) and vice versa. Without air there is no breathing, without breathing there is no soul, without air there is no soul. To exhale the last breath is to stop breathing, to die. But the lack of air certainly brings about the last breath, and all dying is, in a way, a gasping for air, for more air, a suffocating. Is air itself, then, the life-force expressed by the term *pneuma*? Is the natural, physical element already pervaded by a spiritual dimension, so as to justify the classical description of the first philosophers as hylozoists, that is, as those who see matter (*hule*) as in itself provided by a principle of animation (*zoon*)? And is this animation the spiritual?

What is ultimately going on in Anaximenes' association of *psuche, aer,* and *pneuma*? Is Anaximenes simply reducing the psychological, what the tradition has later understood as the spiritual aspect of human beings, to its natural, physical, material make-up? This is indeed the sense in which the Stoics understood *pneuma*. But the Stoics also wrote after Plato's theorization of the division between the soul and the body; thus, in a way, they were forced to operate a choice between the materiality and immateriality of *pneuma* (and they opted for the former). Or is Anaximenes spiritualizing nature, physicality, and materiality? The spiritual dimension shadowed in the term *pneuma* was not lost to the Septuagints, who generally translated the Hebrew form *ruah* (wind, breath, but also the spirit of God) with *pneuma*, and also used *pneuma* in a context where pagan Greek would have used *thumos* or *psuche*.[9] What are the nature and status of the *psuche*, this peculiar entity that seems to be at once material (*aer*) and nonmaterial (*pneuma*) except that the apparently nonmaterial aspect, the *pneuma*, is then allegedly solved back into its material dimension as *aer*?

Some suggestions as to how to cast some light on these questions surprisingly come from Hegel. In his *Lectures on the Philosophy of History,* commenting on Anaximenes' fragment, Hegel translates Anaximenes' *pneuma* with *Geist*, spirit,[10] and writes that "Anaximenes shows very clearly the nature of his essence in the soul, and he thus points out what may be called the transition of natural philosophy into the philosophy of consciousness."[11] Certainly Hegel's understanding of the history of philosophy is oriented by his attempt at reading all moments of such a history as transitional to the full manifestation of spirit accomplished in nineteenth-century German philosophy. With respect to Anaximenes, however, even if one does not subscribe to Hegel's general historiography, one thing becomes clear through his remark: by marking the transition from nature to consciousness, Anaximenes in fact situates himself at the turning point of that transition, as the one who perhaps renders the transition possible but possibly without himself being completely part of it. That is, in Anaximenes the split between nature and consciousness, body and mind, matter and spirit, as well as that between microcosm and macrocosm, which will become evident in Platonic philosophy (although there too it is only by taking care of bodily needs in a certain way that the life of the mind or spirit can develop), is not yet fully at work. *Psuche, aer,* and *pneuma* remain in the ambiguity that enables the transition to occur: they interact and feed on one another in such a way that each nourishes the other, so that nature—or what will later appear as corporeality, physicality, or materiality—is in fact the source, origin, and aliment of spirituality. In other words, nature is itself spiritual while remaining nature, and vice versa. And all this emerges through the somewhat ambiguous notion of *pneuma* in its correlation with *aer* and *psuche.* As Irigaray states in a different context (and remarking on the concept of breathing in terms that do, however, speak the language of the tradition of the split), in breathing "nature becomes spirit while remaining nature."[12]

This very attitude of thought, which situates itself before or beyond the split defining and characterizing so much of Western philosophy between materiality and spirituality with all the conceptual corollaries attached, is present also in Levinas, who explicitly discusses the notion of psychism both in *Totality and Infinity* and in *Otherwise than Being.* In a sense that I will try to elucidate, the two descriptions resemble Anaximenes' double association of the *psuche* with *aer* and *pneuma* respectively, while at the same time they contribute to let emerge and disclose the meaning of the ambiguity contained in Anaximenes' own account.

PSYCHISM AND AIR IN *TOTALITY AND INFINITY*

In *Totality and Infinity* Levinas generally does not speak of the *psuche,* or soul, but of *psychism,* or psychic life; and he understands it as "an *event* in being" (*TI* 54), "a dimension in being, a dimension of non-essence, beyond the possible and impossible" (*TI* 56). As such, psychism belongs to the movement of separation through which the I constitutes itself on the background of the *il y a,* but also on the background of all forms of totalization aimed at encompassing the self. Psychism is what constitutes the I in its individuality; "it is the feat of radical separation" (*TI* 54). In this sense, psychism is not a purely theoretical moment, but rather, an existential one: "It is already *a way of being,* resistance to the totality" (*TI* 54), and thus an act of freedom with respect both to one's own origin and to the universality of history. The tradition has tried to express the irreducibility of the psychism of the

I to the common, totalizing time of history through the notion of "the eternity of the soul" (*TI* 57). But the concept of eternity as "perenniality" does not mark a separation that is radical with respect to common history. Rather, the separation is radical only if "each being has its own time, that is, its *interiority*" that interrupts historical time—that is, only if each being is born and dies. Thus, birth and death are inherent components of psychism, which makes both possible. Psychism means, for Levinas, not existence as eternity, but discontinuity in historical time. The life of the soul is made of birth and death, physical appearance and disappearance. It is human life.

The way in which psychism defines itself is through enjoyment that, according to the description in the section of *Totality and Infinity* devoted to "Interiority and Economy," is grounded on corporeity, sensibility, affectivity, bodily needs that want to be satisfied, happiness. Enjoyment neither relates to the things of the world through an instrumental, "utilitarian schematism" (*TI* 110) that makes the I see them as tools, implements, fuels, or, in general, means, nor do they appear as goals. Rather, enjoyment provides us with an immersion in the fullness of life that in itself is "*love of life*" (*TI* 112)—not life in abstract, but life in its very contents, which are thus lived, and "the act of living these contents is *ipso facto* a content of life" (*TI* 111). In enjoyment, the reliance, the dependency on the contents of life, the "living from . . ." such contents turns the I into an autonomous, independent subject, into an egoism, or, precisely, into a psychism.

As already noticed, for Levinas it is such a psychism, specified as sensibility, "and not matter that provides a principle of individuation" (*TI* 59). That is to say, in Levinas what we would otherwise call spiritual life, what he terms "psychism," is not separated from bodily life, sensibility, and corporeality. For Levinas, the body is not "an object among other objects, but [rather . . .] the very regime in which separation holds sway . . . the 'how' of this separation and so to speak . . . an adverb rather than . . . a substantive" (*TI* 163). Life is a body, and the body is "the presence of [an] equivocation" (*TI* 164) between "on the one hand *to stand* [*se tenir*], to be master of oneself, and, on the other hand, to stand on the earth, to be in the *other*, and thus to be encumbered by one's body" (*TI* 164). The two aspects are not distinct and in succession; rather, "their simultaneity constitutes the body" (*TI* 165), which also means that there is "no *duality*—lived body and physical body—which would have to be reconciled" (*TI* 165). The psychism situates itself before or beyond the distinction into body and soul, body and mind, and thus, unlike much philosophical thinking of Platonic or Platonist (I will not address the difference here) descent, beyond the need for their reconciliation. With a clear reference to Plato's myths of the soul as recounted at various places in his philosophy, Levinas states that "consciousness does not fall into a body—is not incarnated; it is a disincarnation—or, more precisely, a postponing of the corporeity of the body" (*TI*

165–66). That is, consciousness, which Levinas characterizes as a being "related to the element in which one is settled as to what is not yet there" (*TI* 166), is intertwined with the body, has its origin in the body, arises out of the body as a taking time, a taking distance "with respect to the element to which the I is given over" (*TI* 166).

Moreover, sensibility, or rather, this "incarnate thought" (*TI* 164), this psychism, is not made to coincide either with matter or with nature. As sensibility, the body, "a sector of an elemental reality" (*TI* 165), immerses itself in the elementality of matter, elementality that, as we have seen, can be natural as well as artificial or technological. But sensibility is already separation, already psychism; whereas matter, or the elemental, is pure quality in which no separation is possible, since "as qualities, the differences still relate to the community of a genus" (*TI* 59), that is to say, to a totality. On the other hand, the body is not immediately nature because the body exists as already animated by its psychism, the body is its psychism, or better, psychism is "sensible self-reference" (*TI* 59); whereas for Levinas nature is not animated, is not separate, does not possess an interiority of its own. Nevertheless, matter as well as the elemental (both natural and technological) for Levinas can only and always be approached from the perspective of the psychism of the I, through the "sensible self-reference" that in enjoyment bathes itself in such dimensions and that through dwelling, possession, labor, and consciousness gains a stable hold on such dimensions. In other words, it is not only the body but also matter and the elemental that are already spiritual, inscribed in the economy through which the I attains its own individuality and separation—or matter, the elemental, the body are already cultural because in fact they are before and beyond the distinction between nature and culture as a specific dimension of humankind. As Levinas writes against a whole tradition that has instead mainly equated bodily pleasures with animality, "To enjoy without utility, in pure loss, gratuitously, without referring to anything else, in pure expenditure—this is the human" (*TI* 133). As in Anaximenes, psychism is air, being steeped in the elemental as the source of one's independence and happiness, sensible enjoyment, nourishment.

The love of life that Levinas displays in these pages of *Totality and Infinity* is the feeling of innocent, sinless, guilt-free *eudaimonia* with which the Presocratic philosophers were generally capable of approaching the universe; of being completely present to it while representing its *genesis*, its *arche*, to themselves; of being in harmony with it. The injustice of which Anaximander speaks has precisely to do, according to Levinas' reading of Heidegger's interpretation in "The Anaximander Fragment," with a "put[ting] into question [of] the ego's natural position as subject, its perseverance—the perseverance of its good conscience—in its being. It puts into question its *conatus essendi*, the stubbornness of its being" ("Diachrony and Representation," *TO* 108). If it puts such "an indiscreet—or 'unjust'—presence" into question, however, this does not mean the uprooting or elimination of such a "positive moment" of separation (*TI* 53), since "the plurality required for conversation [and, one could add, for the ethical relation] results from the interiority with which each term is 'endowed,' the psychism, its egoist and sensible self-reference" (*TI* 59).

In *Totality and Infinity*, the psychism is characterized as an egoism that actually enables the I to separate itself from the anonymity of the *il y a*, of pure being. As such, it represents an ontological moment in the activity of self-constitution of the I—it is a moment through which the I establishes *its own being*, its having its own beginning and end, its own birth and death—in short, its own time. What animates such a moment, however? As Anaximenes indicates, the *psuche* is *aer*, substantive presence, substantiality, that is, in Levinas' language, persistence in one's own being; but it is also *pneuma*, verbality, vital force, breathing. What gives the psychism its life, its animation, its *pneuma*, according to Levinas? What is "the very pneuma of the psuche" (*OB* 69, 141)?

THE PNEUMA OF PSYCHISM IN *OTHERWISE THAN BEING*

In *Otherwise than Being*, the psychism of the I (which Lingis' translation renders as psuche) is discussed once again in relation to concepts already associated with it in *Totality and Infinity*, such as sensibility, enjoyment, the body. But here psychism undergoes a "coring out [*dénucléation*]" for which "the nucleus of the ego is cored out" (*OB* 64). Thus, psychism is no longer described as egoism, as separatedness of the I, but rather as "the form of a peculiar dephasing, a loosening up or unclamping of identity: the same prevented from coinciding with itself" (*OB* 68). This emptying out, which does not entail "an abdication of the same" but rather "an abnegation of oneself fully responsible for the other" (*OB* 68–69), is brought about through the notions of responsibility, substitution, the one-for-the-other; by the presence of the Other, who then constitutes the very *pneuma* of psychism, its animation. As Levinas defines it, psychism now signifies "the other in me, a malady of identity, both accused and *self*, the same for the other, the same by the other. Qui pro quo, it is a substitution" (*OB* 69).

From substantive identity, like the air-like psychism of *Totality and Infinity*, the I now turns into verbality, movement, breathing, through which the other penetrates the I and, through a "traumatic hold" (*OB* 141), a claim and a command placed on the same, destabilizes the substantive identity of the I and renders it verbal, responsive, responsible, for-the-other rather than for-itself, active of an activity that is, in fact, a passivity, a receptivity, a welcoming, and, ultimately, a donation—the donation of hospitality. "An openness of the self to the other . . .

breathing is transcendence in the form of opening up," Levinas writes in the concluding pages of *Otherwise than Being* (181). Psychism is then a deep inspiration (*OB* 141)—an inspiring, breathing the other in as well as a being inspired, animated by the other who thus constitutes the I in its very substantial identity as a destabilized self. Yet "this pneumatism is not nonbeing; it is disinterestedness, excluded middle of essence, besides being and nonbeing" (*OB* 181). As for Anaximenes, *aer* and *pneuma* are synonyms, and the *psuche* is both. It is the breathing, the verbality, the animation by the other that ultimately gives the soul its identity, its nonsubstantive substance, its being—its *aer.*

Such an animation does not occur at the level of cognition, theory, or intentionality, claims Levinas. Rather, it is only possible at the level of the body, through an incarnation. "The animation, the very pneuma of the psuche, alterity in identity, is the identity of a body exposed to the other, becoming 'for the other,' the possibility of giving" (*OB* 69). The other lays claim on the I, inspires the I as an other who is hungry, thirsty, naked, in need of protection, of a home. Thus, the counterpart of such an inspiration, the movement of expiration through which the breath makes itself breathing, what Levinas will call elsewhere in *Otherwise than Being* testimony, or "witness," can only unfold itself through the donation of bodily, corporeal, material goods. Once again, as in *Totality and Infinity,* psychism, which the tradition has understood as nonmaterial, spiritual being, is described and defined through the body, corporeal donation, giving one's body, one's breath as nourishment, as source of life—"psychism in the form of a hand that gives even the bread taken from its mouth" (*OB* 67).

The body thus is retrieved from its confinement in that Cartesian (but, even before, Platonic) order of materiality for which the body and the soul "have no common space where they can touch" (*OB* 70). Rather, the body is already an "animated body or an incarnate identity" (*OB* 71), and psychism is defined as "the way in which a relationship between uneven terms, without any common time, arrives at relationship" (*OB* 70). That is, psychism is neither spiritual nor material; it is "an accord, a chord, which is possible only as an arpeggio" (*OB* 70). As for Anaximenes, the *psuche* is *aer* and *pneuma,* or the proximity of both, and psychism results into a subject "of flesh and blood," an individual "that is hungry and eats, entrails in a skin, and thus capable of giving the bread out of his [or her] mouth, or giving his [or her] skin" (*OB* 77). Ultimately, Levinas identifies psychism with "the maternal body" (*OB* 67), the only one for which even the activity of breathing for itself, the in-taking of the air that gives the I its substantiality, becomes a breathing for the other, "a further deep breathing even in the breath cut short by the wind of alterity" (*OB* 180). In turn, the subject is defined as "a lung at the bottom of his substance" (*OB* 180).

To say that psychism is an animated body, a lung, does not imply, however, a return to or a lapsing into animality. Animality (or the organic body) and the animated body are not the same thing. An animal is driven by its *conatus essendi;* it is entirely caught in the sphere of ontological self-assertion. The animal lives in being, and the signification of sensibility as signifyingness for-the-other completely escapes it. Conversely, the incarnate body may certainly give in to its own *conatus essendi,* since "there is an insurmountable ambiguity there: the incarnate body . . . can lose its signification" (*OB* 79), and the human subject ends up engaging in an animalistic lifestyle, which is what ontology ultimately is. But the incarnate body, psychism, can also live what we may call the "spirituality" of the elemental, that is, sensibility as ethical signification. Rather than a deficiency, the ambiguity is then "the condition of vulnerability itself, that is, of sensibility as signification" (*OB* 80). As Levinas phrases it, "perhaps animality is only the soul's still being too short of breath" (*OB* 181), that is, the soul's inability to engage in the movement of inspiration by the other "that is already expiration" (*OB* 182). This movement "is the longest breath there is, spirit," Levinas remarks, asking: "Is man not the living being capable of the longest breath in inspiration, without a stopping point, and in expiration, without return?" (*OB* 182).

This also means that it is not the body in itself that belongs to animality or to ontology, since the body is already the possibility of being for-the-other. Ethical subjectivity is distinct from animals' life but not thereby from nature, since nature is alien to the distinction between body and mind, matter and spirit or soul. By engaging in an ethical life, by inspiring the air of the Other as the *pneuma* of one's own breathing, psychism does not relinquish its natural status, does not distance itself from its own nature; if anything, it separates itself from animals and *their* way of being within nature. Ethics is not unnatural for the psychism; in this sense, for Levinas as well as for Anaximenes, *pneuma* is *aer;* the vital principle is proximity with and not distance from the natural element, since the natural element is alien to—it is before or beyond—all dichotomies.

The *pneuma* of psychism, its inspiration and animation, is the appeal by the other so that the elemental that the I enjoys becomes a gift and a donation for the other. Without the elemental, which is not pure being (*il y a*) but already a way of being, ethical subjectivity, the breathing subject, a subject inspired by and responsive to the other would not be possible. Matter, the elemental (whether natural or technological) and its transformation through labor and work, in which the ontological I bathes so as to constitute itself in its substantiality, are already potentially spiritual in the sense that they are already open to the dimension that properly constitutes the psychism in its breathing aspect—or rather, they are beyond such a distinction between materiality and spirituality. As Levinas very clearly puts it, "Matter is the very locus of the for-the-other" (*OB* 77); that is to say, matter and the elemental are the place of the ethical not only because they are instrumental to the ethical but also because they are already open to it, they are what makes the ethical responsiveness concrete and actual. As Levinas has it, in order to be ethical, in order to be able to give the very bread one eats, "one has first to enjoy one's bread, not to have the merit of giving it, but in order to give it with one's heart, to give oneself in giving it" (*OB* 72). Nature belongs not to pure being, toward which the ontological movement of the hypostasis is necessary for the constitution of an identity, but rather to a pre-ontological way of being that, precisely because it is pre-ontological, allows for a beyond being, for hospitality. Thus, *aer* is *pneuma* also in the sense that physical, natural elements contain within themselves, rather, are the possibility for, the welcoming of the other.

Once again, let us ask the question Levinas asks: "Are not we Westerners, from California to the Urals, nourished by the Bible as much as by the Presocratics?" Is Levinas influenced by Anaximenes as much as he is by the Bible in his understanding of psychism as egoism of the self, enjoyment, sensibility, incarnate body, subject of flesh and blood, maternal body? Very likely the answer to the question is "No," and an analysis of the biblical concept of *ruah* would probably show the Jewish ground of Levinas' understanding of such a notion. My point in this essay, however, is not retracing the roots of Levinas' thought as much as it is showing the proximity between the Jewish inspiration and the Greek tradition of the origins regarding the notion of psychism. Such a proximity becomes possible precisely through Levinas' own understanding of psychism. Within that psychism that Western philosophy has understood mainly as a spiritual and immaterial principle, Levinas retrieves the naturalistic, material element and thus situates himself, with Anaximenes, before—or rather beyond—the split between materiality and immateriality, body and soul, nature and spirit that Anaximenes has contributed to originate while remaining at its threshold, at least according to Hegel's interpretation quoted earlier in this essay.

There is no doubt that such a Greek understanding of psychism is obliterated throughout much of the rest of the history of Western philosophy, covered up and bent in a more immaterial, spiritualistic direction by a certain interpretation of Plato known as Platonism, and further elided by Christian metaphysics. But what would it mean, for Western philosophy, to reread its own origin, its own history, its own conceptualizations in light of such a different and yet not foreign understanding of psychism, the breath of which can be perceived through the inspiration of Levinas? What would it mean, for philosophy, to read itself against the grain of its own interpretative tradition, inspired by the presence of the Other that the Jewish religious tradition represents? If led by such an inspiration, could it find within itself those very themes to which the inspiration has opened it up? Could the breath become its air, so that the inspiration would not suffocate philosophy by changing its nature—from philosophy to religion, or theology, or religious thinking? So that, rather, it would only redirect, deflect, or inflect the movement and direction of its breathing, not toward itself, but for-the-other, "wisdom of love" rather than love of wisdom, as Levinas has had occasion to say (*OB* 162)? Would this not be the only possible sense of proximity, of a "contact across a distance" (*TI* 172) between the two traditions, a contact in which the other manifests itself in "a mastery that does not conquer but teaches" (*TI* 171)? "In Greek philosophy one can . . . discern traces of the ethical breaking through the ontological," Levinas remarks.[13] Not only one can, but rather one does indeed, I would argue.

Notes

1. See Friedrich Nietzsche, *Philosophy in the Tragic Age of the Greeks,* trans. Marianne Cowan (Washington, D.C.: Regnery, 1996).

2. It should be noted that the term *arche* is not used by the Presocratics; it is instead Aristotelian in the sense that Aristotle uses it when classifying his predecessors according to how many "first causes" they postulated (*Physics* A, 2 184b15ff.).

3. See Theophrastus, *Physicorum Opiniones,* fr. 2.

4. Diogenes Laertius, *Life of the Philosophers* 5:42.

5. John Burnet, *Early Greek Philosophy* (New York: Meridian, 1957), 78ff.

6. This is not to say that such a theory did not have a previous origin in the popular tradition or that it was not formulated in previous authors such as Homer, for example.

7. Aetius I, 3, 4.

8. In conformity with their physical theories, the Stoic doctrine reads *pneuma* in entirely materialistic terms, and because of this it will be rejected by the later Christian thought, which, through a peculiar Neoplatonist interpretation of the Platonic legacy, will consign such a rejection to medieval and modern philosophy. In this essay I wonder, however, about the reduction of *pneuma* to a purely material dimension.

9. The cultural history of the term *pneuma,* as well as that of "spirit," is complex indeed. For such a history, see Gerard Verbeke, *L'évolution de la doctrine du pneuma du stoicism à S. Augustine* (New York: Garland, 1987), and Marie Isaacs, *The Concept of Spirit* (London: Heythrop, 1976).

10. See G. W. F. Hegel, *Lectures on the History of Philosophy,* trans. E. S. Haldane and Frances H. Simson (New York: Humanities Press, 1974), 1:190.

11. Ibid.

12. Luce Irigaray, "A Breath That Touches in Words," in *I love to you,* trans. Alison Martin (New York: Routledge, 1996), 123.

13. See Emmanuel Levinas and Richard Kearney, "Dialogue with Emmanuel Levinas," in *Face to Face with Levinas,* ed. Richard A. Cohen (Albany: State University of New York Press, 1986), 25.

THE ETERNAL AND THE NEW:

SOCRATES AND LEVINAS ON DESIRE

AND NEED

2

Deborah Achtenberg

For Socrates, in the *Symposium*, eros is a type of desire, and desire is a type of need. For Levinas, in *Totality and Infinity*, desire is contrasted with need. Are their views of desire, then, completely different? No, I will argue, they are not as different as they seem, since Socrates invokes need for the same reason Levinas rejects it: in order to highlight human vulnerability—for Socrates, to reject a decayed masculine ideal of self-sufficiency; for Levinas, to eliminate the return to the self predominant in Western philosophy.[1] How, then, do their views of desire differ? After all, as Levinas rightly points out, Socrates rejects Aristophanes' view that love reunites a split being, a view Levinas appropriately takes to imply that love is a return to the self (*TI* 254; cf. *TI* 292, *GP* 67–8, *EI* 188). Why, then, does Levinas nonetheless charge Socrates with an egoist understanding of love (*TI* 63)? One answer, I will argue, is found in the centrality, for Levinas, of a concept of creation (*TI* 63, 104, 292–94), a concept that, as Levinas claims, is lacking in Plato, who, in the *Timaeus*, substitutes instead the demiurgic informing of matter (*TI* 63).[2] Love and desire, for Levinas, are accomplished in fecund production, for example, the production of a child who, though the father's issue, is nonetheless absolutely other than the father—a creation *ex nihilo*, a true other (*TI* 63). The created other is, according to Levinas, absolute upsurge (*TI* 89), where the absoluteness of the upsurge indicates that the other's coming-to-be is not the informing of matter or the development of potential, but the coming-to-be of something entirely new. Love, Levinas says, aims at the other, the stranger, and not, as Socrates would have it, at immortality (*TI* 63).[3]

Levinas is not consistent, however, in contrasting his view of desire with Socrates' view of it. For though Levinas contrasts his creation *ex nihilo* or absolute upsurge with the informing of matter in the *Timaeus,* he also associates desire both with his absolute other and with Socrates' good beyond being (*TI* 292; *Republic* 509b6–10). For Socrates, the beautiful is a closely related transcategorial to the good beyond being, and the beautiful and the good are the ultimate objects of love. If Socratic transcategorials are the same as Levinas' good beyond being, then the Socratic and Levinasian views of desire do not really differ, and Levinas' critique of Socrates on love and desire collapses. If instead Levinas and Socrates have different ways of thinking of the good beyond being, as I will maintain, desire is different for them as well: for Socrates, desire is responsiveness to form, while for Levinas, desire is an open responsiveness, a responsiveness beyond or before form.[4] Each type of responsiveness is necessary for ethics, I will maintain, since each points to a fundamental type of human vulnerability. On my interpretation, then, creation *ex nihilo*—absolute upsurge—distinguishes the Socratic and Levinasian views of love and desire.

In what follows, I will show, first, that Socrates invokes the concept of need for the same reason Levinas rejects it, namely, to highlight human vulnerability; second, that their concepts of desire are nonetheless different owing to the presence or absence of a concept of creation *ex nihilo;* and third, that Levinas' *good beyond being* is not the same as Socrates', so that the outlined difference in their concepts of desire due to creation remains and points to two fundamental types of human vulnerability.

NEED

References to human vulnerability are legion in the *Symposium,* beginning with the dramatic date of the drinking party itself: 416 BCE, the year that Agathon put on his first tragedy. The dramatic background, as a result, is the Peloponnesian War, during which a self-confident Athens overextended itself and fell. Even more, Socrates claims for himself a teacher, Diotima, who, as a woman, is hardly a symbol of heroic self-sufficiency, not to mention the fact that she identifies eros with pregnancy, a paradigm of being taken over by another.[5] Diotima is from Mantineia, too, where in 418 BCE the Athenians overestimated themselves and were defeated by the Spartans. And she teaches Socrates that love is not all-good or all-beautiful but in between, a peculiar combination of ability and vulnerability, power and need, *poros* and *penia*—a lot like Socrates himself, a powerful, magnetic figure sought out by the young for his wisdom though the only wisdom he claims is awareness of ignorance, and a lot like philosophy, too, which is not wisdom, according to Socrates, but the loving pursuit of it based on awareness of its lack. According to Diotima, "love is a philosopher" (*Symposium* 204b4).[6]

The critique of the male model of heroic self-sufficiency begins early in the dialogue in the frame dialogue between Apollodorous and his companion. The companion wonders about Apollodorous' nickname, *the soft*, given how savage Apollodorous is in his attacks on those who spend their time in pursuits other than philosophy (*Symposium* 173c2–d3). Apollodorous is a comic image of Socrates, comic because he goes too far both in his savagery and, as his nickname suggests, his softness.[7] The dramatic foreshadowing continues when Aristodemus and Socrates, in the next frame dialogue, are on their way to the party, according to Socrates, "to corrupt the proverb" *to a good man's feast the good go uninvited* (*Symposium* 174b3–c4). The superficial corruption is the pun on Agathon's name, which means *good*—as if the proverb were to say *to Goodman's feast the good go uninvited*—while the deeper corruption is a disagreement with the claim that the good go to the good, the beautiful to the beautiful. Instead, the soft or vulnerable, such as Menelaus, *the soft warrior,* go to the good, such as Agamemnon (*Symposium* 174c5–d1). Clearly, the heroic model is under attack in this dialogue.

Soon, too, those present in the central dialogue, the dialogue that takes place at the symposium itself, are divided into those who are capable and those who are incapable—again foreshadowing the ability/vulnerability theme of the dialogue—though in this case, ability and vulnerability regarding drink—with Aristophanes, Pausanias, and Agathon on the side of those who are capable; Eryximachus, Aristodemous, and Phaedrus on the side of those who are incapable; and Socrates, not surprisingly, in the middle, since he can go either way. The capacity to drink large quantities of wine is associated with madness and incapacity with soberness, leaving Socrates in the middle, associated with what we might call sober madness. Socrates can drink or not. He is able and vulnerable, sober and mad, in his mind and out of it. It sounds like the son of Poros and Penia is Socrates and not, as Diotima claims later in the dialogue, Eros. That's not surprising, though, since not only does Diotima describe eros as a philosopher, but Socrates identifies himself with eros when he says that the only subject he knows is *ta erōtika* (love matters, or erotic things) (*Symposium* 177d6–e3). The *Symposium* is another dialogue in which Socrates is identified with a more-than-human figure—for example, with Achilles in the *Apology*, with Heracles in the *Republic*, and here in the *Symposium* with Eros.

Before considering the central dialogue's series of speeches about love, what in general were the issues about love in classical Athens? Homosexuality was not the issue, nor was the age of those involved in homosexual love (since youths had relationships with men at about the same age that girls were married). Instead, what was at issue was aggression (*hubris*) and insatiability.[8] That Plato was concerned about the former is clear from the dramatic framing of the *Phaedrus'* discussions of love in the context of the mythical rape of Oreithyia by Boreas (229b4–5). Insatiability comes up in the *Gorgias* when Socrates caricatures Callicles' view of the hedonistic good life as being like the life of the *charadrios*, a mythical bird that constantly eats and immediately excretes (*Gorgias* 494a6–7). In the background of the *Symposium*, then, as in the background of the *Phaedrus*, is the Greek male concern with the idea of control—represented in Greek iconography by the heroic small penis.[9] It is a concern with not overstepping the boundaries of others, as in rape, and with not allowing others—other things, such as food, drink, or sex, or other people—to overstep one's own. Here again, Socrates is a peculiar, and striking, middle figure. Aware of the problem of aggression, he nonetheless is comfortable with the idea that in love, we're out of our minds. In fact, according to Socrates, the greatest good things come to human beings by way of madness if that madness is divine (*Phaedrus* 244a6–8). So there is divine and human, all-too-human, madness and moderation—the divine represented by love, philosophy, or Socrates, and the human, all-too-human by the comic figure of Apollodorous as well as various less-savory figures: Callicles, who pictures the good life as constant inflow; Lysias, who, in the *Phaedrus*, would seduce Phaedrus for sex through a lie about love (namely, that he is not in love with Phaedrus and that non-love is better anyway since it is moderate, not mad).

At the drinking party, Phaedrus, a sober speaker, makes love, a great god, something useful. Great benefits would be derived from having a city or army composed of lovers and their youths, since before their boyfriends, lovers would be inspired toward virtue by shame and love of honor and would even die for their boyfriends' sake. There is nothing better for a youth, Phaedrus maintains, than a "good lover" (*Symposium* 178c3–5). But Phaedrus' language is the language of heroism, all about avoiding shame and being motivated by love of honor to do great deeds. He neglects love as vulnerability or as a source of incompetence. In quoting Hesiod's description of Eros, Phaedrus leaves out the description of Eros as the limb-loosener who weakens the mind in the breasts of human beings and gods (*Symposium* 178b5–7; *Theogony* 117–122[10]). For Phaedrus, love is all about seriousness, virtue, and boldness, and not at all about being soft or vulnerable. His example of vulnerability is Orpheus, who, soft and lacking the boldness to die for the woman he loves, dies at the hands of women (*Symposium* 179d2–e1).

Pausanias, a mad speaker and Agathon's lover, is less sanguine about love. He does not think all of it is good and describes better and worse types, Uranian (heavenly) and Pandemian (popular). Uranian lovers are manly. They love only youths—stronger youths who have mind—and love them only after their minds have begun to form. Pandemian lovers, to the contrary, love both women and mindless youths. They care only about the sex act itself and, unlike Uranian lovers, leave the youths they have sex with rather than loving for life (*Symposium* 180c3–182a6). There is a queasiness in Pausanias' feelings about love that is evident even when he argues for what he takes to be the better type of it. In attending to their youths, Pausanias maintains, lovers "are willing to perform slavish acts not even a slave would perform"—acts that would be seen as flattery and as unfree if done to attain wealth, office, or power. Beloveds, too, he goes on, are voluntarily slavish when they have sex with their lovers—though they are justified in engaging in those slavish acts if the acts are for the sake of virtue (*Symposium* 183a2–c2). Pausanian willing slavery foreshadows Socratic eros as ability and vulnerability, power and need, *poros* and *penia,* but differs since Pausanian love has an extrinsic aim—sex for the lover and virtue for the beloved. For Socrates, love's vulnerability is for its own sake, since it is vulnerability to the good or the beautiful itself—the good or beautiful the youth instantiates. For Socrates, service is not something shameful endured for the sake of something else that is good. Instead, the service itself is something good.

Eryximachus, one of the sober speakers, is a doctor. An orderly technician, he is puzzled by Heraclitus' view that opposites are unified. If they are unified, they cannot be opposites. If things differ, they cannot agree. That, he says, would be "quite absurd" (*pollē alogia*) (*Symposium* 187a6–8). But is he right? Love relationships suggest the opposite, since often it is because two people differ that they are agreeable to one another. It seems it is the very tension—their very vulnerability to the other—that they crave. In addition, separation often brings us together. "Absence makes the heart grow fonder," as we proverbially say. Perhaps, then, Heraclitus is right to say, presumably about all of reality, that "being brought apart (differing), it is brought together with itself (agrees); there is a back-stretched connection, as in the bow and lyre."[11] Perhaps, as Heraclitus suggests, unity, at least for human beings, requires a certain tension and vulnerability, requires something brought apart that is brought together, as the unity of a bow results from the fact that, at one and the same time, the string pulls in and the bow pulls out.

Not so for sober Eryximachus, whose idea of eros is of a great and wonderful god, found not just in love relationships but in all things, an all-powerful source of happiness. For Eryximachus—Phaedrus's lover—all sciences are erotic sciences and the better eros is an orderly eros that makes hostile elements come to love one another (*Symposium* 186b2–188d3). Love, in other words, is harmony of elements that previously differed, not of elements that currently do (187a8–c2). It is unity with no difference, tension, or vulnerability, whether in relationships or in medicine, music, astronomy, or other areas (186b2–188d3).

The drama of the dialogue suggests a different view of love. Eryximachus' speech is preceded by Aristophanes' hiccups (*Symposium* 185c4–e5). Their rhythmical quality mimics the sex act and reminds us that human beings willingly engender its tension. Eryximachus' suggestion that, to cure the hiccups, Aristophanes should tickle his nose and induce sneezing mimics the sex act, too, as well as all activities in which we induce tension in order to resolve it. Love, the dialogue suggests at this point, is not an orderly unity without tension and difference. Instead, in love we intentionally make ourselves vulnerable and tense in order to enjoy the tension's resolution.

For Aristophanes, whose well-known speech follows, human beings are, to the contrary, a paradigm of vulnerability. Previously we were circle people, terrible in our strength and power, who thought great thoughts and tested the gods (*Symposium* 190b5–6). We had two heads and necks, four arms, four legs, and two sets of genitals, and we moved by rolling around with great force. Now we are sick and need healing because the gods, frightened of our power and *hubris,* sliced us in half (190d6–7). Love draws our archaic nature back together and tries to make us one out of two. What lovers desire is to be fused together into one. Love, then, is the desire and pursuit of wholeness (192d2–193a1). For Aristophanes, eros is not a sign that human beings are manly, powerful, and invulnerable, as the first three speakers suggest, but a sign that human beings are wounded and need healing. His comic speech critiques the heroic ideal that stresses human ability and downplays human need. It makes fun of manly pretensions and points to what we lack. Eros is a sign that we are missing part of ourselves, part of what it is to be complete, to be fulfilled, to be whole.

The fact that there are more speeches about love at this climactic point suggests that some aspect of the critique of the heroic ideal of self-sufficiency may remain to be discussed. Agathon, the tragic playwright, provides the need for continuing the critique when, in his speech, he praises eros as most beautiful and best—beautiful because young, tender, and graceful; good because possessed of all the virtues. Eros is just, not violent, since people willingly serve it; moderate, because stronger than all other desires and pleasures; courageous because Aphrodite defeated Ares; wise because eros makes every person a poet, creates all living beings, and brings renown to the varied craftsmen it teaches (*Symposium* 195a5–197b9). Eros, Agathon says, is of beauty. There's nothing ugly about it. And eros is the cause of peace, intimacy, goodwill, and more. Eros, in other words, is all-good.

Agathon's vacuous tragic speech gets the most applause, presumably because it is a *tour de force,* beautiful in poetic form. In content, it is similar to the part of Phaedrus' speech that makes eros fundamentally good. Socrates refutes Agathon in short order, using wisdom he received from his female teacher, Diotima. Love, Socrates argues, is a species of desire, and desire is a species of lack or need. If love is of what is beautiful, then love lacks what is beautiful and is not itself beautiful. Since beautiful things are good and love lacks beautiful things, then love lacks what is good as well (*Symposium* 200a2–e6). Socrates has learned well his lesson from Diotima—whom, presumably, he made up—that love involves vulnerability, lack, or need. As a young man, he, like Agathon, thought love was beautiful and good. Instead, love is not a god but a *daimon,* the son of Poros (resource) and Penia (need)

(203c5–6). Human beings are not utter vulnerability, as Aristophanic comedy suggests, nor are they complete ability, as Agathon's tragic poetry maintains. Instead, Socratic philosophy teaches, human beings are in between—as is awareness of ignorance. Ignorance makes us needy; awareness is the resource for overcoming our need. In Socratic eros, awareness of need becomes the resource to overcome it. In addition, eros is not a desire for wholeness. It is not a desire for one's lost other half but for what is good. Socrates agrees with Aristophanes that eros is a sign of need or lack. But he disagrees that what is needed or lacking is a part of oneself. For Socrates, eros does not return to the self.

It does not return to the self even though, as Socrates learned from Diotima, eros is desire for immortality (*Symposium* 207a3–4). For immortality, according to her, is found most of all in form, as she suggests in remarking on the fact that a body remains even though all its material parts—hair, flesh, bones, and blood—pass away (207d4–e1). Similarly, the pregnant lover reproduces eternal form, for example, in a child who reproduces human form or, for another, in speeches about what makes a man good, speeches he shares with a youth he educates, which are reflective of the beautiful itself—the form of the beautiful, which is eternal (208e1–209c7). Love begins as a desire to have what is good forever (206a11–12). Since that is not literally possible, love becomes the desire to generate and reproduce in someone beautiful (206e5). As such, it is a desire for immortality (207a3–4). Love is not, then, a desire for one's missing half, but it is a vulnerability or need that results in generation and reproduction, realization and sharing, of eternal form. We begin by loving beautiful bodies, then beautiful souls, then beautiful practices, laws, and knowledge, and then beauty itself, the form of the beautiful—beauty in all its universality and of every type. Then, as a result of our love, we generate and reproduce it. Socrates introduces need, then, to highlight human vulnerability and to critique the heroic ideal of masculine self-sufficiency dominant in his time. In fact, the *Symposium*'s carefully crafted critique of self-sufficiency culminates with Socrates' speech, a speech portrayed as superior to Aristophanes' in its turn away from the self to the beautiful and good, which are eternal.

Unlike Socrates, Levinas argues that desire is not a type of need.[12] In striking contrast, though, he does so to underline, not deny, fundamental human vulnerability. As a result, the two philosophers' views of desire are not as different as they seem, since they share a common aim. Socrates underlines human vulnerability by rejecting heroic male self-sufficiency. Levinas, in a similar vein, does so by rejecting the return to the self that, according to him, dominates Western philosophy. Western philosophy, Levinas says, most often is ontology, "a reduction of the other to the same" (*TI* 43). Like Aristophanes and Socrates, Levinas rejects the idea of human invulnerability. Like Socrates and unlike Aristophanes, however, Levinas rejects the idea that love aims at fusion. "Man's relationship with the other," Levinas says, "is *better* as difference than as unity: sociality is better than fusion. The very value of love is the impossibility of reducing the other to myself, of coinciding into sameness. From an ethical perspective two have a better time than one (*on s'amuse mieux à deux*)!" (*EI* 188). Aristophanes' mistake, he says, is thinking that love "can be reduced to . . . fundamental immanence, be divested of all transcendence, seek but a connatural being, a sister soul, present itself as incest. The myth Aristophanes tells in Plato's *Symposium*, in which love reunites the two halves of one sole being, interprets the adventure as a return to self " (*TI* 254). Desire, for Levinas, is about the other, not about the self. The objective of desire's movement is "the other, the Stranger." Desire "is absolutely non-egoist" (*TI* 63).

For Levinas, desire is metaphysical, and need, ontological, where ontology is comprehension of beings and metaphysics is respect for exteriority, that is, respect for the other as other (*TI* 42–43). Desire is not a species of need, he says, though it is customarily interpreted that way, interpreted to "be at the basis of desire" such that desire is thought to "characterize a being indigent and incomplete or fallen from its past grandeur" and to "coincide with the consciousness of what has been lost." When understood as a type of need, desire is "essentially a nostalgia, a longing for return" (*TI* 33).

For Levinas, however, desire is not a longing for return and "does not rest on any prior kinship" (*TI* 33–34). It is not about the self—not about returning to it, nourishing it, or completing it: "The metaphysical desire has another intention; it desires beyond everything that can simply complete it. It is like goodness—the Desired does not fulfill it, but deepens it" (*TI* 34). The other deepens desire, or even hollows it out (*le creuse*). The other does not feed me: "The other metaphysically desired is not 'other' like the bread I eat, the land in which I dwell, the landscape I contemplate" (*TI* 33). Ontology, for Levinas, promotes freedom, specifically, "the freedom that is the identification of the same, not allowing itself to be alienated by the other" (*TI* 42). But I am not essentially defined by freedom. In metaphysics, the other critiques my freedom: metaphysics "discovers the dogmatism and naïve arbitrariness of its spontaneity, and calls into question the freedom of the exercise of ontology." It "calls into question the exercise of the same" (*TI* 43).

In metaphysical desire, then, I am confronted by my vulnerability. The other, who cannot be integrated, who cannot be consumed by me or reduced to me, disrupts me, disrupts my sense of my self as all there is, a sense I achieve at the very same time that I achieve a self—an I, an egoism, a psychism—namely, in the "atheist stage," as Levinas calls it, the stage in which I resist the totality of what is to form a self. Atheism, for Levinas, is separation. Resistance takes place through a process of taking in and feeding on what is outside myself while at the same time remaining distinct from that on which I feed (*TI* 112, 122). Atheism is accomplished, concretely, in a home, since a home, with its doors and windows, enables me to connect to what is outside while retreating to recollect and retain myself (*TI* 154, 156). In the atheist stage, I move from enjoyment, and sensibility broadly speaking, to perception, to consciousness, that is, comprehension, representation, intentionality, or knowledge. In comprehension and representation, I dominate the other by capturing him or her in a concept, a concept that reduces the other and prevents me from seeing that other as other (*TI* 163–68).

The other, like myself, however, resists the totality and cannot be fully integrated or reduced. The other contests me (*TI* 171), opposes me (*TI* 197), masters me (*TI* 176). The other breaks the ceiling of the totality, breaks totality's closed circle (*TI* 171). For Levinas, as for Socrates and Aristophanes, desire is not a sign of heroic mastery but an indication of fundamental human vulnerability. And as with Socrates, the vulnerability is not harmful since, to use Levinas' term, the other as such is a marvel (*TI* 292). The other who disrupts me opens a new dimension (*TI* 171). The opposition is pacific (*TI* 197), the resistance nonviolent (*TI* 197), the opposition nonhostile (*TI* 171). The other is a master who does not conquer but teaches (*TI* 171). What the other teaches is his or her very otherness, sometimes referred to by Levinas as height (*TI* 171), sometimes as surplus (*TI* 97). The teaching of the critique of heroic or Western self-sufficiency is that there is a type of vulnerability, a type of openness, that does not leave me vulnerable to harm, but instead is positive— positive, though, in different ways for Socrates and for Levinas as we will see.

Desire, according to Levinas, is accomplished in the face-to-face relation with the other and in fecundity. The face-to-face relation, the relation in which I relate to the other as other and the other relates to me as other, takes place in language— not in the content of language but in language's function of direct address, not in the speaking about but in the speaking to, not in the said but in the saying, as Levinas says in *Otherwise than Being*. Language, Levinas says, is "contact across a distance" (*TI* 172), where *distance* is metaphorical and suggests that I can never know or represent the other in his or her otherness, that the other's otherness can never be a given for me. The personal other for Levinas is infinite where *infinite* means indefinite but in such a way as to be contrasted with the way in which the elemental world is indefinite and which Levinas designates with a Greek term for indefinite, *apeiron*. What is *apeiron*, such as a forest of which I only see a part or sea all of whose elements I cannot perceive from my current position, can be disclosed. What is infinite, the other, cannot (*TI* 158–59, 192–93). The infinite can only be revealed, while revelation, for Levinas, is distinct from disclosure. The one who speaks is not disclosed. He or she is not placed in the light of another but, in articulating the world, is announced across what he or she presents (*TI* 65–66).

Fecundity, the second accomplishment of metaphysical desire, is a type of relation with the future that is "irreducible to the power over possibles" (*TI* 267). The biological sense of fecundity is the father's production of the child, but fecundity is broader than that (*TI* 247). Fecundity, in general, is found in relations between one person and another, and between the I and itself (*TI* 306). In fecundity, we surmount the passivity to which our will is exposed. Our will is free—the possibility of its freedom is produced when, in the atheist stage, we resist the totality to form an egoism—but the will is immediately exposed and vulnerable. The work of the will can be taken or sold (*TI* 227). The will itself, because of its necessarily material manifestation, is subject to violence, and we are subject to death (*TI* 229, 224). This suffering and death are surmounted in fecundity (*TI* 236–40). Human existence, for Levinas, is not, as Heidegger avers, being-toward-death, but is the *not yet* or a way of being against death (*TI* 224). We surmount our passivity and death in fecundity, in the production of inexhaustible youths. "Fecundity," Levinas says, "continues history without producing old age." In fecundity, he continues, the I "meets with no trammels to the renewal of its substance" (*TI* 268). In this way, the I exists infinitely, since fecund desire produces another who desires: "Here the desire which in the first pages of this work we contrasted with need, the desire that is not a lack, the desire that is the independence of the separated being and its transcendence, is accomplished—not in being satisfied and in thus acknowledging that it was a need, but in transcending itself, in engendering desire" (*TI* 269)

CREATION *EX NIHILO*

How, then, are Socrates' and Levinas' views of love and desire different? Each, as we have seen, rejects the idea that love is a return to the self: for Socrates, love is first of all a desire to have the good for oneself forever—but then it is the desire to generate and reproduce and, by doing so, to produce immortality; similarly, for Levinas, love in one respect is need—but in another, it is fecund desire and exists infinitely, beyond death (*TI* 254–55). Each sees love as a sign of human vulnerability, an example of the central other-directedness of human beings and of human subjectivity or soul.

The difference is in what that generativity or fecundity is like. Here is a real difference between the two philosophers, not that one is a proponent of self-sufficiency or autonomy and the other of vulnerability or heteronomy, but that one sees immortality in the persistence of form while the other sees it in a series of creations *ex nihilo*. One draws a relation between immortality and the eternal, while the other connects what is beyond death to the upsurge of something new. Levinas is wrong when he states that the way in which he differs with Socrates on love is that Socrates thinks immortality is the object of love while he, Levinas, thinks love's aim is the other, the stranger: "Love as analyzed by Plato does not coincide with what we have called Desire. Immortality is not the objective of the first movement of Desire, but the other, the Stranger" (*TI* 63). Instead, both philosophers believe love defeats death and, as we have seen, both believe love is fundamentally a directedness to something outside oneself. The difference in their views is, instead, the difference between the eternal and the new.

Levinas says "desire in its positivity" is "affirmed across the idea of creation *ex nihilo*" (*TI* 104; cf. 63). By associating love and desire with creation *ex nihilo*, Levinas does not mean to refer to the creation of the universe and its contents in six days. Instead, he wants a "rigorous concept of creation" (*TI* 292), by which he means a philosophic idea that carries its own weight and is not grounded in appeal to religious text. The other in his or her singularity is a creation *ex nihilo* for Levinas because singularity is lack of determination—since determination implies generality—and production out of anything determinate—that is, out of anything whatsoever—would be production of something determinate. Creation *ex nihilo* is not the development of potential, not the realization of projected possibility: "This future is neither the Aristotelian germ . . . nor the Heideggerian possibility" (*TI* 267). Instead, it is the production of something that is its own beginning.

How can that be? Creation *ex nihilo* is found, in the most concrete case, in the production by the father—or, dare we say, by the father and mother—of a child who in some way is nonetheless his or her own beginning: "The separated and created being is thereby not simply issued forth from the father, but is absolutely other than him" (*TI* 63). In fecundity, being is "produced not as the definitiveness of a totality but as an incessant recommencement" (*TI* 270). Every human being begins as a child who is immersed in the totality of what is and is not clearly distinct from it due to an original inability to distinguish subject from object. Each one produces his or her self, ego, psyche, or singularity by resisting the totality: "The psychism constitutes an *event* in being" and "is already *a way of being*, resistance to the totality" (*TI* 54). The resisting is a resistance to all concept, all determination. In that respect, the self is not composed of or produced out of anything, but is instead a resistance to everything determinate. The resistance continues throughout life since the self, though essentially its contents, always remains distinct from them (*TI* 112, 122). This is Levinas' core metaphysical idea, of a self that constantly emerges in or offers a variety of forms while at the same time resisting the forms in which it emerges or which it offers, a self that is essentially in relation while at the same time absolving itself from the relations (*TI* 110).

Both in its biological meaning and in its extension to the relation of one person to another and of the I to itself, fecundity denotes a relation to another's future that is not a power: "The relation with such a future, irreducible to the power over possibles, we shall call fecundity" (*TI* 267). Fecundity, the very accomplishment of desire, is not heroic. Like Socrates, Levinas is a critic of the heroic masculine ideal, in his case perhaps best represented by aspects of Heidegger's philosophy, for example, resolute and authentic being-toward-death. The erotic relation involves "a characteristic reversal of the subjectivity issued from position, a reversion of the virile and heroic I" (*TI* 270). The erotic subject is initiation, not initiative (*TI* 270).

Similarly, for Socrates, love is not heroic. In the *Phaedrus*, the helmsman or governor of the soul, who is identified with reason (specifically with *nous*), falls on his back at the sight of the beloved and as a result loves him and serves him. The helmsman is knocked out by the sight of the youth and is no longer in the things of himself (*Phaedrus* 250a6–7). He even serves like a slave to his beloved (252a1–b1). The lover's nonheroic service to his beloved, though, is differently characterized than the relation to another that is not a power which Levinas describes. According to Socrates, at the sight of the beloved, the lover ascends to the place beyond the heavens up to the very forms themselves, a process Socrates calls recollection of those eternal forms, then descends and, in the best cases, joins together with the beloved in philosophy, that is, in a sharing of the very eternal forms the sight of the beloved has spurred him to recollect. The lover and his beloved youth come together over an eternal third which they share in common (248d2–4, 252e11–253b1). Similarly, in the *Symposium*, as we have seen, immortality is illustrated by Diotima's example of matter that changes while form persists, and is exemplified by the production of a child who shares human form and by the educative function of sharing with a youth speeches about what is good in the hopes that the youth will be influenced by such conversations to become beautiful and good, that is, to share in those forms (*Symposium* 206c1–212a7).

For Levinas, to the contrary, the effect of fecundity is not to reproduce eternal form. Instead, fecundity involves relating to an other in such a way as to facilitate the arising of something that has not in any sense been before. The ability to relate in this way to the future is fecundity, and the way of relating is contraction—"contraction that leaves a place for the separated being" (*TI* 104). For Levinas, the fundamentally ethical way of relating is a contraction that enables the wholly other and his or her projects to be. Fecundity plays this role, not just in erotic relations narrowly speaking, but in all desire—since fecundity is the accomplishment of desire—and in our face-to-face relations with others and our relation to ourselves—since fecundity extends from the biological to both of these. Antiheroic reversion, initiation, and contraction play a role in all desire for Levinas, then, since all desire is a type of contraction in relation to an other that allows the other and his or her future projects—in their newness—to be. For Levinas, love and desire are generative vulnerability to what is fundamentally other or new.

GOOD BEYOND BEING

Levinas is not consistent in contrasting his view of love and desire with Socrates' view of them. Though he contrasts his creation *ex nihilo* or absolute upsurge with the informing of matter in the *Timaeus,* he nonetheless identifies Socrates' *good be-yond being* in the *Republic* with his own *metaphysical separation.* If they were the same—that is, if Socrates' *good beyond being* were the same as Levinas'—the dis-tinction between Socratic and Levinasian love and desire would collapse. If they were the same, Socratic eros would have to be for the new, not for the eternal, since the object of Socratic eros is the good (or the beautiful, a closely related transcate-gorial). But it is not for the new, as Diotima's example of the matter that changes while the form persists indicates. Socrates must mean something else, then, when he says that the good is beyond being.

There is more reason to think that Socratic transcategorials are different than Levinas' *good beyond being* than just this textual argument. For one thing, if the ob-ject of desire for Socrates were the good beyond being in Levinas' sense—that is, radical singularity—then we would expect Socratic virtues to be different than they are. We would expect Socrates to discuss virtues of the same general type as kind-ness, compassion, and faithfulness—virtues that go past knowledge of an individ-ual's characteristics and are directed instead to the singular individual him- or herself. Virtues of this type do not in fact play a central role in the Platonic corpus. Instead, the whole point of Socratic virtue seems to be to critique the heroic male ideal of power or force and replace it with knowledge—not with what is beyond or before knowledge, but with knowledge. A central argument for Socrates regarding virtue is that we all desire good, so virtue is not desire but knowledge or wisdom: we all desire what is good, Socrates argues, so if we do not pursue it, it must be that we do not know what it is (*Meno* 77b2–e2).

Of course, Socrates' goal is to replace the ideal of virile force with knowledge un-derstood as wisdom, not merely with being intelligent or smart (as the suggested re-jection, at *Meno* 88a6-b6, of the equation of virtue with *eumatheia* demonstrates) so that someone could object that the idea that virtue is not simply knowledge but wis-dom could be translated into the claim that virtue is the encounter with the other as singular. Justice, they might say in support of their objection, could be equated with wisdom in this sense. What, though, I want to reply, about moderation and courage? These seem to have nothing to do with singularity and more to do with awareness of what is appropriate or best. We perhaps are asking too much of Socrates if we ask both that he endeavor to eradicate an old ideal of virtue as power and replace it with virtue as knowledge or wisdom and, at the same time, that he introduce the ideal of response to human singularity. Moreover, if he had introduced that ideal, would it not be likely that Aristotle, his follower and great critic, would respond to such a crucial conceptual innovation? He does not respond to any such idea but instead responds to what he thinks is an overly intellectualist idea of virtue in Plato, which he moderates by stressing the importance of emotional development. Virtue, for Aristotle, is not simply knowledge, as it is for Plato, but also requires suitable emotional development.

What, then, is the good beyond being, according to Socrates? It comes up during a discussion in the *Republic* of the mathematical and eidetic or formal aspects of beings, aspects that are known, respectively, by discursive rationality (*dianoia*) and by rational intuition (*nous*) (511d2–5).[13] As a result of this location in the dialogue, the strong suggestion is that the good beyond being is not a non-being but a hyper-being or second-order being—beyond (*epekeina*), hyper or second-order because it is beyond the mathematical and the eidetic aspects of beings (as I have argued elsewhere), that is, beyond both what we might call the *this* and the *what*.[14] Beings, in the *Republic*, are called *originals* to distinguish them from images. In images, such as the image of a tree on water, the mathematical and formal or eidetic aspects are very separate. In originals, such as a tree, they are more together. The good is responsible for their being together. The good is the togetherness of the *this* and the *what*, the mathematical and the eidetic and, as such, we may call the good *the fitting*, meaning the fit between a thing and its qualities or the conformity of a thing to its type.

That Socrates identifies the good with the fitting, or with related terms such as *sufficient, proper, complete,* or *perfect,* is indicated by numerous passages: in book 1 of the *Republic,* Socrates suggests that only if *owed* means *fitting* (*prosēkon*) is justice giving the owed to each (332c1); in book 4, he suggests that justice is doing one's thing or doing the proper (*to ta hautou prattein, oikeiopragia*) (433b4; 434c8); in book 8, he suggests that the best for each is also what is most proper to it (*oikeiota-ton*) (586e2); in the *Gorgias,* he suggests that moderation is doing the fitting (*prosēkon*) concerning gods and people, justice is doing the fitting concerning people, and piety is doing the fitting concerning gods (507a7–b3); in the *Philebus,* he says two signs of the good are the complete or perfect (*teleion*) and the sufficient (*hikanon*) (20d1–6). All these terms have to do with the fit of *this* to *what,* mathematical to eidetic, with *complete* and *perfect* indicating that something entirely fits while *sufficient* or *proper* are deficient cases of the complete or perfect: the sufficient just meets the mark, we could say, while the perfect meets it entirely.[15]

The beautiful, for Socrates, would be another such second-order being or trans-categorial (to use a somewhat Aristotelian term) but one that emphasizes another aspect of mathematico-eidetic beings than togetherness. Instead, the beautiful points, not to the togetherness, but to the separation of the mathematical and the eidetic, to the transcendence by a *this* of its *what*. In the case of a painting of a tree, the painting is in one sense simply shapes and colors on a surface, but those shapes and colors point beyond themselves. The beauty of something is beyond that something's qualities, as the use of the term "surpassing" (294b2) in the *Hippias Major,* the dialogue on the beautiful, suggests. A more complete interpretation of that dialogue would be required to show this, but suffice it here to assert that the definitions of the beautiful in it fail because they reduce beauty to a set of qualities rather than seeing that beauty is in and through those qualities but beyond them.

So also in the case of every being—every original, to use the term from the *Republic*—form not only is together with a thing but transcends it, as the generality or universality of form indicates. The good and the beautiful for Socrates, then, indicate two aspects of one puzzling phenomenon, namely, the relationship between *this* and *what*, between the mathematical and the eidetic, in all beings, with the good indicating their togetherness and the beautiful indicating their separation. This type of interpretation of Socrates' *good beyond being* fits the overall Platonic problematic better than Levinas' interpretation does and, in addition, makes it possible to preserve the difference between Socrates' and Levinas' views of love and desire that the second section of this essay delineates.

We are left, then, with not one but two types of vulnerability, one a Levinasian open vulnerability, a vulnerability not to form but to singularity, and the other a Socratic-Platonic vulnerability to form—to the complexity of the relationship of form to thing—that involves responding to what things are and relating to them based on what fits them as a result of what they are. Each type of vulnerability, it seems to me, is important for ethics because each is necessary for our good dealing with ourselves and with other people. It is necessary and good both to respond to people based on what fits them and thus to play a role in enabling them to be what they are and, as well, to respond to them beyond or without reference to what they are at any particular time, and by so doing to participate in enabling them to be or do something that is utterly new.

NOTES

1. The Socrates referred to in this essay is the Platonic Socrates of the dialogues, not the historical Socrates. As a result, some views that originated with Plato will be referred to as Socrates' views since they are views attributed to Socrates in the dialogues.

2. Another answer, not discussed in this essay, is found in Levinas' critique of what he takes to be Plato's understanding of need as mere lack.

3. The idea of creation is discussed also in *Otherwise than Being*, where it is connected to a variety of central concepts taken up and developed in that book such as absolute passivity. In order not to pass too quickly beyond *Totality and Infinity*, which has its own concepts, terms, and trajectory and as a result is worth considering in its own right, the focus of this essay is on *Totality and Infinity*. It is important, though, that in *Otherwise than Being* Levinas draws a contrast between the Aristotelian idea of prime matter as pure potentiality and Levinas' idea of absolute passivity, which, according to him, is related to the idea of creation (*OB* 110). This contrast between prime matter and absolute passivity is relevantly similar to the one stressed in this essay between the eternal and the new.

4. In *Totality and Infinity* Levinas speaks of openness—for example, of transcendence as "openness par excellence" (193; my translation)—while in *Otherwise than Being* he

speaks of anarchy. The resonances of openness that are missing for anarchy (a term with its own resonances that openness lacks) are a good example of the benefits of not passing too quickly beyond *Totality and Infinity* in discussions of central Levinasian ideas.

5. For pregnancy, see David M. Halperin, "Why Is Diotima a Woman?" in *One Hundred Years of Homosexuality and Other Essays on Greek Love* (New York: Routledge, 1990), 117, 137–42.

6. Translations from Greek in this essay are my own.

7. In the *Phaedo,* his weeping at Socrates' death causes everyone present but Socrates to break down (117d).

8. Eva Cantarella, *Bisexuality in the Ancient World,* trans. Cormac Ó Cuilleanáin (New Haven, Conn.: Yale University Press, 1992), 17–27, and James Davidson, *Courtesans and Fishcakes: The Consuming Passions of Classical Athens* (New York: St. Martin's Press, 1998), 167–82; contra K. J. Dover, *Greek Homosexuality* (Cambridge: Harvard University Press, 1978), 100–109, and Halperin, "Why Is Dotima a Woman?" 124.

9. Dover, *Greek Homosexuality,* 124–28.

10. G. S. Kirk and J. E. Raven, *The Presocratic Philosophers: A Critical History with a Selection of Texts* (Cambridge: Cambridge University Press, 1957), 24.

11. With Kirk and Raven, reading *palintonos* in fragment 51; ibid., 193.

12. A similar distinction is made by Renaissance Jewish philosopher Leone Ebreo (Judah Abravanel), who has Philo argue that truer and more unalloyed desire and love does not involve lack and gives as among his examples God's love for his creatures and a father's love for his child (*The Philosophy of Love,* trans. F. Friedeberg-Seeley and Jean H. Barnes, with introduction by Cecil Roth [London: Soncino, 1937], 180, 250–52; a new translation by Rossella Pescatori is forthcoming).

13. To associate form only with *eidos,* the fourth level of the divided line, though useful for making verbal distinctions in this essay, is somewhat misleading since the mathematicals (third level), the *eidē* or forms (fourth level) and the idea of the good (beyond the line) are all, broadly speaking, formal for Plato.

14. Deborah Achtenberg, "What Is Goodness? An Introduction," Ph.D. dissertation, New School for Social Research (Ann Arbor, Mich.: University Microfilms International, 1982), 148.

15. Ibid., 149.

LEVINAS QUESTIONING PLATO
ON EROS AND MAIEUTICS

Francisco J. Gonzalez

3

In a 1961 outline of the doctoral thesis that would become *Totality and Infinity*, Levinas provocatively characterized his project as "a return to Platonism."[1] This is certainly a surprising description of a book that carries out a radical critique of the entire history of ontology and whose project one would therefore expect to be anti-Platonist. Yet the influence of Plato is indeed evident throughout *Totality and Infinity*, not only in the explicit citations of Plato's texts, which exceed in number the references to any other philosopher, including Descartes, but also, and even more importantly, in the very frequent and unattributed use of Platonic ideas and language. But why this appeal to Plato? And what is the nature of this "return" to Platonism, assuming that it is not simply a repetition? These are difficult questions to answer because, as will be seen, both Levinas' appropriation and his critique of Plato are characterized by a certain ambiguity. Once both the ambiguity and its source are recognized, however, a genuine *Auseinandersetzung* between Plato and Levinas becomes not only possible but indispensable.

LEVINAS' RETRIEVAL OF PLATONIC THEMES

Probably the best-known Platonic theme in *Totality and Infinity*, and that in which Levinas' main debt to Plato is usually located, is the transcendence of the Good. In Plato's description of the Good as "beyond being," Levinas sees a transcendence that resists the totalizing tendency of ontology as the study of beings in their being. Thus Levinas observes that the thesis expressed in Plato's description of the Good's transcendence "should have served as a foundation for a pluralist philosophy in which the plurality of being would not disappear into the unity of number nor be integrated into a totality" (*TI* 80). Later in the text Levinas makes his own retrieval of the Platonic idea of the Good even more explicit: "If the notions of totality and being are notions that cover one another, the notion of the transcendent places us beyond categories of being. We thus encounter, in our own way, the Platonic idea of the Good beyond Being. The transcendent is what can not be encompassed" (*TI* 293).

Yet what Levinas retrieves is not only the idea of a transcendence beyond the totality of beings, but also Plato's characterization of what transcends as the *Good*. Here he finds the priority of ethics to ontology or, more specifically, the idea that the good, as good in itself, resists all reduction to relations between beings. "The Good is Good *in itself* and not by relation to the need to which it is wanting; it is a luxury with respect to needs. It is precisely in this that it is beyond being" (*TI* 102–103). In confronting the Good as in itself Good, we confront not something relative to our needs, not something that fulfills a lack in our being and can thereby be assimilated to our being, but rather a surplus, an excess, beyond what we need and what we can thus make our own. It is in the Good, therefore, that we encounter something genuinely other, and it is only in the ethical relation that we can relate to another *as other*. If my relation to you has the character of *a need* (for example, a need for money, for sexual gratification, for companionship), then I am making you a part of me, or *the same* as me. But if I relate to you in the name of what is good in itself, then I recognize you as irreducible to my own needs and my own being. You are then, like my relationship to you, a surplus and a luxury. Thus in the 1987 preface to the German edition, Levinas expresses his debt to Plato simply as follows: "Wisdom that teaches the face of the other man! Was it not already announced by the Good beyond essence and above the Ideas in Book VI of Plato's *Republic*?" (*TI* iv, my translation). Here we see most clearly the extent to which *Totality and Infinity* is indeed "a return to Platonism."

Yet it would be wrong to confine Levinas' retrieval of Plato to the Idea of the Good. The key opposition in Levinas' thought is that between the Same and the Other. Levinas sees in traditional ontology, as the study of beings *as beings,* the attempt to reduce the Other to the Same. Levinas' own task is to indicate a way of relating to "the face of the other man" that allows it to remain *other* as an uncontainable excess that defies assimilation: a relation that could never constitute a totality and must therefore be infinite. But the very terms Same and Other, as well as the opposition between them, are a retrieval of Plato's *Sophist*. In that dialogue, the Stranger describes the Other (*to heteron*) as distinct from, and irreducible to, the Same and Being. One could therefore see here, as Levinas apparently docs, an attempt to think the Other without making it the same as anything else—not even the same as being. In this case, the *Sophist* would indicate a path of thinking from which later ontology diverges and to which Levinas wishes to return. That the *Sophist* is nowhere explicitly cited in *Totality and Infinity* does not disprove this debt to Plato but rather shows that it has been so fully appropriated by Levinas' own thinking as not to need a citation. Whether or not a Levinasian reading of the *Sophist* is ultimately defensible,[2] in thinking in terms of the Same and the Other, Levinas is returning to what is at least a possibility indicated by the Platonic text.

Yet another important Platonic retrieval can be seen in the central importance Levinas grants to interpersonal dialogue (see *TI* 71, 96, 177). Indeed, the Platonic text Levinas most frequently refers to in *Totality and Infinity* is the description in the *Phaedrus* of a *logos* that can help itself by responding to questions, elaborating, and defending what it says. Levinas takes this description as his model for the self-expression that constitutes the appearance of the Other as "face" (*TI* 66, 98, 200, 253, 298). Here it is important to note Levinas' claim that the "face" is not "seen" but rather "speaks" (*TI* 66). What I see is something I can grasp, capture, and make my own. What is merely seen cannot help itself, cannot resist my attempt to possess it—is, in short, *faceless*. It is in speaking, in expressing himself, that the other defends himself against being assimilated and possessed and shows a "face." Even Plato's characterization in the *Phaedrus* of dialogue as being dialogue with God and not with one's equals (*TI* 297) is retrieved as an expression of the *exteriority* of the Other, that is, the Other's resistance to assimilation in dialogue. In speaking, the other is not the passive object of an unconcealment, but takes part in his own manifestation (*TI* 200, 253). "Man is really apart, non-encompassable only in expression, where he can 'bring aid' to his own manifestation" (*TI* 298). But this also means that the face of the other is not an *object* of speech, not something we speak about, but rather something that speaks to us (*TI* 99). Therefore, I encounter the face of the other, not in any intuition, and not in any set of propositions, but rather only *in dialogue*.

This dialogue is understood by Levinas, and in his view by Plato, not as a logical concatenation of impersonal ideas that happens to be carried out by two persons—what would be only the external form of dialogue—but rather as the site in which persons manifest themselves as such. In dialogue with one another, we manifest ourselves at least as much as we manifest the topic about which we are speaking. This is not to say that the dialogue is *about us:* we manifest ourselves only in expressing ourselves on the topic under discussion (*TI* 96). "Thought, for Plato, is not reducible to an impersonal concatenation of true relations, but implies persons and interpersonal relations" (*TI* 71). On Levinas' view, then, that a discussion of virtue is carried out by the specific characters named Socrates and Meno is not irrelevant to what is thought and shown in such a discussion. This means that for Levinas the Platonic dialogue is not merely an external form whose content could be just as well expressed in another form. What Levinas finds in Plato and wishes to retrieve from Plato is precisely the idea that interpersonal dialogue is essential to thinking because it is only such dialogue that can resist the totalizing tendencies of intuition and discourse and think the "other" in a way that allows it to manifest itself as other. In other words, genuine dialogue is never a totality but is always "open" and therefore infinite. If metaphysics, for Levinas as for Plato, necessarily takes the form of dialogue, that is because they both recognize the *who* to be as fundamental a notion as the *what* (*TI* 177–78).

Another way of characterizing what Levinas here retrieves from Plato is to speak of a *dialogical conception of truth* in both. Thus at one point Levinas asserts that "Truth can *be* only if a subjectivity is called upon to tell it" (*TI* 245). To characterize truth as "objective" is to reduce persons to objects over which the truth holds sway. Truth becomes "universal" only through a reduction of all beings to the same. On the other hand, to characterize truth as "subjective" is to reduce it to the self-sameness of the ego and destroy its transcendence altogether. These two extremes can be avoided by arguing that truth has its being only in dialogue, that is, neither in each person nor outside all persons, but in the addressing of one person by another. The site of truth is neither in the self nor outside the self, but rather in the *self-expression* that takes place through dialogue.

Given the above, it comes as no surprise that Levinas also retrieves Socrates' argument in the *Phaedrus* regarding the priority of oral over written discourse.[3] Written discourse cannot defend itself against our attempts to make it our own through interpretation; it cannot object to how we construe it nor respond to our own objections. Written discourse has no face. If language is a relation that preserves the absolute independence of its two terms (*TI* 64), that is, that allows me to relate to the Other without reducing the Other to me (*TI* 39), then language fully realizes its essence only in oral dialogue. Thus Levinas characterizes oral discourse as "the plenitude of discourse" (*TI* 96). He also speaks of the "surplus" of spoken language over the written language that has become sign (*TI* 182). Oral discourse is an infinite relation that resists totalization because its two terms are always in excess of what is signified.

Yet despite the above-mentioned affinities, Levinas did not follow Plato in writing dialogues. Is not, then, the form of Levinas' text, which is that of the traditional philosophical treatise, in contradiction with his Platonic prioritizing of oral and interpersonal dialogue? Levinas acknowledges at least a tension here, but he attempts to resolve it by suggesting that his text is addressed to another and is thus implicitly a dialogue. Arguing at one point that a conception of truth as unconcealment for contemplation suppresses pluralism (*TI* 221), Levinas anticipates the objection that pluralism is in this case suppressed by his own description of the social relation as preserving pluralism and his presentation of this relation as the truth. "The very utterance by which I state it and whose claim to truth, postulating a total reflection, refutes the unsurpassable character of the face to face relation, nonetheless confirms it by the very fact of stating this truth—telling it to the Other" (*TI* 221). If his presentation of the truth in a treatise appears to dispense with the indispensable face-to-face relation, it is nevertheless the case that even this presentation is an expression of the truth and as such a speaking of the truth to another.

Levinas makes a similar point when it comes to the danger of thematizing and thus totalizing the face-to-face relation itself. This danger is not as serious as it might seem, because even if Levinas' description of the face-to-face relation inevitably thematizes it and totalizes it, in expressing this totality to the reader he inevitably creates another separation in being that ruptures the totality. "The description of the face to face which we have attempted here is told to the other [*à l'Autre*], to the reader who appears anew behind my discourse and my wisdom. Philosophy is never a wisdom, for the interlocutor whom it has just encompassed has already escaped it" (*TI* 295). Any text that addresses a reader thereby forsakes any claim to an absolute or totalizing wisdom, because the reader is the one thing it can never encompass and assimilate. Thus one can say, rather paradoxically, that Levinas' description of the face-to-face relation succeeds only to the extent that it fails.[4] Instead of writing dialogues, Levinas maintains that every treatise is inescapably a dialogue.

This recognition of the inherent finitude and negativity of human wisdom points to another Platonic inheritance, one articulated, though not explicitly labeled as such, by Levinas' assertion that "Critique or philosophy is the essence of knowing" (*TI* 85). What most properly belongs to wisdom is its privilege of bringing itself into question, of penetrating beneath its proper condition. This "critique" is not, for Levinas, an attempt to justify knowledge through an objective knowledge of knowledge, because assuming that liberty can found itself on itself results in an infinite regress. A critique that would get beyond both such viciously circular liberty and objective knowledge would have to take the form of a welcoming of the Other. "The knowing whose essence is critique cannot be reduced to objective cognition; it leads to the Other. To welcome the Other is to put in question my freedom" (*TI* 85).

It is hard not to think of Socratic wisdom here. If Socrates knows that he does not know something, this is not because he possesses an objective knowledge of what knowledge is and what it is not, but rather because he recognizes himself to be always open and vulnerable to the claims of the Other. Socrates is in constant discussion with others because he possesses no wisdom that could preempt what others have to say. Again, one can not help but think of Socrates when Levinas describes the possibility that "the non-knowing with which the philosophical knowing begins coincides not with pure nothingness but only with a nothingness of objects" (*TI* 24). In his commitment to remain in conversation about virtue with another, Socrates can objectify and thus "know" neither the other nor virtue. This inability to objectify what expresses and manifests itself in dialogue is Socrates' ignorance. This ignorance in the face of no-thing, however, is also the highest wisdom for Levinas as well as for the Platonic Socrates.

LEVINAS' APPROPRIATION OF THE PLATONIC FORMS

Levinas, it can be concluded, is in no way exaggerating when he characterizes the project of *Totality and Infinity* as "a return to Platonism." And yet it is, of course, a return to Platonism with a difference. It is this difference that now needs to be articulated. First, however, it is important to stress that, counter to what might be expected, the so-called Theory of Forms is *not* what separates Plato and Levinas. This is because Levinas does not see in the notion of Forms per se a reduction of the Other to the Same. On the contrary, he suggests that, *as invisible,* the Forms are an Other to which no vision is adequate (*TI* 34). And like the Other, the Forms do not exist in another place but *exist in no place* (*TI* 38). Furthermore, *as perfect,* the Forms surpass any concept (*TI* 41), which for Levinas explains the praise of madness in the *Phaedrus* (*TI* 49–50), a madness that he identifies with a desire that knows no satisfaction and with a thinking that thinks more than it thinks (*TI* 62). Thus Levinas emphasizes precisely those characteristics of the Forms that make them resistant to assimilation into any rational and systematic totality: their invisibility, their being *atopos,* their transcendent perfection, and their inability to be known by reason alone. The clearest indication that Levinas, far from opposing the Platonic notion of Forms, instead makes it his own, is his frequent use of the term by which Plato expresses the non-relative character of the Form (*kath'auto*) to express the non-relative character of the Other (*TI* 64–65).

In accordance with the above, Levinas questions the traditional characterization of the Platonic Forms and suggests instead an interpretation that reconciles them with the centrality of interpersonal dialogue in Plato. In doing so, Levinas makes an important contribution to a vexed problem in Platonic scholarship: the apparent tension, if not contradiction, between the claim that there exist absolute Forms as objects of cognition and the insistence on the dialogical form of philosophy. If there exists a Form of Virtue directly cognizable by my reason, then what need is there to converse with another about virtue? "But is the Platonic Idea attended to by the thinker equivalent to a sublimated and perfected *object*?" (*TI* 71).[5] Levinas suggests an alternative when he asks: "Is the ideality of the ideal reducible to a superlative extension of qualities, or does it lead us to a region where beings have a face, that is, are present in their own message?" (*TI* 71). The suggestion here appears to be that the Platonic Ideas, instead of being super-objects existing for intuition, manifest themselves as something unique and personal. This is because we relate to them in a discourse that for Plato, as indicated above, is always personal, always has a "face" (*TI* 71).[6]

On the other hand, what clearly appeals to Levinas about Plato's Forms is that, while these Forms are personal and have a face as manifested in interpersonal dialogue, they yet transcend any particular practical context and resist being reduced to merely practical principles. If they are not objects of intuition, the Forms also are not instruments of some *praxis*. Levinas can therefore be seen as in part defending the notion of Forms when he defends the supposed "intellectualism" of ancient philosophy and theory against the attempts by Heidegger and others to reduce meaning to practical finality (*TI* 94). Because the Forms are objects neither of mere theory nor of mere practice, they can vouchsafe a metaphysical relation to the Other that for Levinas is itself neither purely practical nor purely theoretical (*TI* 29).

The one thing that appears hard to reconcile with the Platonic Forms is Levinas' insistence on the *nudity* of the Other, by which he means that it appears beyond all attributes, all form, all finality, and all reference to a system (*TI* 74–75). To illumine the Other and thus give it form, to assign it a purpose and a place within a system, is of course to destroy its otherness and assimilate it to the Same. The Other as face signifies prior to and without form and illumination, and in this sense is naked. This nudity of the face is thus quite different from the unconcealment of a thing illuminated by its form, and Levinas significantly finds a description of the latter in the Sun Analogy from Plato's *Republic* (*TI* 74). The face is also naked in its refusal to be assigned its place and its finality by *beauty*. This leads Levinas even to speak of the ugliness (*laideur*) of the Other's nudity (*TI* 74). What, then, could be more anti-Platonic than this characterization of the transcendent Other as formless and ugly?

Yet it is significant that Levinas, in this very context, still uses the Platonic *kath'auto* to characterize the Other as naked, that is, as lacking reference to anything else (*TI* 75). And if one follows Derrida's suggestion that the term "nudity," as conditioned by the plenitude that it negates, must itself be overcome once used to point beyond itself,[7] then there might be less opposition here between Levinas and Plato than at first appears. It is not at all implausible to suggest that even the Form of Beauty, as "itself by itself," neither *possesses* form nor is formless, neither is beautiful nor is ugly. As the source of both form and beauty, it is beyond both and outside any system.

LEVINAS' CRITIQUE OF PLATO

What Levinas in fact most directly and sharply takes issue with in Plato is the Greek philosopher's characterization of Eros and his related thesis that learning is recollection. It is on these two issues, and these alone, that the return to Platonism becomes a radical critique of Platonism. There is some evidence, however, that the critique may be not so much of Plato as of the Socratic element in Plato. At one point Levinas explicitly identifies the lesson of *Socrates* as the primacy of the Same, apparently because he sees in Socrates a sovereign reason that recognizes no limit to itself (*TI* 43). Since both Eros and recollection are especially associated with Socrates in the Platonic dialogues, and since Levinas, as will be seen, finds in both a reduction of the Other to the primacy of the Same, there is reason to think that it is the Socrates in Plato that is Levinas' main target.

What Levinas finds objectionable in the Socratic characterization of Eros is its identification with a lack to be satisfied and the corresponding identification of its object with what belongs to us. As a desire to possess forever a good seen as belonging to it, and thus as a desire for immortality, Eros is an egoism that seeks only to return to and affirm the self in its self-sameness. Far from reaching out to the Other, it is a nostalgia for the Same. In contrast, what Levinas calls "Desire" is the rejection of all egoism in the effort to do justice to the Other: "Immortality is not the objective of the first movement of desire, but the other, the Stranger. It [that is, Desire] is absolutely non-egoist; its name is justice. It does not link up beings already akin" (*TI* 63).

It is important to note that Levinas objects not only to Plato's identification of desire with a need but also to his identification of need (*besoin*) with a lack (*manqué*). For Levinas, even the basic needs that constitute life (what he calls "vulgar Venus") cannot be interpreted as simple lack (*TI* 114). Our enjoyment and happiness lie in these needs and not in their extirpation. Here Levinas' target is Plato's characterization of pleasures that satisfy a need as being illusory (*TI* 116; cf. 136). For Levinas the opposite is the case: true pleasure and enjoyment are inseparable from need and are to be found in need. Far from being mere poverty, need is paradoxically itself what satisfies and gives pleasure. This is because, while needs indeed separate me from the world, these needs, and thus this separation, *are my own and in my power.* It is in my insufficiency that I suffice for myself and am fully myself. It is in my poverty that I am rich. Levinas succinctly captures the paradox of need when he writes: "Happiness suffices to itself through the 'not sufficing to oneself' proper to need" (*TI* 118). Thus to suggest that need is the absence of happiness, that need makes a pleasure illusory, is to completely misunderstand the nature and paradox of need.

But even need as thus understood is not for Levinas the same as desire, since the latter does not admit of self-fulfillment nor therefore of happiness or pleasure. While in need I find happiness and pleasure in affirming myself, in desire I find myself and my happiness themselves needy and poor in relation to the Other. At one point Levinas characterizes the distinction thus: "In need I can sink my teeth into the real and satisfy myself in assimilating the other; in Desire, there is no sinking one's teeth into being, no satiety, but an uncharted future before me" (*TI* 117). What makes need paradoxically self-sufficing and satisfying is that in it I assimilate the other and make it my own as my own need. In desire, the self-sufficing self characterized by need becomes itself open to what can never be assimilated, to what is absolutely other. Having enjoyed itself in its need, the self becomes poor in its very self-enjoyment because confronted with a future that can never be planned for and can never satisfy. Thus Levinas explains the difference by suggesting, with implicit reference to the account of eros in the *Symposium*, that while need is *penia* (poverty) as source of *poros* (wealth), desire is the *penia* of *poros* itself (*TI* 114–15). In this case neither need nor desire is a mere lack: the former is finding self-sufficiency and happiness in lacking, while the latter is finding this self-sufficiency and happiness to be themselves lacking. Whether as *poros* in *penia* (need) or *penia* in *poros* (desire), both collapse the apparently Platonic opposition between *penia* and *poros*.

In his description of love as a relation to another, Levinas suggests that love, by its very nature, is ambivalent between desire and need: either it can become a metaphysical desire that is open to the genuinely and absolutely Other, or it can deprive itself of all transcendence and "seek but a connatural being, a sister soul, present itself as incest" (*TI* 254). In the latter case, love becomes the mere *jouissance* of a need. Socratic eros represents for Levinas this latter possibility of "incestuous love." The reference here to "incest" highlights another aspect of Levinas' critique: to object to the characterization of desire as a lack is also to object to the characterization of the object of desire as what belongs to and is akin to me. As a desire for what is akin, eros is incestuous—and in the most extreme sense, since what is erotically desired is not even another related person, such as a brother or sister, but *oneself*. Far from desiring another as other, eros is a desire for what is the same as oneself. Rather than an openness to what is unpredictable and yet-to-come, eros is a desire to return to what one had and thus back to oneself: it is nostalgia. In contrast, what Levinas claims to be true of language is also true of the love that realizes itself as metaphysical desire: "The same is in relation with an other that was not simply lost by the same" (*TI* 172). Only a love that does not identify the Other with what has been lost by, and therefore belongs to, the Same can be genuinely open to the Other and thus free of the charge of incest.

What Levinas opposes to the Socratic conception of eros is therefore a conception of metaphysical desire as neither seeking satisfaction nor capable of being satisfied. It is desire as caress rather than possession. Rather than seeking to regain what it once had, it is a desire that reaches out for a future beyond any object, form, or project (*TI* 257–60). It is a *volupté* that intends without seeing, experiences without conceptualizing (*TI* 260), since what it desires it not an object that can be seen or conceptualized. What Levinas opposes to Socratic eros, in short, is a ravishment beyond all project, a movement that does not uncover what already exists as hidden, but that instead moves toward what does not yet exist and has no quiddity (*TI* 264).

Here one can begin to see why Levinas also takes issue with Socrates' maieutics, that is, the characterization of learning as the recollection of what is already within us.[8] To claim that all learning is recollection is to deny any exteriority, that is, any possibility of relating to what as Other is exterior, and to insist that all relation is a form of interiority, that is, a return to what is already within. It is because Levinas thus sees in the notion of "recollection" a reduction of the Other to the Same and thus a denial of that transcendence to the Other otherwise expressed by the famous reference to the transcendence of the Good, that he so vehemently insists on the possibility of a learning and reasoning that is in no sense "recollection." Thus he characterizes the relation to the Other as one of *being-taught* in the sense of "to *receive* from the Other beyond the capacity of the I" (*TI* 51)—"beyond my capacity" because to receive only what accords with my capacity is only to realize what is already within me and therefore *not* to be *taught*. Levinas therefore proceeds to assert that this being-taught is not maieutic because "it comes from the exterior and brings me more than I contain" (*TI* 51). Thus the conception of being-taught that characterizes our relation to the Other is, as a receiving from outside more than what is contained within, as radically opposed as possible to the notion of "recollection"; and this is because being-taught interpreted as "recollection" would not be a relation to the Other at all, but only the self-assertion of the Same.

Opposed to the notion of recollection is also the notion of the "face" as "an exteriority that does not call for power or possession, an exteriority that is not reducible, as with Plato, to the interiority of memory, and yet maintains the I who welcomes it" (*TI* 51; cf. 69, 86). To encounter the "face" is to encounter something irreducibly exterior and unassimilable and thus to "learn" without "recollecting." To encounter the other only as an incentive to recalling what is within me is not to encounter the other *as* other, is not to "see" the face of the other.

This is why Levinas at one point makes the important suggestion that the idea of recollection is incompatible with the priority of dialogue: "Thought can become explicit only among two; explicitation is not limited to finding what one already possessed" (*TI* 100). He states the incompatibility even more clearly a little later: "The transitivity of teaching, and not the interiority of reminiscence, manifests being; the locus of truth is society" (*TI* 101). According to the notion of recollection, the place of truth is within the soul (*Meno* 86b1–2) and therefore not in the society created by dialogue. To use dialogue with another only as a means of discovering what one already possesses is not to genuinely engage in dialogue with another.

Francisco J. Gonzalez

To assert the priority of dialogue is to assert that the truth is never *mine* but always *ours*. As Levinas observes in again opposing teaching to recollection, "Teaching is a way for truth to be produced such that it is not my work, such that I could not derive it from my own interiority" (*TI* 295). In making all teaching and learning intransitive, the notion of recollection reduces all exteriority to interiority and therefore all dialogue with another to the soul's dialogue with itself.

THE AMBIGUITY OF LEVINAS' CRITIQUE

It should be immediately and painfully obvious that the above does not provide a coherent account of the relation between Plato and Levinas. The reason is that Levinas does not simply praise some things in Plato while criticizing others. Instead, what he praises is the opposite of what he criticizes: if he praises Plato for expressing in the Idea of the Good the transcendence of the Other and for granting priority to dialogue, he criticizes Plato for reducing the Other to the Same and for undermining the priority of dialogue. Are there, then, as has been suggested,[9] two Platos in Levinas? That Levinas' reading of Plato is indeed conflicted is suggested by the fact that even the apparently clear and direct critique of the notions of eros and recollection analyzed above is not without ambiguity. This is because Levinas himself sometimes indicates that in Plato eros, and perhaps even recollection, can be interpreted in a way not incompatible with transcendence. After showing this, the next and final task of this essay will be to answer the following questions: Is the conflicted character of Levinas' relation to Plato due to a conflict in Plato's own thought, or rather to a failure on Levinas' part to see in Plato what is a consistent position behind the apparent conflict? And in the latter case, does this Platonic position suggest a way of overcoming the oppositions that characterize Levinas' own thought and thus a possible Platonic critique of Levinas?

It is significant that Levinas repeatedly cites Aristophanes' account of eros in the *Symposium* (*TI* 254, 292). He does so because Aristophanes' description of eros as the desire to rejoin with one's other half and thus become whole again best describes what Levinas is criticizing. But then is Aristophanes Plato? And can one see Levinas as asserting here that a radical difference separates him from Diotima and Socrates, as Peperzak maintains?[10] The Socrates/Diotima speech, it must be recalled, explicitly criticizes Aristophanes' identification of the object of love with what is one's own, insisting that we do not love our own when it proves bad, so that the object of love should instead be identified with the *good* (*Symposium* 205d–e). It is true that the speech begins by implicitly adopting Aristophanes' identification of love with a desire for what we lack against Agathon's characterization of love as itself possessing all that is good and beautiful (*Symposium* 199e–201b). But when Diotima proceeds to argue that love is not simply lacking, but rather, as a spirit

50

(*daimon*), is in between lack and possession, in between poverty and wealth, as philosophy is in between ignorance and wisdom (*Symposium* 203c–204b), is she not moving toward a conception of love closer to that of Levinas than to that of Aristophanes?

Levinas himself sees this possibility. Plato's rejection of Aristophanes suggests to him that Plato's account of eros as the child of poverty and abundance could perhaps be interpreted "as the indigence of wealth itself, as the desire not of what one has lost, but absolute Desire, produced in a being in possession of itself and consequently already absolutely 'on its own feet'" (*TI* 63). In other words, in the departure from Aristophanes' characterization of eros as mere lack and poverty, Levinas see the possible overcoming of the opposition between *penia* and *poros* and the movement toward a characterization of eros as that *penia* in *poros* that has been seen to characterize metaphysical desire for Levinas. It is this possible interpretation of Platonic eros that is in question when Levinas asks, in the 1987 preface to the German edition of *Totality and Infinity*, if the love of wisdom could be understood as the wisdom of love or wisdom in the guise of love (*TI* iv). And to this question the answer must be positive if, instead of looking to Aristophanes, we look to Socrates. For in the *Symposium,* Socrates is characterized, not as ignorant, but rather as wise with regard to love (177d7–8, 212b6). Socrates' knowledge or *techne* is erotic, not in the sense that it has eros as its object (as if eros could ever be an object!), but rather in the sense that it takes the form of, and is carried out as, eros. Socrates *knows* only in and through how he *loves,* which means that, like the philosopher described by Diotima, he is neither ignorant nor in possession of wisdom. His knowledge is not a knowledge *about* love or a love of knowledge, but rather a knowledge of *how* to love.

The second correction to Aristophanes, that is, the identification of what is loved with what is good rather than simply with what is one's own,[11] also points in the direction of a conception of love in Plato that is much closer to that of Levinas. Even if the Socrates/Diotima speech begins with a characterization of desire as lack, does not the identification of the object of desire with the *good* rather than with what belongs to one radically transform the nature of this desire? In desiring the good, does not desire transcend the mere satisfaction of a need? Levinas indeed sees in the idea of a Good beyond being, as articulated in the *Republic,* a recognition that desire is not necessarily need: "The Good is Good *in itself* and not by relation to the need to which it is wanting; it is a luxury with respect to needs. It is precisely in this that it is beyond being" (*TI* 103). Levinas therefore proceeds to claim that Plato, besides needs whose satisfaction is the filling up of a void, also catches sight of (*entrevoit*) "aspirations that are not preceded by suffering and lack, and in which we recognize the pattern of Desire, the need of him who lacks nothing, the aspiration of him who possesses his being entirely, who goes beyond his plenitude, who has the idea of Infinity" (*TI* 103). In being directed toward the Good, desire ceases to aim at the mere satisfaction of a need and becomes the aspiration toward a luxury, toward a surplus to being. The City of Pigs gives way to the fevered city of luxury that is the Kallipolis. Thus, while Levinas may sometimes criticize Plato for dismissing need-conditioned pleasures as illusory, he also credits Plato's analysis of "pure pleasures" with having discovered "an aspiration that is conditioned by no prior lack" ("Meaning and Sense," *BPW* 51).

Finally, if there is in Plato an ambiguity between characterizing eros as need/lack and characterizing it as "superfluous" metaphysical desire, this is an ambiguity that Levinas locates in love itself. What he characterizes as "the ambiguity of love" in the section of *Totality and Infinity* thus titled is "the simultaneity of need and desire, of concupiscence and transcendence" (*TI* 255). If love contains within itself the possibility of transcending to the Other, it also holds the possibility of the egotistical self-satisfaction found in need: "If to love is to love the love the Beloved bears me, to love is also to love oneself in love, and thus to return to oneself. Love does not transcend unequivocally—it is complacent, it is pleasure and dual egoism" (*TI* 266). Thus, if Plato's account of eros is equivocal, this is because the transcendence that characterizes love is itself equivocal. In desiring the other, it can just as readily find satisfaction in itself; in seeking dialogue with another, it can just as readily content itself with an egoist monologue for two voices.

It might be more difficult to see ambiguity in Levinas' critique of maieutic, yet even here a more positive attitude toward maieutics is detectable. For Levinas sees Socrates' maieutics as motivated by a demand that Levinas makes his own, that is, what he calls "the ancient Socratic exigency of a mind nothing can force" (*TI* 219; cf. 204, 295). Violence, understood as subjection to another, as the imposition on me of a perspective and teaching in no way my own, is precisely what Socrates' maieutics, on Levinas' reading, is intended to oppose. In taking up this opposition to violence, Levinas is taking up the cause of Socrates' maieutics. The difference is that Levinas sees Socrates' maieutics as opposing one type of violence only by enabling another: the violence of assimilating the Other to myself and thus recognizing no limit to my self-assertion. If slavery is violence, then so is self-assertive liberty that acknowledges no other. Yet despite this difference, Levinas sides with Socrates' maieutics in opposing the violence of reducing the Same to the Other, that is, of a relation to the Other that would annihilate the self. This agreement with the Socratic "exigence" is expressed in the very critique of recollection cited above when Levinas adds that the exteriority of the face nevertheless "maintains the I who welcomes it" (*TI* 51). But the agreement is expressed most clearly in a passage that immediately precedes another critique of maieutics:

> The face in which the other—the absolutely other—presents himself *does not negate the same, does not do violence to it* as do opinion or authority or the thaumaturgic supernatural. It remains commensurate with him who welcomes; it remains terrestrial. This presentation is preeminently nonviolence, for instead of offending my freedom it calls it to responsibility and founds it. *As nonviolence, it nonetheless maintains the plurality of the same and the other.* It is peace. (*TI* 203; my emphases)

The debt to Socratic maieutics is to be found in this determination to preserve the autonomy of the Same in the face of the Other. Levinas can therefore be seen, not so much as rejecting Socrates' maieutics in favor of its opposite, but rather as trying to a find a reconciliation between the two extremes: a reconciliation one could name, following the passage cited above, *plurality*.[12]

The Fundamental Divergence between Levinas and Plato

With this last point we have already begun a critical assessment of Levinas' reading of Plato. Therefore, the question asked above can no longer be avoided: why the ambiguous and apparently conflicted character of Levinas' relation to Plato? The answer I wish to venture here is that all the above hides a more fundamental difference between Plato and Levinas, and that it is the failure to confront this difference directly that allows Levinas and Plato to appear sometimes akin and sometimes not. I also suggest that it is at the level of this difference that a true *Auseinandersetzung* between Plato and Levinas becomes both possible and imperative.

The difference to which I refer is to be found in the opposition between what Levinas calls "separation" and the Platonic notion of "participation." By "separation," Levinas means the complete self-sufficiency, createdness, and atheism of the being that is the same as itself. With the notion of "participation," Plato attributes to the self-same-being the opposite characteristics: it does not suffice for itself, is dependent on what transcends it, is not created, and is theistic. For Levinas, the absolute transcendence of the Other requires the absolute immanence and self-sufficiency of the Same (*TI* 77, 148). For Plato, the Same is in its very nature a transcending toward the Other.

In pursuing this difference we can consider one by one the characteristics that Levinas considers synonyms. With regard to self-sufficiency, Levinas has already been seen to claim that even in its needs, or rather precisely in its needs, the *Moi* suffices for itself (*se suffit*) because these needs are its own and in its power (*TI* 118–19). This leads Levinas to maintain, clearly against Plato, that for the "*moi,*" *being* does not mean *aspiring* to something, but rather *enjoying* it (*en jouir*) (120). If for Plato the soul is winged in the sense of having a natural tendency to ascend toward what transcends it (*Phaedrus* 246d6–e1), for Levinas the "*moi*" is wingless. If for Plato metaphysical desire is the very essence of the soul, for Levinas this desire is adventitious and counter to the self's natural tendency. The self is absolutely egoist, "without ears, like a hungry stomach" (*TI* 134). If for Plato the soul is a dialogue with itself as if it were another and thus in its very being always has reference to another, for Levinas the self is a deaf self-satisfaction to whom communication and dialogue are completely foreign. This is why it does not *need* the Other; the Other is for it completely superfluous.

If Levinas appeals to the fundamentally un-Greek idea of creation *ex nihilo*, this is because such creation opens up an absolute rupture in being and thus a radical separation between one being and another. The existence of the created being, once created, is completely separate from that of other beings as well as from that of the creator: its being is not an ongoing emanation from, or participation in, the being of the creator. For Levinas, therefore, only the idea of creation can do justice to radical transcendence. Absolute transcendence requires radical separation. If I am dependent in my being on another being and am not created out of nothing, then that other being does not transcend me but rather belongs to me as I belong to it. Participation destroys transcendence by having me *share in* the being that transcends me. The creature, in contrast, shares nothing with the creator. The following passage clearly summarizes the significance of the notion of creation for Levinas: "But the idea of creation *ex nihilo* expresses a multiplicity not united into a totality; the creature is an existence which indeed does depend on an other, but not as a part that is separated from it. Creation *ex nihilo* breaks with system" (*TI* 104). Plato's characterization of dependence on an Other as participation in this Other creates a totality and a system that needs to be broken in the name of transcendence. With the idea of creation *ex nihilo*, we have a radical multiplicity that cannot be unified; we have, in other words, what from the perspective of the Greek *cosmos* must look like *chaos*.

This "rupture of participation" is what Levinas means by "atheism" (*TI* 58) when he characterizes the soul as naturally atheistic. To say that the soul is "atheistic" is to reject the Platonic characterization of the soul as erotic or spiritual in the sense of by nature communicating with, and sharing in, the divine. It is highly significant that Levinas, in this context, appeals to the Protagorean and Heraclitean doctrines in the *Theaetetus* (*TI* 59–60). He does so because it is in those doctrines, rather than in Socrates' refutation of them, that Levinas finds a recognition of the fundamental egoism that on his view is the natural state of the soul. In the immediacy and identity of sensation and sensed, the self suffices for itself; and in this way "Sensation breaks up every system" (*TI* 59). If Socrates later argues against the Protagorean and Heraclitean doctrines by maintaining that the soul *in and through itself* strives (*eporégesthai*) (*Theaetetus* 186a4) for a being and truth not given by the senses (186c–e), this is an argument Levinas chooses to ignore. Levinas here clearly takes the side of Protagoras and Heraclitus against Socrates: if the former, in making man the measure and reducing being to the flux of what is immediately sensed, ignore transcendence and all relation to the Other, they are absolutely right to do so, since the soul in its very nature is completely deaf to the Other.

If Levinas ignores the Socratic argument in the *Theaetetus,* he explicitly takes issue with the claim at *Phaedrus* 246b that the soul takes care of what does not have soul, a claim that would make a relation to what is other than itself essential to the soul's nature. Against this claim, Levinas insists that the soul is absolutely independent and self-sufficient—even in, or precisely in, its needs—since these, for reasons indicated above, are not mere lacks. This is what Levinas calls "the atheist separation," which, "deformalized," means "the existence at home with itself of an autochthonous I" (*TI* 115). The thesis of such an "atheistic separation," of course, runs directly counter to the whole thrust of the myth of the *Phaedrus,* according to which the soul is anything but autochthonous, instead having its home "elsewhere," in "a place beyond the heavens," to which it seeks to return after having been exiled from it.

The elucidation of the above characteristics finally puts us in a position to understand what is perhaps the strangest recurring Platonic reference in *Totality and Infinity:* the frequent reference to *Gyges.* For Plato in the *Republic,* Gyges is a model of extreme injustice: possessed with a ring that can make him invisible, he commits injustices without restraint. For Levinas, Gyges is a model of separate being as described above. Because he can see the world as a spectacle without being seen or, perhaps more importantly, without being talked to (*TI* 90, 173), he exhibits the interiority, liberty, and certitude that naturally characterize the soul in its separate being. In other words, Gyges is a model for the being of the Same. While in the *Republic* it is a question whether the injustice represented by Gyges is the natural and irremediable state of the soul, only restrained and covered up by convention, for Levinas there is no question that each one of us is a Gyges before being confronted by the Other. More importantly, even having been confronted by the Other we do not lose the nature of a Gyges; at best we become a Thrasymachus, that is, someone who is seen and cannot escape through silence, but whose being still remains characterized by self-sufficiency, atheism, liberty, and thus injustice toward the other (*TI* 201). What the frequent appeal to Gyges ultimately signifies is Levinas' assumption of *egoism as a fundamental ontological fact:* "Egoism is an ontological event, an effective rendering, and not a dream running along the surface of being, negligible as a shadow" (*TI* 175). In our *being* we are invisible and unseeing, deaf and mute: fully caught up in our self-enjoyment.

Yet if Levinas insists on this ontological egoism, it is only to make way for the possibility of ethics. His fundamental argument is that the relation to the

Other can be an ethical one only if it is not an ontological one. I can enter into a genuine relation with the Other only if such a relation does not belong to my very being. This is why Levinas at one point insists that atheism is a necessary condition of a genuine relation with the Other (*TI* 77). If I am not radically separate from the Other in my being, I cannot relate to the Other *as Other*. If I am not unjust in my being, then I cannot be just, that is, recognize the Other *as Other*. Injustice as an ontological fact is the condition of justice as an ethical possibility. Levinas' most fundamental criticism of Plato is therefore that Plato, in transforming the ethical relation into an ontological one, destroys ethics by absorbing it into ontology.

A PLATONIC REPLY TO LEVINAS

This is where a genuine *Auseinandersetzung* between Plato and Levinas becomes both possible and profitable. For can one not reply, in Plato's defense, that his characterization of eros, recollection, and participation, rather than reducing the Other to the Same, instead opens up the Same to the Other, shattering the apparent autonomy and self-sufficiency of the Same? Can one not reply that rather than reduce ethics to ontology, Plato opens up ontology to ethics and that this is in no way the same thing? Is not the source of the ambiguity in Levinas' relation to Plato the fact that Plato offers an alternative to the Levinasian dichotomy between separate, self-same, and self-sufficient being, on the one hand, and the absolutely Other, on the other? That eros, recollection, and participation defy the dichotomy between absolute interiority and absolute exteriority?

So that these suggestions do not remain abstract, it is worth returning again to the *Phaedrus* and noting in particular the ambivalence of Levinas' reference to Plato's description there of the soul nourishing itself, or specifically its wings, on truth (248b6–c2). On the one hand, Levinas must oppose this description because the whole thrust of his argument in the book is to reject any identification of truth with nourishment and satisfaction: "Throughout this book we are opposing the full analogy drawn between truth and nourishment, because metaphysical Desire is above life, and with regard to it one cannot speak of satiety" (*TI* 114). Truth as the object of metaphysical desire is for Levinas something absolutely exterior, superfluous, and luxurious that does not answer to any need or lack in the soul. Yet Levinas continues by observing that Plato's image captures the nourishment that Levinas has been calling *jouissance* (*TI* 114). Thus, because Plato's image of the soul feeding on truth in the place beyond the heavens does not fit what Levinas calls metaphysical desire, he interprets it as expressing that self-sufficient self-enjoyment that he calls *jouissance*. But of course, Plato's image suits the latter as little as it suits the former: the truth on which the soul feeds and which it enjoys is not the soul itself nor anything immediate or imminent, but instead a truth that transcends it. One could argue, of course, that this lack of a fit demonstrates the incoherence of Plato's image as an image that expresses a transcendent immanence or an immanent transcendence (being nourished on what is beyond oneself!) (*Phaedrus* 248b7). But one could also argue that rather than being simply incoherent, Plato's image suggests a genuine third alternative distinct from both the self-satisfaction and self-sufficiency of *jouissance* and a metaphysical desire external to the being of he who desires.

The need for such a third alternative, furthermore, could be defended through a Platonic critique of Levinas. This critique would be that Levinas' insistence on the autonomy and self-sufficiency of the Same makes metaphysical desire impossible (and incomprehensible, though he might grant that[13]) rather than possible. If a being in *jouissance* is "absolutely closed over upon itself," as Levinas insists, then it appears not only not to entail metaphysical desire, but even to positively exclude its possibility. Levinas must therefore state paradoxically: "In the separated being the door to the outside must hence be at the same time open and closed" (*TI* 148). What makes this more than a paradox and an outright contradiction is that Levinas clearly cannot say that the door is *partly open* and *partly closed*: it must be *absolutely open* and *absolutely closed*.

The logical contradiction is not in itself an objection, since Levinas grants that the relation between the Same and the Other defies logic; strictly speaking, it is not even a "relation," of course. But one can still object that, given his assumption of egoism as an ontological fact, Levinas cannot make any sense at all, logical or otherwise, of the possibility of an openness toward the Other. Levinas apparently tries to provide some explanation of the "open door" by asserting (*TI* 149) that within the heart of *jouissance* itself a heteronomy can produce itself that "furnishes the *occasion* for" (earlier on the same page he unjustifiably writes the stronger "incites"—a revealing slip?) a reprise of relations with exteriority. The insecurity that provides this occasion, that is, the indetermination of the future and the dependence on the elemental (cf. *TI* 143–44, 164), cannot, however, be one that undermines *jouissance* and thus requires or even incites it to open up to the Other. This is why Levinas speaks only of an "occasion" here. But then one can ask not only why, but *how* a radically separate, self-sufficient being seizes this occasion. In later summarizing the relation between the Same and the Other, Levinas again insists that the invocation of the Other "leaves room for a process of being that is deduced from itself, that is, remains separated and capable of shutting itself up against the very appeal that has aroused it, but also capable of welcoming this face of infinity with all the resources of its egoism: economically" (*TI* 216). But then one can ask: *What* are the *resources* of ontological egoism such that it is *capable* of receiving the face of the infinite? From whence this mysterious capability?

By the claim in the last quote that we receive the face of the infinite *economically*, Levinas means that we must always receive the Other within a home:

> No human or interhuman relationship can be enacted outside of economy; no face can be approached with empty hands and closed home. Recollection in a home open to the Other—hospitality—is the concrete and initial fact of human recollection and separation; it coincides with the Desire for the Other absolutely transcendent. (*TI* 172)

Only such a reception of the Other within a home prevents the relation to the Other from being a violent one in which the Other annihilates the Same. But now we can ask: How can we welcome the Other within our home, and thus enter a non-violent relation with the Other,[14] if our home is not in its being open to the Other, if it is fundamentally "egoist" (*TI* 157, 173), and if the Other does not in its being belong there? The Platonic alternative would be to characterize the Other as *oikeion*: as *belonging to* the Same in a way that does not destroy its transcendence, that is, that does not make it merely "in" the Same. The objection to Levinas is that he wishes to claim that the Other is received *economically* while insisting that the Other is in no way *oikeion*.

Levinas is indeed willing to speak of human fraternity or paternity (cf. *TI* 213–14), and at one point he even claims that fraternity is not something added to man but something that constitutes his ipseity: "Because my position as an I is *effectuated* already in fraternity, the face can present itself to me as a face" (*TI* 280). Here, then, we have the suggestion that what makes it possible for the face to present itself to me as face is the fact that my position as me has already been effectuated in fraternity: a suggestion that comes close to the Platonic notion of *oikeiotes*. Yet at the same time, there is the insistence that the Other does not in any way belong to the Same and defies any "economy." Especially revealing in this regard is the claim that the Other transcends the hermeneutics by which it is initially understood by involving "a signifyingness of its own, independent of this meaning received from the world. The Other comes to us not only out of context but also without mediation; he signifies by himself" ("Meaning and Sense," *BPW* 53). The Other also transcends its phenomenal presentation and thus phenomenology: "His presence consists in divesting himself of the form which does already manifest him. His manifestation is a surplus over the inevitable paralysis of manifestation" (*BPW* 53). Levinas then proceeds to ask the following crucial questions: "How can the coming of the Other, the visitation of a face, the absolute not be—in any way—converted into a revelation, not even a symbolism or a suggestion? How is a face not simply *a true representation* in which the Other renounces his alterity?" (*BPW* 53; cf. 59). The problem for Levinas is again how the alterity of the Other can be preserved in being "economically" received and welcomed. Because he refuses to see the Other as in any sense belonging to, or at home in, the Same (or vice versa), there appears to be an irresolvable dilemma here.[15]

Significantly, Derrida, after insisting against Levinas that "the other cannot be absolutely exterior to the same without ceasing to be other," turns for support to none other than Plato—or, more precisely, to the Stranger in the *Sophist* who "knows that alterity can be thought only as negativity, and above all, can be *said* only as negativity, which Levinas begins by refusing; he knows too, that differing from being, the other is always relative, is stated *pros eteron,* which does not prevent it from being an *eidos* (or a *genre,* in a nonconceptual sense), that is, from being the same as itself."[16] Derrida thus finds in Plato an important objection to Levinas: because what is other is always *other than,* something *absolutely other* would not be *other at all.* The Other is *other* only in relation to the Same, only in being welcomed into the home of the Same.

The question ultimately at issue here can be expressed in the words of Jean-François Mattéi: "Is ethics definitely opposed to ontology, the ethical primordial sin being the fall, not into non-being, but into being . . . ?"[17] If one can find in Plato a conception of metaphysical desire that identifies it neither with a lack or need to be satisfied nor with absolute transcendence and exteriority, neither with the *jouissance* of a self-sufficing, separate being nor with a self-emptying into the absolutely Other, then the answer may well be, contra Levinas, negative. In this way the debate between Plato and Levinas might point toward a "third way" of the kind recently called for by Richard Kearney:

> Confronted at the same time with the traditional philosophy of sameness and the postmodern fixation with alterity, we need to construct bridges between these extremes represented by tautology and heterology. It is in this way that philosophy might perhaps aid us to discover the other in our self and our self in the other, without abjuring either the one or the other.[18]

The opposition of extremes described here is precisely that found in Levinas. That Plato can help us get beyond this opposition is suggested by the way in which Kearney describes what he sees as the "third way": "Between the *logos* of the One and the anti-*logos* of the Other, one finds the *dia-logos* of oneself as another."[19] As stretched out toward a transcendent truth in desire and reminiscence, the soul as understood by Plato can think this truth only in dialogue with itself *as another* and therefore only in dialogue *with others.* Neither a reduction of the Other to the Self-Same nor the postulation between the two of a deaf and mute silence that must miraculously be overcome, Plato's thought is a dialogue between the Self-Same and the Other, or rather, between the Self-Same as Other and the Other as Self-Same.

Notes

1. Cited in Adriaan Theodoor Peperzak, *Platonic Transformations: With and after Hegel, Heidegger, and Levinas* (Lanham, Md.: Rowman and Littlefield, 1997), 113, 121. For a counting of Levinas' many references to Plato, both in this work and in others, see Jean-François Mattéi, "Lévinas et Platon," in *Emmanuel Lévinas: Positivité et Transcendance*, ed. Jean-Luc Marion (Paris: Presse Universitaire de France), 74–75. See also Levinas' description of a "return to Platonism in a new way" ("Meaning and Sense," *BPW* 58).

2. See Stella Sanford, "Plato and Levinas: The Same and the Other," *Journal of the British Society for Phenomenology* 30, 2 (1999): 141.

3. For Derrida's critique of this retrieval and his attempt to reverse all of Levinas' propositions on this point, see Jacques Derrida, "Violence and Metaphysics: An Essay on the Thought of Emmanuel Levinas," in *Writing and Difference*, trans. Alan Bass (Chicago: University of Chicago Press, 1978), 101–103.

4. See Derrida's reflections on the inescapable negativity of Levinas' thought/speech: how it must work both within and against the traditional conceptuality ("Violence and Metaphysics," 90, 112–17).

5. Part of what is at issue in this question is the problem of the self-predication of Forms. For a discussion of the debate and an argument that the Forms are not to be understood as ideal instances of themselves, see Francisco J. Gonzalez, "Plato's Dialectic of Forms," in *Plato's Forms: Varieties of Interpretation*, ed. William A. Welton (Lanham, Md.: Lexington Books, 2002), 31–83.

6. On this important passage, see Peperzak, *Platonic Transformations*, 117; see also Jacques Taminiaux, *Sillages Phénoménologiques: Auditeurs et lecteurs de Heidegger* (Bruxelles: Éditions OUSIA, 2002), 247–48. Sanford, in contrast, completely overlooks it in asserting that "the Platonic *eidos* stands alongside the Parmenidean 'One,' the Aristotelian 'categories,' the Hegelian 'Concept,' and the Heideggerian 'Being' as one of the great mediating and neutralizing gestures of Western philosophy," so that "the notion of a Platonic Idea of the other would be no other at all according to Levinas' rigorous requirements" (Sanford, "Plato and Levinas," 138). Derrida also ignores Levinas' question in simply asserting that what Plato, along with Descartes, fails to recognize is "that the expression of this infinity is the *face*" (Derrida, "Violence and Metaphysics," 98).

7. "The word 'nudity' thus destroys itself after serving to indicate something beyond itself " (*TI* 106).

8. Derrida sees in this critique of anamnesis the repetition of a Kierkegaardian critique, though Kierkegaard attributes this idea to Plato and not to Socrates (Derrida, "Violence and Metaphysics," 314 n. 27).

9. Mattéi, "Lévinas et Platon," 79.

10. Peperzak, *Platonic Transformations*, 115.

11. The passage leaves open the possibility that what is good is what is most truly our own (205e6–7). And as I argue elsewhere, this is precisely the thesis suggested by the end of the *Lysis;* see Francisco J. Gonzalez, "Socrates on Loving One's Own: A Traditional Conception of Φιλία Radically Transformed," *Classical Philology* 95 (2000): 393–95. For reasons given below, I think that even this thesis can be defended against Levinas' critique that it destroys the transcendence of the Other (the good) by reducing it to the Same (what is my own).

12. I have also argued elsewhere for an alternative interpretation of *anamnesis* that does not identify it with some absolute interiority: "How is the Truth of Beings in the Soul? Interpreting *Anamnesis* in Plato," *Elenchos* 28, 2 (2007).

13. At least he grants that it defies logic and dialectic (*TI* 150).

14. But Levinas must also characterize the relation as *war* to the extent that it exists only between beings that "refuse to belong to a totality, refuse community, refuse law; no frontier stops one being by another, nor defines them" (*TI* 222). He must also claim that violence is possible only in such a relation (223, 225).

15. It is not clear that in the discussion of the notion of the "trace" that follows Levinas does or can provide a satisfactory answer to the cited questions.

16. Derrida, "Violence and Metaphysics," 126–27.

17. Mattéi, "Lévinas et Platon," 79; my translation.

18. Richard Kearney, "Entre soi-même et un autre: l'herméneutique diacritique de Ricœur," in *L'Herne Ricœur,* ed. Myriam Revault d'Allonnes, and François Azouvi (Paris: Éditions de l'Herne, 2004), 206; my translation.

19. Ibid., 212; my translation. In a note, Kearney describes what he proposes: "The model which I propose here, as a hermeneutical melding of ethics and ontology, is a 'third way,' an alternative to the extremes represented by expropriation *à la Levinas* and appropriation *à la Husserl.* I am attempting to negotiate a new dialogue between ethos and logos, to reveal a chiasm of asymmetry and reciprocity" (ibid., 218 n. 22); my translation.

GETTING UNDER THE SKIN:

PLATONIC MYTHS IN LEVINAS

Tanja Stähler

4

> Interiority must be at the same time closed and open.
>
> —Levinas, *Totality and Infinity*

> Next, they must be judged when they're stripped naked of all these things, for they should be judged when they're dead. The judge, too, should be naked, and dead, and with only his soul he should study only the soul of each person immediately upon his death, when he's isolated from all his kinsmen and has left behind on earth all that adornment, so that the judgment may be a just one.
>
> —Plato, *Gorgias*

In an interview conducted in 1981, Philippe Nemo asks Emmanuel Levinas: "How does one begin thinking?" (*EI* 21). Levinas answers that thinking arises from certain traumatisms, from certain events that cannot be considered full-fledged experiences because we cannot name or describe them. Levinas gives examples of separation from a loved one or scenes of violence; he could also have mentioned sudden encounters with death, solitude, or vulnerability. It is essential that these events happen in a moment; once we start thematizing them, we have already moved beyond them. We can proceed to analyze the situations from which they arose, explain them, and thereby overcome our shock. An analysis and rationalization of this sort, however, is not philosophical thought. Another possibility is to turn the shock into a question, which is the beginning of thinking. Levinas says that books help us in this transformation: "It is from the reading of books—not necessarily philosophical—that these initial shocks become questions and problems, [inspiring] one to think" (*EI* 21).

The influence of literature becomes obvious throughout Levinas' work. The Russian Realists (especially Dostoyevsky) and Shakespeare are arguably most important for his thinking. Allusions to literature provide density for Levinas' philosophy, and sometimes a particular philosophical thought is inextricably tied to a specific citation from literature or an invocation of a literary *topos*.[1] In fact, references to literature are so rife in Levinas' writings that one might be tempted to wonder whether he wants to overcome the split between philosophy and literature, between argumentation and narrative, between *logos* and *muthos*. Or perhaps he does not so much want to overcome the split as to go back behind it, to the philosopher who combined *logos* and *muthos* so skillfully and yet was always (and much more so than Levinas) very concerned about their difference: Plato.

Platonic myths play a significant role in Levinas' work. Levinas refers to the myth told by Aristophanes in the *Symposium,* to the myth of Theuth in the *Phaedrus,* to the myth of Gyges from the *Republic,* and to the myth at the end of the *Gorgias.* The most conspicuous myth in *Totality and Infinity* is the myth of Gyges, whereas in *Otherwise than Being or Beyond Essence,* the myth of the last judgment at the end of the *Gorgias* plays the more important role. I focus on these latter two myths in this essay not just because of the prominent place they take in those major works but also because there are interesting connections between the two myths themselves. Both stories are based on the ambiguous relationship between visibility and invisibility, exposure and secrecy.

Levinas' philosophy has been strongly influenced by Plato; he acknowledges Plato particularly for realizing that the Good is beyond Being, or in other words, that the Good transcends any given totality. Both Plato and Levinas are philosophers of verticality. In Plato, we ascend from the cave to the sunlight, and from the lower to the upper part of the divided line. Each of the two Platonic allegories is designed to illuminate the progression from the perception of various appearances to an insight into the Forms. In Levinas, the Other is essentially unforeseeable and comes to me from the ethical height with which he or she confronts me. Doing justice means recognizing and acknowledging this asymmetry between the Other and me.

In what follows, I trace out the connections between Levinas and Plato with regard to the two myths mentioned; in doing this, a number of themes will be touched upon: not only the relation between *muthos* and *logos*, hiddenness and exposure, but also matters of nakedness, vulnerability, and responsibility. For Plato as for Levinas, these themes are all interconnected, and they are all relevant to the two myths I single out. My goal is to illuminate several main concepts of Levinas' philosophy—interiority, exteriority, and infinite responsibility—through his reading of the two myths and, in turn, to shed new light on these myths in Plato.

By focusing on the two myths that play the most important roles in *Totality and Infinity* and in *Otherwise than Being*, respectively, this essay also takes a position regarding the relation between Levinas' two main works. While it might appear as if the terminology of interiority and exteriority becomes obsolete in Levinas' later work, these terms can actually still be understood in a coherent fashion if certain misunderstandings about their relation are avoided. The myth of Gyges helps to prevent such misconceptions. Even though developments and modifications in Levinas' work are undeniable, it turns out that the two main texts form a cohesive whole, complementing each other rather than rendering the earlier work superfluous.

INTERIORITY AND THE MYTH OF GYGES

The Platonic myth of Gyges will be our guide for exploring interiority, since Levinas claims that this myth is not a fictional story, but describes our human condition. It is possible for us, so Levinas claims, to sever our connection to the world and to others, to close ourselves off within ourselves and indulge in egoistic enjoyment. This would be a state of seeing without being seen, observing without participating; and this state neither creates internal contradictions nor can easily be detected by others. The ring of Gyges symbolizes a state of radical injustice at the core of our existence.

I consider the myth of Gyges here because it will help us to discuss some important questions about the dimension Levinas refers to as "interiority"—questions such as: What is interiority? Is interiority a state that precedes my encounter with others and perhaps even my encounter with the world? Why does Levinas deem it necessary to investigate interiority, and do such investigations not run counter to his "philosophy of alterity"?

A provisional response to the first question could take its departure from terms Levinas brings up as he explores interiority, most importantly, "separation," "closing oneself off," and "being at home with oneself." Separation designates a division, a severance of the ties between me and those parts that I am connected to, or the world that surrounds me. Such a manner of speech, along with the expression "closing oneself off," indicates that this separation severs a connection and is, in that sense, secondary or derivative in relation to the original connection. Levinas strengthens this impression when he says that separation "breaks" with participation or "no longer" participates (*TI* 61, 90). However, a response to the second question will be more complicated than these preliminary quotes imply: the state of interiority is primordial as well as secondary; it is both anterior and posterior—and it is this paradox that Levinas inflicts on us and our ways of thought.

Furthermore, it seems that interiority is not a "real" state that occurs in any "pure" form. If I ever exist as true interiority, it would be in a moment of egoistic enjoyment, a moment where I do not lack anything. It is this observation, namely, the fact that "in a certain sense one lacks nothing" (*TI* 61), that the idea of interiority expresses. Levinas explores this dimension to show that at the basis of my existence there is not a lack but self-sufficiency. Thus, my encounter with otherness is not based on deficiency; the Other does not complement me, but rather ruptures my interiority.

After these very preliminary remarks on interiority, which need to be fleshed out, we will explore the myth of Gyges in order to elucidate our complicated human condition. The myth of Gyges tells a story about Gyges, a shepherd in the service of the king of Lydia (*Republic* 359d–360b). One day, after a thunderstorm and an earthquake has broken open the ground, Gyges finds a corpse in the chasm created by the earthquake.[2] The corpse is wearing nothing but a golden ring, which the shepherd takes with him. After some time, he realizes that the ring makes him invisible if he turns it inward and visible again if he turns it outward. Gyges abuses the power that the discovered ring gives him by seducing the king's wife, killing the king with her help, and taking over the kingdom. Glaucon tells this story to Socrates to show that we only act in a just fashion because we want to avoid punishment. Nobody, so the common opinion goes, would stay on the path of justice if given the chance to do whatever they wanted to without being seen, and thus without having to be accountable. This, of course, is not Socrates' conviction; he wants to show that we not only want to *appear* just, but in fact *be* just.[3] However, the myth makes it obvious that Socrates has a very difficult task if he wants to show that justice indeed belongs to the highest goods, which are valued both for their own sake and because of their consequences.

Glaucon tells the myth of the ring of Gyges because he wants to represent the common opinion about justice. According to the common view, justice is an intermediate between two extremes. The best would be to do injustice without being punished, the worst to suffer injustice without being able to take revenge (*Republic* 359a). Out of fear of suffering injustice, people make laws and contracts. So the myth of Gyges is told in the context of discussions about justice, the main topic of the *Republic*. More precisely, the myth forms the transition between the ordinary views about justice as they are represented by Cephalus, Polemarchus, and Thrasymachus in Book I of the *Republic*, and Socrates' account of what justice is as he develops the idea of a perfect *polis*.

For Levinas, on the most general level, this myth represents our condition of being separated from each other, being enclosed in ourselves, and not acknowledging the call of the Other. We can exist in a state of injustice without encountering any apparent contradiction. Levinas calls this state the ego's interiority or separation, and he says that the myth of Gyges is a myth of the I and interiority:

> Separation would not be radical if the possibility of shutting oneself up at home with oneself could not be produced without internal contradiction as an event in itself, as atheism itself is produced—if it should only be an empirical, psychological fact, an illusion. Gyges' ring symbolizes separation. Gyges plays a double game, a presence to the others and an absence, speaking to "others" and evading speech; Gyges is the very condition of man, the possibility of injustice and radical egoism, the possibility of accepting the rules of the game, but cheating. (*TI* 173)

The state of the ego that closes itself off is not a contradictory state but a self-sufficient one. There are no internal contradictions because there is no lack that the presence of the Other would fill. If egoism is interrupted, this happens, not because there are logical contradictions in this position or because I realize that I want to live my life differently, but because the Other makes me aware of my egoism. It is not possible to develop an ethics grounded in egoism, but rather, ethics happens as the Other calls my selfishness into question. Egoism will then still be a moment in ethics, yet it will not be the basis of ethics. It is the possibility of—and temptation toward—playing the game of Gyges.

The ego's interiority is ambivalent; it opens the possibility both of error *and* of truth. Gyges is the very condition of man because we can radically close ourselves off from others. We have the option of seeing without being seen. If necessary, we can turn away, lower our heads, and remain inconspicuous. And we can excel in this attitude to such an extent that we do not even notice the imbalance between seeing but not being seen.

We can be invisible; we have the ability to act as an invisible person in that realm which we take to be the realm of the visible. Being on the border between visibility and invisibility, being present in the absence and absent in the presence is what Levinas calls "phenomenality." The phenomenon is the being that "appears, but remains absent" (*TI* 181). In order to explain this absence, Levinas refers to another Platonic myth that figures prominently in his work, the myth of Theuth from the *Phaedrus*. In the case of a written speech, the author does not come to the assistance of his speech but remains absent, opening the possibility of misunderstanding and misuse.[4] Similarly, the state of interiority means that I am not taking responsibility for my actions, but hiding away like Gyges. "As long as the existence of man remains interiority it remains phenomenal" (*TI* 182).

The absence that characterizes phenomenality is an essential absence; it is not the absence of some future revelation or light. Some things cannot be drawn into any light; others can, but are not meant to be drawn into the light. Levinas is suspicious of vision in general. Gyges exploits the possibilities of visibility and invisibility that speech and silence, for example, do not offer. Vision gives us the illusion of power; it means to have things on display, at our disposal. The visual metaphors in the history of Western philosophy (among which *theoria* is the most prominent, but certainly not the only one) had a major influence on the violent and totalizing character of philosophy, Levinas believes.

To illustrate such dangers, it might be helpful to consider briefly another version of the myth of Gyges, told not by Plato but by Herodotus in *The Histories*. According to Herodotus, a strange episode occurred in Lydia when King Candaules had the idea of asking Gyges, his favorite spearman, to confirm the beauty of Candaules' wife. Candaules was so in love with his wife that praising his wife's beauty was not enough; he suggested that Gyges hide behind the door to watch the queen undress and see her beauty with his own eyes. Gyges, though reluctant at first and quite willing to confirm that he completely trusted the king's judgment, finally agreed. But when he left the bedchamber, the queen spotted him. She was ashamed, and yet she remained silent. The next day she called Gyges and gave him the choice to die himself or to kill the king and take his place. She said: "Either he must die who formed this design, or you who have looked upon me naked." So Candaules was killed and Gyges became king. A story about the ambiguity of love, about shame, secrecy, and possessiveness—and a story about visibility and invisibility, about breaking the secret of Gyges, in this case not broken by Gyges himself but by the queen who discovers his secretive looking. The king who succumbed to the power of vision in the end loses it all.

The ring of Gyges plays a significant role throughout Levinas' thought. Yet Levinas undertakes some modifications and even reversals in regard to the original myth. For him the myth is not about an unreal thought experiment, but it actually presents an ability that we, as humans, have. We can hide in our invisibility, in the interiority of the ego. We can do so—but we cannot be right as we do so. Using the ring of Gyges is radical injustice.

In *Totality and Infinity*, Levinas examines interiority to emphasize that it is possible to ignore the call of the Other. Such ignoring is itself a response, namely, the response of denial. Analyzing this possibility is important since Levinas has to acknowledge the fact that the command coming from the Other is frequently denied. Yet such denial does not refute Levinas' ethical philosophy, which we examine below. Moreover, he points out that I encounter the Other, not on the basis of a lack or need, but from a self-sufficient basis. As the Other enters the scene, his or her demands solicit the separated being who is satisfied and autonomous. The face of the Other that speaks to me calls into question the security of my dwelling.

The approach taken in *Totality and Infinity* is helpful since it enables phenomenological analyses (in the widest sense) of interiority, the body, enjoyment.

However, this line of analysis can easily be misunderstood as implying that the sphere of interiority is existent *prior* to my encounter with the Other. This is not the case: "The light of the face is necessary for separation" (*TI* 151). Yet interiority is not strictly speaking posterior either; it is both anterior and posterior. "Anterior" and "posterior" are not temporal categories here (given Levinas' request that we rethink time on the basis of alterity and ethics), but rather they designate conditions for the possibility of certain experiences, if these Kantian expressions may be used in an entirely different framework. My autonomous dwelling and enjoyment are conditions for encountering the Other (that is, for an encounter that is not based on a lack); and at the same time, this encounter conditions my enjoyment, since such egoistic happiness depends on the fact that I am retreating, no longer participating. This relation could be called a co-dependence if we are capable of thinking co-dependence in the strong, emphatic sense that maintains the original paradox.

Another reason for Levinas to present interiority as if it were a prior state is his concern that it might be taken as a mere counterpart or reversal of my relation with the Other. Although it is important to understand interiority and exteriority in relation to each other, a flawed image of interiority would arise if it were just the reverse of exteriority. Interiority is not solitude or longing; it has its own modes, such as sensibility and enjoyment. Levinas claims that "the relation with the Other is the only relation where such an overturning of formal logic can occur" (*TI* 180ff.). Interiority cannot be understood as the reverse of exteriority or vice versa. The story of Gyges helps to show that the state of separation consists of its own stories and ways of being.

An additional line of explaining interiority is introduced through the term *psychism*, which is Levinas' word for the "inner life" (*TI* 54). It is an important term already, because he will refer to this idea in *Otherwise than Being* under the heading of "psyche." The inner life, the life of the psyche, is not contrasted with the physical life; interiority actually encompasses corporeality. Rather, it names a resistance, a "resistance to the totality" (*TI* 54). Against the tendency to attribute a place in the world to every being, thereby making it part of the totality, the ego strives to maintain its uniqueness. Realizing that I am also part of a whole does not take away from my sense that I am opposed to this whole and that the singularity of my enjoyment depends on my resistance and separation.

Levinas acknowledges the difficulty of thinking interiority and separation. The structure of *Totality and Infinity*, where the section on interiority precedes the section on exteriority, facilitates his investigation while at the same time inviting misunderstandings about the order and relation of these two modes. In *Otherwise than Being*, Levinas moves away from the systematic structure of his earlier work to avoid such misunderstandings. He now stresses that the Other is in me from the very beginning, and his name for this invasion is "psyche."[5] The Other is under my skin, as we will see with the myth from Plato's *Gorgias*.

INFINITE RESPONSIBILITY AND THE MYTH OF THE *GORGIAS*

"Infinite responsibility" is an idea that runs throughout Levinas' work, even though *Otherwise than Being* introduces it in a different fashion than *Totality and Infinity*. In *Otherwise than Being*, Levinas emphasizes that I only become a subject in my encounter with the Other, and as a subject, I am always already "obsessed" or held "hostage" by the Other. I neither choose to encounter the Other, nor do I ever exist in a state of not having experienced such an encounter. Moreover, the expression "call" from Levinas' earlier work could be misconceived as connoting a rather harmonious and uncompromising situation, whereas the language of *Otherwise than Being* makes it obvious that I have the Other "under my skin" no matter how much I try to free myself from him or her. When the Other says *no* to my killing him or her, this is not so much a *no* from a being in front of me as it is a *no* that touches me in my core, as if coming from inside me, threatening to rip apart my existence if I go against it.

In order to explore further the concepts of responsibility and having the Other "under my skin," we now turn to Plato's *Gorgias*, which proves a crucial dialogue for Levinas' *Otherwise than Being*. Levinas' claims about infinite responsibility strike many contemporary readers as outrageous in a way similar to the anger caused among Socrates' interlocutors by his claims about the happiness of the just person. This anger motivates the extensive discussions about justice that form the *Republic*. In the *Gorgias*, Socrates holds the extreme position that doing injustice without being punished is the worst thing that can happen to a person (since there is no chance for improvement), and that such a person would be most unhappy (*Gorgias*, 479d).

The arguments for this statement go through various twists and turns. When arguing with Polus, Socrates defends the argument by examining different meanings of shamefulness. Since Polus admits that doing injustice is more shameful than suffering it and also agrees with Socrates that what is more shameful surpasses what is less shameful either in pain or in badness, he has to agree that doing injustice is worse than suffering it (for it clearly does not seem more painful) (*Gorgias* 475b). When Callicles, unhappy about Polus' capitulation, picks up the discussion, Socrates refutes the thesis that good equals pleasant, that is, a certain form of hedonism, as part of his argument for the thesis about the happiness of the just person. Following this argumentation step by step would require a substantial analysis; however, the argument underlying both of these considerations is ultimately a simple one that involves the nature of the soul.

The soul, so Socrates argues, has a certain purpose, and this purpose is being just, which is what the soul aims at, what the soul is good at, and what fulfils the nature of the soul. Justice of the soul, according to Socrates, connotes being well organized and self-controlled (*Gorgias* 506d). If our soul is able to fulfill its function, this will make us happy, whereas disharmony or chaos in the soul induces misery.

Socrates likes to use an analogy between body and soul to point out that just as a sick body does not make the person happy, so a sick, unjust soul will also lead to unhappiness. Therefore, the unjust person who is being punished is better off than the unjust one who escapes, since there is a chance for improvement in the latter case. Socrates does not specify, and the Greek concept of *eudaimonia* makes it unnecessary to specify, that he means happiness in the long run, as it were, and true happiness in contrast to an illusion of happiness. The rich tyrant may assume that he is happy, but he will turn out not to be. And in the long run, this will even become obvious to other people, as Socrates shows in the myth about the last judgment; those who have an unjust soul at the time of dying will receive their due punishment.

Would Levinas embrace the Platonic conception of the just soul? Levinas' ethics is quite obviously not based on a conception of the just soul as harmonious and thus happy. Such a conception would focus too much on the ego and his or her soul, neglecting the Other. Furthermore, any theory of a soul divided into parts would nowadays have to take a stance regarding psychoanalytic ideas, and Levinas does not wish to engage in such a debate. The rare reflections on the psyche that we find in *Otherwise than Being* are striking, however, since Levinas writes, "The psyche in the soul is the other in me" (*OB* 69). He establishes where the Other who is obsessing me can be found, namely, in my soul. More precisely, as a footnote specifies, "The soul is the other in me" and is thereby "already a seed of folly," of madness (*OB* 191). And madness, as we learn from the *Phaedrus*, is highly ambiguous. Eros turns out to be a divine madness, and so is the madness inspired by the muses, but there are also several forms of human madness.[6]

While it seems futile to look for the soul's harmony in Levinas, there are two points of proximity between Plato and Levinas in addition to the rigor that connects their positions and separates them radically from everyday assumptions about justice. First, both regard the soul as a connection between interiority and exteriority. For Plato, this connection takes the shape of mirroring; the individual soul mirrors the state (and vice versa). According to Levinas, the Other enters my soul as an obsessive power, but the Other also transcends my soul. A situation of mirroring, as described by Plato, appears more peaceful and harmonious. Yet when we think of the mad and delirious soul in the *Phaedrus*, driven by a desire for ideas or Forms, which it has partly forgotten and which nevertheless obsesses it, it becomes obvious that Platonic harmony of the soul is not a simple achievement either.

Secondly, and on a more general level, both Plato and Levinas attempt an ethics that does not involve *bad conscience* as a motivating factor—and yet both philosophies can easily be misconstrued as harboring this idea. When Plato discusses the harmony of the soul as leading to happiness, a modern interpretation might tend to read disharmony as bad conscience, as the chaos that inhabits remorseful souls. But harmony of the soul is very different from a mere strategy to avoid bad conscience. Such harmony refers to the balance of the soul, and having a well-balanced soul does not presuppose experiencing and avoiding bad conscience. Furthermore, the chaos that designates an unjust soul is a more encompassing and precarious condition than bad conscience. Bad conscience has already realized that something went wrong and is focused on particular occurrences. Disorder needs a more thorough diagnosis, since the person whose soul is affected by it may only have a very vague sense of something going wrong. For this reason, Socrates has to engage his interlocutors in long discussions about the soul, its parts, and its state of being. Yet if someone recognizes that Socrates is right, this can lead to a fundamental turn of character like the *periagoge* described in the allegory of the cave.[7]

The element in Levinas' philosophy that might seem to resemble bad conscience is the "impossibility of murder." In what sense can I not kill the Other, in what sense can I not kill the face? It is tempting to assume that I cannot kill the Other because I will continue to feel bad about it. Levinas might even admit that the Other's face will haunt me and that this haunting is part of the impossibility of killing; yet this is not the same as the psychological risk of bad conscience. Bad conscience would partly be in my control, and I could provide reasons why I do not have to feel bad about my deed. But the face of the Other as haunting me is entirely beyond my control. I am responsible for the Other even after his or her death; even if I have killed the Other on the physical level, my responsibility does not come to a close. On a practical level, this responsibility would extend to those who were close to the deceased one, to everything and everyone left behind, but also to the victim's corpse and soul.

These two points of proximity between Plato and Levinas are countered by what may seem to be an opposition at the very core of their ethical theories, an opposition concerning their respective concepts of justice. According to Levinas, "justice consists in recognizing the Other as my master" (*TI* 72). How does this statement of Levinas' relate to Plato's definition of justice? In the *Republic,* we learn that "justice is doing one's own work and not meddling with what isn't one's own" (*Republic* 433b).[8] "Not meddling with what isn't one's own" seems to imply that we should leave the Other alone—but what Socrates means is that we ought not undertake tasks for which we are unsuited, since the three parts of the soul should be in harmony. "Doing one's own work" could well mean to be responsible for the Other (for example, in health care); moreover, it might turn out that it is exactly my "work" to recognize the privilege of the Other and to do everything this recognition demands of me. Hence, there exists no real contradiction regarding the different concepts of justice.

Yet the fact that the two concepts of justice do not conflict in such an obvious way does not necessarily mean that Plato and Levinas would be in agreement about the nature of justice. They do agree that justice is not a matter of law courts and that it belongs to a more fundamental level. This is a conviction that virtually all philosophers share and, ever since Kant, discuss under the heading of morality versus legality. However, for Plato as well as Levinas, justice is something immediate, neither mediated by a concern for consequences (as in consequentialist ethics) nor by a version of the categorical imperative (as in deontological ethics). In Plato, this immediacy is expressed through his considerations on the Good beyond Being and all of the myths that involve the soul's contact with justice.[9] According to Levinas, the myth at the end of the *Gorgias* serves particularly well to show this immediacy. This myth plays a crucial role for Levinas' philosophy; there are indications that the significance of skin in *Otherwise than Being* can be traced back to this Platonic myth.

The myth at the end of the *Gorgias* is told by Socrates, who claims that it is not a mere tale but an account, a *logos* (523a). The myth, which goes back to Homer, reports that during Cronus's time, Zeus realized that the cases of the people judged for their lives were badly decided because the people were judged the day they were going to die, when they were still alive and fully dressed. The judges were awestruck by the clothes of the people they had to judge but also by the beauty or ugliness of their bodies. In order to come to a fair judgment, both the judge and the person judged have to be stripped not only of their clothes but even of their bodies, so that soul encounters soul. Socrates says that just as the corpse, after the soul has left it behind, still shows whether someone was fat or skinny, healthy or sick, so too the soul, after being stripped naked of the body, shows its true nature and what has happened to it. Since the soul is more naked than a naked body, no deception is possible, and fair judgments are passed.

The role of this myth at the end of a dialogue about justice is problematic since it could undermine Socrates' general claim that we want to be just for the sake of itself rather than for the sake of some external reward. According to the myth, the final judgment decides whether the dead souls go to the Isles of the Blessed or to Tartarus. As he seems aware of conflicts with his earlier claims, Socrates does not present this myth as an argument for his thesis that the just person is the happiest person. He merely holds that "to arrive in Hades with one's soul stuffed full of unjust actions is the ultimate of all bad things" (*Gorgias* 522e), a further horror after having already been unhappy during life due to the disorder of the soul. It is also possible that Socrates presents this final myth for those listeners who, after the philosophical discussions, still wonder about the afterlife.

The myth from the *Gorgias* forms an interesting contrast with the myth of Gyges. Both myths explore issues of visibility and invisibility, and both involve a reversal. When Gyges, with the help of his ring, becomes invisible, he still moves in the realm of the visible, so that he can be unjust without being punished. In the myth of the *Gorgias*, souls encounter each other in the realm of the dead. Everything that constitutes visibility for human beings is taken away, and it is presumed that exactly through this removal it will be possible to see more.

For Levinas, on the most general level, the myth of Gyges represents our condition of being separated from each other, being enclosed in ourselves, and not acknowledging the call of the Other. The myth of the *Gorgias*, on the other hand, symbolizes radical openness to the Other, an encounter from soul to soul, a proximity that gets under the skin.

Levinas interprets the myth of the *Gorgias* as a description of the Other approaching me. This approach is immediate, and external attributes do not play any role in it. The removal of external attributes takes place in two steps. First, everything that covers the body is removed, like clothes and jewelry. But this removal is not yet radical enough; the skin and the body have to be removed as well. The skin color, for example, should not play any role in my encounter with the Other. Such removal suppresses "all conditions for knowledge" (*OB* 199 n. 25), Levinas claims. An encounter in the original and emphatic sense, that is, an ethical encounter, is not an epistemological endeavor. In contrast to a judgment in a legal court, such an encounter does not benefit if more and more information is gathered and laid out.

While Levinas appreciates how Plato describes the ultimate insignificance of all specific attributes, he does not fail to point out that in some sense, the origin of the Other makes a difference. When it comes to choosing the final judges, Plato takes care to establish a "certain community," as Levinas calls it, between the judge and the judged. If the judge stems from the same general region of the world as the judged one, a fairer judgment can be expected. This is a Platonic insight that Levinas reports but perhaps does not fully utilize. When Levinas discusses the connection between an ethical one-to-one encounter and a political community, he tends to move immediately from the dyad to all of humanity, stressing that all others come to appear in the eyes of the Other. In the political domain, however, it is necessary to attend to communities that share a certain history and culture. Sharing a "certain community" is relevant in the political, although not in the ethical register. The difficult relation between the political and the ethical that troubles Levinas' philosophy could benefit from a sustained consideration of the myth from the *Gorgias;* yet this is an issue we cannot examine further here.[10]

UNDER THE SKIN

There are two main lessons that Levinas would like us to draw from these Platonic myths, and each of these lessons goes along with a correction from Levinas' side. First, "we can note that for Plato the approach of the other is beyond experience, beyond consciousness, like a dying" (*OB* 190 n. 35). The approach of the Other is like a dying—it is traumatic, immediate, and pure. It ruptures my world and transforms it in a way that is as fundamental as the transition from life to death. However, and this is the correction, Levinas brings those myths (the myth from the *Gorgias* as well as that of Gyges) back into our world, the world of the living. It is not after our death that we encounter the Other in this radical fashion, but the very condition of our existence is the proximity of naked soul to naked soul. Similarly, the condition of Gyges is not a mere thought experiment but describes our human condition. Levinas shows that the Platonic myths are about the here and now, about *this* world.

The second lesson concerns the possibility of the Other speaking to me from soul to soul, straightforwardly without any mediation. When the Other speaks to me and calls on my responsibility, vision and hearing are inessential; eyes, ears, and mouth are only secondary. Levinas calls this radical proximity "saying," and the myth from the *Gorgias* helps to indicate that there is a "signifyingness" in the saying that is "not 'poorer' than the said" (*OB* 199 n. 25). However, Plato misconceives this primordial contact when he describes it as a judgment. The original encounter with the Other, according to Levinas, is not a situation of being judged but one of being accused in the literal sense: called upon. Judgments only arise and become necessary when someone else enters the face-to-face relationship, namely, the third (*OB* 190 n. 35).[11] Judgments lead away from the ethical level to political considerations.

Both of these lessons are to be learned from myths; Levinas takes the Platonic myths seriously as myths in the sense that they call for an interpretation and that this interpretation is by no means an arbitrary matter. It cannot be our goal here to discuss the extensive theme of the relation between *muthos* and *logos* in Plato, nor to provide a solution to the tension between the critique of *muthos,* on the one hand, and the employment of myths, on the other. Let it suffice to say that Plato's proximity to the beginnings of Western philosophy and the resulting proximity to *muthos* makes it particularly important for him to delimit *logos* from *muthos:* he has to explicate and justify a way of thinking that had only recently emerged. The need to define philosophy, to the extent that this is possible, is also a need to distinguish it from what is so close to it that the two might be confused: *muthos.* Both philosophy and myths are concerned with language or speech, and both take up questions at the margins of what can be talked about. Yet philosophy, according to Plato, is directed at the truth, that is, at that which can stand up to thorough questioning.[12]

When Socrates justifies his myths, as outlined above, he alerts us to some interesting aspects. First, myths are something essentially human, related to our limited intellectual capacities. When we cannot give a fully reliable, necessarily true account, we would rather approach the matter in some other way and possibly speculate about different options than dismiss the topic altogether, especially if it is a topic of special significance to humans, such as the Good or the soul.[13] Second, Socrates argues that his myths are more reliable than other myths. Even though it may strike us as exaggerated to call them *logoi* (as Socrates does in the *Gorgias*) or to deny altogether that they are myths, it seems plausible that they are more than mere stories. How are they more? They arise in the context of a specific question and are meant to account for something, even if they themselves are not accounts. And Socrates always interprets his myths, integrating them into the philosophical framework.[14] Because myths pose questions rather than giving fixed answers, they call us to think.

The myth of Gyges calls us to consider our human condition between interiority and exteriority, between separation and openness. It turns out that interiority and exteriority are co-dependent. The encounter with the Other relies on a self-sufficient situation of enjoyment in which I do not need anything, yet which enables me to desire the Other who overwhelms me. At the same time, interior enjoyment is so exceptional because it signifies stepping outside of participation, and in this sense, it is dependent on exteriority. Such a description still remains valid if I realize that the Other is under my skin, since it is possible to ignore this fact and indulge in egoistic hedonism. In other words, Levinas' late philosophy does not render his earlier examinations invalid.

Yet can myths really teach us about ethics, especially if we are dealing with a myth as peculiar as the *Gorgias'* last judgment about an encounter with the Other unmediated by skin? The original face-to-face encounter is immediate, such that the attributes of the Other do not matter. However, is skin not a rather unfortunate image, given how difficult it is for us to imagine a skinless encounter in this world rather than after our death? Why is skin so important for Levinas' ethics? Levinas wants to show the significance of a "'contact' without the mediation of the skin" (*OB* 199 n. 25). We are familiar with at least one relation in which I encounter the Other without the separation of skin: pregnancy. Pregnancy, or maternity, is Levinas' model for explaining the Other in me, me being obsessed by the Other, and me being there for the Other. Maternity, Levinas points out, is a "gestation of the other in the same" (*OB* 75). It is immediately linked to, and in fact sometimes equated with, the Levinasian concepts of vulnerability and responsibility, showing how neither of them is taken over voluntarily. Is the analogy of pregnancy helpful? Levinas is certainly not retreating to biologism here. The analogy shows that there indeed exists a relation to the Other that does not link two independent beings, and a contact that is not mediated by language. Yet we expect Levinas to provide an account of the ethical relationship that extends beyond the example of pregnancy, which, to state the obvious, is not even accessible as an experience to half of humankind.

Pregnancy is an extreme case in which the Other is literally under my skin, but beyond this case, there are various ways in which the Other can get under my skin. "Getting under the skin," "*unter die Haut gehen,*" "*avoir dans le peau*"—several languages acknowledge the possibility of being approached in a way that penetrates my cover and protection. A phenomenological description of skin yields that skin is indeed the cover protecting my body, but a cover with several gaps and holes, and a cover that can be pierced.[15]

When Levinas states that the face of the Other calls me to give away the bread that I am tasting in full enjoyment and even calls me to offer my skin to the Other (*OB* 77), a number of questions arise: Does the Other have the right to ask so much of me? Is not the skin that I am giving away still *my* skin, and is it not *me* who is giving it away?[16] A philosophy of encountering the Other has to account for my need to protect myself, including my wish to establish some borders in this encounter—the most original border being my skin. Levinas acknowledges the need for protecting myself; yet there is something more fundamental, something that "all protection and all absence of protection already presuppose: vulnerability itself " (*OB* 75). Protection is secondary to the most primordial vulnerability that the notion of skin signifies.

In *Otherwise than Being,* Levinas seems to toy with the idea of replacing, or at least supplementing, "face" with "skin." At times he talks of "the unity of the face and the skin" (*OB* 192 n. 27). When he discusses the face as a strange phenomenon, present and absent, he starts his analysis with "a face approached, a contact with a skin—a face weighed down with a skin" (*OB* 89). Both face and skin are surface phenomena that Levinas wants to understand in a non-superficial fashion. The face of the Other is a non-phenomenon; it is beyond visibility and invisibility. The face is beyond the body, although the body is the trace of it. The myth of the *Gorgias* shows, similarly, that the face lies beyond the body, that it is under the skin. For Levinas, it is especially the "skin with wrinkles" (*OB* 88, 90) that exposes my vulnerability and fragility. While it is more difficult for us to imagine an encounter without mediation of the skin than a face-to-face encounter, a careful examination of skin shows how skin immediately alerts us to a depth dimension that may remain more hidden in the notion of face, and a fragility that is hard to endure.

Skin represents the vulnerability that is the condition for encountering the Other. Whereas the Other approaches me by facing me, my skin represents the need for protecting myself—until I realize that the Other is already under my skin. If we take the call of the Other seriously, we encounter him or her soul to soul, as in the myth of the *Gorgias.* We can respond to this call, or we can ignore it by turning the ring of Gyges to the inside and hiding in our invisibility, in the interiority of the ego.

Notes

I thank Benjamin Grazzini for his help with the style of this essay and for his questions and suggestions.

1. For example, when Levinas talks about infinite responsibility, he likes to quote Fyodor Dostoyevsky's *The Brothers Karamazov:* "We are guilty of all and for all men before all, and I more than the others" (trans. Constance Garnett [New York: New American Library, 1957], 264).

2. Some translations name Gyges as the main protagonist of the story, whereas others ascribe it to an ancestor of Gyges. This divergence is based on two slightly different versions of the Greek text. Since my concern lies with the general idea of the myth, this difference does not really matter.

3. The discussion between Sachs and Demos about the relation between justice in the Platonic sense and justice in the ordinary sense does not convince me, since it appears to be the point of philosophy (exemplified in the allegory of the cave) that it does not need to coincide with ordinary views on a given subject, even though there should certainly be some connection to the ordinary view. See D. Sachs, "A Fallacy in Plato's *Republic,*" *Philosophical Review* 72 (1963): 141–58, and R. Demos, "A Fallacy in Plato's *Republic?*" *Philosophical Review* 73 (1964): 395–98.

4. In addition to Derrida's well-known engagement with this myth in "Plato's Pharmacy," there exists an insightful interpretation by Heidegger in his lecture course *Plato's Sophist.* Heidegger suggests that Socrates would not reject writing as such, but rather, "free-floating (*freischwebend*) speech" in contrast to a speech that stays closely connected with its subject matter. See M. Heidegger, *Platon: Sophistes,* Gesamtausgabe 19 (Frankfurt: Klostermann, 1992), 339.

5. The idea of an otherness in the same is rather common in contemporary philosophy. However, otherness in the same is usually either approached from an epistemological or an ontological perspective, acknowledging that something in the "ego" evades me, or from an ethical perspective, indicating that such an otherness in the same is what we all share and what allows us to understand others better. Levinas rejects the epistemological perspective, but he also diverges from the usual ethical perspective since to establish a common ground between me and the Other is to misunderstand who the Other is.

6. For a detailed account of madness in the *Phaedrus,* see Ferit Güven, *Madness and Death in Philosophy* (Albany: SUNY Press, 1995).

7. An interpretation of the cave allegory from a Levinasian perspective can be found in Brian Schroeder, "Breaking the Closed Circle: Levinas and Platonic *Paideia,*" *Dialogue and Universalism* 8, 10 (1998): 97–106; reprinted in *Emmanuel Levinas: Critical Assessments,* Vol. 2: *Levinas and the History of Philosophy,* ed. Claire Katz with Lara Trout (London and New York: Routledge, 2005), 285–95.

8. Plato, *Republic,* trans. G. M. A. Grube, in *Plato: Complete Works,* ed. J. M. Cooper and D. S. Hutchinson (Indianapolis: Hackett, 1997).

9. Levinas regards the Good beyond Being as one of the most valuable insights in the history of philosophy. It is one of the most enigmatic topics in Plato's philosophy. For an elucidating account, see Adriaan Peperzak, "Heidegger and Plato's Idea of the Good," in *Reading Heidegger: Commemorations*, ed. John Sallis (Bloomington: Indiana University Press, 1993), 258–85.

10. The relation between ethics and politics has been discussed by several Levinas scholars. While Levinas undoubtedly acknowledges the need to move beyond the ethical realm and consider the political dimension, it seems implausible to claim, as does Simon Critchley, that in Levinas, "ethics is ethical for the sake of politics"(*The Ethics of Deconstruction. Derrida and Levinas* [Edinburgh: Edinburgh University Press, 1999], 223). Rather, the tension between ethics and politics can never be resolved. Helpful is Robert Bernasconi's insistence that "Levinas, in spite of the criticisms often directed against him, is not so much the thinker of ethics in distinction from politics, as the thinker of the space between the ethics of suspicion and politics, ethics and justice" ("The Ethics of Suspicion," *Research in Phenomenology* 20 [1990]: 15). Alternatively, the tension between ethics and politics could be described in terms of ambiguity. I plan to explore this topic in a study on the ambiguity of ethics in Plato and Levinas.

11. For a thorough discussion of the issue of "the third" in *Totality and Infinity* and *Otherwise than Being*, see Robert Bernasconi, "The Third Party: Levinas on the Intersection of the Ethical and the Political," *Journal of the British Society for Phenomenology* 30, 1 (1999): 76–87.

12. In a similar way, Plato takes pains to distinguish the philosopher from the sophist and from the statesman. Both the philosopher and the sophist are concerned with speeches, but the philosopher never engages with speech for its own sake or to turn a weak argument into the stronger. The statesman and the philosopher, in turn, share a concern with the whole of human affairs, yet the philosopher cares for the soul rather than the body, takes a more general perspective, and starts from ethical questions rather than straightforward political issues. However, discussions of the perfect rhetorician (*Phaedrus*) and the perfect statesman (*Gorgias, Republic, Statesman*) seem to show that both end up being philosophers if they indeed take their task as seriously as it can be taken, that is, search for the truth.

13. This does not mean that some Platonic myths can be said to "*teach* in concrete language what an unsophisticated audience would otherwise have trouble following" (Nickolas Pappas, *Plato and the Republic* [London: Routledge, 1995], 136). Such an explanation sells both Plato and his audience short.

14. Pappas' suggestion that the myths told by Plato are deliberately imperfect in order to "draw attention to their own inadequacy" does not strike me as particularly convincing (ibid., 215).

15. See Rudolf Bernet, "Encounter with the Stranger: Two Interpretations of the Vulnerability of the Skin," in *Phaenomenologische Forschungen*, special volume on Interculturality (Freiburg: Alber, 1998).

16. Ibid.

LENDING ASSISTANCE ALWAYS TO ITSELF: LEVINAS' INFINITE CONVERSATION WITH PLATONIC DIALOGUE

5

Michael Naas

THE LAST WORD

In a text written in the hours immediately following the death of Emmanuel Levinas and read at a service at the cemetery in Pantin on December 27, 1995, Jacques Derrida pays tribute to the remarkable life and work of Emmanuel Levinas and to the unique role Levinas played in twentieth-century thought both inside and outside of France and inside and outside of philosophy. In his tribute, Derrida praises and celebrates Levinas' life and work in order to say at the end "Adieu," in order to pronounce in his own voice the word he says he learned to hear and pronounce otherwise from Emmanuel Levinas. Continuing a conversation that began more three decades earlier, Derrida speaks to Levinas in Levinas' absence and concludes by offering him a final "Adieu," a final word both to mark the interruption that Levinas' death brought to their conversation and to recall what was at the very origin of that conversation.

In his eulogy for Levinas, Derrida speaks of what Levinas' death means for philosophy and of what it means for him and for the dialogue he had with him for more than thirty years. But because this text was read publicly, and because we perhaps never speak only for ourselves, Derrida also imagines what others might have wanted to say in honor and praise of Levinas. It is thus in the course of these reflections that Derrida not only mentions but actually evokes, even reanimates, a singular friendship in the life of Levinas that dates back all the way to Levinas' time at the University of Strasbourg in the early 1920s. Those familiar with Levinas' life and work know well the friendship to which I refer. Derrida writes: "For many among us, no doubt, certainly for myself, the absolute fidelity, the exemplary friendship of thought, the *friendship* between Maurice Blanchot and Emmanuel Levinas was a grace, a gift; it remains a benediction of our time."[1]

Since Blanchot was not present at the cemetery in Pantin, Derrida not only speaks of this friendship but puts it on the scene by recalling one of the episodes in what might be called the "unavowable conversation" between Blanchot and Levinas, a singular conversation that spanned some seven decades. Honored, it seems, to have been witness to this friendship, Derrida continued: "In order to hear once again today, right here, Blanchot speak for Levinas, and with Levinas, as I had the good fortune to do when in their company one day in 1968, I will cite a couple of lines" (*A* 8). These lines, the only ones Derrida cites in this text that do not come from Levinas himself, are from Blanchot's 1961 "Knowledge of the Unknown," one of the essays gathered near the beginning of *The Infinite Conversation* under the section heading "Plural Speech."[2] With neither Levinas nor Blanchot there to speak, Derrida stages or hosts, in his own gesture of friendship or hospitality, it seems, this brief "conversation" between Levinas and Blanchot by citing a passage in which Blanchot—or one of the voices in the polylogue of *The Infinite Conversation*—praises Levinas' work, especially the then recently published *Totality and Infinity*. Instead of turning to other words of Blanchot on Levinas, other more current words, Derrida cites a text more than three decades old in which Blanchot praises Levinas but then also, later in that same piece, raises a couple of critical questions regarding Levinas' understanding of the relationship between speech and writing in *Totality and Infinity* and elsewhere.

But that is not all. In returning in this 1995 text to Blanchot's reservations with regard to Levinas' understanding of conversation, speech, and writing, and to the relationship between these and ethics, Derrida is also returning to his own conversation with Levinas, to his own dialogue with Levinas *and* Blanchot. For Derrida, in his eulogy of Levinas, returns to the very text of Blanchot that he himself had cited more than three decades earlier in his 1964 essay "Violence and Metaphysics" in order to ask Levinas a series of questions about his understanding of ethics in relation to speech and writing as it is developed out of a reading of Plato's *Phaedrus*. Between Levinas, Blanchot, and Derrida, everything thus seems to come down to a *reading* of Plato, to a reading of the myth of *writing* at the end of the *Phaedrus*, and to everything this implies for conversation, speech, and writing in relationship to ethics.

Derrida's final word to Emmanuel Levinas could thus not be more overdetermined. Thirty-one years after "Violence and Metaphysics," Derrida returns to the very same place in the very same texts, that is, to the very same written words, *not,* I will ultimately argue, in order to reanimate an old debate, *not* in order to reinterpret what Levinas might have meant by his comments on Plato's understanding of the relationship between speech and writing, *not* in order to go behind Levinas' words or lend assistance to them so as to refute or affirm them, but in order to renew an *infinite conversation in writing.* My aim here is thus not to come down on one side or the other of this debate between Levinas, Blanchot, and Derrida over the role and importance of writing, but to clarify the terms of the debate and demonstrate why Levinas and Blanchot could, in the end, remain in absolute proximity despite some absolutely striking differences. I will end up arguing that while it appears that Levinas adopts the Platonic hierarchization of speech over writing—and so falls prey to Blanchot's critique of Plato's humanism and Derrida's charge of phonocentrism—his understanding of conversation in relation to writing ultimately avoids such a critique, though it does so, as we will see, only at the price of a risky analogy between the face and God, speech or human speech and the divine word. In a rather uncanny curvature of space, we will see that the place where Levinas and Blanchot would appear furthest apart is the place where they enter into a strange proximity—and perhaps into conversation. Today, in the wake of the deaths of all three of these thinkers, we are, I would like to believe, enjoined to listen and admire, to bear witness to this conversation but also, perhaps, to add a word of our own, beginning from that final word, a word that is *written "à-dieu."*

To set the stage for this conversation between Levinas, Blanchot, and Derrida, I will begin with a very brief overview of Levinas' reading of Plato in general before turning to his use of Plato in *Totality and Infinity* and, especially, his adoption of certain key notions and terms from the *Phaedrus.* Along the way I will consider Blanchot's reading of Plato on these same points and the discreet objections Blanchot voices to Levinas' understanding of speech and writing. Though the relationship between Blanchot and Levinas extends well beyond their respective readings of the *Phaedrus* or of Plato more generally, this conversation over the myth of writing in the *Phaedrus* is crucial to understanding their relationship in the late 1950s and early 1960s, a pivotal time for both in their reading of Plato and in the development of their own thought. The limited scope of this analysis is further justified by the fact that the *Phaedrus* is the only dialogue that Blanchot has, to my knowledge, commented on extensively, in his essay "The Beast of Lascaux"; and it is the dialogue that Levinas names in *Ethics and Infinity* as one of the four or five greatest or most beautiful texts in the Western philosophical tradition (*EI* 37).[3] After determining how each reads Plato in general and the *Phaedrus* in particular, we will finally be able to ask what this debate about speech, writing, and conversation can teach us about the conversation between Blanchot and Levinas themselves, about that friendship that, as Derrida says, "remains a benediction of our time."

LEVINAS ON PLATO I: BEFORE AND AFTER *TOTALITY AND INFINITY*

Though one could certainly find examples that run counter to this tendency, there is in Levinas, as there is in Blanchot, a general "rehabilitation" of Plato during the late 1950s and 1960s. Before this time, Levinas seemed to find in Plato a foil for most everything his own philosophy would attempt to overcome. In *Time and the Other* (1946–47), for example, Levinas reproaches Plato for his Eleatic tendencies, for his absorption of multiplicity into unity, his avoidance of the specificity of the feminine in the erotic relationship, his idealization of a world of light without time in imitation of the ideas, his neglect of the specificity of death, and his positing as the ideal for the social realm a fusion of self and other (*TO* 91–93). A couple of years later, in his 1951 essay "Is Ontology Fundamental?" it is the same "primacy of ontological thought," from Plato and Aristotle through Heidegger, that Levinas finds problematic (*BPW* 2), the same "unmixed rationalism," as he puts it in another essay from the same period.[4] Time and again during the 1940s and 1950s, Levinas uses Plato's dialogues as the ontological and epistemological backdrop against which to develop his own ethical thought.

But then begins the progressive rehabilitation of Plato as Levinas turns toward the ethical rather than the ontological and epistemological dimensions of Plato's thought. This rehabilitation is already evident, as we will see later, in *Totality and Infinity* and other texts of the 1960s, and it appears more or less complete by the mid-1970s. To give just a single indication, in his 1975 lectures that would come to be published in *God, Death, and Time*, Levinas begins, not with Plato's neglect of the singularity of death, as he well might have done in the 1940s, but with a reflection on the death of Socrates in the *Phaedo* as a struggle between discourse and its negation and as an excess and scandal that cannot be wholly absorbed or occulted in dialogue (*GDT* 9, 14). He goes on to say that the Platonic soul contemplating ideas is to be described "phenomenologically as a *face*" (*GDT* 14) and that an exception to philosophy's original identification of death with *my* death can be found in Plato's doctrine that "committing an injustice is worse than undergoing one" (*GDT* 97).

The *mot d'ordre* of this more positive evaluation of Plato is, of course, Levinas' frequent invocation of the famous description in *Republic* 509b of the Good as *epekeina tēs ousias*, that is, as a Good beyond being or essence, an exemplary thought, as Levinas reads it, of the priority of ethics over ontology within the Western philosophical tradition. Levinas opens *Otherwise than Being* with this insight, and he returns to it regularly throughout both this book and his corpus (*OB*

3, 8, 19; *EN* 100). While philosophy is thus normally caught in a thinking of being alone, there are in the history of philosophy, and particularly within Plato, certain "*instants d'éclair*," certain "flashes," that break with the primacy of ontological thought (*OB* 4). Though in Plato "the essence claims to recover and cover over every ex-ception—negativity, nihilation, and . . . non-being, which 'in a certain sense is,'" there is also a thinking of a beyond of being not only in the Good of the *Republic* but in the One of the *Parmenides*.

Beginning with Plato, then, Levinas is able to find these little strokes of good fortune, these "*instants d'éclair*" or moments of insight, throughout the history of philosophy.[5] Though the history of philosophy is sometimes pre-sented as relatively uniform—since, according to Plato's doctrine of anamnesis, truth is always *re*-discovered, and is thus always the same[6]—there are moments within the Platonic dialogues (from *Republic, Phaedrus, Gorgias,* and *Symposium* to *Timaeus* and *Parmenides*), and within the rest of the tradition, that break with this seemingly monolithic tradition. "Against the irrupturable identity of the Same," then, we would find the "beyond being" of Plato and Plotinus, the intel-lect of Aristotle, the Cartesian idea of God that is in us and exceeds our finite capacity, even Bergson's notion of duration and the sobriety of reason in Hei-degger ("Ideology and Idealism," *LR* 245; see also *GCM* 12; *EN* 89). Levinas thus insists that his thinking remains quite classical to the extent that it adheres to the Platonic thought that it is not consciousness that founds the Good but the Good that calls consciousness (*EN* 204). It is here that philosophy as the circle of the Same is broken and the outside of philosophy—call it God or the other—is approached.[7]

In Levinas' Talmudic commentaries, not surprisingly, Plato is rarely men-tioned or cited, but when he is, it is often with reference to a thought of justice that exceeds ontology or epistemology (*BV* 26–28). Hence, Plato's critique of rhetoric in the *Phaedrus* and *Gorgias* would be motivated not so much by rhetoric's lack of knowledge or its manipulation of appearances, that is, because of its onto-logical or epistemological shortcomings, but because justice is perverted by means of it. As Levinas succinctly puts it elsewhere, "Plato's denunciation of rhetoric presupposes the moral scandal of Socrates' condemnation" ("Ideology and Ideal-ism," *LR* 248). Levinas thus refers in several places to the myth of the last judg-ment in the *Gorgias* as setting forth a "*beyond* of institutional justice," since both the judge and the judged are stripped of clothes, ranks, and reputations, made to appear naked before one another, not the object of the other's gaze but, in Lev-inas' terms, already a "neighbor." This Platonic myth helps Levinas to develop a notion of judgment without common ground, beyond any perceptible attribute, a purely dis-inter-ested judgment that approaches the other without reducing them through some shared concept to an indifferent knowledge, where the other approaches beyond appearances, beyond experience, and beyond consciousness, which is why, for Plato, such a relation can only be between the dead ("Ideology and Idealism," *LR* 243–44; *OB* 199 n. 25).

From the 1960s onward, then, Levinas often cites Plato, or certain aspects of Plato, as having opened up the possibility of his own thought and writing. Though still sometimes ambivalent toward Plato even in these later works, he is no longer as hostile toward him as he once was. Our question will thus ultimately be whether Levinas' rehabilitation of Plato is not, in the end, simply too generous, too "ecumenical," since it seems to accept not only the ethical moment of the "Good beyond being" but many other of Plato's metaphysical distinctions, from presence and absence to speech and writing. Levinas seems to accept, in the end, so much of Plato's language that we will want to ask whether he has not fallen prey to the Socratic humanism of which Blanchot speaks.[8]

To test such a charge, it is essential to read in context those objectionable or problematic passages of *Totality and Infinity* in which Levinas would seem to be using the *Phaedrus* to privilege speech over writing, those passages to which Blanchot refers in "Knowledge of the Unknown" and then Derrida in "Violence and Metaphysics." Before turning to *Totality and Infinity*, however, and to Blanchot's discreet objections with regard to certain of its theses, we need to put this text of 1961 in the context of Blanchot's own reading of the *Phaedrus* just a few years before.

BLANCHOT ON PLATO I: "THE BEAST OF LASCAUX"

While references to Plato can be found throughout Blanchot's corpus, from the novel *Thomas the Obscure* to *Writing of the Disaster*, the closest thing to a commentary or reading of a Platonic dialogue comes in Blanchot's 1953 "La bête de Lascaux," translated just three years later into English by David Paul as "The Beast of Lascaux."[9] Though Blanchot's interpretation of the myth of writing at the end of the *Phaedrus* is intended to help illuminate his reading in the second part of that essay of the poetry of René Char, Blanchot's comments on the *Phaedrus* are echoed in other texts and so can be read outside their immediate relation to Char. Since Levinas was himself no doubt developing his own understanding of the relationship between speech and writing, language and the Other, during this very same time period, and in part as a result of his reading of the *Phaedrus*, it is important to see where Blanchot's reading of this same dialogue confirms or conflicts with the reading Levinas would later give it.

Blanchot begins "The Beast of Lascaux" with a relatively straightforward and unsurprising reading of the well-known myth Socrates recounts at the end of the *Phaedrus*. Like many commentators, he takes Socrates at his word, or rather, identifying Plato with Socrates, he takes Plato at Socrates' word when the latter denounces the dangers of writing. Blanchot writes:

> In the *Phaedrus,* Plato defines and condemns a strange kind of speech: a language spoken by someone, and yet by no-one; a speech whose words always say the same thing, without thinking of what they say, a speech incapable of choosing its speakers, incapable of replying if they question it, or of defending itself [*se porter secours à elle-même*] if they attack it; whose character compels it to turn as chance guides, in any direction, forcing the truth to become the child of that chance: to entrust such speech with the truth is, in fact, to entrust it to death. Socrates proposes therefore that we should avoid this speech as much as possible, as if it were a dangerous infection, and that we keep to the true speech, the spoken one, in which each word finds a living guarantee in the person who speaks it. (*BL* 29)

Notice, first, that Blanchot attributes these views not simply to Socrates but to Plato; it is *Plato* who "defines and condemns a strange kind of speech." While Blanchot might ultimately wish to qualify Plato's condemnation of writing or read a kind of ambivalence into it, he does not evacuate it, as others have, by appealing to a sort of Socratic or Platonic irony. Second, Blanchot begins his reading of the *Phaedrus* at the very same place to which Levinas will turn in *Totality and Infinity* when he wishes to define discourse in its relation to the Other. As we will see, it is precisely speech's ability to "defend itself" or "come to its own assistance" that will lead Levinas, like Plato, to privilege conversation and the spoken word over writing.[10] Levinas writes, for example, in a passage in which he tries to give an orientation to the aimless and enchanting flow of significations without a face, "Speech disenchants, for the speaking being guarantees his own apparition and comes to the assistance of himself [*se porte secours*], attends his own manifestation" (*TI* 98).

Levinas and Blanchot thus enter the *Phaedrus* at exactly the same point; both understand Plato and not just Socrates to be condemning the anonymous character of writing, with Levinas seeming to endorse this critique in his emphasis on speech, and Blanchot seeing the threat but also the promise of what is being criticized. Blanchot continues:

> The written word: word of death, oblivion. This extreme distrust of writing, to be shared by Plato, shows what doubts were born, what problems arose from the novel use of written communication. What are we to make of the word that has behind it no support from the personal caution of a real man, anxious to state the truth? The humanism of Socrates, already grown old, stands at an equal distance from two worlds which he sees for what they are and vigorously rejects. (*BL* 29)

Writing against the backdrop of a whole host of thinkers interested in the influence of technology on the mediation and transmission of thought, thinkers as diverse as Heidegger and Leroi-Gourhan (of whom Derrida will also speak at some

Michael Naas

length in *Of Grammatology*), Blanchot, following Plato, situates Socrates between two epochs of technology and two epochal relationships to language.[11] Socrates rejects at once "the impersonal knowledge of books" and the "impersonal language" that "gives voice to sacred things," that is, the voice of oracles and divinely inspired poets where it is not the prophet or poet but the god who speaks. Both forms of impersonal language are condemned because there is no one behind their words to guarantee or back them up, no one to defend or lend assistance to them if they are attacked. What Socrates values in speech is thus indeed the human living presence behind it. But in order to escape his own critique of rhetoricians who pay more attention to the identity and reputation of the speaker than to the truth of what he says, this human presence must be, so to speak, stripped of all rank, origin, and reputation—indeed, of all appearance—a naked living presence that would not be unlike the souls being judged in the myth of the final judgment in the *Gorgias*.

After analyzing Plato's or Socrates' comparison of writing to painting and pointing out that what "dismays" Socrates about both is their immutable silence behind which there is but a "void," "a scandalous semblance of truth, an image," an essentially "inhuman" force, Blanchot writes: "This is why both Plato and Socrates, in this same passage, are eager to reduce writing, like art, to a pastime in which the truth is not compromised, a thing reserved for hours of recreation . . . capable at the utmost of commemorating the achievements or the stages of wisdom, without having any part in the labor of their discovery" (*BL* 31–32).

In the second part of "The Beast of Lascaux," Blanchot, much like Levinas in the 1940s, uses Plato's critique of writing to develop his own positive conception of writing in the poetry of René Char. Blanchot there compares the poetry of Char to the fragments of Heraclitus, arguing that both establish a relationship with "first things, a relationship not so much confident and stable, as fragmentary and agitated" (*BL* 38).[12] Hence, Blanchot praises Char and Heraclitus for the very things for which Plato and Socrates condemn writing. The famous Heraclitean fragment "The Lord whose oracle is at Delphi neither expresses nor conceals, but indicates" is, for Blanchot, a "kind of retort to Socrates, by situating the true authority of language in that which makes the impersonal words of the oracle at Delphi a danger and a scandal" (*BL* 32). Socrates wants "a word of certainty, vouched for by a living presence," rather than "the word which initiates," rather than a "language directed towards first things, whether it be the oracle, or the work of art which gives voice to the beginnings" (*BL* 33). Socrates thus rejects what Blanchot calls "prophetic" speech, by which he means not a speech that "dictates future events" but one that "does not rely for support on something already existing, or on a current truth, or even on language as it is already spoken and verified" (*BL* 33). Because such a speech does not rely on any past speech, says Blanchot, it is "fundamentally unjustified" (*BL* 33).

We have, then, the groundless, unjustified, and essentially *inhuman* utterances of Heraclitus and the poetry of Char opposed to the humanist speech of Socrates, which is justified, vouchsafed, and defended by the living human presence behind it. Speaking of Char's poetry, Blanchot writes: "The words do not repeat or make use of themselves, or speak of present things; they have nothing of the tireless give-and-take [*le va-et-vient inlassable*] of Socratic dialogue, but like those of the Lord of Delphi, are the voice which has said nothing yet, the voice that wakes and rouses, harsh and rigorous at times, coming a long way and calling far" (*BL* 35–36).

Between two epochs of anonymous, inhuman language, one of speech (pre-Platonic poetry and the oracles of the gods) and one of writing (the technologies of the book), Socrates' humanism condemns him to a tireless taking up of what has *already* been said and, thus, to a perpetual avoidance of first things. Insofar as both the anonymous language of the oracles and the poetry of Char are concerned with nothing but this perpetual commencement, both might be thought in Blanchotian terms as being involved in the "prophetic" practice of *writing*. Between two epochs of writing, Socrates would truly be "the one who does not write."

LEVINAS ON PLATO II: *TOTALITY AND INFINITY*

Read in the context of Blanchot's interpretation of the *Phaedrus* in "The Beast of Lascaux," Levinas' use of Plato's *Phaedrus* in *Totality and Infinity* appears all the more extraordinary. How, we will want to ask, can Levinas' reinscription and seeming endorsement of Socrates' condemnation of writing escape the charge of Socratic humanism and the reduction of language to a perpetual re-saying of what has already been said?

On the one hand, Plato still belongs, in *Totality and Infinity*, to the history of ontology as totalization. Near the very end of this work, Levinas writes: "For common sense but also for philosophy, from Plato to Heidegger, panoramic existence and its disclosure are equivalent to the very production of being, since truth or disclosure is at the same time the work or the essential virtue of being" (*TI* 294).[13] But there are many more passages in this work of 1961 where Plato is praised or used by Levinas to help justify or support some of his most important thoughts, sometimes with and sometimes without caveats or reservations. Levinas thus refers in a note in the opening pages of *Totality and Infinity* to *Republic* 529b, where the invisible or, in his language, "the very dimension of height is opened up by metaphysical Desire" (*TI* 34–35), and he refers approvingly, as he will in many texts thereafter, to Plato's understanding of the Good as transcending totality (*TI* 103, 218, 293). The Aristophanes myth of the *Symposium* is here also seen as being true to the ambivalence of love, since the desire to return to an original self would describe an event that is at once immanent and transcendent (*TI* 254). In addition, several aspects of

Michael Naas

Plato's work are used as heuristic devices to help explain certain key notions. To illustrate, for example, the exposure of the I to the Other, to help dispel "the very myth of the I and interiority" (*TI* 61) and develop the asymmetry of the Other in relationship to the I, Levinas speaks of a reversal of Gyges, where instead of being able to see without being seen, the I is seen and summoned without itself being able to see (*TI* 90, 170, 173, 222; cf. *GDT* 196).

It is in the opening divisions of *Totality and Infinity*, however, that Plato, and particularly the *Phaedrus*, is used by Levinas not simply to justify, explain, or support his position but actually to develop it. Though Levinas' most salient comments concern the myth of writing at the end of the dialogue, other parts of the dialogue are used in the development of the argument. Levinas thus refers to the way in which ideas in Socrates' second speech are presented and recognized by the metaphysician as other, and, citing Aristotle, not "in a site" (*TI* 38). Though Levinas will ultimately oppose the Platonic notion in the *Phaedrus* of the soul feeding on truth, since, as he puts it, "metaphysical Desire is above life, and with regard to it one cannot speak of satiety" (*TI* 114), he will seemingly endorse this Platonic notion of ideas.

In the beginning of the section of "Metaphysics and Transcendence" entitled "Transcendence as the Idea of Infinity" in *Totality and Infinity*, Levinas refers to Socrates' rejection of suicide at the beginning of the *Phaedo* as the rejection of "the false spiritualism of the pure and simple and immediate union with the Divine." Instead, Socrates "proclaims ineluctable the difficult itinerary of knowledge starting from the here below" (*TI* 48). These observations lead to a discussion of Descartes and the idea of the infinite, an idea whose *ideatum*—which is precisely the infinite distance of the idea from its *ideatum*—exceeds this idea. Levinas then argues that such an idea can be found already in Plato, and he proceeds to cite three different phrases from the *Phaedrus*.

> We find that this presence in thought of an idea whose *ideatum* overflows the capacity of thought is given expression not only in Aristotle's theory of the agent intellect, but also, very often, in Plato. Against a thought that proceeds from him who "has his own head to himself" (244a), he affirms the value of the delirium that comes from God, "winged thought" (249a). Delirium here does not have an irrationalist significance; it is only a "divine release of the soul from the yoke of custom and convention" (265a). The fourth type of delirium is reason itself, rising to the ideas, thought in the highest sense. Possession by a god, enthusiasm, is not the irrational, but the end of the solitary (and which we will later call "economic") or inward thought, the beginning of a true experience of the *new* and of the noumenon—already Desire. (*TI* 49–50)

This idea of infinity in me, which is produced, not as a Desire for some thing I might possess, but as disinterested Desire, as goodness, is produced positively, says

Levinas, in a relationship that can then be understood as *conversation.* Having used Socrates' second speech in the *Phaedrus* to develop a notion of ideas as other, having related these ideas to the Cartesian idea of the infinite in me, and having referred to divine madness in the *Phaedrus* as a model of his own notion of Desire, Levinas turns to the myth of writing at the end of the *Phaedrus,* obliquely at first but then explicitly, and he enters in, as I noted earlier, at the very same place Blanchot did in "The Beast of Lascaux" and, it should be noted, at the very place Derrida will enter in "Plato's Pharmacy."[14] Speaking of the way in which the face expresses itself, the way it expresses not some content but an expression that every content would presuppose, Levinas writes:

> To approach the Other in conversation is to welcome his expression, in which at each instant he overflows the idea a thought would carry away from it. It is therefore to *receive* from the Other beyond the capacity of the I, which means exactly: to have the idea of infinity. But this also means: to be taught. (*TI* 51)

This teaching is an ethical teaching, says Levinas, since it comes from the other and not from myself, as it would in Socratic maieutics. Ethical teaching is thus opposed to maieutics in just the same way that revelation is opposed to disclosure and clarification.[15] Levinas writes several pages later:

> *The absolute experience is not disclosure but revelation:* a coinciding of the expressed with him who expresses . . . the manifestation of a face over and beyond form. . . . The face is a living presence; it is expression. The life of expression consists in undoing the form in which the existent, exposed as a theme, is thereby dissimulated. The face speaks. The manifestation of the face is already discourse. He who manifests himself comes, according to Plato's expression, to his own assistance [*porte . . . secours à lui-même*]. He at each instant undoes the form he presents. (*TI* 65–66)

One might see here why Blanchot might question Levinas' privileging of speech, of live presence, over writing, his privileging of an expression that can come to its own assistance if attacked. For Levinas, as for Plato, the live word or expression can assist itself if questioned or attacked, while the word of writing cannot. But unlike Plato, it seems, there is no content, no meaning, beyond the expression of the face, no difference, distance, or depth between expression and its content—no living speech or being "behind" the face, behind expression, and no truthful disclosure beyond this expression. The phrase "coming to one's own assistance" thus cannot mean here, as it would seem to mean in Plato and as Blanchot seems to interpret it in "The Beast of Lascaux," coming to *clarify* a previously questioned meaning or coming to justify something that has previously been said; it would suggest, it would *mean,* perpetually to interrupt the meaning and the form given to any expression. Indeed, while works or objects of knowledge would give us only an oblique relation to the other through something past, the face, for Levinas, expresses itself presently, that is, as Blanchot would say about writing, *incessantly*. Levinas writes:

> The object of knowledge is always a fact, already happened and passed through. The interpellated one is called upon to speak; his speech consists in "coming to the assistance" of his word—in being *present*. This present is not made of instants mysteriously immobilized in a duration, but of an *incessant* recapture of instants that flow by by a presence that comes to their assistance, that answers for them. This *incessance* produces the present, is the presentation, the life, of the present. (*TI* 69)

Speaking, then, is understood not, as Socrates would seem to understand it, as the ability to clarify or justify a past statement or thought, but as the incessant taking back up of the instant. Even if Levinas later speaks of *clarifying* and of *clarification* as the activity of speaking, what is clarified is not some previous signification or meaning but simply the manifestation of expression. While Levinas calls speech "a taking up again of what was a simple sign cast forth by it, an ever renewed promise to clarify what was obscure in the utterance" (*TI* 97), what is obscure cannot be some signification that was once given and is now past but the very manifestation of language. That is speech's sole teaching. To put it in terms that Levinas will develop more fully in *Otherwise than Being* and elsewhere, what is obscure is not some Said that needs clarification but a Saying that must be perpetually taken back up since it is never exhausted in the Said.[16] Speech or conversation thus has little to do with dialectical thought understood as a "dialogue of the soul with itself" or as a clarification of what is already contained in the self. Speech does not return to some previous thought and is not simply an expression of thought; it is but "the ever recommenced effort of *language* to clarify its own manifestation" (*TI* 97; my emphasis).[17]

These passages indicate that while Levinas is indeed deploying the Platonic categories of speech and writing, presence and absence, he is doing so in order to wrest them loose from their Platonic context, that is, from the context that Blanchot, among others, assumes, and perhaps rightly assumes, in his reading of Plato. Such an operation is at once bold and extremely risky, for even if one were to grant that Levinas is not simply misreading the Platonic text for his own purposes but trying to reinscribe its categories anew, such reinscriptions always risk being contaminated by their older inscriptions in the Platonic text. And while such a contamination might lead to what Blanchot generously calls a "necessary ambiguity," it would also make Levinas vulnerable—despite all his protestations and attempts to clarify his use of terms—to the charge of phonocentrism that Derrida, in "Plato's

Pharmacy" and elsewhere, levels against so much of Western philosophy, beginning with Plato.

And yet, in speaking in the above passage of language and not just speech, Levinas would seem to echo many of the things Blanchot would say about language—and, indeed, about *writing*. In the unavowable conversation between them, in, as Levinas puts it just a page before, the "conversation [*entre-tien*] which *proposes* the world" (*TI* 96), Levinas and Blanchot might themselves be read as being engaged in something quite other than a mere exchange of ideas. While their respective interpretations of the *Phaedrus* initially appear radically opposed, once their interpretations and terms have been clarified, Blanchot and Levinas demonstrate a very strange proximity, even in—perhaps especially in—those places where they would seem to be furthest apart.

BEHIND THE SIGN: THE INFINITE CONVERSATION BETWEEN LEVINAS, THE ANCIENTS, AND HIS CONTEMPORARIES

I began by recalling that in his 1995 memorial essay for Levinas entitled *Adieu* Derrida feels compelled to cite a 1961 text by Blanchot in which Blanchot praises Levinas but then expresses some reservations with regard to his understanding of speech and writing and his use of the *Phaedrus* and its categories in *Totality and Infinity*. Having seen Blanchot's own reading of the *Phaedrus* a few years earlier and Levinas' original use of terms from this dialogue in *Totality and Infinity*, we are in a better position to understand the force of Blanchot's reservations and the resources Levinas has open to him for a response.

In *Adieu*, Derrida does not, of course, cite Blanchot's reservations with regard to Levinas' view of writing, only Blanchot's praise for the importance of Levinas' thought. He does not cite or even recall his own foray into these questions in "Violence and Metaphysics," only his long friendship and enduring admiration. And yet, by pointing us back in 1995 toward Blanchot's 1961 text on Levinas and to this entire nexus of texts surrounding the *Phaedrus*, Derrida's gesture could not have been more equivocal.

In a first moment, Blanchot's "Knowledge of the Unknown" could hardly be more complimentary or enthusiastic, with one of the voices in this polylogue praising the newly published *Totality and Infinity* for its radicality, rigor, and beauty, going so far as to declare it a "new departure for philosophy." Yet near the very end of the polylogue, a simple parenthetical remark risks opening up a seemingly unbreachable gap between Blanchot and Levinas on something no less important than the relationship between the face, speech, and writing. This remark is set up earlier in the work as Blanchot comments on Levinas' reading of the *Phaedrus* and adoption of its terms. Speaking of what Levinas calls magisterial speech and the privilege Levinas in *Totality and Infinity* accords oral discourse, which "alone would be a plentitude of discourse," Blanchot writes:

> Levinas often invokes Socrates on this point, recalling the well-known pages of Plato where the pernicious effects of writing are denounced. But I wonder whether this comparison doesn't introduce into Levinas' thought some ambiguity—unless it is a necessary ambiguity. On the one hand, language is the transcendent relation itself, manifesting that the space of communication is essentially non-symmetrical . . . *Autrui* is not on the same plane as myself. . . . But here, I believe, is the ambiguity. This speech of eminence, which speaks to me from very far away, from very high above (or very far below), is the speech of someone who does not speak with me on equal footing . . . —yet, suddenly [*tout d'un coup*], this speech once again becomes the tranquil humanist and Socratic speech that brings the one who speaks close to us since it allows us, in all familiarity, to know who he is and from what country, according to Socrates' wish. Why, then, does oral discourse seem to Socrates (and to Levinas) to be a manifestation without peer? Because the man who speaks can assist [*porte secours*] his speech; he is always ready to answer for it, to justify and clarify it, contrary to what happens with what is written. (*IC* 56–57)

Some twenty-five pages later, Blanchot, having put forward the hypothesis of a "necessary ambiguity" with regard to speech and writing, suggests that "what is proper to all language—spoken, *but also, and perhaps to a higher degree, written*—is that it always lends assistance to itself, never saying only what it says but always more and always less" (*IC* 82; my emphasis). Considering everything Levinas says about the superiority of speech over writing in *Totality and Infinity*, considering his use of the phrase "lends assistance to itself" throughout his analysis of conversation, this little addition by Blanchot threatens to take back much of the praise he so generously lavishes on Levinas in *The Infinite Conversation*.

Blanchot's reservations of 1961 do indeed appear absolutely legitimate, even necessary. Levinas, like Socrates, does seem to privilege speech over writing, the presence of face-to-face speech over the absence of writing. Though Levinas clearly does not *mean* to repeat the Platonic opposition and hierarchy of speech and writing as it has been traditionally understood, since there is no living presence *behind* speech in Levinas, no thought or meaning to be clarified, Levinas in these pages does suggest his own priority of speech over writing and he does relate speech to presence, to the face, and, as if adopting the entire Platonic matrix, to the living, speaking, human face of the master able to justify his words. Levinas writes:

> This *incessance* produces the present, is the presentation, the life, of the present. It is as though the presence of him who speaks inverted the inevitable movement that bears the spoken word to the past state of the written word. . . . The unique actuality of speech . . . brings what the written word is already deprived of: mastery. (*TI* 69)

Though this mastery has no doctrine, being an expression that teaches nothing but itself, it is related, as in Plato, to life, presence, and speech and *not* to writing. Like Socrates in the myth of the final judgment in the *Gorgias*, Levinas appears to be positing a face-to-face, a present encounter, where the masks, the clothes, the plastic appearances come off and one is left with the naked face of the other—an expression that we could never grasp and that would always exceed our perception and our understanding.[18] But is there not, as Blanchot would ask, and as Derrida would have Blanchot ask, an incessance in writing, a perpetual manifestation of language and a return, not to some previously determined signification, but, as in Heraclitus, to the perpetually beginning word?

Blanchot's questions about the status of writing in relationship to the face and the Other, seemingly minor in light of the overwhelming agreement between Blanchot and Levinas, threaten the very proximity of Blanchot's and Levinas' work, and thus the very basis for the friendship that Derrida describes as exemplary and as a benediction for our time. For who could deny that, for Blanchot, what is at stake in this rereading and reinterpretation of the *Phaedrus* and this revaluation of writing ("what is proper to all language—*spoken, but also, and perhaps to a higher degree, written*—is that it always lends assistance to itself") is not simply another critical perspective on Plato, another debate over what Plato said or meant, but the very relationship between speech and writing, speaking and reading, self and other—in other words, the *ethical relationship*? What is at stake in Blanchot's reservation lodged in the midst of his praise for Levinas is nothing other than the question of language and the way in which we *read* the entire history of philosophy—beginning with Plato.

It should perhaps come as no surprise then that Derrida would turn to *this* text rather than to some other in 1964 in "Violence and Metaphysics" and then again in "Adieu" in 1995 when putting Blanchot back in "communication" with Levinas. It should come as no surprise that Derrida would be drawn to this intersection of themes in Blanchot and Levinas when he himself would end up offering his own highly original and influential interpretation of this same Platonic dialogue just a few years later in "Plato's Pharmacy." Finally, it should come as no surprise that he, like they, would turn to a Platonic dialogue that concerns not only the relationship between speech and writing but the question of lineage, legacy, and legitimacy—the question of what it means to be a legitimate heir.

Seeing the problem, then—or perhaps the potential for dialogue—between these two longtime, legendary friends, Derrida in "Violence and Metaphysics" enters into the conversation between Levinas and Blanchot at exactly this point. In this important essay of 1964, Derrida initially appears to be quite sympathetic to Blanchot's reservations before going on to express a reservation of his own with regard to Blanchot's reading of Levinas. Before turning to Blanchot's "Knowledge of the Unknown," Derrida summarizes Levinas' adoption of the language of the *Phaedrus* in *Totality and Infinity*. After arguing that, in Levinas, "the face is not a metaphor, not a figure," he goes on to explain why, for Levinas, speech is said to be, according to terms taken from the *Phaedrus, behind* the sign, able to lend assistance to the sign if it is attacked:

> The face does not signify, does not present itself as a sign, but *expresses itself*, of-fering itself *in person*, in itself, *kath'auto*. . . . To express oneself is to be *behind* the sign. To be behind the sign: is this not, *first of all*, to be capable of attending (to) [*assister (à)*] one's speech, to assist it [*de lui porter secours*], according to the expres-sion used in the *Phaedrus* as argument against Theuth (or Hermes)—an expression Levinas makes his own on several occasions. Only living speech, in its mastery and magisteriality, is able to assist itself [*se porter secours*]; and only living speech is ex-pression and not a servile sign. . . . The written and work are not expressions but signs for Levinas. (VM 101)

After this summary of Levinas' reading of the distinction between speech and writing in the *Phaedrus*, Derrida wonders aloud—in anticipation of Blanchot's objection—whether it might not make sense to reverse all of Levinas' claims about speech and writing, expression and sign. He asks himself—and thereby asks Levinas:

> Are not height and magisterial instruction an aspect of writing? Is it not possible to invert all of Levinas' statements on this point? By showing, for example, that writing can assist itself [*se porter secours*], for it *has time* and freedom, escaping bet-ter than speech from empirical urgencies. . . . That the writer absents himself bet-ter, that is, expresses himself [*s'exprime*] better as other, addresses himself to the other more effectively than the man of speech? . . . The thematic of the *trace* . . . should lead to a certain rehabilitation of writing. Is not the "He" whom transcen-dence and generous absence uniquely announce in the trace more readily the au-thor of writing than of speech? (VM 102)

It is at precisely this point in his own treatment of Levinas that Derrida turns to Blanchot's "Knowledge of the Unknown." He begins: "Maurice Blanchot speaks of his disagreement with this preeminence of oral discourse, which resembles 'the tranquil humanist and Socratic speech which brings us close to the speaker'" (VM 106). With Blanchot behind him or behind his words, Derrida proceeds to pose a supplementary question to Blanchot. The question concerns the relationship be-tween speech and writing in Levinas, to be sure, but more exactly the relationship between philosophy and theology, the face and God, the human speaker and the divine word. Derrida asks, "How could Hebraism belittle the letter, in praise of which Levinas writes so well?" He then continues:

> The aspect of living and original speech *itself* which Levinas seeks to save is clear. Without its possibility, outside its horizon, writing is nothing. In this sense, writing

will always be secondary. . . . But it is only in God that speech, as presence, as the origin and horizon of writing, is realized without defect. One would have to be able to show that only this reference to the speech of God distinguishes Levinas' intentions from those of Socrates in the *Phaedrus;* and that for a thought of original finitude this distinction is no longer possible. And that if writing is secondary at this point, nothing, however, has occurred before it.

    As for Levinas' ties to Blanchot, it seems to us that despite the frequent rapprochements he proposes, the profound and incontestable affinities between them all belong to the critical and negative moment. . . . Blanchot could probably extend over all of Levinas' propositions what he says about the dissymmetry within the space of communication: "Here, I believe, is what is decisive in the affirmation which we must hear, and which must be maintained independently of the theological context in which it occurs." But is this possible? Independent of its "theological context" (an expression that Levinas would most likely reject) does not this entire discourse collapse? (VM 102–103)

Derrida thus appears to agree with Blanchot in this critical questioning of Levinas, but his subsequent questioning of Blanchot's phrase "theological context" from "Knowledge of the Unknown" suggests an even more serious problem: yes, writing, not speech, would seem to be a more appropriate way to understand the *incessant* nature of a language that perpetually begins, the way in which a tranquil Socratic humanism is perpetually interrupted by the asymmetry of writing; but, Derrida asks Blanchot—and thereby Levinas—can Levinas' discourse on speech really be understood "independent of its 'theological context,'" that is, without the exemplary *analogy* between the face and God?[19] "To be behind the sign which is in the world," writes Derrida, is "*afterward* to remain invisible to the world within epiphany" (VM 103). To be behind the sign thus cannot mean to be a tranquil human presence ready to justify the sign and defend it. It cannot mean that there is a prior meaning behind the sign to which the sign can return for clarification. To be *behind* the sign, able to lend assistance to the sign, would be the work not of maieutics but of ethical teaching, not of disclosure but revelation, not a phenomenal appearance but an epiphany. Levinas is thus able to avoid Socrates' tranquil humanism, not by emphasizing the force of an inhuman *writing*, as Blanchot seems to do, but by invoking an analogy between *speech* and the divine word, the face and God, the human face of the stranger, widow, or orphan in the world and the Other as "non-phenomenal," as "not 'of this world,'" indeed, the Other as "the origin of the world" (VM 103).

    Both Blanchot and Levinas thus speak of origins but in very different terms. Whereas Blanchot speaks of *writing* as an incessant return to first things, Levinas writes about *speech* as an origin of the world. For neither, however, will this turn out to have been their last word on speech and writing. Indeed, each has for the other not only a supplementary take or turn on the question but something like a reversal, one that either draws these two friends even closer together or, this time, sets them worlds apart.

BLANCHOT ON PLATO II: SOCRATIC WRITING

As we have seen, Blanchot's "The Beast of Lascaux" appears to read in a rather straightforward manner the Platonic critique of writing set forth in the *Phaedrus*. Writing, like sacred poetry or like the word of the oracle, is dangerous because there is no one behind the word to defend or lend assistance to it. Plato's *Phaedrus* expresses a mistrust of the technologies of writing and a certain faith in the humanism of speech, a Socratic humanism that emphasizes the living presence behind speech. Blanchot himself will thus argue against this humanism and emphasize the inaugural word of both sacred poetry and writing. Hence, Blanchot attributes to Plato a position on writing that he himself will want to reject or, rather, reverse. For Blanchot, writing is to be preferred to speech insofar as it is closer to the inaugural word. This is how Blanchot reads Plato, how Blanchot reads what Plato *meant to say*.

Blanchot thus rejects Plato's position on writing but not necessarily the status of Plato's dialogues—or even Socrates' speech—*as writing*. Indeed, in the very conclusion of "The Beast of Lascaux," Blanchot suggests that even Socrates, in his insistence on the speech of a live interlocutor, was perhaps also involved in the perpetual commencement that is writing. After citing Char's "the Beast unnameable," a poem about the famous cave paintings at Lascaux, Blanchot speaks of the "indistinctness of a primal word" and concludes: "A strange wisdom, too ancient—and too novel—for Socrates, and yet, for all the distaste which alienated him from it, we must believe that he is not shut out from it; for it was he who, accepting nothing but a man's living presence as guarantee of his word, yet went to his own death in order to keep his word" (*BL* 40).

In this striking conclusion, Blanchot prefigures many of the things he will say about Socrates and Plato in later texts, allowing him at once to accept as serious the Socratic and Platonic critique of writing and yet see not only Plato's dialogues but Socrates' speech, even his privileging of speech and his fear, condemnation, and avoidance of writing, as a sort of writing *avant la lettre*. In *The Step Not Beyond*, for example, Blanchot suggests that the one who does not write was, in effect, already writing, already involved in the incessant recommencement that is writing: "Not to write a line (like Socrates) is perhaps not to privilege speech, but to write by default and in advance, since, in this abstention, the space of writing in which Plato already works is prepared and is decided."[20] In *The Infinite Conversation*, too, Blanchot opposes a spherical, Parmenidean language to the discontinuous and fragmentary language of literature, a language of *writing* that includes not only Heraclitus, Pascal, Nietzsche, Bataille, and René Char, as we might expect, but the dialogues of Plato (*IC* 6–7). In deciding to write, in betraying the prescriptions of his master Socrates, Plato too would have given himself over to the "the madness of writing, a movement that is infinite, interminable, unceasing" (*IC* 229).

While Plato and Socrates might thus in all seriousness condemn writing in the *Phaedrus*, what they are engaged in is a sort of writing. Could it be that this writing is what Levinas *calls*—what Levinas *means by*—conversation?

LEVINAS' LAST WORD—"*ECRITURE!*"

Blanchot thus suggests that even in the humanist Socrates, and even in the dialogues of the one who disparaged, and disparaged in earnest, writing in the name of speech, there was already a kind of writing. Should we be surprised to find Levinas, who in 1961 seemed to suggest that Plato was right to condemn the facelessness of writing, suggest, and perhaps without contradiction, that the face is actually the site, not simply of speech, but indeed of writing—or at least of *Ecriture*?

The face as *Ecriture*? That is arguably what Levinas *meant* back in 1961 in *Totality and Infinity* when he spoke of conversation and, more than a quarter of a century later, in a preface to this same work, that is exactly what he *said*. In his 1987 preface to the German edition of *Totality and Infinity*, Levinas writes, as if responding to the questions Blanchot had asked him some twenty-five years earlier: "Face, already language before words, an original language of the human face stripped of the countenance it gives itself . . . origin of value and good, the idea of the human order within the order given to the human. The language of the inaudible, the language of the unheard of, the language of the non-said." And then Levinas adds a final word with an exclamation point—"*Ecriture!*" (*EN* 199).

How is one to translate this last word, this extraordinary final word? One trembles before the task. Does one translate it as "Writing!" (this is, after all, a preface to *Totality and Infinity*), a sort of Blanchotian "Writing"—or, indeed, as "Scripture!"? Just a few lines later, Levinas continues and makes the decision for us: "A phenomenology of the face: a necessary ascent to God, which will allow for a recognition or a denial of the voice that, in positive religion, speaks to children or to the childhood in each one of us, already readers of the Book and interpreters of Scripture [*Ecriture*]" (*EN* 199). Less ambiguous, this reference to *Ecriture*—to Scripture—raises anew all the questions of speech and writing in relation to the Other (and the Other in relation to God) that we have been pursuing throughout this essay.[21] Can *écriture* and *Ecriture* be at all compared? What does it mean for a "voice" to speak to children who are already *readers* of the Book and *interpreters* of

Ecriture? Might it be that when Blanchot and Levinas converge on the word "*écri-ture/Ecriture*" in relationship to the incessant recommencement, the simple differ-ence between a lower case and a capital letter signals an irreducible difference between them, a difference between inhuman writing and the divine word? But then what kind of difference is that?

Levinas can affirm the Platonic critique of writing, he can be critical of the Platonic dialogue understood as a dialogue of the soul with itself, and yet he can suggest that in the very writing of the Platonic dialogue there is a participation in *Ecriture*—that is, perhaps, a participation of the written dialogue in Scripture, a participation of national literature in the *Livre des Livres* or Book of Books (see *EI* 117).

Between writing and Scripture, the technologies of the book and the voice of the Book of Books, between *écriture* and *Ecriture,* the plural *Livres* and the singular *Livre*—differences, notice, that cannot be heard in speech and so must be marked out in writing, or else in translation—we are at the very heart of the question of the relationship between language and ethics, speaking and writing, at the very heart of the relationship or *conversation,* infinite or otherwise, between Emmanuel Levinas and Maurice Blanchot. Can it be said, can it actually be affirmed, that there is or has been a face-to-face encounter, a conversation or friendship between Emmanuel Levinas and Maurice Blanchot, a conversation or friendship that Levinas might have referred to in terms of speech and Blanchot in terms of writing, a conversa-tion and a friendship that would have been, nonetheless, the same, unique, unsub-stitutable? Speech, writing—what's the difference, we might say, if what is *meant* is the same, that is, something that precedes both meaning and the same, something that could be justified by neither meaning nor the same, something that perpetu-ally begins, like the inhuman force of writing or the divine word. Either Blanchot and Levinas *mean* the same thing with *different* and even opposite words, or else they mean different and perhaps quite opposite things with the *same* words. In the section of *Totality and Infinity* entitled "Discourse and Ethics," Levinas writes, cit-ing the *Phaedrus:*

> Plato maintains the difference between the objective order of truth, that which doubtlessly is established in writings, impersonally, and reason *in* a living being, "a living and animated discourse," a discourse "which can defend itself, and knows when to speak and when to be silent" (*Phaedrus* 276a). This discourse is not the unfolding of a prefabricated internal logic, but the constitution of truth in a strug-gle between thinkers, with all the risks of freedom. The relationship of language implies transcendence, radical separation, the strangeness of the interlocutors, the revelation of the other to me. In other words, *language is spoken where community between the terms of the relationship is wanting,* where the common plane is wanting or is yet to be constituted. (*TI* 73; my emphasis)

It is this discourse, part of this conversation, I believe, that Derrida attempted to stage or to host one last time in his eulogy of Emmanuel Levinas on December 27th, 1995—one last time, but then again another time, and yet again today, in the text entitled "Adieu."

Notes

1. Jacques Derrida, *Adieu—To Emmanuel Levinas,* trans. Pascale-Anne Brault and Michael Naas (Stanford, Calif.: Stanford University Press, 1999), 8. Hereafter abbreviated *A.*

2. Maurice Blanchot, *The Infinite Conversation,* trans. Susan Hanson (Minneapolis: University of Minnesota Press, 1993), 49–58; hereafter abbreviated *IC.*

3. The other works cited are Kant's *Critique of Pure Reason,* Hegel's *Phenomenology,* Bergson's *Essai sur les données immédiates de la conscience,* and Heidegger's *Being and Time.*

4. In this essay, originally published in 1955 and later published in *Difficile Liberté* (1963), Levinas opposes the "unmixed rationalism" of Plato and Aristotle to the "mixed rationalism" of Spinoza.

5. Asked during an interview at the end of *In the Time of the Nations* whether he would still say as he once did in *Proper Names* that "all philosophy is Platonic," Levinas responds: "That is a quote from an early text, I believe. I do not reject it, to the extent that the link between philosophy and transcendent alterity is affirmed in the Platonic theory of ideas, in which the problem or the anxiety of that radical alterity—even though there is an attempt to reduce it—seems to me to authenticate philosophy. I have already said that. I do not reject my attachment to Platonism, because to owe the daring formulation *beyond being* to Plato is good luck [*une bonne chance:* a stroke of good fortune]" (*TN* 178). This is a rather curious moment. Levinas in this interview from 1985 defends his claim from 1955 by referring to the ethical, non-ontological dimension of Plato's thought. But a reading of the passage in question from "Jean Wahl and Feeling" (*PN* 113) suggests that Levinas was referring in 1955 to the ontological, totalizing dimension of Plato's thought. Here is the passage in its entirely—with the line "All philosophy is Platonic," curiously missing from the English translation, restored:

> The mastery of self through the mastery of the universe is an integral part of European thought. All philosophy is Platonic. It is through participation in ideas, which are *yonder,* that becoming can work toward a pale existence. From Plato to Hegel and even to Heidegger, the thinker can only return to himself by completing a large circuit that takes him far from himself. He grasps himself in his objective concept, his act, his historical efficacy, his universal work. He *is* through the state. And all the rest is zoology. The *I* is determined at the heart of a totality, becomes itself in forgetting its uniqueness. The uniqueness of an individual, of a hunger, a need, a love—the child of indigence and abundance.

Despite the veiled reference at the very end of this passage to Eros as the child of poverty and resource, or indigence and abundance, Plato is still here presented as the essentially ontological thinker he was seen to be in the 1940s and most of the 1950s.

6. Levinas makes reference to the doctrine of *anamnesis* when he says, "Truth has been *re-discovered* ever since Socrates showed us that learning was only a *return* to a forgotten knowledge" (*EN* 136). See also *GCM* 114.

7. Cf. *EN* 54; *GDT* 126. In *Entre Nous* and in many other places, Levinas calls the impersonal Idea of the Good in the *Republic* Plato's God, a God who would be beyond being or beyond essence. As we will see, the question of the *analogy* between the face of the Other and God will be at the very center of Jacques Derrida's "Violence and Metaphysics," in *Writing and Difference,* trans. Alan Bass (Chicago: University of Chicago Press, 1978); hereafter abbreviated VM.

8. In a text from the same year (1961) that would eventually be collected in *Difficult Freedom,* Levinas writes, recalling the beginning of the *Phaedrus* and Socrates' preference for exile in the city rather than being rooted to the land: "Technology wrenches us out of the Heideggerian world and the superstitions surrounding *Place.* From this point on, an opportunity appears to us: to perceive men outside the situation in which they are placed, and let the human face shine in all its nudity. Socrates preferred the town, in which one meets people, to the countryside and trees. Judaism is the brother of the Socratic message" (*DF* 232–33).

9. "The Beast of Lascaux," trans. David Paul, in *René Char's Poetry* (Rome: Editions de Luca, 1956), 27–40; "La Bête de Lascaux" was first published in *La Nouvelle Revue Française* 4 (1953): 684–93 and then as a book by Fata Morgana (Paris, 1982); hereafter abbreviated *BL.*

For an excellent analysis of Blanchot's reading of Platonic dialogue, see Françoise Collin's *Maurice Blanchot et la question de l'écriture* (Paris: Gallimard, 1971), 94–98.

10. Both Levinas and Blanchot appear to be using the Léon Robin translation of the *Phaedrus* in the Pléiade Edition of 1950. Since Levinas often has the Greek in mind, he may have also been consulting the Guillaume Budé Greek-French Edition of several of the dialogues, including the *Phaedrus.* Léon Robin had himself translated a few of the Platonic dialogues for the Budé Edition many years earlier and then retranslated these dialogues for the Pléiade Edition. In his preface to the Pléiade Edition, Robin explains that he has corrected earlier translations but also made many changes because of the different demands and audiences of the Pléiade and Budé editions. In Robin's 1933 translation of the *Phaedrus* for the Belles Lettres Edition, Socrates says that written words are unable to "*se porter assistance à eux-mêmes,*" a formulation that is very close to the one used by Blanchot in his critique of *Totality and Infinity* in *The Infinite Conversation.* In Robin's retranslation of this same dialogue for the Pléiade Edition of 1950, Socrates says that written words are unable to "*se porter secours à eux-mêmes,*" the very phrase Levinas uses to describe speech in *Totality and Infinity.*

11. Just a couple of years later, Blanchot will repeat this reading of the *Phaedrus* and refer explicitly to Heidegger's shared distrust of writing and of technical reproduction. See Maurice Blanchot, "Museum Sickness," in *Friendship,* trans. Elizabeth Rottenberg (Stanford, Calif.: Stanford University Press, 1997), 43.

12. In an essay in *The Work of Fire,* trans. Charlotte Mandell (Stanford, Calif.: Stanford University Press, 1995), 107, Blanchot again compares René Char's writing to that of Heraclitus.

13. Elsewhere in *Totality and Infinity,* Levinas criticizes Plato's theory of negative pleasures (136), his understanding of need in the *Philebus* (116), and his theory of *anamnesis* as a truth to be found in memory *within us* (50–51).

14. Jacques Derrida, "Plato's Pharmacy," in *Dissemination,* trans. Barbara Johnson (Chicago: University of Chicago Press, 1981), 61–171. The essay first appeared in *Tel Quel* 32–33 (1968).

15. On the contrast between revelation, where "truth is expressed and illuminates us before we [seek] it," and disclosure, see *TI* 103. Levinas opposes teaching to maieutics, emphasizing that the "primacy of the same was Socrates' teaching: to receive nothing of the Other but what is in me. . . . The ideal of Socratic truth thus rests on the essential self-sufficiency of the same, its identification in ipseity, its egoism. Philosophy is an egology" (*TI* 43–44; see also 171).

16. Levinas writes in the essay in *Proper Names* devoted to Derrida: "But the Saying is not exhausted in the *Said,* and the sign did not spring from the soil of the ontology of the Said, to receive from it its paradoxical structure of relation (which astonished Plato to the point of pushing him to parricide) and make up for a self-eluding presence. The sign, like the Saying, is the extra-ordinary event (running counter to presence) of exposure to others, of subjection to others; i.e., the event of subjectivity. It is the one-for-the-other" (*PN* 61).

17. Levinas speaks frequently of the Platonic dialogue as a kind dialectic or "conversation of the soul with itself," Plato's definition of thought in the *Sophist* (*GCM* 106, 140, and *OB* 25). Levinas writes: "Dialectic is not a dialogue with the Other, or at least it remains a 'dialogue of the soul with itself, proceeding by questions and answers.' Plato precisely defined thought thus. According to the traditional interpretation of discourse that goes back to this definition, the mind in speaking its thoughts remains no less one and unique, the same in presence, a synchrony despite its coming-and-going where the ego could be opposed to itself " ("Diachrony and Representation," *TO* 100–101).

18. Levinas adopts Plato's critique of rhetoric for similar reasons. See the section "Rhetoric and Injustice" in *TI* 70–72, which makes frequent reference to the *Phaedrus.* Levinas there argues that rhetorical discourse is not a relation with exteriority, not a face-to-face conversation with the Other, what he calls "justice," but an oblique discourse of ruse and artifice, a discourse of violence, corruption, and injustice. Levinas concludes that section: "Justice is the recognition of his privilege qua Other and his mastery, is access to the Other outside of rhetoric, which is ruse, emprise, and exploitation. And in this sense justice coincides with the overcoming of rhetoric."

19. Blanchot himself seems to have come to share these concerns. In the republication of his original 1961 essay in the 1969 collection *The Infinite Conversation,* Blanchot adds a supplementary footnote. To the original line running "I believe this is what is decisive in the affirmation we must hear and must maintain independently of the theological context in which it presents itself," Blanchot adds this note: " 'Context' here, as Jacques Derrida very aptly observes, is a word that Levinas could only deem inappropriate—just as he would the reference to theology" (*IC* 441 n. 2). Both would be inappropriate, it seems, because metaphysics and theology have a common root, a common "context," and so could never be taken "independently" of one another.

20. Maurice Blanchot, *The Step Not Beyond,* trans. Lycette Nelson (Albany: State University of New York Press, 1992), 39. See also *The Writing of the Disaster,* trans. Ann Smock (Lincoln: University of Nebraska Press, 1995), 65.

21. Derrida writes in "Violence and Metaphysics": "The foundation of metaphysics—in Levinas' sense—is to be encountered in the return to things themselves, where we find the common root of humanism and theology: the resemblance between

man and God, man's visage and the Face of God. 'The Other resembles God.' Via the passageway of this resemblance, man's speech can be lifted up toward God, an almost unheard of *analogy* which is the very movement of Levinas' discourse on discourse" (108). And just a bit further on: "The face is neither the face of God nor the figure of man: it is their resemblance" (109).

ETHICS AS FIRST PHILOSOPHY: ARISTOTELIAN REFLECTIONS ON INTELLIGENCE, SENSIBILITY, AND TRANSCENDENCE

6

Claudia Baracchi

One of Levinas' crucial contributions to contemporary thought is the understanding of ethics as first philosophy. This view calls for a radical critique of the priority traditionally accorded to rational-scientific knowledge, with respect to which the various disciplines would be construed in their derivativeness, merely as fields in which purely rational structures would find their application. In this perspective, theoretical knowledge, far from autonomous and self-grounding, is exposed as emerging out of practical involvements and, more broadly, out of the involvement in sensibility and phenomenality. Such an involvement is irreducible to experience understood as the content of formal and formalized knowledge as always already brought back to, contained in, and owned by self-consciousness. Rather, it points to experience as that which cannot be thematically circumscribed. It points to the "vivacity of life" as a matter of "excession (*excession*), the rupture of the container by the noncontainable" (*EN* 88). Such would be the "very event of *transcendence* as life" (*EN* 87) in its anarchic precedence with respect to all *arkhe*.

The present essay undertakes to show that a consonant understanding of the relation between the practical and the theoretical may be found in Aristotle.[1] Such a way of receiving Aristotle's thinking is called for by Levinas himself. To be sure, he pervasively refers to Aristotle as one of the paradigmatic figures in a philosophical tradition obsessed with logic/ontology and culminating with Heidegger.[2] And yet, Levinas also lets transpire, with occasional and sudden gestures, the irreducibility of

Claudia Baracchi

Aristotelian thinking to the hegemonic aspirations of the metaphysics it inaugurates. For instance, he notes the resourcefulness of Aristotle's thinking of the plurivocity of being vis-à-vis the concern with justice (*EN* 27). In the essay "Totality and Totalization," he highlights the inexhaustibly disruptive power of sensibility at work both in Aristotle and in Kant: "Discovering a rationality at the level of the sensible and of the finite, in contrast with the inordinate rationality of the Platonic Idea, rediscovering the Aristotelian intelligibility inherent in things (which expresses itself in the Kantian doctrine of schematism, in which the concepts of the understanding are exposed in time), Kant's [critical] philosophy seriously shakes the foundations of the idea of totality" (*AT* 46). Again, Levinas repeatedly underlines the way in which Aristotle's understanding of the agent intellect splits open any pretense at rational as well as subjective self-containment and self-sufficiency. Various philosophies at their "heights," he says, make it apparent that the "questioning of the Same by the Other, and what we have called 'wakefulness' or 'life,' is, outside of knowledge, a part of philosophy." Among the symptoms of such a questioning, he mentions "the beyond being in Plato . . . the entrance through the door of the agent intellect in Aristotle; the idea of God in us, going beyond our capacity as finite beings" (*EN* 89).

Levinas is especially captivated by the phrase "through the door," *thurathen*, which he borrows from Aristotle. It occurs twice in the treatise *On the Generation of the Animals* (736b28 and 744b22) and refers to the intellect, *nous*, which enters from the outside and is "divine." Levinas takes this phrase to indicate the radical exteriority haunting interiority, and he returns to it more than once. Already in 1954, he affirms that justice "comes from the outside, 'through the door,' above the fray; it appears like a principle external to history" ("The Ego and the Totality," *CPP* 40; in the footnote on the same page, the Aristotelian expression is said to be specifically related to "the agent intellect [*nous poietikos*]," while this is at most implicit in *Generation*). Levinas speaks of the "Other calling the Same" as "a heteronomy of freedom that the Greeks have not taught us" (*GCM* 24). And yet, in a note, he immediately adds, with caution: "Unless they suggest it, both in the Daimon of Socrates and in the entry, *by the door*, of the agent intellect in Aristotle" (*GCM* 189 n. 24). Again, Levinas mentions "the entry, 'through the door,' of the agent intellect in Aristotle" as showing the "relation of transcendence" (*GCM* 119).

What follows is an approach to Aristotle informed by these intuitions recurring in Levinas' work. It is an attempt to take them seriously as interpretive indications and rigorously unfold their implications. Thus, the discussion here presented is not "comparative," comparing two bodies of work presumed in their constitutive separation, unproblematic availability, and inertness. Rather, following Levinas' suggestions will disclose the movement of Aristotle's thinking in altogether unorthodox and unusual ways, disrupting a crystallized tradition of Aristotelian systematization and allowing for the articulation of unheard-of possibilities. Such a reading of Aristotle constitutes the main body of the present essay, but the Aristotle thereby emerging can be encountered precisely thanks to Levinas' directives and orientation. Thus, while we will be thematically focusing on the Aristotelian texts, our inquiry will at once provide an elaboration of Levinas' abbreviated statements and draw out their consequences. In this sense, despite appearances, it is the demand inherent in Levinas' thinking that dominates the essay, determining its turns as well as the transgressive character of its perspective on antiquity.

The perils, discontinuities, and irreducibility inherent in juxtaposing Aristotle and Levinas must, of course, be acknowledged. In particular, it is crucial to observe that, while the concern with the infinitely, indeterminately pre-logical or pre-discursive may be common to both Aristotle and Levinas, the Levinasian elaboration of infinite priority in terms of injunction and persecution is remote from Aristotle's horizon. Likewise, it should be granted that, in the treatises gathered under the title of *Metaphysics*, Aristotle often calls first philosophy *episteme*. However, the question imposing itself in this regard is what *episteme* could possibly mean and be like, if understood as "science of principles." For principles, on Aristotle's own terms, are not the subject matter of science but rather constitute science's very premises and presuppositions. Rigorously speaking, then, as first philosophy *episteme* would turn out to be prescientific.

In the wake of Levinas' intimations, I propose that Aristotle acknowledges theoretical knowledge as integrally involved in the movement of life—in becoming, sensibility, and hence action. In this sense, ethics should be seen as first philosophy, that is, as the structural study of conditions and of the principles arising from them. This line of inquiry would demand a comprehensive assessment of Aristotelian thinking, ranging from the ethical treatises and the *Politics* to *De anima,* from the *Physics* and *Metaphysics* to the treatises of the *Organon*. However, in the present study I will approach this issue in the perspective of the primacy that Aristotle accords to sensuous perception, especially in the *Posterior Analytics.* I will then consider certain aspects of Aristotle's meditation on *nous,* especially as regards the convergence of sensibility and intelligence (intellect, intuition) and the irreducibility of both to *logos*.

Through this line of inquiry, the theoretical emerges as always informed by a set of practices, by the modality of comportment toward phenomena. Encountering phenomena, the world, or nature in the broadest sense is always a matter of *ethos.* As will be expounded in what follows, *this apparently "modern" intimation is to be found at the heart of Greek thought.*

Of course, "ethics as first philosophy" cannot here mean a normative or prescriptive compilation. Nor can it signify a self-founding, all-encompassing, and rationally self-contained discourse. Understood as ethics, first philosophy may not retain such privileges, which would be the privileges of rational autonomy. Rather, the phrase "ethics as first philosophy" indicates that ethics is characterized by a certain comprehensiveness vis-à-vis all manner of human endeavor. At the same time, precisely qua ethics, the discourse coming first exhibits the consciousness of its own openness vis-à-vis that which exceeds it, that is, vis-à-vis that which is not discursive and in which all discourse as such belongs. This *logos* cannot fully account for its "differing and wandering" subject matter, nor can it itself bring about that which it strives to clarify, namely, the good or happiness. In other words, the *logos* of ethics is manifestly aware of its own incapacity for self-enclosure and remains open to that which can neither be discursively exhausted nor simply formalized. Such a *logos* understands itself in its openness to the infinite. Once again, central to this investigation will be tracing the limits of reason—or more precisely, acknowledging how Aristotle draws such a delimitation.

ARISTOTLE ON *AISTHESIS* AND *NOUS*

> Sensation breaks up every system . . .
>
> —Levinas (*TI* 59)

At various junctures of the *Posterior Analytics,* we find the intimation of the indissoluble concomitance (if not the identity) of noetic and sensible perception, *nous* and *aisthesis.* Here Aristotle gestures toward *aisthesis* as both informed by and implicated in *nous,* and deepens his examination of the intertwinement of the two.

The treatise begins with the observation that scientific knowledge rests on premises that are better known than the conclusions to which scientific demonstration leads: better known by their nature, without qualification, or *simply,* and not relative to us.[3] Premises, principles, or causes are prior in the order of what is and hence eminently knowable, although they may be posterior in the order of human coming to know. The priority here at stake, however, may not simply be said to be ontological without qualification, just as the meaning of the knowledge pertaining to it requires further clarification. Priority in the order of being designates a priority indeterminately exceeding ontology as the distinctively human philosophical discourse. It designates the priority inhering in nature itself, in that which imposes itself on the human prior to any attempt at discursive systematization—the priority of what is and, in virtue of this, compels assent. Knowledge here indicates precisely the compelling, inevitable character of that which can only be affirmed.

The premises of demonstration are more known, that is, they compel assent to *begin with.* Yet as beginnings, *arkhai,* they exhibit a certain elusiveness, an excess vis-à-vis the procedures of knowledge that they initiate. They are knowable above all, and yet not according to the demonstrative/scientific procedures. This irreducible distinction and discontinuity, in Aristotle, between knowing demonstratively and knowing otherwise, that is, the perception of principles, is of incalculable consequence. At stake is the unbridgeable rift between *logos* and *nous,* even though at this juncture Aristotle is not explicitly casting the discussion in these terms.

In the context of discursive or apodictic knowledge, the principles or premises appear as given. Within the procedures of knowledge, the question concerning principles can at most be formulated but not addressed. Indeed, the principles remain radically extraneous to the demonstrative practices: the latter base themselves on principles but cannot examine, assess, and clarify them. The principles remain liminal and therefore ungraspable vis-à-vis the discourses they make possible.

The sciences must *begin* with and from principles that have always already elicited conviction. This means that knowledge of the principles, in the mode of intuitive belief and reliance, is experienced primordially and decisively. From within the logic of demonstration, the priority of the principles is incalculable and hence neither merely logical nor chronological. Principles enjoy an altogether excessive, in(de)finitely anterior priority. Says Aristotle:

> [Demonstrated knowledge, *apodeiktike episteme,* must be acquired] from [premises which are] first and indemonstrable. . . . [The premises] should be the causes, more known (*gnorimotera*), and prior [to the conclusion]. They must be the causes [of the conclusion] since we know (*epistametha*) a thing when we know (*eidomen*) a cause of it; they must be prior (*protera*) [by nature to the conclusion], if they, as such, are its causes; and they must be previously known (*progignoskomena*), not only in the other manner, that is, by being understood (*xunienai*), but also by being known that they are (*eidenai hoti estin*). (*Posterior Analytics* 71b27–34)[4]

It is telling that, in order to point to the intuitive apprehension of principles, Aristotle repeatedly switches from the language of *episteme* to that of *gnosis* and "having seen," *eidenai.* It is such an indeterminately prior vision that sensibly grounds the syllogistic procedures of scientific knowledge in the proper sense. It is such a perception that constitutes the principle and beginning, the *arkhe,* of discursive articulation and analysis. And such a beginning is first simply and absolutely. It is origin, and as such its priority is a matter of the always already of immediacy—of that which is immediate and has no middle, no beyond, no further reference. Aristotle says: "A principle of demonstration is an immediate (*amesos*) premise and a premise is said to be immediate if there is no other premise prior" (*Posterior Analytics* 72a8–9).

Not only, then, are the principles acquired through intuitive perception and ultimately a matter of belief, but they constitute the an-archic *arkhe,* the non-logical ground of demonstrated knowledge. The latter is derived from the premises intuitively acquired and is therefore marked by a certain secondariness with respect to them. What comes to the fore is thus the irreducibility of knowledge, even of *epis-teme* itself, to the order of demonstration. Knowledge, *episteme* itself, would have to be understood in light of a rupturing dynamic, constitutively exposing knowledge in its openness and heteronomy. On this point Aristotle could not be more explicit:

> We on the other hand say that (1) not all knowledge (*epistemen*) is demonstrable but that (2) knowledge of immediate premises is indemonstrable. And it is evident that this is necessary; for if it is necessary to know (*epistasthai*) the prior [prem-ises] from which a demonstration proceeds, and if these [premises] eventually stop (*histatai*) when they are immediate, they are of necessity indemonstrable. Such then is our position, and we also say that there is not only knowledge (*epistemen*), but also a principle of knowledge (*arkhen epistemes*) by which we know (*gnori-zomen*) the limits (*horous*) [of that knowledge]. (*Posterior Analytics* 72b19–25)

It is noteworthy that Aristotle, on the one hand, preserves a certain distinction be-tween the modes of *episteme* and of *gnosis*, reserving the latter for knowledge in the comprehensive sense, which includes but exceeds demonstration. On the other hand, however, he also proposes a loose usage of the language of *episteme* in order to signal a kind of overflowing of scientific knowledge with respect to itself: sci-ence seems to be characterized by a centrifugal movement according to which it finds its boundaries and stability only in its other, in the nonscientific, nondemon-strable beginnings. It founds itself on principles it cannot found, and this means that it is neither self-sufficient nor self-enclosed. In this sense, the principle ap-pears in a way as an end: as that which brings to an end the concatenation of causes and cannot itself be grasped causally; as that which stands secure and past which no further movement can be thought. It is only thus that the field and scope of science is delimited.

What Introduces Itself into One

First principles, then, whether axioms or principles pertaining to the particular sci-ences, are known, not by demonstration but otherwise. As we shall see, this will re-ceive further elaboration in the course of the ethical discussion. But what is crucial in this context is Aristotle's insistence on the connection between intuitive appre-hension and induction, *epagoge*—on the belonging of the phenomenon of noetic perception in the broader experience of the physical, sensible surroundings. From the point of view of the human condition, *noesis* gives itself in and through the per-ceptual acknowledgment and ensuing investigation of the environment, whether we should call this *phusis* or *kosmos*. The final section of the *Posterior Analytics* (Beta 19) is devoted to this issue, but this articulation is variously foreshadowed at earlier stages, most notably at Alpha 18, which deserves to be quoted extensively:

It is also evident that, if a [power of] sensation is lacking, some corresponding science must be lacking, for a science cannot be acquired if indeed we learn either by induction or by demonstration. Now a demonstration proceeds from universals (*ek ton katholou*), whereas an induction proceeds from particulars (*ek ton kata meros*). But universals cannot be contemplated (*theoresai*) except through induction (and even the so-called things from abstraction [*ta ex aphaireseos*], although not separable, are made known by induction, since some of them belong to each genus insofar as each is such-and-such), and it is impossible to learn by induction without having the [power of] sensation. For of individuals (*ton . . . kath'hekaston*) [there can be only] sensation, and no knowledge of them can be acquired; and neither can we [demonstrate conclusions] from universals without induction, nor can we [acquire universals] through induction without sensation. (*Posterior Analytics* 81a38–b9)

While sensing may pertain to the perception of individuals, of which there can be no knowledge *stricto sensu*, it is also the case that the manifold power of sensation is a necessary condition for the development of scientific knowledge. For sensation is the ground of inductive investigation, and it is through such an investigation that the universals are obtained. Indeed, Aristotle emphasizes, even universals that appear to be abstracted from the sensory *datum*, those which appear to be removed from the sensible and are thematized separately, as though autonomous, are indeed taken in, thanks to the experience of the sensible surrounding. As laid out in *Metaphysics* Mu and Nu, the mathematical beings, such as numbers, are not separate from the sensible beings, though they can be separated in thinking or discourse, *logos*.

This, however, crucially extends the claim with which the section opens. To be sure, if a specific power of sensation is lacking, the corresponding science also will be lacking. For instance, in the absence of the power of hearing, the scientific investigation of acoustic phenomena will be unthinkable. But saying that even universals arrived at through discursive abstraction are ultimately acquired in virtue of induction means that science as such could not develop aside from the basic involvement in sensibility.

Induction, *epagoge*, then, is the operation whereby the surrounding is taken in (*epago*), comes into one, and thus makes possible the lighting up of an intuition that is no longer limited to the contingent particular or configuration one is sensing. Rather, such an intuition illuminates something *katholou*, "according to the whole"—universally, so to speak. It keeps open to that which opens its way into one, sensing at once its uniqueness and what it shares in common. More precisely, thus, induction names that *possibility* that introduces (*epago*) itself into one in the sensuous experience. Indeed, sensation brings (*ago*) into and upon (*epi*) one the possibility of an insight exceeding the scope of one's immediate sensing or observing—the possibility of revealing and actualizing the capacity for such an insight, the power of *nous*. Strictly speaking, sensation pertains to being affected by individuals, undergoing their coming into one, and yet it implies the possibility of grasping that which cannot be reduced to individuals and that, rather, gathers and configures them. The interpenetration of affection (*pathos*) and formative involvement should be noted in this regard.

As though implicated in, folded into sensibility, the possibility of contemplating universals is led into one as one senses. Apprehending by induction, therefore, means realizing the possibility that is imported into one by the very fact that one is alive and sensitive, that one is stirred up by what comes in and is responsive to it. But of course to speak of realizing the possibility implicit in sensing (the potential of sensation) also raises the question whether sensation may always already be ordered, structured, and informed—whether, that is, instead of attempting to isolate the moment of sensation as the mere report of raw and chaotic data, we should see in the articulate differentiation yielded by the senses the intersection of *aisthesis* and *nous*. While we are not in the position of elaborating on this question further at this point, we can minimally say that induction presents itself as a certain conjunction of sensation and noetic perception, as the advent of noetic insight out of the basic, repeated undergoing of the sensible. It is striking that Aristotle, in the passage just quoted, refers to the inductive grasp of universals in terms of *theorein*, properly contemplative or theoretical understanding: in one's exposure to the sensible, one comes to see, to discern what is not itself sensible, not a "this," not a thing among things, but belongs in the sensible as its shapes and rhythm.

Sensuous Thinking

Later in *Posterior Analytics* Alpha 31, Aristotle underlines again that knowledge (*episteme*) is not through sensation, for sensation is of the "this," which "of necessity is somewhere and now," while "that which is universal and belongs to all cannot be sensed" (*Posterior Analytics* 87b30). Accordingly, sensation is found to be less "honorable" than the knowledge of the universals, which (1) reveals the cause and (2) enables demonstrated knowledge. Nevertheless, here once more the bond between sensation and intuition of universals is restated. It is indeed formulated in terms of dependence of the latter on the former:

> It is evident, then, that it is impossible for one to know something demonstrable by sensing it, unless by "sensing" one means having knowledge through demonstration. In some problems, however, reference may be made to lack of sensation; for we might not have inquired if we could see (*heoromen*), not that we would understand (*eidotes*) by seeing (*toi horan*), but that from seeing (*ek tou horan*) we would have the universal. For example, if we would see (*heoromen*) that the burning glass had holes in it and the light passing through them, by seeing (*toi horan*) each instance separately it would also be clear why it burns and simultaneously (*hama*) the thought (*noesai*) that such is the case in every instance. (*Posterior Analytics* 88a9–17)

Witnessing various instances of a certain phenomenon reveals its cause, as though, by repeated experience, the intimate structure of what is experienced would be laid bare. Mediated through iteration, the immediate intuition arises that what has been revealed holds in all analogous cases, according to the whole. In this sense, cause and universal are simultaneous, or even identical. Here Aristotle's effort seems especially acute, to convey in the linear unfolding of discourse the simultaneity or coincidence (*hama*) of thinking and sensing, the interpolation of the immediate into the temporal, the unmediated intuition at once breaking through repeated perceptual exposure.

Singularity Arising

It is in *Posterior Analytics* Beta 19 that we find, however, the decisive statement concerning the arising of universals or first principles out of repeated sensible perception. The way in which Aristotle here pursues the issue of "the principles, how they become known and what is the knowing habit (*gnorizousa hexis*) of them" (*Posterior Analytics* 99b18–19), parallels the analysis in *Metaphysics* Alpha 1, situating the preconditions and development of intellectual perception in the field of life broadly understood. It does, however, introduce a few points of decisive importance that are not illuminated in the "metaphysical" discourse.

Sensation, the innate (*sumphuton*) power (*dunamis*) that all animals possess and that is less honorable than knowledge in accuracy, is in and of itself said to be "discriminating" (*kritike*) (*Posterior Analytics* 99b36). In certain living beings, however, the sensation presents an abiding character (*mone*): it is retained in the soul. Here, unlike in the discourse of the *Metaphysics*, Aristotle elaborates on the mnemonic power (*mneme*) in terms of the ability to "draw out a *logos* from the retention of such [sensations]" (*Posterior Analytics* 100a3–4). For certain animals, the formation and formulation of *logos* seems to occur out of (*ek*) the constancy of sensation harbored in the soul and constituting memory. Thanks to the persistence of the impression, they can divine, out of the phenomenon, the *logos* at the heart of the phenomenon. Again, as is said in the *Metaphysics*, many similar memories lead to one experience. Here, however, experience seems to be equated with the formation of the universal: the latter seems to give itself immediately alongside the former, out of the memory of sense impressions—out of that abiding that also lets the *logos* transpire and be grasped. From this level of experiential seizing of the universal would proceed the principles of science and of art:

> Again, from experience[s] or from every universal which has come to rest (*eremesantos*) in the soul and which, being one besides the many, would be one and the same in all of them, [there arises] a principle (*arkhe*) of art and of science, of art if it is a principle about generation (*genesin*), but of science if it is a principle about being (*to on*). (*Posterior Analytics* 100a6–9)

At this point Aristotle distinguishes the universals from the principles properly understood, suggesting that it is from the distinct and abiding character of the universal that a principle would issue. What is important to note, however, is the characterization of the formation of universals as a halt, a stabilization. Out of the indefinite flow of sensations, the universal names the endurance of a comprehensive insight, of an intuition that, because according to the whole, does not simply pass away:

> So neither are these [knowing] habits present in the soul [from the start] in any determinate way, nor do they come into being from other more known habits, but from sensation (*apo aistheseos*), like a reversal (*tropes*) in battle brought about when one makes a stand (*stantos*), then another, then another, till a principle (*arkhen*) is reached; and the soul is of such a nature as to be able to be affected in this way. (*Posterior Analytics* 100a10–14)

The disposition to know universals issues from sensation in a way similar to the countermovement that arrests a retreat in the course of a battle. As the flux of men fleeing is countered by one of them halting, others similarly take position in succession; in this way an order is found and, at least for a while, held. As in the passage previously quoted concerning immediate and indemonstrable premises (premises "of necessity indemonstrable," which "eventually stop, *histatai*, when they are immediate"; *Posterior Analytics* 72b19–25), seizing universals appears to be not simply a matter of resting in the soul but, more precisely, a matter of stopping and standing upright. Knowing, most clearly in the mode of *epistamai*, is illuminated in terms of setting up, over, and steadfastly (*histemi, ephistamai*). It is such a crystallization, such a steady posture bespeaking reliability, that allows for discernment. Aristotle elucidates further, this time making it emphatically clear that universals broadly understood and first principles alike stem in the end from the exposure to the sensible:

> When one of those without differences (*adiaphoron*) has made a stand (*stantos*), [there is formed] in the soul the first universal (for though one senses an individual [*to kath'hekaston*], sensation is of the universal, for example, of a man, not of the man Callias), and then again another among these makes a stand (*histatai*), till a universal that has no parts (*amere*) makes a stand (*stei*); for example, "such and such an animal," and this proceeds till "animal," and in the latter case similarly. Clearly, then, of necessity we come to know the first [principles] (*ta prota*) by induction; for it is in this way that sensation, too, produces in us (*empoiei*) the universal. (*Posterior Analytics* 100a15–b4)

As Aristotle also specifies at *Posterior Analytics* 97b29–31, by "those without differences" (*ta adiaphora*) we should understand the singular individual.[5] Mnemonically retained and erected, the sensory impression of the individual gives rise to (rises as) the intuition of a universal. This occurs as though immediately, for, as Aristotle underlines, "sensation is of the universal," it literally "produces the universal in us," makes it actual in our soul. Indeed, let this be said in passing, the intimation here is that there can be no sensation of an absolutely unique individual which would not *also* belong with others and through which a universal could not be discernible. The emergence of the universal rests on the belonging and sharing with others. The fixation of a multiplicity of universals makes it possible for human beings to perceive more comprehensive ones under which the universals brought forth by sensation may be gathered—just as, for example, the delimitations of various animals may belong together under the genus "animal."

Things Themselves

Once the intimate implication of noetic intuition in sensation (and vice versa) has been thus articulated, the remarks concluding the *Posterior Analytics* sound all the more peremptory in their pointing to the experiential, and hence thoroughly practical, presuppositions in virtue of which scientific inquiry may at all take place. Such is the life of scientific practices:

> Since of the thinking habits (*ton peri ten dianoian hexeon*) by which we think truly (*aletheuomen*) some are always true while others (for example, opinion and calculation [*doxa kai logismos*]) may also be false; since scientific knowledge (*episteme*) and intuition (*nous*) are always true and there is no genus [of knowledge] that is more accurate (*akribesteron*) than scientific knowledge except intuition; since the principles of demonstration are [by nature] more known [than what is demonstrated], and all scientific knowledge is knowledge with *logos* (*meta logou*) whereas there could be no scientific knowledge of the principles; and since nothing can be more true (*alethesteron*) than scientific knowledge except intuition; it follows from the examination of these [facts] that intuition would be [the habit or faculty] of principles (*arkhon*), and that a principle of a demonstration could not be a demonstration and so [the principles] of scientific knowledge could not be scientific knowledge. Accordingly, if we have no genus of a true [habit] other than scientific knowledge, intuition would be the principle [beginning, origin] of scientific knowledge. Moreover, a principle would be of a principle, and every [other kind of knowledge] is similarly related to a pertinent fact (*pragma*). (*Posterior Analytics* 100b5–17)

Of the dispositions to know, only noetic intuition and science are always true, disclose the true (*aletheuein*), and pertain to that which is necessary and abiding. But again, noetic intuition appears to enjoy higher honor: intuition itself is said to be "more true" than science and to surpass it in accuracy, while the principles intuition yields are found to be in themselves more known. It could be said that the *aletheuein* that intuition names releases truth to a higher degree than *episteme*. But these two modes of knowledge are not compared as though their difference were

Claudia Baracchi

merely a matter of degree in exactness. They are, instead, essentially heterogeneous. The knowing of intuition does not take place with and through *logos:* it is not discursive; it does not share in the demonstrative and inferential procedures constituting scientific knowledge. Intuition of principles is not mediated by the articulation in and of *logos.* While scientific knowledge is established and firmed up by its apodictic strategies, the contemplation of principles involves another kind of certainty, namely, the unshakeable conviction immediately compelled by the evidence of the phenomena themselves. Without proof or syllogism, what is experienced induces assent. In Aristotle's words, "[In the case of induction,] the universal is proved through the being clear of the particular (*dia tou delon einai to kath'hekaston*)" (*Posterior Analytics* 71a8–9). Accordingly, it is far from accidental that in the *Metaphysics* the "science of wisdom," the strange science endowed with an awareness of itself as resting on an intuitive "ground," is said to be necessitated and guided by the truth itself (*aute he aletheia*) (*Metaphysics* 984b10), that is to say, by the things themselves (*auto to pragma*) (*Metaphysics* 984a18) or phenomena (*Metaphysics* 986b31).

Noetic perception, the principle and origin of scientific inquiry, then, concerns principles. The apprehension of principles is not knowledge *meta logou,* accomplished through *logos,* although it grounds *logos* and discerns it in the phenomena giving themselves to perception according to the whole. Awareness of the noetic stratum by nature prior to scientific investigation may, alone, grant *logos* its proper positioning. It alone may acknowledge *logos* as emerging out of phenomena (100a3–4) and anchor *logos,* the discursive elaboration of scientific demonstration, to experience. The possibility, always inherent in *logos,* of an emancipation from experience and the corresponding need to prevent such an alienation, such a drifting away that makes *logos* abstract, indeed formal, are central concerns for Aristotle. They constitute a leading thread not only of the ethical discourse but of the meditation in the *Metaphysics* as well.

The Delay of Discursive Knowing

Let us merely note, to conclude this brief excursus through the *Posterior Analytics,* that the remarks on science and intuition in the final section of the treatise only magnify what was already stated at the very beginning. The inquiry had opened with a proposition both laconic and pregnant with consequences: "All teaching and learning through discourse (*dianoetike*) come to be from previous (*ek prouparkhouses*) knowledge (*gnoseos*)" (*Posterior Analytics* 71a1–2). All transmission and reception of knowledge that move across (*dia*) intuition or thinking (*noesis*) in order to articulate themselves discursively presuppose a knowledge that must always already be given in order for any exchange to take place at all. Since the first sentence,

114

with the reference to preceding knowledge, we witness a bifurcation in the language of knowing. We notice, concomitantly, the intimation that knowledge of principles, of that from (*ek*) which discursive knowledge begins, cannot be taught or learned—not, anyway, conveyed according to the way of human dialogue. The apprehension of principles emerges out of the silent unfolding of life itself: it is inscribed in my own constitution, or rather, inscribes my constitution as never simply my own. I never subsist aside from the apprehending, but am constituted in this subjection to that which arrives, in this permanent openness and exposure.

The problem of prior and unmediated knowledge, adumbrated in the beginning of the treatise, is retained in its disquieting, unsettling potential. For such a knowledge is a prerequisite for all human mediation, communication, and scientific practices; yet it is not humanly established and remains, as a matter of fact, only dimly illuminated. Discursive knowing is, in a sense, always already late: always already requires and finds a ground that exceeds it in worth and originary force. Such is its constitutive delay.

To be sure, the prior knowledge always already required does provide an absolute beginning. As we saw above, first principles as such constitute a halt, the term beyond which no causal concatenation may continue. And yet such an unqualified priority remains by definition impervious to analysis. In virtue of itself, it poses difficulties that, for the scientific endeavor, are hardly less severe than the abyss of infinite regress. As Levinas surmises, sensation does indeed break up every system.

"THROUGH THE DOOR"

> . . . the Daimon of Socrates and . . . the entry, *by the door,* of the agent intellect in Aristotle.
>
> —Levinas (*GCM* 189 n. 24)

That which enters "through the door" from an infinitely inappropriable outside, which forms and informs me, which I am besieged by and exposed to: we have already considered the dynamic of that which comes and imposes itself, that which introduces itself into one in *epagoge,* that is, through the thresholds of *aisthesis* and *nous,* sensibility and intelligence. Entrance "through the door" is a figure of transcendence, of the transcendence that life is, of life as transcending, perturbing, and splitting open reason's self-referential games—its foreseeable histories and hegemonic aspirations. In this regard, a further consideration of Aristotle's thinking on *nous,* in its excessive character and indeterminate implication in *aisthesis,* may be desirable.

In the *Nicomachean Ethics* the inquiry concerning *nous* is introduced as follows: "Since scientific knowledge is *belief* (*hupolepsis*) of universal and necessary things, and since there are principles of whatever is demonstrable and of all scientific knowledge . . . a principle of what is scientifically known cannot be scientific knowledge . . . we are left with intuition [as the disposition] of those principles" (*Nicomachean Ethics* 1140b31–1141a9; my emphasis). It is significant that, consistently with William of Moerbeke's institution of the Aristotelian terminology in Latin, *nous* should be rendered as either "intellect" or "intuition," depending on the context. *Nous* undecidably oscillates in the semantic range disclosed by both terms, while being exhausted by neither. Yet quite remarkably, in the history of systematizations and (con)versions of the Aristotelian *corpus*, *nous* as *intellectus* has been assimilated to *ratio*.

Nous names the intelligence pervading *aisthesis*.[6] It yields the perceived in its nakedness, not as an object that has been cognitively mastered, but rather as that which announces itself onto the threshold of awareness in its sudden evidence, disclosing itself in an articulation indeterminately prior to the articulations and mediations mastered by discourse. As the sudden intuition of the universal inherent in the particular, *nous* bespeaks the grasping of axioms and definitions—hence its role in granting principles and, subsequently, in the grounding of science. Across science and sensation, *nous* lights up the range from sensation to perception of the universal or definition. *Nous* is the element of insight.

Crucially, then, *nous* is said to be nondiscursive, nonlinear, that is, to entail a certain immediacy. As Aristotle repeatedly puts it, it does *not* involve *logos*, "[f]or *nous* is of definitions (*horon*), for which there is no *logos*" (*Nicomachean Ethics* 1142a26–27). The rift between *nous* and *logos*, then, can in no way concern only the so called "practical" *nous*, as is often surmised—as if one could simply subdivide *nous*, the intelligence at work and involved in life, into practical and theoretical "parts." *Nous* without any further qualification is excessive to *logos*. This is shortly afterwards reiterated in a passage remarkable in particular for its association of *nous* with judgment, intelligence, and the practical-deliberative virtue of *phronesis*, let alone for its rapprochement of the language of nature and of virtue, habituation, experience. Such considerations represent an outstanding development in the treatment of *nous* and deserve to be quoted extensively:

> Now all matters of *praxis* (*ta prakta*) pertain to the order of particulars (*ton kath'hekasta*) and ultimates (*ton eskhaton*); for a prudent man should know them, and also intelligence (*sunesis*) and judgment (*gnome*) are concerned with matters of *praxis*, which are ultimates. And *nous*, too, is of ultimates, and in both directions, for of both primary terms [definitions] and ultimates there is *nous* and no *logos*; and *nous* according to demonstrations is of immovable (*akineton*) definitions and of that which is primary, whereas in practical [matters] it is of the ultimate and variable objects and of the other [that is, minor] premises, since these are principles of final cause; for it is from particulars that we come to universals. Accordingly, *we should have sensation* (aisthesis) *of these particulars, and this is* nous. (*Nicomachean Ethics* 1143a33–b6; my emphasis)

116

Nous pertains to the perception of what is ultimate, both in the sense of "this" and "according to the whole." It perceives individuals as well as definitions or even particulars in their definition, definiteness, and delimitation. *Nous* is of both, and the distinction between *nous* as perceiving definitions and *nous* as perceiving singularities is only perspectival: seen from the operation of demonstration, *nous* provides the principle, the universal; seen from the operation of practical deliberation, *nous* provides the perception of the circumstances to be assessed. Here we come to appreciate the twofold nature of *nous,* as intellectual *stricto sensu* and intuitive or, in fact, sensible. In both cases, *nous* names a certain grounding. Of such an intellectual-sensible grounding there is no discursive knowledge, no *logos.* Indeed, it constitutes the ultimate limit of *logos* and remains inassimilable to *logos.*

It is important to underline that Aristotle here is not proposing a dichotomy of "practical *nous*" and "theoretical *nous*," as it were, so much so that he emphasizes the fundamental role of particulars in the formulation of universals and hence the implication of sensation in intellectual perception. Indeed, because of this he once again intimates the conjunction, if not the simple identity, of *nous* and *aisthesis*—a conjunction that it will be hard to write off as solely applying to some subdivision of *nous* that would concern practical matters alone.[7] After stating the concomitance of *nous* and sensation, Aristotle continues:

> In view of this, it is thought that these [powers] are natural (*phusika*) and that, while no one is by nature wise, one [by nature] has judgment and intelligence and *nous.* A sign of this is the fact that these [powers] are thought to follow certain stages of our life, for example, that such-and-such an age possesses *nous* or judgment, *as if* nature were the cause of it. Hence intuition is both a beginning and an end; for demonstrations come from these and are about these. Consequently, one should pay attention to the undemonstrated assertions and opinions of experienced (*empeiron*) and older and prudent human beings no less than to demonstrations; for they observe rightly because they gained an eye from experience (*ek tes empeirias omma horosin orthos*). (*Nicomachean Ethics* 1143b6–14; my emphasis)

That *nous* should be "both a beginning and an end" corroborates the unity of *nous* as a matter of both intellectual and sensible perception. We should also highlight that the coincidence, if not the identity, of *aisthesis* and *nous* is situated within the broader framework of a certain, however qualified, belonging of *nous* in the order of the "natural."[8] According to these suggestions, it would seem hardly possible even to understand *nous* as a virtue in the strict sense of the term. The aporia of *nous* begins to be manifest. On the one hand, *nous* comes to be disclosed as somewhat discontinuous with respect to the dimension of habituation and repeated practice defining the virtues. It is said to belong in the order of *dunamis* (*Nicomachean Ethics* 1143a29)—indeed, to be (*like* sensibility, or even *as* sensibility) a power actualized by nature. In this sense, *nous* designates the unmediated intelligence at work in and as sensation. Yet on the other hand, the activation of noetic insight, however "natural," appears to be neither automatic nor simply immediate. In fact, the insightful "eye" of *nous* becomes actual *through* time, as though refined and fulfilled by experience. Aristotle insists on this distinction between *nous* and what is simply by nature, "observing" that those with "natural dispositions" but "lacking *nous*" are like a "mighty body" that "mightily stumbles" because "lacking vision (*aneu opseos, me ekhein opsin*)," and that only if one "acquires intellect (*labei noun*)" will one's disposition, "though similar to the corresponding natural disposition," be "a virtue in the main sense" (*Nicomachean Ethics* 1144b9–14).[9] *Nous* indicates a unique "natural power" to grow, to develop further.

Oddly enough, then, *nous* must be understood by reference both to (1) the immediacy of its activation and operation, and to (2) a process of "acquisition" in virtue of which *nous* seems to ripen, as it were. The statement that we should "pay attention to the undemonstrated assertions and opinions of the experienced" once again suggests a certain secondariness and non-self-sufficiency of the sciences, recognizing the nonscientific condition of scientific-discursive articulations. Science in its highest sense, that is, wisdom (*sophia*), precisely entails the awareness of its intuitive/experiential root. Most importantly, experience, age, and prudence itself are involved in the coming to "have" *nous,* in a certain "correctness or conformity of the gaze"—in the "seizing" or "apprehending" (*lambano*), as it were "at a glance," which noetic perception names.

This is in line with another remark just preceding the passage now considered, where Aristotle remarkably associates wisdom, *sophia*, with the investigation of nature (physics) and contrasts them both to mathematics, which can be practiced even by the inexperienced:

> A young man is not experienced, for much time makes (*poiei*) experience. (And if one were to inquire why it is possible for a boy to become a mathematician but not wise or a physicist, the answer is this: the objects of mathematics are by abstraction while the principles of philosophy and physics are from experience; and the young have no conviction [*pisteuousin*] of their principles but [only] speak [*legousin*], while the what-it-is [of the objects] of physics and of wisdom is not unclear.) (*Nicomachean Ethics* 1142a16–21)

Philosophy in its highest accomplishment manifests itself as the practice of reason, aware that its own principles exceed reason. It consciously proceeds from experience and recognizes experience as its beginning. This realization constitutes the difference between wisdom and the merely scientific posture (here exemplified by mathematics). In this perspective, philosophy as the exercise of wisdom is at one with physics, the study of nature. Indeed, if the principles are a matter of experience, in no way could the pursuit of wisdom be construed as "metaphysics." The latter enterprise would remain an issue, at most, for boys and those who can only develop their reasoning in abstraction from its experiential ground, that is, from the uncontainable content that life is. In this case, *logos* becomes formal, divorced from life, from the trust on which *logos* rests and of which *logos* speaks.[10]

Nous must, then, be understood within the compass of *phusis* or, at any rate, in continuity and coextension with natural-physical motifs. As for the concomitance, if not the identity, of *nous* and *aisthesis,* let us mention, in the margins of the present discussion, that this hypothesis is further corroborated in the *Physics.* In arguing that the being of nature is a matter of primordial self-evidence, Aristotle says:

> As far as trying to prove that nature is, this would be ridiculous, for it is evident (*phaneron*) that there are many such beings; and to try to prove what is evident (*phanera*) through what is not evident (*aphanon*) is a mark of a man who cannot judge what is known through itself from what is known not through itself. That this can take place is not unclear (*adelon*); for a man born blind may make syllogisms concerning colors, but such a *logos* must be about names without intellectual perception (*noein*) [of what the names indicate]. (*Physics* 193a3–9)

The immediacy of the apparent imposes itself, its phenomenal evidence compels assent. Such is the force of what is more known by nature, in virtue of itself, of its being. One must know when it is appropriate to stop asking for demonstrations, Aristotle urges, for demonstrations come to an end at some point, coming to rest in that which cannot be demonstrated, indeed, that which, if attended to, does not require any further discursive effort. If/when unable to receive the ground of evidence in its givenness and rest in the ensuing trust, one produces uprooted reasonings, alienated from what is. Just like the inexperienced young one considered above or the blind man making syllogisms about what he cannot experience and hence cannot conceive (*noein*), in this case one speaks without knowing what one is talking about.

After all, even in the *Metaphysics* we find indications to the effect that noetic apprehension is still thoroughly involved in the sensible and phenomenal. Let us limit ourselves, here, to mentioning a couple of statements. The first is near the beginning of Alpha Elatton, where Aristotle observes that the attainment of truth may be difficult, for "as the eyes of bats are to the light of day, so is the intellect of our soul to the objects that in their nature are most evident (*phanerotata*) of all" (*Metaphysics* 993b9–11). The second is in Kappa, where it is said:

> In general, it is absurd to form (*poieisthai*) our judgment of the truth from the fact that the things about us (*deuro*) appear to change and never to stay the same. For, in hunting (*thereuein*) the truth, we should start from things that always hold themselves as the same and suffer no change. Such are the heavenly bodies (*ta kata ton kosmon*), for these do not appear to be now of one kind and now of another, but are always the same and share in no change. (*Metaphysics* 1063a10–17)

What can be drawn from both moments is the irreducibly phenomenal character of evidence and hence of the ground or beginning. Even the intellection of that which is immutable entails a contemplation altogether implicated in sensibility, namely, the contemplation of those (in the plural) which are "most phenomenal," "most apparent"—those which "most shine forth." They, the celestial bodies, are eternal yet visible. They are unchangeable, and yet they move—whether returning every night in the same configuration (as the fixed stars do), or wandering and changing their positions with respect to one another, all the while exhibiting a certain regularity in their orbiting and always returning back to the same point (as the planets do). Their eternity and immutability are not due to absolute fixity but to a more tenuous, suggestive manifestation of self-sameness—to the phenomenon of a celestial body coming back to the same, repeating the same course in such a way as to remain by itself, close to itself, endlessly reasserting the same course in proximity of itself and through the same beginning point. The noetic perception, then, seems to be not so much a matter of transcending phenomenality in order to attain a contemplation of the purely intelligible, but rather a matter of a certain reorientation of the gaze from the things "here," "about us" (*deuro*) to the shining bodies in the sky—a reorientation not leaving the sensible behind, as it were, but thoroughly consistent with it. Such would be the gaze of *sophia* (*Nicomachean Ethics* 1141a19–1141b8).

The concurrence of *nous* and *aisthesis*, however succinctly addressed here, raises problems analogous to those occasioned by *De Anima* 430a11–12 and 24–25, which gave rise to the Peripatetic and neo-Platonic contrast between active (productive) and passive, or actual and potential intellect. So far, despite the tension thus engendered, we have emphasized the coincidence of *nous* and sensibility, while at the same time maintaining the unity of *nous* (that is, rejecting the subdivision of *nous* into "practical" and "theoretical"). This means understanding *nous* in its inseparability from embodiment, experience, and practical considerations, in accordance with a number of Aristotelian remarks analyzed. However, precisely by turning to *De Anima* and the dominant interpretive tradition, one might object that Aristotle does acknowledge there the distinction between agent and patient intellect as well as the separability (and immortality) of the former. To this paradigmatic objection we must reply by proposing an incipient problematization of the distinction and separation at stake here. Of course, a close consideration of these passages would lead us into the enormous complexities of Aristotelian psychology and theology that have engendered centuries of interpretive battles and a virtually endless scholarly literature, not to mention trials and executions at the stake.[11] Since a study of such matters clearly exceeds the scope of the present essay, we shall limit ourselves to delineating our reply in the barest terms. At stake in the reading of these lines is the understanding of transcendence and of the relation between divinity and sensibility, or god and life.[12]

The passages in question must be brought to our attention, not so much in order to rely on their clarity, but rather so that their obscurity may be appreciated.[13] Aristotle introduces the distinction between potentiality and act, and based on this, between passive and active or productive *nous:*

> Since in each genus of things there is something, for example, matter, as in the whole of nature (and matter is that which is potentially each of these things), and also something else which, by bringing forth (*poiein*) all [those things], is the cause and that which brings forth (*poietikon*), as in the case of art (*tekhne*) in relation to matter, these differences must belong in the soul also. On the one hand, the intellect becomes all things (*panta ginesthai*) while, on the other, it makes all things (*panta poiein*), just like a certain habit (*hexis*), as with light; for in a certain sense light, too, makes (*poiei*) potential (*dunamei*) colors be actual (*energeiai*) colors. (*De Anima* 430a10–17)

The role of *tekhne* in the characterization of a certain aspect or "part" of *nous* should deserve our attention, especially since within the framework of Aristotle's reflection on this matter, it may be arduous to understand *tekhne* in purely active terms. Indeed, art may not necessarily, or not at all, proceed unaffected, simply imposing on matter a self-subsisting eidetic pattern: creativity and receptivity or responsiveness may demand to be thought together.[14] Along these lines, of course, the recognition of a "productive" mode of *nous* may hardly amount to the isolation of a purely active intellect opposed to a purely passive one. Also, in light of the discussion preceding the passage just quoted, it is unclear whether the intellect would potentially be and become "all things," both in their intelligibility and in their materiality, or only in their intelligibility (*De Anima* 429b30–430a9). The former would seem problematic, given that even sensation is said to be perception "without matter" (*De Anima* 425b24). Finally, the parallel between the bringing forth of *nous* and the work of light reveals "production" in a highly qualified sense: bringing forth appears to be less a matter of constitution than of laying bare, shedding light on, unveiling in the sense of discovering and uncovering. Such is the sense of the transition from potency to act. In this sense, making is making actual, or even letting be actual. Aristotle continues:

> And the latter intellect is separable (*khoristos*) and is impassible (*apathes*) and unmixed (*amiges*), and in beingness (*ousiai*) it is as an actuality (*energeiai*); for that which brings forth (*poioun*) is always more honorable than that which undergoes (*paskhontos*), and the principle (*arkhe*) than matter. (*De Anima* 430a18–19)

It is curious and remarkable that the argument on the separability of the *nous* that brings forth should be based on issues of worth and honorability. Indeed, we could say that this is no argumentation at all—that the separable, unaffected, and unadulterated character of *nous* thus understood is simply posited, or even more precisely, undergone in its inexplicability:

> Actual knowledge (*kat'energeian episteme*) is the same as the thing (*pragmati*) [known]; potential (*kata dunamin*) [knowledge], however, is prior in time in the one (*en toi heni*) [individual], but, as a whole (*holos*), it is not [prior] in time. But the [active intellect] is not at one time thinking (*noei*) and at another not thinking (*ou noei*). When separated (*khoristheis*), it is as such only that, and only this is immortal (*athanaton*) and eternal (*aidion*) (but we do not remember [*ou mnemoneuomen*], for, although this is impassible, the passive intellect [*nous pathetikos*] is destructible), and without this nothing thinks. (*De Anima* 430a20–25)

Without even broaching the strictly textual difficulties in this section—for example, (1) how to understand the temporal priority of potential knowledge, whether or not what is at stake here is the contrast between the experience of a single individual and knowledge experienced collectively, "as a whole"; or (2) the nature of the "it" without which "nothing thinks"—let us simply highlight the clause "but we do not remember." Added as a parenthetical remark, it is hardly marginal.

This remark implies a twofold reflection on transcendence. On the one hand, in no uncertain terms it announces the impossibility, for human beings, of overcoming the strictures of the "passive" or "destructible" intellect—that is to say, the inability simply to transcend the finitude and impurity of human intellect, simply to remember and maintain all intellectual activity in the fullness of its exercise (*ergon*).[15] On the other hand, transcendence is affirmed precisely in its ungraspability—not the transcendence that would confer further controlling power on the separate, unaffected, subjective, and sovereign exercise of reason, but the transcendence, infinite and unaccountable, of that which exceeds reason, which traverses and disrupts reason. Such would be the transcendence of (and as) that which comes from the outside (outside the subject, self-constitution, autonomy), irreducible and unforeseen.

"But we do not remember" means that whatever we may speculate around an intellect that would never relapse into inactivity, whose insight would never fall back into latency or oblivion, we know nothing of it, at least not straightforwardly. We *are* it, and we cannot conceptually, reasonably recapture that which we are. In virtue of what we essentially are, we cannot rationally hold in view that which crosses us, the infinite in us. We forget. And all we may venture to say regarding the simply creative, active intellect, immortal and untouched by mortal conditions, is marked precisely by that—by our forgetfulness, by our inability fully to comprehend and fill with meaning the phrase "active intellect." The infinity that we are (the infinity that, however, is neither "I" nor mine) marks the limits of language and reason, of the language of reason, *logos*.

It is in the crevices of such problems that the battles were fought, most notably between the broad fronts of Thomism, on one side, and Averroism, on the other side (the latter inheriting certain unorthodox Peripatetic motifs, especially through Alexander of Aphrodisia and Themistius). It is here that comprehensive contrapositions came to be crystallized, for instance between (1) the view upholding the separability, and hence eternity and immortality, of the whole intellect (passive and active), that is, of the "personal" or individual soul; and (2) the views variously maintaining that what is separable and immortal is transcendent in the special sense of common, shared, received "from outside," as it were, and hence in no way "personal"—whether this is to be understood as (a) the active intellect only (Alexander, Avicenna, possibly the Averroes of the commentary on *Metaphysics* Lambda), or as (b) both the active and passive intellect, where the latter is "in us" but belonging in the intellect transcending us (Averroes). These latter positions, and particularly Averroes' so-called monopsychism, hold noteworthy implications regarding the question of separation and, more broadly, the focus of the present essay. Their elaboration of separation does not require dualistic assumptions: the immortal, eternal, and separate is not understood in terms of disembodiment, but as nonindividual, impersonal. It may be separate in the sense that it is separate from *me*, from *this* particular being that I am. It may be transcendent in the sense that it transcends me, even as it is "in me" ("in the soul"). But then separation or transcendence comes to indicate commonality, sharing in common—with vital consequences concerning the basic approach to the political.[16]

Let us, to conclude, come back to our reading of *Nicomachean Ethics* Zeta. In addition to the complex cluster of problems laid out above, the further question arises concerning the proper location of *nous* within the domain of *logos*. Situating *nous* in the context of reason now appears to be both necessary and impossible: necessary because, as an "intellectual virtue," *nous* would pertain to the rational part of the soul, to the part that "has" *logos;* and impossible because, as has become manifest, *nous* is nondiscursive and without *logos*. Strictly speaking neither communicative nor communicable, yet the condition of communication and communion, *nous* indicates a non-logical operation at the heart of *logos*—a trace, divine indeed, having in itself *nothing to do* with the various doings, with the commerce, negotiations, and procedures of discourse, including demonstrative discourse and practices.

Its location within the rational part is therefore highly problematic, indeed, unrepresentable. Above all, what is in this way disclosed is the questionability of the map of the rational domain—in its internal divisions, in its general designation as "rational," and even in its topological assumptions. For it turns out that the part that "has" *logos* is not (or not simply) thereby rational or logical. It turns out that the authority of *logos* is not coextensive with the region it inhabits, that *logos* dwells there less as an absolute ruler than as a guest. *Nous*, which is said to be "both beginning and end, for demonstrations come from these and are about these" (*Nicomachean*

Ethics 1143b10–11), remains somehow impervious to *logos* and lends itself to discourse only in a highly qualified way. Because of this, to whatever extent it may develop in the direction of *phusis*, Aristotle's discourse on *nous* can hardly be seen as a kind of "philosophical naturalism" or, in general, as a "naturalizing," legitimizing move. Indeed, far from discursively appropriating the natural and setting it to work in the service of discursive logic, Aristotle is here exploring the limits of such a logic, those borders at which discourse meets silence and its own end (or origin), the way in which speaking (in its very articulation) harbors the unspoken and unspeakable within itself.

Nous is the condition for *logos*, its outside and abode—that through which, in virtue of which (*dia*), *logos* as well as *dianoia* and all dianoetic exercise become possible. An unspoken or unspeakable so radical, indeed, as to be irreducible to what would "remain to be said," to the projection of a future task.

NOTES

1. In the context of recent scholarship, Christopher Long's work seems to be pervasively provoked by the task of reading the ancient texts in light of Levinas' thinking of alterity. See in particular *The Ethics of Ontology: Rethinking the Aristotelian Legacy* (Albany, N.Y.: SUNY, 2004).

2. A few examples: "Is Ontology Fundamental?" *BPW* 4; "Truth of Disclosure and Truth of Testimony," *BPW* 100; "God and Philosophy," *CPP* 157; *TIH* 154; *EN* 40–41, 44–45, 72; *EE* 38; *GDT* 22–91, 121–66; *TN* 157; *NTR* 127; *GCM* 107; *OE* 56; *PN* 128.

3. The reverse is the case with induction, *epagoge*, which moves from what is clearer and more known to us (*Posterior Analytics* 72b29–30). See also 71b35–72a6.

4. I have fruitfully consulted, whenever available, Hippocrates G. Apostle's translations of the Aristotelian texts—even though my own rendition often diverges from his. The following translations by Apostle were published by the Peripatetic Press (Grinnell, Iowa) in the year indicated in parenthesis: *Metaphysics* (1979), *Physics* (1969), *Nicomachean Ethics* (1975), *Categories* and *Propositions* (1980), *Posterior Analytics* (1981), *On the Soul* (1982), *Politics* (with Lloyd P. Gerson, 1986). I have utilized Werner Jaeger's edition of the *Metaphysics* (Oxford: Oxford University Press, 1957) and all the dual editions in the Loeb Classical Series (Cambridge: Harvard University Press).

5. "It is also easier to define the particular (*to kath'hekaston*) than the universal, so one should proceed from particulars (*apo ton kath'hekasta*) to universals; for equivocations, too, escape detection (*lanthanousi*) in universals more than in those without differences (*en tois adiaphorois*)." The "therapeutic" tenor of this remark, aiming at preserving any inquiry from straying too far from experience, that is, from particulars, is noteworthy as well.

6. On the connection between sensation and perception of universals, see Alexander of Aphrodisia's commentary on *De Anima* (83, 2–13), in which it is said: "This comprehension (*perilepsis*) and the grasping of the universal by means of the similarity among particular objects of sensation, is thinking (*noesis*); for the synthesis of similar things is already a function of *nous*."

7. Contra Heidegger's claim; see Martin Heidegger, *Plato's* Sophist, trans. Richard Rojcewicz and André Schuwer (Bloomington: Indiana University Press, 1997), 108–13.

8. In the *Physics*, an interchangeability of *nous* and *phusis* seems at times to be signaled by certain terminological oscillations. For instance, in the passage 1984a6–13 the conjunction of *nous* and *phusis* occurs three times, intimating their equivalence as "first or prior cause" of "the all" (*tou pantos*).

9. Virtue "in the main sense," here said to be acquired through *nous,* is shortly afterward said to come to be thanks to *phronesis* (*Nicomachean Ethics* 1144b15–17). Aristotle seems somehow to intimate a convergence of the latter and *nous. Phronesis* itself seems to exhibit an *insightful, illuminative* function analogous to that of *nous.*

10. See *Republic* 409b–e, in which it said that "the good judge must not be young but old, a late learner of what injustice is."

11. As has frequently been noticed, the section of *De Anima* under consideration (430a10–25) constitutes the pinnacle of Aristotelian psychology. Presenting his translation of *De Anima,* Willy Theiler observes that no other segment from an ancient philosophical text has given rise to such a range of disparate readings; Aristotle, *De Anima: Über die Seele* (Berlin: Akademie-Verlag, 1959). Along the same lines, Ingemar Düring points out that, rather than clarifying Aristotle's doctrine in this text, most commentators have expounded their own thought on the subject; *Aristoteles: Darstellung und Interpretation seines Denkens* (Heidelberg: Winter, 1966). See also Franz Brentano, *Die Psychologie des Aristoteles, insbesondere seine Lehre vom nous poietikos* (Mainz, 1867; reprint Darmstadt: Wissenschaftliche Buchgesellschaft, 1967).

12. In Levinas' words, at stake is the possibility of "[a] transcendence perhaps in which the distinction between transcendence toward the other man and transcendence toward God should not be made too quickly" (*EN* 87). Concerning the concurrence of "animal psychism" and theology, see *IRB* 271.

13. W. D. Ross comments on the relatively negligent writing of chapter Gamma 5; Aristotle, *De anima,* edited with introduction and commentary by David Ross (Oxford: Clarendon Press, 1961), 296.

14. It would take a detailed exposition to show how, especially by reference to the ethical treatises, *tekhne* cannot be understood as mere manipulation of matter by the application of eidetic paradigms. Here I will limit myself to recalling the incidence of the language of *tekhne* to characterize the ethico-political inquiry in its formative work. Ethics-politics is the "most authoritative and most architectonic" of the "sciences or faculties" (*Nicomachean Ethics* 1094a28), even though it is an architecture without geometry, that is, without the guidance of geometrical knowledge (1094b13–28, 1098a21–b8). Indeed, it is a *poiein* in which the paradigm (the good, living well) is that which is pursued.

15. In this connection, see also the earlier passage at *De Anima* 408b24–29.

16. Despite many prejudices to the contrary, on Aristotelian terms not even the transcendence of *nous* as the god of *Metaphysics* Lambda should be taken as absolutely unqualified and uncontroversial—that is, as rationally, dualistically appropriable as the separation from body and life. On the one hand, Aristotle says that the first immovable mover ("the first what-it-was-to-be") "has no matter, for it is actuality" (*Metaphysics* 1074a35–36). On the other, he also states that this "beingness," however "eternal," "immovable," and "separate from sensible beings," as well as "without parts and indivisible," nevertheless "has infinite potentiality," for it causes motion for "an infinite time" (1073a3–8). In Mu, moreover, Aristotle says that "the good is always in action (*en praxei*)"

(1078a32). In "Infinity," Levinas observes that "Aristotle, in admitting the eternity of the world and its movement . . . allows something like an actual infinity in the cause of this eternal movement. The act, purified of all potential, or form, purified of all matter, the Prime Mover or the God of Aristotle, sufficient onto itself as thought of its thought, is infinite in this new sense" (*AT* 61).

ARISTOTLE AND LEVINAS ON WAR AND PEACE: THE ONE AGAINST THE OTHER

7

Catriona Hanley

Who would desire war? Apart from the obvious forms of political manipulation through propaganda, disinformation, and appeal to economic interest that rouse a people or peoples to desire war, there is another reason war succeeds so well in holding a population in thrall. Wars have long been justified by the very criterion of achieving a situation other than war, which, though it might better be named truce, we call peace. War for peace! The idea of fighting for peace seems prima facie contradictory. What are the grounds of such a notion?

In what follows, I will discuss how the propaganda that drives war is rooted in a conception of what it is to be human, and specifically what it is to be a good, rational, ethical human; it is a conception that springs from the Western ontological tradition. Against this tradition, the thought of Levinas (re)introduces us to a notion of peace, one that comes from beyond the Western ontological tradition but that resonates with us.

Levinas lived through the horrors of the Second World War—horrors he experienced very closely—and somehow emerged against all odds neither to defend a Hobbesian worldview nor to write about revenge, but rather to defend a notion of peace that, though in broad outlines had been heard before, had never been so well grounded in relation to philosophy. What is most interesting in Levinas' view of peace, which could be taken as a cornerstone for the understanding of his entire corpus, is how it is focused, not on the level of the political state, which governs human interaction and works to solidify social norms, but on what is prior to any social formation apart from the relationship of me with you. Peace is built from the ground up, from the real contact of this me here, with a you who is there before me. It begins with the very human, very fragile relationship of the self with another. Where it ends is certainly less clear. For reasons that become evident in reading his work, Levinas is much less voluble on the political that proceeds from the personal than he is concerning the personal relationship that is the foundation, for him, of any ethics, any ontology, any politics, any thought. Still, as I will argue, he is hardly silent on this question, and it is quite possible to trace a path from the one-on-one relationship that for him is the foundation of all ethical theory and action, to the ideal realization of an ethical politics. The state is necessary, but it is essential that it attend to the ethical insight that the Other is primary.

Both of Levinas' greatest works begin with a discussion of war and peace: the remarkable preface (or, in a sense, the afterword, since it was clearly composed after the whole) to *Totality and Infinity* is an essay on eschatological peace; and the first sections of the first chapter of *Otherwise than Being* discuss war as the clash of egos, and true peace as transcendence to the ontology that undergirds this constant warring. But Levinas, a man of peace, has his enemies too. It could be said that he fights the entire corpus of Western philosophy (though there we would renew the idea of war for the sake of peace). It is not so much that he thinks that the West is set purposefully on a course toward war as that he finds the ontological tradition, rooted in Athens, is consistent only with an ethics that results in war. This tradition he opposes philosophically (in his philosophical, as opposed to his religious writings) to the wisdom of Jerusalem and its revealed truths, and he attempts to translate the core of this revelation into philosophical language. One could say that he appropriates elements of Judaic revealed religion, common also to Christians, Moslems, and accessible to other believers in a God who is good beyond comprehension—Jerusalem, in short—and translates these into the language of Western philosophy, while also retaining the tradition and wisdom of Western philosophy—Athens, in short—but making this latter secondary to the primary ethical impulse of Jerusalem. Contrary to the Western philosophical tradition, in other words, he puts Jerusalem first.

Centuries of the scholastic tradition might argue for the placing of Jerusalem prior to Athens, of faith prior to reason, at least in those writings, which after all constitute close to a thousand years of our Western philosophical tradition. Among the scholastics, understanding was in very general terms devoted to the clarification of belief: reason was harnessed to the demands of faith. It could be argued, however, that *credo ut intelligam* was not a foundational doctrine, that the defense of a particular doctrine or doctrines of faith through the use of reason was already a distortion of the insights of Jerusalem. Arguably, the thought was, "We *must* believe, now let us bring belief into the sphere of the rational." Faith was dissolved into the realm of the rational; the beauty of its extra-rational impulse was thus lost in compelling what cannot be rationally comprehended to meet the regime of reason.

Jerusalem requires no argument. It is beyond, before, rational analysis. "Love thy neighbor" is not susceptible to scrutiny because it does not speak to the rational soul. It is a command that is evident in experience and that cannot be shaken by argument. There is no "other side" to this kind of ethical command because it does not present itself within the sphere of reason.

What then of Athens? For Levinas, it is not that the ontological tradition that springs from the Greeks has *forgotten* something—this is Heidegger's analysis of the shortcomings of the Western tradition, in which he accuses the post-Socratics of not being sufficiently attuned to being. Forgetting implies a lost or hidden consciousness—and indeed, Heidegger delights in discovering the hidden within the revealed, the *lethe* within the *aletheia.* For Heidegger, the truth of being is always already there, though undisclosed, awaiting revelation, wrapped up in the layers of human forgetfulness and denial of being. In Levinas' view, the truth that was always there has never been brought to light within the Western philosophical tradition precisely because the tradition is *other* to this truth. The truth Levinas points to—that which is otherwise than being—cannot enter the Western ontological tradition as it has unfolded because it precedes ontology. It transcends ontology in being before the ontological. And for Levinas, as for Heidegger, the Western tradition of philosophy is largely the history of ontology.[1]

This is a long introduction to an essay that will discuss Aristotle and Levinas on the notion of peace. The postponement of my thesis, presented below, is meant to set the stage for the confrontation and reunion I would like to accomplish here. I take Aristotle, especially in the *Politics,* where he discusses peace as the teleological end to war, to represent Athens in this debate. Levinas, throughout his corpus, represents the potential overcoming of that tradition via Jerusalem—but not without the reappearance of Athens. Athens, it turns out, is an ally and not an enemy.

The question at the heart of my inquiry has two parts: first, how does Levinas' notion of peace differ from the political peace described in Aristotle, and how is it grounded philosophically? and second, is Levinas' version of peace possible politically, that is, is it compatible with the existence of a state, or a fellowship of states? Taking Aristotle as representative of the Western tradition, I will argue that Aristotle defends peace as the telos of the polis, for only in a peaceful nation is the highest good of humans—the contemplative life—achievable. Aristotle—never mind the beauty and, one might want to say, the humanity of his arguments (though with several major gaps in this regard)—is nonetheless representative of Western philosophy's defense of war. It is exactly this tradition that Levinas has to overcome, or rather to bracket, in order for his own notion of peace to be grounded. Levinas defends a notion of peace that is prior to the political one Aristotle upholds—peace is experienced, or commanded, in an ethical moment that is itself prior to ontology. The insight of Jerusalem—love of the neighbor and responsibility for one's fellow human as the experience of the divine—is at the heart of Levinas' discussion. For Levinas, peace is framed on the "each," that is, on the recognition of the individual whom I encounter as unique and irreplaceable, and not on the universalizing "all" of our Athenian tradition. I will ask how we can go from this compassionate understanding of each individual as an end in herself to a social-political system in which the many have to interact with each other. The answer will be in reinstating Athens after an adequate understanding of Jerusalem: preserving Jerusalem as fundamental, and building the insights of Athens on the ethical foundation of love for the other. What Aristotle misses, Levinas provides at the outset, and when Levinas' analysis is faced with the political, Aristotle is recalled.

Accomplishing these goals will require a first section in which I analyze Aristotle's notion of peace and discuss how it is rooted in his general ontological project, which sees the individual fundamentally as an instantiation of the universal. In a second section, I will discuss Levinas' version of peace as pre-ontological, and thus pre-political, by way of a treatment of ideology and the limits of reason.

ARISTOTLE'S ONTOLOGICAL PEACE

Aristotle's notion of peace (*eirene*) is firmly rooted in his ontology. He discusses peace in *Politics* book seven, where he is trying to determine the nature of the ideal state. In a well-known passage, he writes, "War must be for the sake of (*charis* + genitive; parallel to *heneka* + genitive) peace, business for the sake of leisure, things necessary and useful for the purpose of things noble" (*Politics* 1335a35: cf. 1334a2, 1334a15; also *Nicomachean Ethics* 1177b6–7). He then adds: "One should be capable (*dunasthai*, from *dunamai*) of engaging in business and war, but more capable of living in peace and leisure; and he should do what is necessary and useful, but still more should he do what is noble" (*Politics* 1333a41–1333b3). The phrase used in this passage, "for the sake of," provides a first clue to the interpretation of peace as metaphysically grounded; a second clue is in the use of the word translated here as "capacity." I will look at each of these concepts as a way to expose the metaphysical underpinnings of Aristotle's concept of peace.

The relationship of potentiality and actuality (*dunamis* and *energeia*) is the key relationship in Aristotle's metaphysical project. His perennial focus—outlined in the *Physics* and carried through, mutatis mutandis, in the *Metaphysics, Nicomachean Ethics,* and *Politics*—is on the shift from potentiality to actuality in all natural beings, their tendency to become what they already are as determined by their form (or to become what they already "have been," in the sense of having been already determined—*to ti en einai*). Change and movement, *metabole* and *kinesis,* occur in natural things according to a pattern that is laid out already in the very being of a thing by virtue of what it most essentially is. Rocks degrade in ways that are predictable, since they change according to the nature of rocks; bats develop from babies to full-grown according to the laws that rule being a bat.[2]

The teleological movement in Aristotle's work is commonly expressed in his use of "for the sake of" (*charis* or *heneka*), a future-oriented construction that underlines the way in which what is currently evident in a given particular natural being, or—in the case of the polis—a particular state of affairs, is a moment of movement toward completion. Heidegger's analysis of Dasein as primarily futural owes a lot to Aristotle, as does his discussion of the ontological structures that are already in place in human being. For natural beings apart from rational beings— and unlike for Kant, only humans fit this category here—the notion of "purpose" is as foreign to Aristotle as it is to Darwin. Things change, not in order to achieve some kind of "otherly" fulfillment, but simply in accordance with how they are already set to change. "For the sake of" is explanatory of the direction of change within an internal system, the rules of which are governed by the function (*ergon*) of a particular as a member of a given species.

The *Metaphysics,* particularly book Lambda, asks what change *as such* is for the sake of. If the why of each member of a species can be answered by reference to the form of the species, that is, to the need of each particular to accede to the demands of species-form, then what is the why of the whole of the movement as such? The larger why turns out to be answered by appeal again to final, and not efficient, causality. Things do what they do because it accords with reason for them to do so—it just makes sense that movement should be cyclical and thus predictable (which implies rational understandability). There is no telos that reduces the species telos to a step on the path of some greater purpose, but only a principle of reason in the universe, a god, who in pursuing his own rational end—in being his own rational end—inspires the universe with the rational impulse and makes each particular attain to its species-end.

Capacity, *to dunasthai,* then, is first of all another way of saying potentiality, that not-yet which is implied in all natural beings who have still to attain entelechy. "To be capable of" means to have the power, the potency, to be other. Yet once again, any otherwise than being this here now, this *tode ti,* is prescribed already in the being of the *tode ti* as an exemplar of a given genus.[3] For any given individual, to be is to be a particular and a universal at the same time—thus the difficulty of translating and interpreting Aristotle's concept of "*ousia*": while Aristotle wishes to save the particularity of the individual, insisting on the importance of his definition of a natural being as one that is embodied, he argues at the same time that rational comprehension of what is can only be accomplished on the level of the universal. *Ousia* refers thus both to a being in its particularity and to a being understood as an instance of the universal.

It is arguable that for Aristotle ethics is metaphysics applied to human beings. Since human beings are rational beings, they have the capacity of choice, and thus their path to entelechy is more complicated than for other natural beings. The determining characteristic of human beings—their form, or that which determines the path of the development of their potentiality—is their capacity for reason, their possession of a rational soul. The first line of the *Metaphysics*, "All humans by nature desire to know," sets the theme in that book for a description of the kind of knowledge most exclusively typical of human beings in the highest attainment of their *ergon,* and describes the object(s) of that kind of knowing. In the *Nicomachean Ethics,* on the other hand, Aristotle acknowledges the necessity of human beings—by nature—to live among their fellows, and determines the best way for humans to do so. In that book, it emerges clearly that the life of contemplative activity is the most perfect form of human happiness. "Happiness" here is the word used to describe the activity of living well that best suits human nature, or best accords with the form of human being as rational. The life of moral virtue (the development of good character by the formation of good habits) fits best the human part of human nature, and the intellectual virtue (*theoria*) expressed in the contemplative life fits the divine part of humans, thus "the virtues of our composite nature are purely human; so therefore is the life that manifests these virtues and the happiness that belongs to it, whereas the happiness that belongs to the intellect is separate" (*Nicomachean Ethics* 1178a22).

Insofar as it is possible for humans to attain to the divine and imitate the activity of god, they should strive to devote themselves to contemplation. But here is the rub: Aristotle notes that "the philosopher, being human, will also need external well-being, since human nature is not self-sufficient for the activity of contemplation, but he must also have bodily health and a supply of food and other requirements" (*Nicomachean Ethics* 1178b33–35). It is exactly the composite nature of human beings, their nature both as political creatures, creatures of the city with animal needs, and as sharing in the spark of the divine, that draws the intellectual into the life of the city.

Aristotle explicitly refers in these chapters of the *Nicomachean Ethics* to the politician and the philosopher, setting one form of life against the other and arguing that the philosophical life is the best for humans, the happiest, the most in conformity with the highest feature of human capacity, that which indeed sets the human on the plane of the gods. *Eudaimonia,* as the human end, involves leisure (*skole*), since again, "we do business that we may have leisure and carry on war that we may have peace" (*Nicomachean Ethics* 1177b5). Philosophy, contemplative activity, is a pursuit that we do in leisure and not for any instrumental purpose. It produces no results beyond the activity itself, whereas in practical pursuits, we always seek some advantage beyond the action. Politics—whether it be the pursuit of authority or honors, or concern for the happiness of citizens—and war, though they may be occasions for the display of virtues, are thus unleisured activities: indeed, the pursuits "of war [are] entirely so, for no one desires to be at war, nor deliberately takes steps to cause a war" (*Nicomachean Ethics* 1177b9–11). If contemplation is desired above all else because of its self-sufficiency, war is despised beyond all else because it is purely and only a means. Not only is the content of contemplation the most universal and thus highest kind of knowledge but also, qua activity, it is the highest, given its non-instrumental nature and its character unsullied by application to the material world.

One would think that having established the superiority of the philosophical life so clearly in the *Nicomachean Ethics,* the question of the end of the ideal state would follow clearly in the *Politics.* Yet Aristotle writes, "It remains to say whether the happiness of a state is to be pronounced the same as that of each individual human, or whether it is different" (*Politics* 1324a5–7). Everyone would say it is the same, he says, but then which kind of life is the best: active participation in the affairs of the state, or theoretical detachment—that of the alien? Though there is no question that the ideal state should be devoted to virtue, as should be the lives of the individuals who compose the state, the question of which kind of virtuous life is more desirable is raised again. Both the political life and the contemplative life seem adequate candidates for the focus of the ideal state. Aristotle seems to distinguish between the task of the "business of political study and speculation" and "the question of what is desirable for the individual" (*Politics* 1324a2–23); that is, having already argued that the best possible life for the individual is the one of contemplation, he now needs to see how this would in fact work out in the practical circumstance of the individual's relationship to the state.

To review: Aristotle notes the essential, that is, natural, connection of the individual to other humans, both in the physical way outlined in the first book of the *Politics,* through sex, procreation, and the founding of community, and in the spiritual sense described in books eight and nine of the *Nicomachean Ethics.* It would seem strange, then, for Aristotle to advocate the happiest kind of life for the individual considered in relation to the state as that removed from human involvement or political engagement in the broad sense: in short, the philosopher lives in the city. As noted above, it is quite clear that Aristotle thinks the philosophical life, a life devoted to the activity of contemplation, is the best for any given individual, the political life being secondary. But it is also evident that Aristotle does not imagine the contemplative individual as apart from the society in which he lives, or as not having to face the moral and physical struggles that result from being an embodied human within a state.

The state has to be set up in a way that permits, encourages, and values the contemplative life above all other possibilities of human action. But it cannot justifiably do this at the expense of the happiness of those citizens who are not engaged in this life. An entire population of human, and thus embodied, contemplators is a practical impossibility. After all, Aristotle thinks that not all citizens are capable of contemplation (*Politics* 1333a26–30). Thus either one has to argue that the many live at the expense of the few, that is, many are unhappy, pursuing a life that is not in conformity with human nature, or that *phronesis,* practical virtue, is also a possibility of human happiness. Aristotle takes the latter route while preserving some elements of the former.

But let us return to the *Politics* and the question of peace and war. The passage under consideration (make war only as a means to peace) appears in the context of an excursus into psychology, revisiting the parts of the soul as laid out in book one of the *Nicomachean Ethics.* The primary division of the soul is between the rational and irrational elements, the rational directing the irrational appetites and thus being superior to it.[4] The rational soul has two "divisions," the theoretical and the practical, and this is the seat of the difficulty in determining the end of the ideal state, exactly because of the implication that there are two natural ends for individual humans. But it also provides an "out" for Aristotle. Those involved in the virtuous life of action are pursuing a natural and good end, as are those involved in the life of contemplation. For the state to function, both are necessary, although there is a clear hierarchy. It is not the case that the practical life has value only because it serves the end of the contemplative. Political engagement does not simply serve the needs of theoretical life but has its own justification. Still, the less instrumental the political activity, the better it is.

As David Depew points out, Aristotle notes that the proponent of the political life is wrong in thinking that happiness is tied to exercising power over others, though right in thinking that the key to the happy life is activity. But the defender of the apolitical contemplative life is right to think that a happy life is free from debilitating dependence on external goods and from the task of securing them, but wrong to think that all ruling is domination and to imagine that his life has virtue by being inactive (*Politics* 1325a24–35).[5] Political activity must take place in recognition of the highest value of contemplation for which peace and leisure are required as well as acting in accordance with the moral virtues,[6] as Aristotle argues extensively (*Politics* 1334a17–27). Again, "it is evident that while all military pursuits are to be deemed honorable, they are not so as being the ultimate end of all things but as a means to that end" (*Politics* 1325a6–9). The intellectual, on the other hand, must recognize the importance of the political activity that makes her pursuit possible and must see herself as engaged in an activity, not as disengaged from the city.

Ultimately, just as the individuals who make up the state are involved in different activities but one is highest of all, the state is involved in different activities but has one primary aim—peace. Just as the philosopher attains to the highest rational end of contemplation without abandoning his body, which puts him into relation with others in the city, so the state, in order to attain to the highest rational end of peace, needs to devote itself also to political activity. Just as the virtuous person of action acts for the sake of achieving leisure and not for the sake of action alone, so the state should aim at peace. Just as the intellectual is focused on internal activity, so also should be the state. Aristotle then expressly denies that the good state should dominate its neighbors, remarking that it would be strange indeed if a statesman were focused on conquest of neighboring peoples whether they desire it or not (*Politics* 1324b24–27). Useful and necessary things must be done, but only to accomplish a noble purpose: permitting citizens to thrive in accordance with their rational ends.

It is worth noting, for the purposes of comparison with Levinas below, that left out of the above analysis is the activity of the slaves, tradesmen, craftsmen, farmers, and those who actually produce and process goods for the citizens, as well as women occupied with children and the household. Aristotle solves the problem of their purely instrumental activities by not permitting them citizenship in the ideal state—a bit of a stretch by contemporary standards.

LEVINAS' PRE-ONTOLOGICAL PEACE

My analysis of Aristotle's notion of peace is meant to show how deeply embedded the concept of political peace is in a theory of human nature that has had incalculable influence on the Western tradition and that is itself deeply embedded in a reductive ontology. However beautiful the systematic unity of Aristotle's texts might be, the guiding thread is an ontology that diminishes—if not obliterates—the particularity of the individual (who counts for Aristotle as a citizen, which is to ask, who counts at all?). Even accounting for the breadth that Aristotle allows ethics and politics as unscientific pursuits, permitting them some consideration of the particular case over against study of the universal, the individual is nonetheless never taken as fully legitimate (free?) unless she acts according to the demands of universal form.

There is an impulse to see one's own singularity suppressed by this demand. Levinas, however, sees the problem, not as the reduction of the one to the other, but precisely as the reduction of the other to the one. It is not that the tradition of Western ontology has not left place for the ego—on the contrary, it has granted it all the room. Insofar as I set the agenda for determination of the universal, textually or otherwise, I reduce the other to a case of me.[7]

Counter to this, one could claim that the foundation of political peace has been laid through the universal recognition of the rights of all human beings, itself grounded in Greek ontology: since you are identical to me in your being, you must be accorded the same rights and privileges that I expect for myself. We are equal. But the limitation of the Greek notion is evident historically and phenomenologically, given that we are still at war, as were the Greeks, almost constantly. Levinas speaks of the egology latent within Western ontology: the rational identification of you with me fails to recognize that you are not me. It ignores the unicity of you, as distinct from me. Ontology, spoken from the perspective of the I who is the subject, is bound to a notion of the universal that proceeds from this subject. The reduction of you to me, of the other to the same, leads to the destruction of the uniqueness of you and feeds my need to encompass all as an expression of my own development as ego.

Levinas writes in the preface to *Totality and Infinity*, "Everyone will readily agree that it is of the highest importance to know whether we are not duped by morality." The context here is peace and war: "The art of foreseeing war and of winning it by every means—politics—is henceforth enjoined as the very exercise of reason. Politics is opposed to morality, as philosophy to naiveté" (*TI* 21). The interminable cycle of war and peace is for Levinas the core of the political realm. War and peace are two sides of the same coin, each understood only in relation to one another. We need an ethical, not a political foundation for the practice of justice that cancels this paradigm.

The unexamined problems in the West's universal and rationalist approach are treated by Levinas in his 1973 essay "Ideology and Idealism." Here Levinas discusses the role and fate of thought in a global industrial society. In this age, reason has become suspect—and not without justification, given what Levinas calls the "spreading desert," the "increasing spiritual misery" of the era of industrialization. Since Hegel—and through Hegel, Marx—the culprit has been seen as ideology, a notion elaborated and grounded in the critiques of Freud and Nietzsche. In disavowing ideology in its pretension to science, we disavow also reason, and with reason, the hope of an ethics. Ideology can then be seen as dealing the "most severe blow" to morality that it has ever suffered. The concept of ideology is grounded on the view that what appears as rationality is a disguised mystification, one that resists the power of logic to penetrate and unravel. If reasoning is just masked ideology, if ethics is logocentric, then to unmask ideology is to unmask reason's failure and to dispense with the possibility of ethics. As Levinas puts it, "Ethics becomes the first victim of the struggle against ideology that it inspired" ("Ideology and Idealism," *LR* 238).

Another phase of the critique of ideology, according to Levinas, is that expressed in thinkers who argue that reason is a *necessary* source of illusions ("Ideology and Idealism," *LR* 238). Here consciousness is determined by material and social conditions, and ideology expresses this relationship; science is able to identify the determinative conditions. Ideological illusions are then at least in principle dispersible by means of a gradual perfection of science. But this science separates the subject and reality: the subjective experience of love, pain, enjoyment, are distinct from the "objective conditions"—physical, psychological, sociological—that underlie and guide them, and that are calculable and determinative. Levinas writes that "[a] kind of neo-scientism or neo-positivism dominates Western thought" (*LR* 239), in which no role is assigned to human subjectivity and theoretical reason reigns supreme. At the same time, we witness the production of a rhetoric that "eats away the very substance of human speech" (*LR* 241), a rhetoric that merely flatters, that bears no relation to truth or works in the absence of truth. His "parable" example is that of American astronauts reciting biblical passages—what Levinas calls an ideological recitation—either a lip service to some Other that cannot truthfully enter the paradigm they are defending in all other ways, or the profound recognition of the limits of the efforts of science. In other words, the parable points either to signs detached from meaning—"an ideology more desolate than all ideology" (*LR* 241)—or to the acknowledgement of an Other that cannot enter the ontological paradigm expressed by science.

Levinas offers some hope, however. Though our age is characterized by the demand for scientific rigor and the critique of ideology, it is also permeated by the rebellion against injustice. Demanding justice for the other human is a return to the very core of morality, but without the trappings of ideology. The validity of philosophizing is clearly put into question by critique of ideology; taking this critique seriously means to step outside the traditional philosophical boundaries. A place for ethics needs to be found outside the traditional assimilation of ethics to ontology; ontology needs to be reinterpreted, restored, in the light of an inassimilable ethical command.[8]

The youthful idealism that demands justice for the human other, "a prophetic cry . . . the rebellion of Marx and some Marxists, beyond Marxist science" ("Ideology and Idealism," *LR* 238), is not philosophy; it is a break with philosophy, in the recognition of another outside the economy of being.[9] Placing oneself into question as the unrivalled center of the ethical is not an ideological move, but one contrary to all ideology and rational discourse. Here my responsibility for the other precedes my self-concern. I am disinterested (dis-inter-est-ed), in the sense of removing myself from the self-interest that is the *esse* of my interrelation with the other.

It is, finally, the experience of my responsibility for the other that breaks the paradigm, that opens me up to the ethical dimension. It is not, in Levinas' view, endless discourse about the tricks of the subconscious, or social conditions, or bad faith that liberates us from the warring of egos. Rather, the acceptance of what was already there, before the rational analysis, before the solidity of the written word, and that is a condition of any discourse whatsoever, is brought to the philosophical table. This other human before me (the nakedness of her face, the heavy curve of her back, her greeting me), this unique person, who is not an instantiation of a universal and who obliges me to respond, *this one here* obliges me, by her very presence, to put her needs before mine. This other human, who is (from the point of view of ontology) so surprisingly not me, is yet not necessarily the one whom I see. The neighbor is not, most of all, the acquaintance, but the one whom I do not "know," whom I cannot ever know.

The shifting of the I from the center of moral discourse through the transcendence of ontology is not a purely negative moment. Putting the self into question is the welcoming of the absolutely other ("Transcendence and Height," *BPW* 17). There is no reduction in the I in this move, but rather a raising of it. The I, far from being displaced from a height, is restored to its rightful height in the experience of infinite responsibility for the Other. There is clearly an asymmetrical relationship between the self and the Other who appears before me, through whom my autonomy gives way to the heteronomous dimension of recognition of the other as "higher" than me. But in this movement the I is in no way annihilated—rather, it is opened, "put into question" as Levinas describes it in "Transcendence and Height," bound to the Other in an asymmetrical relationship that releases it from the prison of egology, from its "imperialism and egoism." Here this recognition of responsibility that frees the I is shown to be one that defines the I as unique, but without transforming it into a particular member of a universal species. Thus Levinas writes:

> Responsibility confirms the I in its ipseity, in its central place within being, as a supporter of the universe. Such an engagement is happy; it is the austere and noncomplacent happiness that lies in the nobility of an election that does not know its own happiness, tempted as it is "by the slumber of the earth" ("and yet, Lord, I am not happy . . ."). (*BPW* 18)

How does this happiness differ from that of Aristotle's contemplator? Aristotle's intellectual hero is exactly removed from social intercourse, to the extent that it is even possible within Aristotle's argument for the ideally intellectually virtuous person to be morally lacking in virtue. Levinas rebels against this notion. The I is most truly defined in its recognition of the other and in its acting for the other; happiness is not in the quest for theoretical satiety but in the practical response to the need of the other.

The I does not disappear in the face of the other (how could it?), but in the relationship in which the other is apprehended as higher, is confirmed to itself as a *this here*. The *this here* of the I in this new economy is not defined through the reduction of the other to the same (as me), but rather in the painful happiness of living the responsibility ordained by the presence of the other. This responsibility "does not originate in a vow to respect the universality of a principle" ("Ideology and Idealism," *LR* 245); it is not a rational obligation formed within the bounds of my *decision* to be an ethical being.

Returning then to the question of peace: since "political" peace is rooted in a universalizing ontology, it is outside this ontology that Levinas must ground his notion of peace. Rooting peace in the sameness of all humans, according to the tradition, has duped us into putting our own interests first, while pretending that they are interests common to all.[10] The assumption that you are me has led to the assimilation of you to me, forgetting your uniqueness—the plainness of the fact that you are not me but are uniquely your own. Indeed, "the concept of man is the only one that cannot be comprehended, since each man is absolutely different from the other. The concept of man has a single extension, and that is human fraternity" ("Transcendence and Height," *BPW* 27). As Levinas points out here, it would be strange if the word "human" designated a genus, for then the move to solidarity would be impossible—how do we get solidarity from a genus? Here bats can do what humans cannot—assimilate, or give up subjectivity to the universal (they have no true subjectivity to surrender).[11] We humans, on the other hand, must begin with the one, with the insight gained from Jerusalem, the unicity of the other, to found an ethics that is not fundamentally disposed to the war of each against all. We are fundamentally in solidarity, first, because of the recognition of the other as distinct from me, and then, through his distinction—by virtue of his uniqueness as other—as valuable and inassimilable.

The other is primary in Levinas' conception of interhuman relationships. It is unsurprising, then, that he offers a view of peace focused on fellowship with the other, "peace independent then of belonging to a system, irreducible to a totality" ("Peace and Proximity," *BPW* 165). Peace here is irreducible to a genus, to a notion of the universal, to the identification of me with a particular *us* versus an other who is *them*. It is "an ethical relation which thus would not be a simple deficiency or privation of the unity of the One reduced to the multiplicity of individuals in the extension of a genus" (*BPW* 166). In short, he says that the unicity of the one is that of the beloved. I love you because you are unique. Peace is love. Peace is the awareness of the precariousness of the other. Roger Burggraeve describes how the appeal of the face "also represents the first and fundamental minimal demand of right, namely the right to life, the right to respect for one's own otherness and history, for one's own personhood. To see a face is to hear, 'Thou shalt not kill.'"[12] To say this another way, "The foundation of consciousness is justice and not the reverse" (*BPW* 169). Human rights are originally the rights of the other person. We come to rational consciousness when we are faced with the conflicting demands of two "others."

The conflict of responsibility that I face in adjudicating between the conflicting needs of two or more others is far from the conflict between you and me that I face within rational ontology. My own interest is apart in the former, Levinasian case: I judge the case on the basis of the need the *other* experiences, and not on the basis of my own desire. But how to make this one-for-the-other work in practice? For Levinas' ethical cry to have political content, we would need a formalization of the ethical command within ontological language.

If the direct relationship with the other is a world unto itself, then ethics poorly serves humanity. After all, we do live in a world of many others, and the many in need call us to task. In "Ideology and Idealism," to take one example of the many texts in which the same message is repeated, Levinas writes that this experience of conflicting needs indicates that there is a need for a state, that legal justice is required (*LR* 247). The responsibility for the other which is so clear in the one-to-one relationship with this person here before me—I must simply give everything I have to meet her needs—is complicated by the competing demands of two or more others. Here we are faced with the famous question of the "third." Levinas makes it clear that "there is a direct contradiction between ethics and politics if both these demands are taken to the extreme" ("Ethics and Politics" *LR* 292). It is all too evident how the political can exclude the ethical. The ethical also risks refusing the political if it cannot go beyond its focus on the one before me toward understanding how the limits of responsibility for this one are defined by the existence of the needs of other others.

In the discussion subsequent to the essay "Transcendence and Height," Levinas notes:

> It is the fundamental contradiction of our situation (and perhaps of our condition), which is called Hypocrisy in my book [*TI* xiii], that the hierarchy taught by Athens and the abstract and somewhat anarchic ethical individualism taught by Jerusalem are both necessary to suppress violence. Each of these principles, left to itself, only furthers the contrary of what it wants to secure. (*BPW* 24)

Commenting on this passage, Peperzak poses the question of whether Levinas points here to an "unconquerable contradiction," or rather to the need to discover a "new form of synthesis."[13] Perhaps to adequately defend the hope of synthesis over contradiction, as I would like to do, we need to examine what Levinas means by "violence."

In "Freedom and Command," an essay inspired by Plato's discussion of tyranny, Levinas describes the supreme violence as a loss of freedom so profound that one no longer knows one has lost it: servitude. "That one can create a servile soul," he writes there, "is not only the most painful experience of modern man, but perhaps the very refutation of human freedom" (*CPP* 16).[14] It is easy to see how lost we are today in the form of servitude that Levinas describes. We are all too willing to submit to a power that relieves us of responsibility for the other—and in so doing, cancels our own freedom as unique beings indebted to each other human. But as such, it is a form of war. It is I against the others.

What then of freedom? If freedom is seen as the variegation of possibilities that are negated by the other, then one ends up again with war, since each one's freedom is seen as limited by that of the other ("Freedom and Command," *CPP* 22). Levinas sees freedom, rather, as the construction of a state, "entrusting the rational to a written text, in resorting to institutions" (*CPP* 17). Freedom is the obedience to law, the commitment to freedom in the name of freedom—this to avoid tyranny. "To conceive of and bring about a human order is to set up a just State," he writes, "which then is the possibility of surmounting the obstacles that threaten freedom. It is the only way to preserve freedom from tyranny" (*CPP* 17).

For Levinas, however, there are problems with the notion of the state as guarantor of freedom. The state is prone, by its very nature, to totalitarian demands. Any individual within a state must be worried about freedom, about the necessary submission to universals that give rise to the element of violence ("Transcendence and Height," *BPW* 23). In this context, Levinas writes, "I do not wish to protest against all the worries that an individual may have in a State" (*BPW* 23). Even when it functions well and everyone submits to the universals that are required for the functioning of the state, still the element of violence appears. The rational order demands terrible cruelties, it seems. In order to suppress violence, it seems necessary within the state to have recourse to violence (*BPW* 15). To counteract this, we need to affirm, and reaffirm, the infinite responsibility that each has to each other, for each and before each (*BPW* 23). Reason is universalizing—it needs the constant corrective of the individual conscience that can strive to remedy the disorder proceeding from Order of universal reason (*BPW* 23). The tears of the other are wasted time to the bureaucrat—but they are the starting point of ethics for Levinas.

What the synthesis of Athens and Jerusalem would look like is not plainly laid out in Levinas' texts. No blueprint is offered of the political state or system of justice that takes the ethical command with utmost seriousness. Peace as eschatological cannot be the property of one people. It is a cry for the peace that is to come—peace in the respectful relationship of the human with the other human and with all that is necessary to sustain us both (all) in life and happiness. Respect for the other before ourselves must govern our politics.

I have described two models of peace in this essay: the political model of Aristotle, which resonates strongly with those of us in the academy, with its emphasis on the state as organized around the thinker, or at least organized in such a way as to make the activity of the thinker both possible and intrinsic to the existence of the state (or at least to its purpose); and the Levinasian ethical model, which is grounded not in ontology but on the demand that before all thought, before all judgment, I put the other's needs before mine. Peace here is love of the other, the impossibility of making war upon her. It is in this sense a refutation of the ontology that underlies Aristotle's defense of the intellectual's role in the state. Yet we see that at the moment Levinas' Jerusalem-inspired thought enters the political, at the moment the question of justice arises, we must return to the wisdom of Athens and to the task of laying out a set of laws that guarantee human freedom against tyranny.

Notes

1. With the difference that Levinas includes Heidegger in the tradition, as one still within the (same) ontological paradigm of the same.

2. For Aristotle, the question of what it is like to be a bat is answered by an appeal to the unchanging form of bats. The subjective nature of any individual bat is, pace Thomas Nagel, entirely irrelevant to Aristotle's inquiry, since any particular member of a species is, for the purposes of his inquiry, simply an instance of the universal.

3. Naturally here, as in all the above, I have to elide some of the greatest problems in Aristotelian metaphysical scholarship in order to prepare a more generic comparison of his thought with that of Levinas.

4. This model of leadership is of course at the root of Aristotle's specious justification of "natural" slaves as well as the natural dominance of men over women. This is not the only topic on which Aristotle let the cultural and social norms of his day cloud his reasoning.

5. See David Depew, "Politics, Music and Contemplation," in *A Companion to Aristotle's Politics*, ed. David Keyt and Fred D. Miller (Oxford: Blackwell, 1991), 349. Depew argues that "the claim that contemplation is an activity serves to cancel both extremes and to construct a space in which political and contemplative engagements can fuse into a *sui generis* way of life, or rather into a pair of lives that have more in common with each other than either has with conventionally political or exclusively contemplative lives" (352).

6. Moral virtue is the cultivation of the mean between two extreme ways of reacting to a particular given emotion or desire. The mean is determined by reference to "what is done" by the best people; in other words, it requires familiarity with accepted and lauded social norms. Moral virtue is at its best a *hexis*, a habit, cultivated through good instruction and repetition.

7. Could it be said that Kant, in his insistence on duty and treating the other as an end, reduces the me to a case of the other? No, since it is I who form a maxim of action and make myself thereby a lawmaker.

8. We see this explicitly confirmed when Levinas asks: "Should we not concede that philosophy cannot confine itself to the primacy of ontology, as has been taught up to now?" ("Transcendence and Height," *BPW* 22).

9. Here Levinas finds hope and further grist for his refusal of Derrida's famous general critique of Levinas' project, when Derrida notes (quoting "a Greek") that "if one has to philosophize, one has to philosophize; if one does not have to philosophize, one still has to philosophize" ("Violence and Metaphysics," in *Writing and Difference,* trans. Alan Bass [Chicago: University of Chicago Press, 1978], 191). In response, Levinas can produce the experience that the I (and the I is transformed post-experientially) has of the other. Here there is no gap in meaning, no interruption, but rather the recognition of what "is" before the "is" that Derrida rightfully holds up to question. See also "God and Philosophy," *LR* 186.

10. Even worse, it has made us susceptible to the propaganda that sells us the idea that the good of the whole is served in each pursuing his own interest. As if my rational interest could coincidentally coincide with that of the other, whom I step on in the way to my own success! As if really my profit seeking were for the benefit of the other! As if my not thinking of the other in the pursuit of my own end of wealth could "trickle down" to the benefit of the other and transform my self-interested pursuit into altruism. In short, as if I for I is "really" I for the other, in some way "behind" appearances.

11. This too is controversial, though not within the problematic that Thomas Nagel presents. The question to be raised here is of the limits of subjectivity, the delimitation of the face. The question of whether nonhuman beings can be considered "faces," that is, beings worthy of the ethical command to place the other before oneself, is not new to Levinas scholarship.

12. Roger Burggraeve, *The Wisdom of Love in the Service of Love,* trans. with concluding essay by Jeffrey Bloechl (Milwaukee, Wis.: Marquette University Press, 2002), 104.

13. Adriaan Theodoor Peperzak, *To the Other* (Lafayette, Ind.: Purdue University Press, 1993), 128 n. 10.

14. In this context, we cannot help but remember Aristotle's argument in defense of "natural slaves." We are complicit, in that we accept and praise his metaphysics and ethics, while writing small footnotes to excuse his oversights. QED.

STOIC ETHICS AND TOTALITY IN
LIGHT OF LEVINASIAN ALTERITY

Julie Piering

8

Bringing together Stoicism and Levinas seems, at first, a peculiar task. A brief survey of their philosophical commitments reveals undeniable disparities. Stoicism introduces a sweeping metaphysical framework that views each individual from the perspective of an ordered *kosmos*. Levinas provides a departure from traditional Western thought by opposing the privileging of ontology and Being over individual human beings. Stoic virtue is achieved through constructing a self able to accomplish moral indifference, *apatheia*, toward everything external.[1] Levinasian responsibility is infinitely felt before the other. Epistemologically, Stoic knowledge centers on the notion of the "grasp," a kind of direct mental apprehension wherein the object of the mind corresponds precisely with that external object being grasped. Levinas moves beyond epistemology and attends to what is ungraspable, overflowing, and in surplus. Said simply, Levinas' emphasis on infinity and alterity runs counter to the Stoic avowal of a rational totality.

The philosophical backgrounds and motivations of Levinas and the Stoics likewise highlight their divergence. Levinas begins with the methods and insights of phenomenology and existentialism while laboring against Heideggerian ontology and Hegelian absolute knowledge. In replacing an ontological "first philosophy" with an ethical one, Levinas connects ethics with an originary event coincident with an unlimited responsibility toward the other. The Stoics, by contrast, inherit ad hoc philosophical tenets from Socrates and the Cynics but develop a metaphysical scaffolding to buttress this almost exclusively ethical inheritance.[2] Whereas the Stoics are the great systematizers of Hellenistic thought, Levinas undercuts the hegemony of the Same.

The disparity of these two positions renders it possible to employ Levinasian insights as a foil for understanding both the compelling and the problematic aspects of Stoicism. In turn, the ontology of the Stoic system and the practical aims of self-transformation offer a helpful revision to Levinas' understanding of ancient Greek metaphysics, responsibility, and the injunction to know thyself. The Stoic ethical imperative to self-knowledge is paired with practices for cultivating a certain kind of self in relation to others. Such concrete practices can provide a welcome companion to Levinas' abstract but crucial imperative to hospitality. Furthermore, the fluid nature of such practices shelters them from the dogmatizing effect of theory. In examining the tension between the Stoic ethical system and Levinasian alterity, questions surface that otherwise might remain obscured. Specifically, how can Stoicism, a philosophy of the self, make sense of or respond to the other? How might Levinasian ethics be aided by this emphasis on the creation of an authentically ethical self?

THE STOIC SYSTEM

Stoicism emerges from an amalgamation of Socratic and Cynic ethical practices that are combined with an emphasis on advances in logic and physics.[3] Stoic theory situates novel metaphysical and epistemological views in relation to detailed practices that support the art of living so deeply rooted in their philosophical progenitors. The Stoic transformation of ethics and *askēsis*[4] maintains, despite the systematic additions to it, an integral sense of intersubjectivity. Moreover, the Stoic creation of duty via natural obligation initiates a new moment in ethics.[5] Perhaps their most striking ethical innovation is the generation of a cosmological system to sustain ethics. Given the coherence of Stoic theory, their ethical claims are only fully appreciated within the system constructed to accommodate them.

The unity of the Stoic structure is so complete that Posidonius develops an organic metaphor for Stoic philosophy: "Since the parts of philosophy are inseparable from one another . . . Posidonius said he preferred to compare philosophy to a living being—physics to the blood and flesh, logic to the bones and sinews, and ethics to the soul."[6] Throughout antiquity, the soul is commonly defined by its function: it animates the being, and consequently, only that which is ensouled is properly called alive. This crucial placement of ethics within the Stoic philosophical system is telling. To follow Posidonius's analogy one step further, if the soul makes the living being what it is, that is, a being which is alive, ethics must be that which makes Stoicism what it is. Though physics and logic are necessary aspects of Stoic philosophy, they serve as support for the life of the "living being"; Stoicism is essentially ethical.

The Stoics are commonly credited with producing the first thoroughly systematic philosophical theory. Posidonius's depiction of Stoicism could be misleading in its simplicity, for each division he cites contains within it a diverse curriculum. Destruction and generation, substance, corporeality and its qualities, universals or concepts, theology, epistemology, and cosmology are just some of the subjects the Stoics catalogue as components of physics.[7] Stoic logic, for example, embraces anything related to *logos*, or reasoning, and thus incorporates dialectic, rhetoric, definitions, language, and so on. The Stoic system encompasses so exhaustive an arrangement of topics that there is only space to glance at those that are initially most germane to a Levinasian critique: cosmology, theology, *physis* or Nature, and the identification of each with the other two.

The sheer quantity of Stoic identities is dizzying. "God is one and the same with Reason, Fate, and Zeus; he is also called by many other names."[8] The *kosmos*, which likewise admits of many identities, not the least of which is "God himself " (*DL* 7.137–38), is ordered by providence and by intellect. Everything that happens does so by providence, and it follows that the *kosmos* is divinely and perfectly ordered. The ordering of the *kosmos* is attributed to God, Nature (*phusis*), and Reason (*logos*), interchangeably.[9] Therefore, Nature, or *phusis*, is wholly equated with Reason, or *logos*, which in turn is equivalent to divine providence and fate, and, of course, to Zeus. The role of reason within these identifications is particularly important. The Stoics conceive of the *kosmos* as a living being, "rational, animate and intelligent" (*DL* 7.142).[10] Reason is not something that orders the universe externally, but spreads throughout it "just as does the soul in us."[11] Reason (*nous* or *logos*) permeates the universe, human beings included. Human beings participate in this divine intellect differently than all else because of their capacity for reason.[12] Human rational powers allow insight into the *kosmos*. This awareness of the workings of the universe, epistemologically, allows for wisdom and even divination.[13] Ethically, it is the ground for tranquility: "Do not seek to have everything that happens happen as you wish, but wish for everything to happen as it actually does happen, and your life will be serene."[14] The serenity Epictetus advocates is the result of a proper understanding of cosmology. Basically, once one recognizes that the universe is ordered such that it is the best possible universe, one is empowered to find happiness by not struggling vainly against this order.

The human relation to the universe is illustrated by way of a slightly severe analogy. "When a dog is tied to a cart, if it wants to follow, it is pulled and it follows, making its spontaneous act coincide with necessity; but if it does not want to follow, it will be compelled in any case. So it is with men too: even if they do not want to, they will be compelled in any case to follow what is destined."[15] Humans are not relieved of their moral responsibility, because the *kosmos* will follow the path of its trajectory; human responsibility is to be understood in terms of choices made that reflect their knowledge of the *kosmos*.

TOTALITY AND LEVINASIAN ALTERITY

Before engaging those questions that Levinasian thought conveys to Stoic meta-physics and ethics, one caveat is necessary: the Stoics are not those Levinas has in mind when he speaks of the Greeks or the origins of Western thought; this position belongs primarily to Plato. Though Whitehead's sentiment that European philosophy is a series of footnotes to Plato might rightly echo here, Levinas is unique in his appreciation of the tension between these footnotes. Plato is both the origin of the problem within the Western tradition and the first hint at the answer to a totalizing ontology. Plato clearly places being in a hierarchical relationship above becoming. In following the Parmenidean division of reality, the eternal forms are the true reality, accessed only occasionally and with great effort by humans attached to and misled by the realm of material illusions. Nevertheless, in his *Republic,* just before he divides reality linearly, Plato places the Form of the Good beyond Being. If the analogy of the sun is consulted, the Good makes Being possible. Levinas' thoughts on the history of Western philosophy tarry with this tension in Plato.[16] As such, a certain amount of care must be taken when turning Levinas' words toward Stoicism. The Stoics might not offer the best representation of the kind of target at which Levinas takes aim.

Levinas famously questions totality. As such, the Stoic system outlined above is ripe for critique. "The same is essentially identification within the diverse, or history, or system" (*TI* 40). In Stoicism, every being is placed within a singular cosmological system and identified with a single providential order. The system enables one to make sense of each particular being within it by viewing the particular through the lens of the whole. This is precisely where the first problem with such a totality rests: "To comprehend the particular being is already to place oneself beyond the particular. To comprehend is to be related to the particular that only exists through knowledge, which is always knowledge of the universal" ("Is Ontology Fundamental?" *BPW* 5). The task of comprehending is itself inappropriate to particularity because comprehension demands universality; comprehension of the particular as particular would cease to be comprehension at all. Thus, in placing the relation with particularity within comprehension's order, particularity is necessarily subjected to the universal.

The Stoic account of the, quite literally, universal standpoint required for proper comprehension of particularity, including and especially an understanding of one's own self, seems to fit this characterization. Stoicism, then, suffers from the same problem all claims to a universal comprehension of particularity contain. "From the moment that one engages in reflection and precisely for the very reasons which since Plato subject the sensation of the particular to knowledge of the universal, one is forced, it would seem, to subject relations between beings to structures of being, metaphysics to ontology, the existentiell to the existential" ("Is Ontology Fundamental?" *BPW* 5). For Levinas, placing the other within an economy of being occurs inevitably when one employs a Platonic epistemic structure. Though the other always overflows comprehension and interrupts the conceit of universal knowledge, the task of reflection and universal comprehension ignores this disrupting force. The question becomes whether the Stoics advance an epistemic and ontological structure similar to the one Levinas identifies with Plato. If not, this critique may fail to apply to them and so highlight where their thought diverges from Platonic metaphysics.

Stoic ontology stems from corporeality not ideality. In exact opposition to the Platonic theory of the Forms, the Stoics claim that ideas are merely "figments of the soul" and Forms are "linguistic conventions" (*HP* 30A, 30H). Universals, such as the concept of man, animal, tree, and so forth, are classified as "not-somethings," and though they prove useful for expression and understanding, they are not, properly speaking, existent.[17] Though the Stoics consider the individual human being from the scope of the universe, the universe is itself a particular, living, rational organism. Within this particular are more and various parts. In fact, the "Stoic world is occupied exclusively by particulars."[18] Stoicism advocates a holistic perspective, but the kind of ontology this perspective is itself subjected to is one of particularity and corporeality. In other words, the existential is not understandable apart from the existentiell. Whereas bodies are classified as "something," *ti*, and are given the status of real, ideas are merely figments of certain souls inhabiting certain bodies. By inverting the Platonic order, Stoicism offers an important corrective to Levinas' view of ancient metaphysics and can help to illustrate a totality that may not be the kind of totalizing system Levinas condemns.

The problem that alterity raises for Stoic totality is attenuated by a proper understanding of Stoic ontology. Levinas' critique of totality, though, is directed more toward an ethics in conflict with ontological commitments than toward ontology itself. By locating the ethical and its primacy in the relationship of the face to face between the I and the Other, Levinas shifts the ground of ethics to a space outside of comprehension, reason, and, in an important sense, philosophy. "The interrupting force of ethics does not attest to a simple relaxing of reason, but to placing in question the *act of philosophizing*, which cannot fall back into philosophy" (*GCM* 4). The ethical does not result in reason's failure, a situation in which ethics would have little to offer to reason, but its overflowing. The ethical interruption of the activity of reason, then, turns philosophy on itself. Alterity and its interruption are outside of reason, and this position permits the other to be revealed both in relation to the self to whom he appears, the I, and in his particularity.

The particularity that places the other in so singular a relationship to the I, in the end, places both outside of the economy of being. "He [the other] is my *part-*

ner in the heart of a relation which ought only to have made him present to me. I have spoken to him, that is to say, I have neglected the universal being that he incarnates in order to remain with the particular being that he is" ("Is Ontology Fundamental?" *BPW* 7).[19] The revelation of the other, in partnership with him, through the face to face signifies the originary moment of ethics. As the other is made present to the I, the philosophical functioning of reason becomes disrupted, compelling the philosopher to experience the unthinkable or that which is beyond comprehension. The universal is the proper domain of comprehension, but the other demands that one forego such comprehension in order to remain with the other as such.

The particularity of the other does not, though, contain those qualities that could render him as this or that particular person. That is, the other is not an individual who can be named, identified, and described as this specific person with these precise characteristics and not another. As a result, the particularity of the other is abstract, even "ghostly."[20]

> The other must be received independently of his qualities, if he is to be received as other. If it weren't for this, which is a certain immediacy—it is even immediacy *par excellence;* the relationship to the other [*autrui*] is the only one to have no value except when it is immediate—then the rest of my analyses would lose all their force. The relationship would be one of these thematizable relationships that are established between objects. (*GCM* 80)

The particularity of the other is given in the face to face, but the best way to encounter the other is to not notice the color of his eyes.[21] In rupturing being, the encounter with the other maintains the human being qua human. An encounter that exceeds reason simultaneously inaugurates ethics.

Given the Stoic conception of an all-pervading *logos,* reason's interruption seems impossible. If reason permeates the universe as the soul permeates the living being, then it seems inconceivable that there could be an experience beyond reason. As such, the Stoic system would fail to account for the encounter with the other in much the same way that other traditional philosophical systems fail. The position of the other in Stoic philosophy is as one to whom a necessarily rational and natural duty is owed. Alterity and the Stoic response to it is, so to say, within the natural order of things. Levinasian alterity, then, will permit a critical reflection upon Stoic duty as well as Stoic totality. What resources does Stoicism possess to respond to the partnership that Levinas sees in the relation with the other, and, more significantly, to the notion that ethics begins with the other rather than the self? The privileged ethical relationship within Stoicism is that of the self to the self. In fact, it is not often that one finds arguments for Stoic intersubjectivity. Levinas, then, challenges us to examine the role of the other in Stoicism and to question whether

Stoicism, given its self-focused conception of virtue and praise of indifference, can provide an account of ethics that includes alterity and responsibility.

STOIC VIRTUE, INDIFFERENCE, AND DUTY

The Stoics, like most Classical and Hellenist schools, are eudaimonists.[22] Their key difference lies in the claim that virtue is both necessary and sufficient for happiness. To support this position, the Stoics separate external states that have no effect on virtue from internal impulses, desires, and aversions that can be labeled "good" or "bad." Many Stoics further this division by parsing out preferred from rejected "indifferents"; health, wealth, and family are extra-morally preferable to illness, poverty, and solitude. The existence or absence of any of these indifferents is, morally speaking, insignificant.

The logical extreme of this position is easily arrived at: since indifferents are of no consequence to virtue or happiness, they are of no consequence at all. Aristo of Chios in particular argues this stance.[23] For Aristo, ethics is the singularly important philosophical topic, and the goal of life is "a perfect indifference to everything which is neither virtue nor vice; recognizing no distinction whatever in things indifferent, but treating them all alike" (*DL* 7.160). The external world and all it contains is to be met with a thoroughgoing indifference. Aristo is intriguing because he exploits the strangeness of Stoic ethical philosophy: namely, that virtue consists in an attitude or disposition toward that which is neither virtuous nor vicious. By forcing Stoic *apatheia* to its furthest reach, Aristo clarifies the relation between the Stoic sage and those around her. The Stoic sage must ultimately be indifferent to others, the Other, and alterity as such. Given this, the Stoic call for responsibility will need to locate its meaning, if it is meaningful at all, within a rather idiosyncratic understanding of one's relation to alterity.

Indifference has its ground in *apatheia*. To make sense, then, of the tension between freedom from passions and responsibility, the passions, *oikeiōsis*, and duty demand examination. The passions are by definition irrational. "Passion [*pathos*] is defined by Zeno as an irrational [*alogos*] and unnatural [*para phusin*] movement in the soul, or again as impulse in excess [*hormē pleonazousa*]."[24] Whereas the goal for a human being is to live virtuously or in accordance with nature (*kata phusin*), passions are contrary to nature.[25] Only by living in accord with nature, which is divinely rational and governed, can one achieve true happiness. In aiming at that which is in accord with nature, one acts virtuously and rationally.

In Stoic ethical thought, one's aim or intention alone deserves consideration. In Cicero's *De Finibus*, the Stoic spokesman Cato employs the model of archery to exemplify ethical activity. It is within one's power to aim straight, and the archer must do so; but the consequence of the arrow actually hitting the target is not within the archer's control, and thus it is not the "purpose" of the activity: "his 'ultimate End,' so to speak, would be what corresponded to what we call the Chief Good in the conduct of life, whereas the actual hitting of the mark would be in our phrase 'to be chosen' not 'to be desired'" (*De Finibus*, 3.22). Stoicism is teleological insofar as an end determines one's present activities, but that *telos* is always internal, and the means by which one reaches it are self-designed.

The distinction that marks something as choice worthy but not desirable rests on a division between that which is and is not within one's power. By desiring or averring something that is not up to oneself, one invites disappointment. Employing the analogy of the archer again, one must aim as carefully as possible without desiring that the arrow hit the target. The moment the arrow is released, it leaves the archer's control. Wind can force the arrow off course, the target can tip over, and any other number of things can cause the arrow to miss the bull's eye, thereby producing disappointment. Desire is a passion that produces tumult in the soul when it goes unfulfilled and leads to the ascription of inflated or false value to external things.[26]

Given the Stoic understanding of virtue as living in accord with nature, it is unsurprising that they held to a unity of the virtues. Interestingly, they also develop a unity of the passions. Passions have a dual nature, and half of this nature is that they are judgments, or by some accounts the result of judgments, which tend toward excess. Galen quotes Chrysippus regarding exactly this: "The passions are called ailments not just in virtue of their judging each of these [external] things to be good, but also with regard to their running towards them in excess of what is natural" (*HP* 65L). There is a subtle point here. It is perfectly natural, that is, rational, for an individual to have an impulse in a certain direction, but passion oversteps the bounds of this impulse. Those impulses which remain in accord with nature are found within the Stoic theory of *oikeiōsis*.[27]

Oikeiōsis concerns, roughly, that which is in the nature of a thing or which conforms to a thing's nature: "So it remains to say that in constituting the animal, nature made it belong to itself. For that is how things that are harmful are repelled and things that belong are pursued" (*DL* 7.85). An animal's first impulse is for self-preservation.[28] From these primary natural impulses human beings are led to appropriate actions or *kathēkonta*. Ever fond of developmental accounts, the Stoics detail a progression from acting to preserve one's constitution, the first of the appropriate actions, through the habituation of choices conditioned by nature, to a fully rationalized sense of choice in which the good emerges. As Annas has pointed out, this is different from egoism or a love of self: "It is the tendency we have both towards developing self-concern and towards developing other-concern."[29] If nature inclines human beings toward concern for both self and other, one is not more rational or natural than the other, and thus one is not to be credited or pursued over the other.

Though humans are essentially rational and are guided toward their proper activity by nature, reason is susceptible to corruption;[30] natural impulses are allowed to run to excess, thereby running contrary to nature. Corrupted reasoning leads to judgments that mistakenly deem externals as good or bad. Galen describes this as an excess of impulse, and his model preserves Chrysippus' representation of the passionate state by a man running. When running, our legs fly before us, making it difficult to stop or change direction at the moment we decide to do so. On the other hand, when walking, the body is well within the control of the will. Once the will decides to stop, the body readily complies. The relationship between running and walking is analogous to that between a passionate and reasonable frame of mind. "When our minds and feelings are passionate, we cannot count on having them respond instantly to a change in our evaluation of the situation we are in. The excessiveness of our emotional response is a matter of our loss of control, once we step outside the framework of reason."[31]

Given this distinction, it is possible to posit certain appropriate relationships and duties with and toward the other which, when approached from the proper state of mind, are in accord with nature. In other words, excessively emotional mind frames with regard to relationships cause tumult, not the relationships themselves. A continuum of appropriate actions exists within which the Stoic sage restricts herself, and it is here that responsibility toward and caring for others resides. It is numerously mentioned that the sage participates in society, feels warm stirrings for fellow humans, and can even serve politically. All such affiliations result from natural impulses and lead to appropriate actions.

In classifying the areas of study that comprise the training of those striving to be good and noble, Epictetus highlights impulses and appropriate actions, *kathēkonta*. "For I should not be unfeeling like a statue, but should preserve my natural and acquired relations as a man who honours the gods, as a son, as a brother, as a father, as a citizen."[32] Certain feelings, namely the *eupatheiai*, are appropriately acted upon. It is natural and appropriate to feel affection and benevolence toward others. This is further illustrated by those duties prevailed on us by reason, such as "honouring one's parents, brothers and country, and intercourse with friends" (*DL* 7.108–109). In fact, Diogenes Laertius credits Zeno with the invention of *kathēkonta*, often translated as "duty."[33]

All human beings have natural impulses toward family, neighbors, friends, and humanity in general. The Stoic sage is likewise appropriately moved toward natural, acquired relations and inclined toward association, not isolation. The distinction between the sage and all others is that the sage can make correct judgments following upon these impulses and is not drawn into excess. For example, grief at the loss of a loved one is an excessive emotion. First, given the unity of the passions, grief evidences a passionate frame of mind. One who grieves has been suffering from other ailments of the soul made manifest in the impossible desire rather than the rational wish for the company of the beloved. Grief is a symptom of a more extensive disease wherein one allows one's own happiness to depend upon something external. Possessing an affiliation and responsibility toward another and rationally wishing for that other to be present is appropriate; to wish for a human being, a fragile and mortal thing, to be always free from disease, injury, and death is not.

Hierocles, a Stoic philosopher circa 100 CE, takes *oikeiōsis* as a starting point for ethics. He recapitulates the standard line: sensation lends itself to the knowledge of that which is appropriate as evidenced in a newborn's perception of itself. He differs in that he immediately locates in *oikeiōsis* the seed for the "elements of ethics."[34] This ethics takes into consideration the duties of the sage. Hierocles directly addresses appropriate disposition, which "to oneself is benevolence, while that to one's kindred is affection. . . . Just as our appropriate disposition relative to our children is affection. . . . We are an animal, but a gregarious one which needs someone else as well. For this reason we too inhabit cities. . . . Secondly, we make friendships easily. By eating together or sitting together in the theater . . . [text breaks off]."[35] Hierocles' choice of the word "need" is significant, but the need for society should be viewed rationally. Nature has given us an impulse toward sociality; it is thus reasonable for all, the sage included, to proceed on the grounds of this impulse.

Nature guides the social leanings of a rational creature and instills certain affections for friends and family. The sage, though, curbs this affection before it becomes a passion and thus cultivates an indifference that supports the sense of duty and responsibility that arrive with natural affection. In conversing with a government official who deserted his ill daughter because, he says, of his great affection for her, Epictetus denies the possibility of a conflict between family affection, a "good and natural thing," and that which is reasonable, for both are in accord with nature. Affection does not trigger the father's abandonment; his judgment that sickness and death are evils leads him to act in a way contrary to nature.[36] Such judgments must be extirpated and eliminated from the soul with care greater than that with which tumors are removed from the body.

Stoic personal attachment, then, is of a curious kind:

> When you become attached to something, let it not be as though it were to something that cannot be taken away, but rather, as though it were to something like an earthenware pot or crystal goblet, so that if it happens to be broken, you may remember what kind of thing it was and not be distressed. So in this, too, when you kiss your child, or your brother, or your friend, never entirely give way to your imagination, nor allow your elation to progress as far as it will; but curb it, restrain it . . . remind yourself that what you love is mortal, that what you love is not your own. [37]

A form of training, or self-discipline, is detailed for the sake of redirecting our emotional attachment. Epictetus is not suggesting that one value one's child similarly to earthenware, for nature and reason guide the warmth one feels toward friends and family. Instead, he advises that the fragility of one's beloved not be forgotten and recommends thinking a contrary impression simultaneously with delight: one might whisper "Tomorrow you shall die" to oneself while kissing one's child or think of a friend's departure while in her presence. Through this vigilance attachments can be kept within the limits of reason.

Epictetus' advice highlights the dual nature of Stoic responsibility. One has a duty to others but is always responsible for one's own desires, impulses, opinions, aversions, and judgments, which may either assist or impede this duty. The Stoic exercises freedom and responsibility within relations to those not within one's power, but given the imperative force of duty, others seem a class of externals that are not wholly extra-moral. In fact, the Stoics endorse practices that buttress this responsibility through the creation of a rational, virtuous self that is interestingly intersubjective.

STOIC PRACTICES

The Stoic practices of the self that aid the cultivation of a virtuous self and creation of a beautiful life are, in some ways, more robustly intersubjective than the Stoic theory of duty. Stoic practices are therapeutic and are taken up for the sake of the health of the self. Like therapies of the body, these have the two functions of maintenance and repair. They include remedies for the passions, remembrance of good things, accomplishment of duties, reading, writing, and listening. Meditation is a specific technique that both embraces and is embraced by other Stoic practices.[38] Since these meditation techniques are less obviously intersubjective than practices such as listening to or corresponding with another, by briefly examining this specific practice in its intersubjective aspects, the method and function of such practices in general can be better illustrated.

Meditations figure largely in Stoic practices and are, to some extent, an expansion of Socratic self-examination. Meditation itself has multiple facets, but these can be gathered under three related topics. The first revolves around review, which involves taking the time to examine one's faults and shortcomings, what one did well and poorly. Seneca suggests that the mind "should be summoned to give an account of itself every day." By reviewing his thoughts, words, and deeds every night, Seneca can discover precisely where he went astray and train himself all the more adeptly.[39] Review, then, is not for self-congratulation or deprecation; it is oriented toward proper habituation for future situations.

The goal of review, that is, creating an ethical disposition, introduces the second aspect of meditation: preparing for future events. Marcus Aurelius distills this preparation during his own *Meditations*. He reminds himself that there are two ways in which he must always be prepared. First, he must constantly act in agreement with the divine prescription to benefit all humankind. Second, he must be prepared to change his "purpose" through the aid of another's guidance and correction.[40] Part of Stoic meditation is the preparation to accept one's faults when another exposes them. When rebuked by parents, teachers, judges, and anyone else who occupies a position to point out shortcomings, "we ought to submit to the chastening they give in the same spirit in which we submit to the surgeon's knife, a regimen of diet, and other things which cause suffering that they may bring profit" (Seneca, *De Ira*, 2.27).

Both Seneca and Marcus Aurelius engage in preparation for the right kind of relation with others. The latter explicitly introduces two sides of the preparation: to improve others, and to be improved by them. The care of the self, which is central to Stoic ethics, is facilitated by the concern others cultivate for us and the demands of concerning ourselves with the well-being of others. This has, then, a prescriptive element: "Never value as an advantage to yourself what will force you one day to break your word, or to abandon self-respect, to hate, to suspect, execrate another, to act a part, to covet anything that calls for walls or coverings to conceal it" (Aurelius, *Meditations*, 3.7). To cultivate an ethical relationship with oneself, one must treat others in a certain way. In exhorting himself, Aurelius discusses the "retreat into oneself" that is reparative. "Recall the judgment that reasonable creatures have come into the world for the sake of one another; that patience is a part of justice; that people do wrong involuntarily" (*Meditations*, 4.3). Though human virtue is entirely internal, the meaning of human existence, that for the sake of whom the human being exists, is found in alterity.

One aspect of meditation takes account of the past, a second prepares one for the future, and so, unsurprisingly, the third aspect is a correlative sense of meditation for the present, namely attention. Epictetus describes the attention one should apply vigilantly to all aspects of life: "So is it possible to be altogether faultless? No, that is impracticable; but it is possible to strive continuously not to commit faults. For we shall have cause to be satisfied if, by never relaxing our attention, we shall escape at least a few faults" (*Discourses*, 4.12). Attention demands an awareness of one's reactions to certain situations and the emotions welling within one in order to discover whether such reactions and passions are reasonable. Once one roots out the judgment that stands behind the passion,[41] one can choose to be swayed by the passion or to deny it.

Marcus Aurelius recommends meditation as the ultimate practice, for "nothing will help more than a meditation on our morality" (*Meditations*, 3.4). These meditations are appealing precisely because they readily and consistently treat the relation of the self to others, reminding us that Stoic morality is, in spite of the independence it offers, intersubjective. In other words, the practices that form the Stoic self do so in such a way that the self is already in relation to others and answers to the responsibility the Stoic demands of herself before the other. The stringency of the Stoic system is paired with an unwavering regard for the other in Stoic practices.

One reading, and subsequent critique, of Stoicism is that its success as a philosophical school is the result of its ability to shield its adherents from the miseries of the human condition by contending that they are not miseries at all. Levinasian ethics, by contrast, seeks to challenge rather than to console. In light of human misery, suffering, hunger, poverty, and weakness, the other appears before us as an absolute responsibility. Is Stoicism, then, merely a consolation for the miserable, suffering, hungry, poor, and weak? Perhaps worse, does the indifference that the Stoic is meant to cultivate leave her insensitive to her responsibility before the other, however well trained this response might be?

LEVINASIAN RESPONSIBILITY

Levinas radically redefines the notion of responsibility by viewing it as an invocation prior to and beyond reason. Numerous philosophical and juridical systems take reason as the *sine qua non* for responsibility, and Stoicism looks to be no exception. The problem with this view of responsibility, as already briefly explored, is that it seems to place alterity and the responsibility felt before the other within the totalizing structure of comprehension and ontology. "Consciousness as a conscious grasp is a possession of the Other by the Same" ("Transcendence and Height," *BPW* 18). Before determining whether the Stoics assimilate alterity, a slightly more developed account of Levinas' position should be offered.

To enclose the other in totality reduces him to sameness and identity, thereby violating the unicity that marks the other as such. The relationship between human beings is, for Levinas, characterized by an utter inability to synthesize this relation. Levinas describes the encounter with the other by drawing attention to its irreducible and nearly indescribable aspects. It is through this aspect of the face to face that Levinas broaches the concept of infinity. Infinity, as that which surpasses thought and cannot be contained by it, names the ethical relationship that binds the I to the Other.[42] "The idea of the infinite consists in grasping the ungraspable while nevertheless guaranteeing its status as ungraspable" ("Transcendence and Height," *BPW* 19). To totality and the structure of the same Levinas opposes infinity, an idea that is characterized by its radical alterity and the surplus it presents to thought. Levinas imagines the responses to his suggestions, especially from the Heideggerian perspective, and finds it necessary "to reply that respect for the person—infinite responsibility for the Other (*Autrui*)—imposes itself on thought with the power of primordial coordinates; that to seek the condition for the personal and the human is already to undermine them" (*BPW* 31). The face to face places one in an asymmetrical relation with the other and calls for absolute responsibility.

The face of the other speaks, addresses, invokes. Levinas turns to language because of its expressive function and presupposition of plurality. Language requires that an addressor make her address to an addressee. Alterity, then, is the very condition of language.

> If, on the contrary, reason lives in language, if the first rationality gleams forth in the opposition of the face to face, if the first intelligible, the first signification, is the infinity of the intelligence that presents itself (that is, speaks to me) in the face, if reason is defined by signification rather than signification being defined by the impersonal structures of reason, if society precedes the apparition of these impersonal structures, if universality reigns as the presence of humanity in the eyes that look at me, if, finally, we recall that this look appeals to my responsibility and consecrates my freedom as responsibility and gift of self—then the pluralism of society could not disappear in the elevation to reason, but would be its condition. (*TI* 208)

Whereas the Stoics view responsibility to the other as demanded by reason, Levinas compels us to think of this initial responsibility as foundational for reason. Pluralism always precedes egoism, and the separation of the I is possible only through the look of the other. Do the Stoics, though, truly conflict with the pluralism that Levinas takes to be the basis of ethics?

The Stoics describe the structures of reason as immanent rather than impersonal. Reason, in the Stoic sense, pervades the *kosmos* and so precedes any universal structure through which the human tries to express human relationships. Society, and the natural human impulses toward it, certainly precede the apparition of universality. Indeed, universals are only ever apparitions, secondary to and contingent upon immanent particulars. In fact, it is the emphasis on the immediacy of reason that separates Stoicism from the traditional philosophical structures Levinas critiques so compellingly. Nevertheless, the Stoic traces this immediacy primarily within the self and seeks to bolster the self in relation to the other, thanks to the former. Though there is a palpable tension in Stoicism between the care of the self and the responsibility toward the other, a tension that surfaces when the Stoics are thought in light of Levinas, Stoic ethics begins with the relationship of the self to the self.

In describing the philosophy of existence, a philosophy that will ultimately "efface itself before ontology," Levinas offers what could here be described as a further salvo against the Stoic concept of responsibility. In addition to surpassing reason, responsibility is for more than one's own intentions.

> We are thus responsible beyond out intentions. It is impossible for the regard that directs the act to avoid the nonintended action that comes with it. We have one finger caught in the machine and things turn against us. That is to say, our consciousness and our mastery of reality through consciousness do not exhaust our relation with reality, to which we always are present through all the density of our being. Consciousness of reality does not coincide with our habitation in the world. (*BPW* 4)

Levinas directs us to what he describes as the drama of human existence. We exist in a way that surpasses our comprehension and our intentions. The Stoics tend to diminish the way in which actions as well as intentions are truly one's own. As such, Levinas offers a more cohesive account of the relationship between selves and their projects. The Stoic is forced to say that one's projects are not really up to one: they are external, and therefore outside of one's control. But this fractures the distinctive relationship one feels with regard to one's own activities, tasks, and creations, however mundane or profound. The asymmetrical responsibility felt before the other calls one to a cognizance of the disparity between one's consciousness of the world, or *kosmos,* how one means to be in this world, and how in fact this existence and habitation proceeds.

Given this disparity, what brings one toward the other? For the Stoics, it is a natural affiliation, innate and rational. Levinas' account is not terribly divergent. In discussing the approach to the other through speech and invocation, Levinas claims that prior to "any participation in a common content by comprehension, it consists in the intuition of sociality by a relation that is consequently irreducible to comprehension" (*BPW* 7). The Stoics not only agree with this intuition to sociality but develop new ethical terminology in order to better make sense of it.

The real difference between the Stoic and Levinasian notions of responsibility is that the Stoics must, due to their cosmological emphasis, claim that the relationship to the other is theoretically within the bounds of comprehension. But in terms of priority, the Stoics would contend that first the intuition of sociality arises, through natural affiliation and duty, and only later is it understood in a way that allows one to support such duty through extirpating irrational emotions. It is precisely through the eradication of emotions such as fear, grief, envy, and anxiety, passions that can cause one to betray the duty owed to the other, that the Stoic can be sure to act appropriately. As the section on Stoic practices intimates, the Stoic seeks to create a self more fully capable of responding appropriately to the other; the care of the self allows for a more robust care for the other. Levinas describes reason through its "impersonal structures." The Stoics, by contrast, see intersubjectivity as fundamentally rational. To deny responsibility and natural duty to the other is to deny humanity.

Though bringing together the Stoics and Levinas is a peculiar task, it is this very peculiarity that renders such a project fruitful. The Stoics fall outside the guise of Levinasian thought. As such, they call into question his characterization of a European tradition of universal ontology and demonstrate another way of viewing alterity.

Stoic ethics focuses on the self. The main thrust of Stoicism is to shore up the self by providing practices and methods, guidelines and discourses, and, in the end, metaphysical and epistemic structures that permit the creation of an imperturbable, virtuous, and flourishing self. Indeed, "vice" defines a relationship of the self with the self wherein reason has failed. This understanding of the ethical is in keeping with a tradition of ethics as an art of living and so is precisely what makes Stoicism appealing to thinkers who find within it a dynamic alternative to juridical models of ethics. In embracing an aesthetics of existence, the Stoic is impervious to social and political patterns and pressures that would otherwise mold the self. It offers the possibility of more or less authentic self-creation.

The primacy of the self that renders self-creation possible is simultaneously that which detaches the Stoic from other human beings. It is this fundamental understanding of human relation that gives a Levinasian reading of the Stoics its force. After thinking through Levinas' view of the human relationship, it is possible that the Stoic view of alterity simply feels wrong. In lacking the possibility of overflow and a relationship that defies any attempt to bring it back into the fold of comprehension, the responsibility of the Stoic sage strikes a note too cold and calculating to describe, with any phenomenological force, the ethical relationships in which human beings have found themselves.

What, though, might the Stoic conception be able to offer Levinasian ethics? One possibility emerges with the concrete practices of duty the Stoics so adeptly advocate. Given the ghostliness and abstract qualities of alterity, it is hard to imagine how one could live up to the asymmetrical responsibility the face to face imposes in practice. Levinas has been critiqued for an ethical view that is stunningly sparse in its practical and political suggestions. If ethics takes place outside of reason, how might one reasonably act ethically? In his 1934 essay "Reflections on Hitlerism," Levinas diagnoses some of the more pressing concerns regarding the "sovereign freedom of reason":

> The whole philosophical and political thought of modern times tends to place the human spirit on a plane that is superior to reality, and so creates a gulf between man and the world. It makes it impossible to apply the categories of the physical world to the spirituality of reason, and so locates the ultimate foundation of spirit

outside the brutal world and the implacable history of concrete existence. It replaces the blind world of common sense with the world rebuilt by idealist philosophy, one that is steeped in reason and subject to reason. (RH 66)

The Stoics, like Levinas, challenge this perspective. Furthermore, the Stoics permit reason to function on the human plane of reality, wherein no gulf is possible between this world and any other, for this world is reality's majestic entirety. Politically, then, the Stoics demand cosmopolitanism.

Cosmopolitanism is among the more enduring and engaging paradoxes of antiquity. The citizen, the *politēs,* is so by virtue of the rights and responsibilities owed to the *polis,* or city-state. The very idea that one would be a citizen of the *kosmos,* and so thereby claim all rights from and honor all responsibilities to others by virtue of one's humanity, would have struck the ancient consciousness not only as novel but as oxymoronic. The Stoic notion of cosmopolitanism is adapted from their Cynic predecessors, and it coincides beautifully with the opening insight of *Totality and Infinity,* namely that morality is opposed to politics. The Stoics redefine the political by making sense of it via the *kosmos* rather than the *polis.* Politics, falsely premised on the arbitrary boundaries of this or that *polis,* artificially imposes a restriction on one's duty to others. The Stoics, without being quite as anarchic as their Cynic forbearers, see politics as bankrupt if it opposes the human perspective of the *kosmos.* In this way, then, the cosmological structure of Stoicism, which initially looked to be such a liability, leads it into Levinasian terrain.

Finally, if in the end the concrete demands of responsibility for both the Stoics and Levinas match each other, one might justifiably wonder whether both are mistaken in seeing so strong a connection between the system one maintains or eschews and the ethical activity one advances. "Concretely our effort consists in maintaining, within anonymous community, the society of the I with the other—language and goodness" (*TI* 47). If one added to this statement the Stoic term *logos,* a term that carries with it connotations of speech and language as well as reason, Levinas might easily be describing the most essential aspects of the Stoic effort.

NOTES

1. For the Stoics, *apatheia* means to be without *pathos* or passion. Though it can denote insensibility, the Stoic use should not be equated with apathy. *Apatheia* does not describe a complete lack of feeling, for the Stoics endorse "good passions," or *eupatheiai.* The good passions are in accord with reason and include such feelings as warmth, sociability, generosity, and caution. For a general account, see A. A. Long and David N. Sedley, eds., *The Hellenistic Philosophers,* 2 vols. (Cambridge: Cambridge University Press, 1987), 65A–E;

hereafter abbreviated *HP* (the second volume employs the same numbering as the first, but produces the passages in the original).

2. It is beyond the scope of this project to distance the historical Socrates, who is almost wholly concerned with ethical questions, from the Platonic Socrates, who becomes acutely interested in metaphysics and epistemology (as well as aesthetics, political theory, mathematics, and so on). Nevertheless, it bears mentioning that the aspects of Socratic ethics that are palpable in Stoicism are carried through the intermediary of Cynicism.

3. The link between Stoicism and Cynicism takes its most legendary form in the story of Zeno's encounter with the Cynic Crates. Shipwrecked on a voyage from Phoenicia, Zeno, a native of Citium, sat in an Athenian bookseller's shop reading Xenophon's *Memorabilia*. Zeno asked the shopkeeper where he might find men like Socrates, and amazingly Crates was passing at precisely that moment. The shopkeeper pointed to Crates, told Zeno to follow him, and Zeno became Crates' pupil. Though this narrative is too convenient to be entirely trustworthy, it accurately depicts an intellectual lineage from the Cynics to the Stoics. See Diogenes Laertius' *Lives of Eminent Philosophers*, 2 vols., trans. R. D. Hicks (Cambridge: Harvard University Press, 1979), 7.2–3. Hereafter abbreviated *DL*.

4. The term *askēsis* is often translated as "exercise," "practice," or "training." In a more general sense, it is a "mode of life" or a "profession." The use Greek philosophers make of the term is far afield from the Christian understanding of asceticism. The Cyrenaic philosopher Aristippus, a self-proclaimed hedonist, offers an obvious example of an utterly un-ascetic *askēsis* in relation to training and virtue. In addition to defining pleasure as the good, Aristippus holds "that bodily training [*tēn sōmatikēn askēsin*] contributes to the acquisition of virtue [*aretēs*]" (*DL* 2.91).

5. Duty stems from doing one's due, *ta kathēkonta*, in order to fulfill one's natural obligation, *oikeiōsis*.

6. This is according to Sextus Empiricus. See his *Against the professors*, 7.19, in *HP* 26D.

7. For a more complete rendering of Stoic "physics," see *DL* 7.132. "Their physical doctrine they divide into sections (1) about bodies; (2) about principles; (3) about elements; (4) about the gods; (5) about bounding surfaces and space whether filled or empty." Under each of these subdivisions additional topics fall: under "bodies" one finds distinctions between corporeality and incorporeality as well as extension; included under "elements" are discussions of astronomy, meteorology, geography, and psychology (*DL* 7.144–46, 152–59).

8. *DL* 7.135. Hicks is translating *nous* as "Reason."

9. Alexander of Aphrodisias summarizes this position: "Well then, they say that this universe, which is one and contains in itself all that exists, and is organised by a Nature which is alive, rational and intelligent, possess the organization of the things that are, which is eternal and progresses according to a certain sequence and order; the things which come to be first are causes for those after them, and in this way all things are bound together with one another" (*De Fato*, 191.30–192.3; in Alexander of Aphrodisias, *On Fate*, trans. R. W. Sharples [London: Duckworth and Co. Ltd., 1983]).

10. This was the opinion of Antipater, Chrysippus, and Posidonius, though there seems to have been some disagreement regarding the ruling principle. See *DL* 7.138–39.

11. The term in *DL* 7.138 for "reason" is *nous*. The reason present in the *kosmos* is of the most perfect and complete kind. See also the argument at Cicero's *On the Nature of the Gods*, 21–34.

12. The infusion of intellect (*nous*) into all aspects of the *kosmos* is somewhat complex. To summarize, though, "intellect" has different powers (*dunameis*) such as that of tenor (*hek-*

tikēn) as well as the physical (*physikēn*), psychical (*psychikēn*), rational (*logikēn*), and calculative (*dianoētikēn*) powers. These different powers are extended to all things: stones and logs (having tenor), plants (having physique, which is tenor in motion), irrational animals (having soul), and rational creatures such as humans (having rational and calculative powers extended to them). See Philo, *Allegories of the laws*, 2.22–23, in *HP* 47P.

13. Or, the truth of human access to the *kosmos* is proved by divination: "The predictions of the soothsayers could not be true, [Chrysippus] says, if all things were not embraced by fate"; Eusebius, *Evangelical preparation*, 4.3.1, in *HP* 55P.

14. Epictetus, *Encheiridion*, 8. In *The Discourses as Reported by Arrian*, trans. W. A. Oldfather (Cambridge: Harvard University Press, 1928). The term that Oldfather is rendering as "serenity" is not *ataraxia*, or tranquility, but *eurhoia*, which is literally "well-flowing," a term that Zeno may have ushered into ethical discourse.

15. Hippolytus attributes this image of human responsibility and destiny to Zeno and Chrysippus. See *HP* 62A.

16. Aristotle likewise figures prominently in Levinas' texts, but in one sense Aristotle is the first of the series of footnotes. Though this is somewhat reductive, given Aristotle's expansion and clarification of philosophical thought, his task owes much to the teacher with whom he so often and importantly disagrees.

17. For the Stoic classification of universals, see *HP* 30E.

18. Long and Sedley give this summary of Stoic ontology in volume 1 of *HP* 164.

19. The importance of language in the relationship with the other is discussed alongside Levinasian responsibility below.

20. In a 1975 interview with Levinas, T. C. Frederikse employs this term in commenting on his experience with Levinas' seminal text: "While reading *Totality and Infinity* I had the impression that the face of the other emerges, as it were, from nothingness, which gives a ghostly character to your philosophy" (*GCM* 79–80).

21. Levinas claims that although perception can dominate the relation of the face to face, this relation is not reducible to perception (*EI* 85–86).

22. Though the most common translation of *eudaimonia* is "happiness," it refers to an enduring activity rather than a fleeting emotional state, hence its alternate translation as "flourishing."

23. Though Diogenes Laertius treats Aristo, a student of Zeno's, as an example of a Stoic who differed from the others, Herillus seems to have been different in the same way, since "everything that lies between virtue and vice he pronounced indifferent" (*DL* 7.165). Aristo the Bald allegedly died from sunstroke, which inspired Laertius to compose a poem in "limping iambics," which I include here only because it is so awful: "Wherefore, Ariston, when old and bald did you let the sun roast your forehead? Thus seeking warmth more than was reasonable, you lit unwillingly upon the chill reality of Death" (*DL* 7.164).

24. This definition is preserved in *DL* 7.110. *Pathos* is characterized by excess, whereas there is nothing essential to *hormē* that is contrary to nature. The feeling of benevolence toward oneself and of affinity toward others is "appropriate," given to every human being *by nature,* and is a "first impulse" or *prōtēn hormēn* (see *DL* 7.85).

25. Cicero's Cato details Stoicism's chief good: "We may now observe how strikingly the principles I have established support the following corollaries. Inasmuch as the final aim—(and you have observed, no doubt, that I have all along been translating the Greek term *telos* wither by 'final' or 'ultimate aim,' or 'chief Good,' and for 'final or ultimate aim' we may also substitute 'End')—inasmuch then as the final aim is to live in agreement and

harmony with nature, it necessarily follows that all wise men at all times enjoy a happy, perfect and fortunate life, free from all hindrance, interference, or want"; Cicero, *De Finibus*, trans. H. Rackham (Cambridge: Harvard University Press, 1931). The same position is summarized at 3.31 and is found throughout *DL* Book 7. See especially *DL* 7.87–88.

26. According to Epictetus, a *pathos* "does not arise except when a desire [*horexeōs*] fails to attain its object, or an aversion [*ekkliseōs*] falls into what it would avoid" (*The Discourses as Reported by Arrian*, 3.2.3).

27. The term *oikeiōsis* is translated variously as "appropriation," "affection," "affinity," and "becoming familiar with." It comes from the term for home *oikon* and from *oikeioi*, which designates the people in one's household. *Oikeiōsis*, then, refers to the affinity or familiarity between human beings. It is a noun used in reference to oneself or other human beings, but not objects.

28. Cicero has Cato phrase this initial self-attachment in similar language but expand the notion to include those things that are adopted "for their own sake." The first and most pressing of these are acts of cognition, or *katalēpseis*. Kataleptic impressions are in accord with nature "because they possess an element that so to speak embraces and contains the truth"; see Cicero, *De Finibus*, 3.17.

29. See Julia Annas, *The Morality of Happiness* (Oxford: Oxford University Press, 1993), 263. The developmental account is more detailed than I here describe it. The concern for others comes from the concern for one's offspring, who are, in a sense, a part of one. Annas describes other-concern and self-concern in terms of innate affiliations, or "primitive forms of instinct" that all human beings have at birth (265). Thus, the feelings of affection are for oneself, one's children, and ultimately, for all other human beings.

30. See *DL* 7.89 on this point: "When a rational being is perverted, this is due to deceptiveness of external pursuits or sometimes to the influence of his associates. For the starting points of nature are never perverse."

31. See Brad Inwood's "interpretive paraphrase" of the Chrysippus fragment in "Why Do Fools Fall in Love?" in *Aristotle and After* (Bulletin of the Institute of Classical Studies, Supplement 68, 1997), 67.

32. Epictetus, *The Discourses, the Handbook, Fragments*, trans. Robin Hard, ed. Christopher Gill (London: J. M. Dent, 1995), 3.2.4.

33. "They say too that he was the first to introduce the word Duty and wrote a treatise on the subject" (*DL* 7.25). The treatise mentioned here is likely *Peri tou kathēkontos*, or *Of Duty*, listed as one of Zeno's works at *DL* 7.4.

34. Hierocles' *Elements of Ethics*, 1.34–9, 51–7, 2.1–9, in *HP* 57C.

35. Ibid., 9.3–10, 11.14–18, in *HP* 57D.

36. Epictetus, *The Discourses as Reported by Arrian*, 1.11. This is my interpretation of the passage; Epictetus does not explicitly state the father's motivation for fleeing.

37. Ibid. 3.24.84–87.

38. It is one of the therapies of the passions, it calls for remembering and projecting, and it often reaches its culmination in the correspondence of the meditation between friends.

39. *De Ira*, 3.36. In Seneca, *Moral Essays*, Vol. I: *De Providentia, De Constantia, De Ira, De Clementia*, trans. John W. Basore (Cambridge: Harvard University Press, 1928).

40. Marcus Aurelius, *The Meditations of Emperor Marcus Aurelius Antoninus*, 2 vols., ed. and trans. A. S. L. Farquharson (Oxford: Clarendon Press, 1944), 4.12.

41. This holds for irrational feelings of frustration or grief or pleasure over that which is not up to one, such as death (Epictetus, *Encheiridion*, 5) and being pleased with one's beauty (6), respectively.

42. The view of infinity as an overflowing of thought has philosophical precedence in such thinkers as Descartes, who in his *Meditations on First Philosophy* famously argues for the existence of God on the basis that the concept of infinity could not have originated independently in such limited and finite creatures.

OF A NON-SAYING THAT SAYS NOTHING: LEVINAS AND PYRRHONISM

Pierre Lamarche

9

Alerting us to a significant fact about Levinas' invocation of skepticism in his parenthetical qualifier, Robert Bernasconi notes, "Levinas draws on the recurrence of (a certain form of) skepticism—in spite of the attempt of logic to exclude its return—in order to suggest that skepticism is witness to reasons that reason does not know."[1] Strangely, though, Levinas himself, and to my knowledge all of the commentators on Levinas' recourse to skepticism's eternal recurrence, fail to pay serious heed to this fact even when they acknowledge it, as Bernasconi does. The basic sweep of Levinas' gloss of skepticism and of the role that the recourse to skepticism plays in Levinas' work has been well documented.[2] Levinas first notes the fact that skepticism constantly returns—famously, as the "legitimate child" of philosophy—despite its self-refutation. He then defends this constant return through the introduction of his distinction between saying and said to show that skepticism does not, really, refute itself—its gesture remains aloof from, and untouched by, a *logos* that, over and over again, would deny its very possibility. He then marshals this discussion in order to defend his own theorization of the priority of ethics over all theory, against criticisms that it too, like skepticism, is self-refuting, aporetic, illegitimate.

To begin to see the stakes of Bernasconi's parenthetical qualification, we can use Adriaan Peperzak's straightforward characterization of the "skepticism" whose recurrence, despite its self-refutation, Levinas invokes: "What skepticism says, its thesis or 'said,' can be formulated in a sentence like the following one: 'All (philosophical) theses are false' or 'None of the possible theses (in philosophy) is true.'"[3] Such a statement, obviously, refutes itself. However, it is also hardly the only possible statement of what skepticism has said, particularly in the context of Hellenistic thought. Indeed, within what is arguably the richest and most interesting vein of Hellenistic skepticism—the pyrrhonian—such a statement would not be considered "skeptical" at all, but rather dogmatic. The theses "all philosophical statements are false," or "nothing can be known," or any of the like express not skepticism but negative dogmatism—an epistemological position wherein a particular thesis concerning the nature of things is believed to be true and thus known, although the thesis expresses only "negative" knowledge: for example, that things are such that nothing can be known about them. So what are the defining contours of pyrrhonian skepticism, and how does it differ from the negative dogmatism to which Levinas takes recourse?

Levinas takes skepticism to be an epistemological position characterized by some form of argument that truth is unattainable—essentially, skepticism is an attack on truth that holds its own position to be true and hence refutes itself. This view is consistent with the broad sweep of modern skeptical strategies inaugurated by Descartes in the first meditation. Hume attacked the means of justifying the validity of any truth held. Philosophers in the Anglo-American tradition have employed Cartesian-type strategies in order to develop skeptical arguments, either to varying degrees of support for, or ultimately, à la Descartes, contra skepticism.[4] Their target is also, uniformly, any process of justifying the validity of any proposition believed true. With reasonable leeway, we can consider Kierkegaard, Nietzsche, and Derrida (the latter clearly implicated by Levinas as situated within a tradition at least sensitive to the possibility of skepticism's return) to be representative of the general problematization of truth, and attempts at rational justification of truths held, characteristic of much of nineteenth- and twentieth-century Continental thought and consistent with the modern skeptical attack on truth and justification emerging in the first meditation.

From the perspective of Levinas' eternal recurrence of skepticism, it is unnecessary to argue that any of the above figures is, in fact, a skeptic. Rather, we need merely to note that a very skeptical incredulity toward truth plays an important role, positively or negatively, in all of their work and hence that all of them take (the recurrence of) skepticism seriously. For my purposes here—and to use a model of "knowledge" as some form of justified, true belief—the skepticism to which Levinas refers takes its target to be truth and the attempt to justify one's true beliefs. As both Bernasconi and Margret Grebowicz have pointed out, on this view of skepticism's stakes, then, Levinas' claim of skepticism's eternal recurrence is not a historical claim but a structural one: as the search for truth, philosophy must always, at some point, confront the possibility of its own impossibility. The key difference between this form of skepticism and the pyrrhonian strain (from which I want to distinguish it) is the fact that pyrrhonian skepticism is concerned only secondarily with truth and its justification. Its real target is belief and belief formation. The pyrrhonist seeks, as we shall see, to rid the subject of skeptical therapy of the propensity to form any belief whatsoever, and hence to leave the "patient" unconcerned, unmoved by merely epistemological concerns of truth and its ultimate attainability. To put it another way, pyrrhonian skepticism is not essentially an epistemological enterprise; rather, it is an *agogē*—a way of life.

WHAT WAS PYRRHONIAN SKEPTICISM?

As a specific tradition within Western philosophy, skepticism emerged in the Hellenistic age. Hellenistic skepticism took a place alongside the other major competing Hellenistic traditions of stoicism and epicureanism, and to a great extent those three movements defined Western philosophy in the centuries following the death of Aristotle in 322 BCE. The great hero of the skeptical philosophy characteristic of the Hellenistic age was the obscure figure Pyrrho of Elis, who flourished ca. 360–270 BCE and who, like Socrates, wrote nothing at all. Its last great figure, at the nether historical reaches of the Hellenistic world, and a vital source of information concerning both skepticism and the dogmatic philosophy it opposed, was the even more obscure Sextus Empiricus.[5] Our direct sources for Hellenistic skepticism are notoriously spotty and include such dubious major sources as Diogenes Laertius, from the third century CE, so our knowledge of who actually said and thought what, when, is almost entirely second, third, or even fourth hand. Be that as it may, skepticism became the official philosophy of Plato's Academy after the succession of Arcesilaus (who wrote nothing at all) as its head, ca. 273 BCE.

For the next two centuries, the Academic skeptics engaged in an ongoing battle with the Stoic followers of Zeno of Citium, a long-running debate that altered the philosophical practice of both schools, forced the skeptics to flirt with dogmatisms of various sorts, and pushed the stoics to the brink of a genuine skepticism. During this period the most significant figure associated with the skepticism of the Academy was Carneades (c. 219–120 BCE), who wrote nothing at all. Ultimately, Aenesidemus (of whose works we have only a brief description in the commentary of the ninth-century Byzantine scholar Photius on the contents of his library) broke away from the Academy, ca. 90–80 BCE, and revived the old pyrrhonian skeptical practice that the Academy had largely retreated from during the two hundred-odd years of its development post-Arcesilaus. Sextus offers the last and most extensive view of pyrrhonism, in the context of its dialectical conflict with stoicism, and of the varying alterations of skeptic and stoic thought that had taken place up until Sextus's time, ca. 200 CE.

Pyrrhonian skepticism may be characterized as a practice in three parts. First, it is characterized by a therapy consisting of arguments—generalized under various systems of "modes"—intended to establish *isostheneia*, or the equivalence of force of competing positions, arguments, claims, vis-à-vis truth. This equipollence is usually established via appeal to the general unreliability of sense perception and to the relativism or conventionalism of normative claims. Equipollence then leads to *apatheia*, or a fundamental impassivity in the face of competing claims to truth, carrying with it a concomitant suspension of belief—*epochē*. For example, I argue that an orange tastes sweet at the end of a savory meal; however, I also point out that if you bite into one after eating baklava soaked in honey, it tastes sour. You feel that both of the points I have made are equally compelling, and this leads you to suspend judgment concerning the issue of whether oranges actually are sweet or sour—you form no belief regarding that issue, you think that sometimes they appear sweet and sometimes they appear sour, and you leave it at that. Saying or thinking that "this orange appears sweet, or seems sweet, or tastes sweet" does not commit you to a belief about what the orange is really, truly like; it is just a report about how things appear to you at any particular moment—as Sextus remarks, the pyrrhonists "assent to feelings forced upon them by appearances."[6] On this view, "belief" requires being committed in some reasonably robust way to a statement about the way things actually are. Philosophers of antiquity might have put their fairly commonsense notion of what counts as a belief in this way: Belief requires assent to the truth of some proposition or statement of fact regarding the essence or nature of some thing or some state of affairs.

Ultimately, the pyrrhonian therapist is to be so successful in establishing the equipollence of competing claims that the propensity to establish any belief with regard to the truth or falsity of any particular matter gradually fades away in the patient. Thus, secondly, having rid oneself of the propensity to form beliefs, the patient lives and acts on the basis of the apparent—*phainomenos*—alone, with absolutely no commitment whatsoever to the truth or falsity of what appears—indeed, with no serious interest whatsoever regarding the issue of truth or falsity itself. The pyrrhonist eats an orange because it appears to be edible, not because the pyrrhonist believes the proposition "oranges are nourishing" is true—the pyrrhonist has no such belief. And finally, third, a life free of belief, utterly unencumbered by any opinions as to what is, in fact, true or false, lived on the basis of appearances alone, leads to tranquility—*ataraxia*, literally, freedom from disturbance.

Ataraxia is the positive goal of skeptical therapy, and as such the pyrrhonian skeptical practice must be seen not merely as a philosophical exercise, but essentially as a practice of everyday life to which the philosophical argumentation characteristic of Hellenistic skepticism—its modes of argumentation, its principles and utterances—is subordinated. Debate does continue concerning the role of *ataraxia* in the skeptical program: whether it should, in fact, be considered the positive goal of therapy—since this could risk a slide into beliefs concerning the relationship between *epochē* and *ataraxia*—or whether *ataraxia* should be considered to follow suspension of belief "fortuitously," as Sextus notes in section 29 of his *Outlines of Skepticism*. Most significantly for my purpose here, pyrrhonian skepticism was not essentially an epistemological position, or a philosophical school, or a manner of argumentation. Sextus also repeatedly notes that pyrrhonists themselves considered skepticism to be an *agogē*—again, a way of life, characterized by freedom from belief and subsequent freedom from disturbance.

While not essentially an epistemological position, the complete dissociation from belief of any kind that is characteristic of the pyrrhonist is consistent with the following metaphysical and epistemological positions: The pyrrhonist does not know if things do or do not have particular essences or natures. If things do, in fact, have particular essences or natures, the pyrrhonist does not know what they are. The pyrrhonist also does not know if knowledge is possible or not possible; the pyrrhonist's ignorance extends to not knowing whether or not things can, in fact, be known. To the question "Is it possible that you will know something—that you will correctly believe something to be true—later this evening?" the pyrrhonist responds "I don't know, maybe, I guess." In this way pyrrhonism differs radically from Levinas' negative dogmatism. Negative dogmatism is, essentially, an epistemological position that holds that it is true that nothing can be known. The pyrrhonist truly does not know whether things can be known or not, does not care whether things can be known or not, and has, appropriately, nothing further to say on the matter.

When the pyrrhonists do offer an account of their methodology and principles, of what they say in dialogue with their dogmatic other, the self-refutation of pyrrhonian utterances is well recognized by them. But their own response to this self-refutation is not to separate diachronically the gesture of their utterance, their saying, from the thesis that their utterance affirms, their said, as Levinas does in attempting to safeguard skepticism's recurrence:

> For [the Skeptics] suppose that, just as the phrase "Everything is false" says that it too, along with everything else, is false (and similarly for "Nothing is true"), so also "In no way more" says that it too, along with everything else, is no more so than not so, and here it cancels itself along with everything else. And we say the same of the other skeptical phrases. Thus, if people who hold beliefs posit as real the things they hold beliefs about, while the skeptics utter their own phrases in such a way that they are implicitly cancelled by themselves, then they cannot be said to hold beliefs in uttering them.[7]

Instead, the pyrrhonist simply points out the fact that they neither affirm nor believe anything that they utter—their saying has said nothing at all. All that is said by them is always already said under erasure, as it were. And in fact, there never was any pyrrhonian saying, any *me voici*, in the first place.

WHOLLY OTHERWISE THAN LEVINAS' "SKEPTICISM": NO *SAYING*, NOTHING *SAID*

Levinas argues that skepticism overcomes its self-refutation by means of the diachrony between the affirmative *me voici* of its saying and the apparent negation of its own affirmation in its said—in its alleged thesis that "nothing can be known." This is the kernel of his invocation of skepticism, which, as I have noted, is ultimately marshaled to counter the objection of self-refutation directed toward Levinas' own thesis of the priority of ethics over all theory. But here, within this kernel, consideration of the pyrrhonist skeptical practice brings the analysis to a complete stop—or perhaps to a suspension and dislocation. I will argue in the final section of this essay that this dislocation carries us from Levinas' concern with the epistemological stakes of skepticism's movement to an encounter between Levinas' own conception of ethical first philosophy and the ethical stakes of living a life devoid of belief.

I have noted—ironically, of course—the fact that several of the main figures within the development of pyrrhonian skepticism wrote nothing at all. However, it is not simply the rather dramatic gesture of official silence on the part of pyrrhonists that begins to trouble Levinas' analysis. Pyrrhonists did engage in debate. They argued with their opponents. Sextus and others did attempt to offer an official and detailed record of what pyrrhonism was—of both its thinking and its practice of life. But the attempt to glean from all of this notions of their Levinasian saying—of their *here I am* "exposure without reserve to [their] other" (*OB* 168)—or of their said—their thesis, their statement of what they believed true—remains quite hopelessly problematic.

The pyrrhonian mode of argument was dialectical, and in this sense entirely parasitic on dogmatic thought. For example, Cicero writes of Arcesilaus's method and its proximity to that of Socrates: "This method was not preserved by [Socrates' immediate] successors, but Arcesilaus revived it and required that those who wished to hear him not ask for [his opinion], but should themselves say what they thought; and when they had done so, he maintained the contrary position."[8] Arcesilaus gave no opinions, put forward no views of his own. He affirmed nothing. In order to hear Arcesilaus, one first had to say what one thought. Then, whatever one said, Arcesilaus "maintained the contrary position" (*ille contra*). Arcesilaus did not affirm the opposite of what was said; rather, whatever an interlocuter's opinion might be, he simply spoke to the contrary. Pyrrhonian discourse, in general, put forward no positive positions, affirmed nothing. Even the elaborate accounts of pyrrhonian methodology and discourse offered by Sextus in *Outlines of Pyrrhonism* and *Against the Mathematicians* should not be understood to present any affirmative positions whatsoever, as the previous quotation from Sextus makes clear. Whatever appears to be affirmatively asserted in pyrrhonist writings is merely a response maintained in the face of an opposing position that is well known and that as such is assumed by the author. The positive assertions are merely negations of what everyone else has said about any matter and are neither affirmed nor believed. *Outlines* clearly indicates this with its seemingly endless series of . . . "if you say . . . if they say . . . when it is said . . . then we say. . . ."

The pyrrhonist invites the dogmatist, the one who believes, to enter into a dialogue, but under one condition—that the pyrrhonist not be asked to say what the pyrrhonist believes, since the pyrrhonist believes nothing and has nothing to say about anything. All that will be said is what the dogmatist believes, followed by the pyrrhonist parroting its contrary, neither affirming nor believing in the slightest—remaining utterly aloof from his own utterance. This parroting really only expresses what dogmatists themselves ought also to believe, given what they say and the rational methodology that guides them. The pyrrhonist merely says to the dogmatist the contrary of what the dogmatist had said and then leaves it to the dogmatist to fill in the blanks, to think what the weight of the contrary claim should carry the dogmatist to think: "If I affirm this, then on the basis of my own beliefs and the rational methodology that guides me, I should also affirm the contrary and hence admit that what I affirmed is unclear and suspend judgment in this regard." The pyrrhonist, in dialogue, will not fill in these blanks for the dogmatist, will not say "if you believe . . . then you should also believe . . ." since this would indeed constitute the pyrrhonist's own saying and said—an utterance that affirms what the pyrrhonist *believes* about what his opponent should be thinking. But since pyrrhonists believe nothing, they say nothing; and in pyrrhonist discourse and writing, in turn, there is also no said—there is only the *vous voilà* of dogmatic thought. There is merely the sound and the encryption of the dogmatist's own undoing, his own self-refutation, the fatal aporia and weightlessness that constitute the thought of those who want to believe.

It is clearly a difficult task for us boisterous moderns—like Levinas and those who have commented on Levinas on skepticism—to come to grips with the complete dissociation from their own thought, from everything going in their heads, that the pyrrhonists sought to cultivate. In a sense, the pyrrhonist gesture constitutes an absolute refusal of the modern subjectivity assumed by Levinas and others as the bearer of skepticism's alleged theses. The pyrrhonists' gesture, *par excellence,* is to refuse to be the subject of their thinking, to refuse to take propriety over anything they thought, anything that thinking itself thought within them. And whether one believes or not that they, or anyone, could ever truly succeed in this enterprise is beside the point if one is interested in truly understanding what pyrrhonism was all about.

Bernasconi forgives Levinas, at least, for this blindness to the radicality of pyrrhonism's movement, by noting that "he gives no indication of having made a detailed study of the history of skepticism."[9] But even after noting the difficulty of discerning what, exactly, the ancient skeptics thought, and the fact there were, clearly, alternative forms of skeptical thinking in the Hellenistic age, Bernasconi still persists in following Levinas in characterizing skepticism as a simple epistemological position that holds, believes, affirms, *says* the claim of negative dogmatism.[10] The pyrrhonists say nothing of the sort and, at the end of the day, have never said anything at all—they merely acquiesce to what appears within them, to what nature forces upon them, about which, however, they will never speak, or think, in the affirmative.[11]

This is all very well and good. In response, though, it can be argued that the apparent hopelessness of Levinas' invocation of skepticism's self-refutation in the face of a reckoning with skepticism's full force and power—with the pyrrhonism that is its most vital core—can be solved by a simple maneuver: simply cross out "skepticism" wherever that word appears in Levinas' text, and write "negative dogmatism" in its place—a fine risk, to maintain what Levinas himself, but not skepticism, has said. But this would be to do violence against the very thinking that Levinas has attempted—though, ironically, inattentively—to sustain, as a kin to his own thought. I will leave the issue of whether we may, simply, let Levinas "off the hook" for his neglect of his skeptical other and, in addressing it, his failure to maintain an unreserved openness. But to simply maneuver around this issue by means of a "find and replace" function would also be to foreclose upon the consideration of what an encounter between Levinasian first philosophy and the pyrrhonist practice of life might have looked like. In the final section, I will briefly sketch what I take to be the possible stakes of such an encounter.

LEVINAS AND PYRRHONISM

In her essay "Between Betrayal and Betrayal," Grebowicz takes up Bernasconi's examination of Levinas and skepticism, which itself is an attempt to intervene within and build upon the exchange between Levinas and Derrida on this issue, centering around Derrida's "Violence and Metaphysics" and "At This Very Moment in This Work Here I Am," and Levinas' *Otherwise than Being* and "Wholly Otherwise." Grebowicz introduces a useful Lyotardian motif in order to both displace and further the polylogue between these figures concerning Levinas' invocation of skepticism. She argues that Levinas, by introducing the distinction between saying and said in order to solve the riddle of skepticism's eternal recurrence and thus to preserve the legitimacy of both it and Levinas' first philosophy, has failed "to attend to the stakes of his own discourse."[12] She says, quite straight-forwardly, that the stakes of skepticism are epistemological, and those of Levinas, ethical. She then mentions Bernasconi's own attempt to finesse this issue by pointing out that, once upon a time anyway, skepticism was "as much a way of life as a philosophical position."[13] Grebowicz remains unconvinced by this tack, how-ever. She argues that skepticism can only have an ethical stake in "the vulgar sense, the sense of how to live a 'good' life,"[14] and that this precludes any serious consid-eration of skepticism as an ethical enterprise on any sort of par with Levinas' ex-traordinary attempt to establish ethics as first philosophy. Bernasconi and Levinas should both have known better and not confused the stakes of first philosophy with the vulgar egoism of skeptical practice.

Though some might consider his gesture somewhat flippant, I have always been attracted to Nietzsche's first attempt at a revaluation of all values in section II of "The Four Great Errors," where he suggests, head-shaking, eyes rolling, that we should just forget about ethics and morality and go about the business of living a happy life; and "virtue" will follow from it as fortuitously, perhaps, as tranquility follows suspension of belief. So I take issue with Grebowicz's dismissal of, let us say, the practical implications of the skeptical practice of life in the face of first phi-losophy. Grebowicz is correct to argue that the stakes of these enterprises are dif-ferent. One is practical, one is ethical, though in what sense "ethical" it is nearly impossible to discern. Certainly, Levinas himself seems to admit that, at least in its said, his first philosophy is theoretical, philosophical, thematic. Be that as it may, I would like to expand, briefly, upon the ethical dimension of Levinas' invocation of skepticism in the light of what I have shown to be an inattention—a carelessness, a certain effacement of the skeptical other—to that which Levinas is addressing in and through this invocation. I will then close with some remarks concerning the ethical dimensions of the pyrrhonian practice of life in the light of Levinas' ethics as first philosophy.

Even a mildly attentive reader will have probably discerned an implicit accusa-tion I have been making against Levinas throughout the course of this essay, so it is time to say it. It is already a kind of violence to say that the skeptic, the other who is the skeptic, has said anything at all, let alone that what the skeptic has said has been refuted, let alone that the skeptic persists in saying what he has said in spite of the fact that he has been refuted.

It has been said that Levinas' challenge to Western thinking may be best ex-pressed by the demand that we "let the other speak," finally, and for the first time. With an enterprise as inscrutable as Levinasian first philosophy, it is, of course, en-tirely problematic to suggest that this or any other such simple formulation goes to its core. It is beyond the scope of this essay to even articulate, let alone resolve, the myriad difficulties presented to us by this articulation of the "Levinasian gesture." I will merely persist, at this point, to speak as though there truly is something to it.

Levinas' non-encounter with pyrrhonism presents us with a very concrete example of one of the central difficulties of his call to open ourselves unreservedly to the other, to address ourselves to the other in such a way as to allow the other to be who she is, as she "speaks" to me. When we consider the pyrrhonists as other, to "allow" these others to speak is already to have done violence to them. And this violence is not simply a matter of "quoting" the other, accurately or inaccurately, of appropriating their saying toward this or that end. Nor is it merely the phenomenological violence that Derrida alluded to when he noted that addressing the other in any way must also involve bringing the other into the sphere of intentionality and meaning, and hence cannot escape the ipseity that dogs phenomenology in general, despite all of its best efforts to the contrary. The violence has already occurred before the other has ever spoken, in the very gesture of *allowing* the other *to speak.*

The pyrrhonist chooses not to speak. To "allow" them to speak is to force them to become the bearer of subjective meaning; to force them to become a subject, which they are not; to force them to act as if they believed in things, as if they were, in some robust sense, attached to that which they utter, there, in or alongside of, their saying. But they are not. To the violent gesture of being allowed to speak, the pyrrhonist reposes in silence. They have nothing to say, about anything, ever. If you want to hear them speak, say what you think, and they will say the opposite but not say it—all that you've heard when their saying is done is the recoil of your own thinking. And let us, please, not get too carried away at this point with the irony of the pyrrhonist having just been spoken for.

I am obviously not the first person to recognize this. Derrida had already done so when he remarked that "the other is not myself—and who has ever maintained that it is?—but it is *an* Ego, as Levinas must suppose in order to maintain his own discourse."[15] The real problem, awkwardly gestured toward here, is the seemingly intractable problem of alterity that plagues any thinking conducted on the basis of a supposition of modern subjectivity, the modern subjectivity with which phenomenology is shot through to its core. Pyrrhonism reminds us of the trace of a way of life wholly otherwise to that conceived on the basis of modern subjectivity, and at the very least, I hope I have managed to remind us of the enormous difficulty of invoking this prior way of being in any modern context.

Recognizing this, and the enormous difficulty of pretending to speak of this prior way of life as I have been pretending to do, can we also at least try to appreciate what it might have been? Shall we reduce this way of life, for example, to a vulgar egoism, in pale contrast to, for example, the sophistication of Levinasian ethics as first philosophy? Or can we do better by it? How did these pyrrhonists live?

The story has been told often enough for it to be believed in contemporary scholarship: Pyrrho lived with his sister and did "women's work." He brought chickens and pigs to the market, cleaned house, washed piglets, and god knows what else. True, out of his indifference, he left his pal Anaxarchus floundering in a ditch, but all was forgiven. He was odd. But he did what appeared to him to be the right thing to do, regardless of how scandalous it was according to the beliefs of the culture in which he was raised. He did not share those beliefs.

In his paper on skepticism and Levinasian first philosophy, Paul Davies approaches the issues involved by focusing on the fundamental asymmetry of the latter.[16] Davies notes that one way of thinking of Levinas' project is as an attempt to, felicitously, capture the very real fact of self-sacrifice, of concrete acts of altruism, within ethical and phenomenological categories and descriptions that seem, by their very nature, to immediately preclude any such attempt. People do, as Davies notes, give their lives for others, in some if not many instances, I suggest, not on the basis of the beliefs that they hold or the principles that allegedly guide them, but because in the very instance of action what they do simply appears to them as what must be done. There, in the instant, the other appears to them, and they simply do what they do.

Can we imagine, then, a nonsubjectivity that refuses propriety, that refuses to attach itself to what thought thinks within it? This would be to believe nothing, but to merely assent to what appears to and within one, and to act on that basis alone. To Pyrrho, it appeared that what was to be done was to clean the house and to wash the piglets. Others, almost all those around him, believed wholly otherwise and mocked him for it. This is not a facile matter. Would a response, devoid of belief, to nothing but the other as the other appears, begin to approach a fundamental priority of what is called "ethical" action, over theory, theme, principle, category—a fundamental asymmetry that demonstrates itself in what people actually, thoughtlessly, do?

Notes

1. Robert Bernasconi, "Skepticism in the Face of Philosophy," in *Re-Reading Levinas,* ed. Robert Bernasconi and Simon Critchley (Bloomington: Indiana University Press, 1991), 152.

2. In addition to Bernasconi, see Jacques Derrida, "Violence and Metaphysics: An Essay on the Thought of Emmanuel Levinas," in *Writing and Difference,* trans. Alan Bass (Chicago: University of Chicago Press, 1978), and "At this very moment in this work here I am," in *Re-Reading Levinas;* Margret Grebowicz, "Between Betrayal and Betrayal," in *Addressing Levinas,* ed. Eric Sean Nelson, Antje Kapust, and Kent Still (Evanston, Ill.: Northwestern University Press, 2005); Paul Davies, "Asymmetry and Transcendence: On Scepticism and First Philosophy," *Research in Phenomenology* 35 (2005): 118–40.

3. Adriaan Peperzak, "Presentation," in *Re-reading Levinas,* 54–55.

4. Most obviously, Putnam's "brain in a vat" and Lehrer's "Googols," which are both simple variations of Descartes' evil deceiver. Others, such as Stroud and Unger, have developed sophisticated skeptical arguments, in the latter case in support of a strong form of skepticism. See Hilary Putnam, "Brains in a Vat," *Reason, Truth and History* (Cambridge: Cambridge University Press, 1981); Keith Lehrer, "Why Not Scepticism?" in *The Philosophical Forum* 2, 3 (1971): 283–98; Peter Unger, "A Defense of Skepticism," in *Philosophical Review* 80 (1971): 198–219; Barry Stroud, *The Significance of Philosophical Scepticism* (Oxford: Clarendon Press, 1984).

5. "About Sextus himself we know very little. He probably lived in the second century CE, and seems to have been a doctor of the Empirical school. It is perhaps fitting that he survives, for us, merely as a name attached to a skeptical position and a host of arguments" (*Sextus Empiricus: Outlines of Skepticism,* trans. and ed. Julia Annas and Jonathan Barnes [Cambridge: Cambridge University Press, 1994], xii). (Sextus's title, *Pyrrhoneae hypotyposes,* is usually given the more literal translation *Outlines of Pyrrhonism.*)

6. "When we say that Sceptics do not hold beliefs, we do not take 'belief' in the sense in which some say, quite generally, that belief is acquiescing in something; for Sceptics assent to the feelings forced upon them by appearances. . . . Rather, we say that [Sceptics] do not hold beliefs in the sense in which some say that belief is assent to some unclear object of investigation" (ibid., 6).

7. Ibid., 6. See also *Life of Pyrrho: Diogenes Laertius,* 9.76, in *Hellenistic Philosophy: Introductory Readings,* 1st ed., trans. Brad Inwood and Lloyd P. Gerson (Indianapolis: Hackett, 1988), 176.

8. Cicero, *On Goals* 2.2, in *Hellenistic Philosophy,* 165.

9. Bernasconi, "Skepticism in the Face of Philosophy," 150.

10. The extent of this misunderstanding can be shown in the following passage by Bernasconi: "Levinas seems to uphold the view of skepticism as self-defeating as soon as its own argument is turned against it. He refers to that moment when skepticism does not hesitate to affirm 'the impossibility of statement while venturing to *realize* this impossibility by the very statement of this impossibility.' Metrodorus of Chios . . . exemplifies what Levinas has in mind. He allegedly said, 'None of us knows anything, not even this, whether we know or do not know'" (ibid., 150). Bernasconi mentions Levinas' reference to skepticism's *affirmation* (Levinas himself says "affirms the impossibility . . .") of the impossibility of statement. As applied to pyrrhonism, this reference is false. Pyrrhonism does not affirm the impossibility of statement—it affirms nothing. If you argue that statement is possible, it merely parrots the contrary argument, that statement is impossible, without affirming or believing any of it. It has no opinion on the matter—the possibility or impossibility of statement is your concern; it is not the concern of the pyrrhonist, who neither knows, cares, nor believes. And yet Bernasconi offers as an example of this skeptical thesis the utterance of Metrodorus of Chios. No one knows (Bernasconi's "allegedly" proviso) what Metrodorus of Chios actually said or thought. But taken as a figure, or really as an utterance representative of the pyrrhonist tradition, which is how he is generally taken, his alleged statement was not anything that he was affirming as true. In fact, the statement could be considered to be just another way of saying, precisely, "I affirm nothing, I believe nothing—when I utter anything there is no *me voici,* there is no 'here I am, here is *my* thought, myself, opened unreservedly to you'; there is nothing but your, you dogmatist's, way of saying thrown back at you, and constituting nothing more than your own undoing." No affirmation. No saying. No said.

11. Blanchot and Barthes' thinking of "the neutral" comes close to capturing the radicality of this way of being that remained a possibility prior to the imposition of modern subjectivity upon everything and everyone.

12. Grebowicz, "Between Betrayal and Betrayal," 79.

13. Bernasconi, "Skepticism in the Face of Philosophy," 150; Grebowicz, "Between Betrayal and Betrayal," 79. I will withhold my urge to correct them both by stating that skepticism was indeed a way of life and *not* a philosophical "position," if, as I assume, holding a position requires affirming some thesis believed true.

14. Grebowicz, "Between Betrayal and Betrayal," 80. And here we should again remind ourselves that in making recourse to the practical, pyrrhonist vein of Hellenistic skepticism, Bernasconi and Grebowicz are no longer talking about the skepticism invoked by Levinas; they are talking about something else altogether.

15. Derrida, "Violence and Metaphysics," 110.

16. Davies, "Asymmetry and Transcendence," n. 2.

THE TIME AND LANGUAGE

OF MESSIANISM: LEVINAS

AND SAINT PAUL

10

Bettina Bergo

LEVINAS AND THE ANCIENTS: SAINT PAUL AS MESSIANIC THINKER

To address the question of Levinas' relationship to the Ancients—which certainly entails more than one question—we should be mindful of Levinas' relation to the Greeks *and* to ancient Jewish thought like that of Philo, who gave us the first exhaustive exploration of the meaning of the name and the letter. Rather than examining Philo, I will turn to a dimension of Jewish thought that has arguably arisen out of prophetism: messianism.

When does messianism begin in Jewish thought? With Isaiah? With Amos? While much of the meaning of Jewish messianism has become skewed by Christian readings of the "Old Testament" as realized by the "New," the meaning of messianism breaks down according to two axes: (1) the time of the temple and the time of the universe; and (2) the resources available to the free creature (to save itself) and redemption from without. The messianism understood as restorative concerns the promise of the reestablishment of the temple, which is also the promise of a *Heimkehr,* or return to a home. Restorative messianism therefore takes on political or mystical qualities. It conjoins with apocalyptic messianism in the question of the end of cosmic time, at which point the Messiah returns. As Levinas reminds us, it is a classic Jewish thesis "that there is a difference between the future world and the messianic era" (*DF* 60). The messianic era would represent an intermediary time before the end of the world and the world to come. It is like a sort of hinge between the future and the atemporal. Levinas writes, "As for the future world, it seems to exist on another level . . . it therefore concerns a personal and intimate order, lying outside the achievements of history that wait for humanity to be united in a collective destiny" (*DF* 60).

The messianic dimension of redemption and return has the paradoxical character of being at once close to the prophets *and* close to what the twentieth century called the New Thinking. In Levinas' recapitulation of the debate between Rabbi Eliezer and Rabbi Joshua—concerning the meaning of and path to salvation—it is important to remember that Rabbi Eliezer is silent at a crucial moment. Rabbi Joshua declares, with a decisive hermeneutic intervention: "And I heard the man clothed in linen . . . [swear] by him that liveth for ever that it shall be for a time . . . [and then] all things shall be finished" (*DF* 74). To this, R. Eliezer says nothing. But R. Joshua means that redemption imposed from without is necessary, because in the fact of human freedom lies an inevitable gnosticism of good and evil. Does this gnosticism touch messianism? Can messianism stand as a pure promise apart from the dangers of freedom and evil? If that were the case, would prophetism serve any purpose? What would messianism be, other than a strange calendaric announcement that we humans, like the earth, are *zum Tode:* beings unto-death? In other words, if redemption from without is inevitable, and constitutive, then the prophet does no more than remind us of our finitude, which is trivial.

In messianism, two axes, that of time, that of redemption, each pose separate difficulties. But the second axis requires the first axis to become meaningful. Messianic time must evince a different quality than world time or the atemporality of the world-to-come if the problem of return and redemption is to move past the aporetic position in which we find it when the debate between R. Joshua and R. Eliezer grinds to a halt. This appears to be the contribution of Paul, when we read him as messianic thinker within and without the rabbinic tradition. This alone recommends a close inspection of a study written in response to Jacob Taubes' seminar on *Paul's Letter to the Romans.*[1] The question is taken up again in Giorgio Agamben's *The Time that Remains.*[2] We will thus read Agamben's Paul as an "ancient" and as an early, post-prophetic messianist. Ultimately, we will show the crossings between Agamben's Paul and Levinas' late philosophy. I believe that this best shows in what way Levinas' philosophy is messianic and how his philosophical messianism undercuts those elements of "restorative" messianism in his Jewish texts without denying them.

Agamben's argument moves through six fundamental themes: service, the inversion of the world, the call, time and presence, the name, and the verb. I will follow, here, the theme of temporality. It is that theme that best elucidates Levinas' messianic temporality as it appears in 1974.

First, let us elucidate the meaning of service. "*Paulos doulos christou iesou, kletos apostolos aphorismenos eis euaggelion*": "Paulus" meaning "little ('*Paulus . . . minimum est*')" (*TR* 10–11) is the messianic *signum* that the "apostle" and "slave" (*doulos*) gives himself. Eschewing the debates about the choice of this *signum*, Agamben argues that this Sha'ul, member of the tribe of Benjamin, designated himself "negligible" following a logic that appears elsewhere in the epistle. Sha'ul, a name of prestige, has become "as if not" Sha'ul: the noble has become the slave. This is the effect of messianic force. The messianic principle, as Agamben shows, performs two transformations. First, it transforms time: between the resurrection of the *christos*—meaning simply the "anointed" or, for Jews, the "Messiah" (*TR* 15)—and the Messiah's return, lived time has contracted. Time has changed from Heidegger's "whiling away" or "not right away" into an awaiting.[3] The essential point is that in the Aramaicized Greek of the *koinè*, the adjective or noun *christos* is not a proper name but simply means "messiah" (*TR* 18). We have projected on the Pauline text "our own forgetting of the original meaning of the term" (*TR* 18). It is to the Messiah that Paul is "slave." But he is a slave without having lost his human freedom, as we will see (*TR* 29). Concerning the inversion of worldly things: Paul's choice of *signum* entails what rhetoric calls "metanomasia" (setting on a different name as sign or surname that better expresses one's status or nature). The change of name "realizes the intransigent messianic principle . . . in which those things that are weak and insignificant will, in the days of the messiah, prevail over those things that the world considers to be strong and important" (1 Corinthians 1:27–28) (*TR* 10).

It is neither Paul's nor Agamben's concern to establish *who* "Jesus" is. He is simply the Messiah, not the creator of a new religion. For Paul, he is the Messiah by virtue of his resurrection. The decisive question concerns the ontological and eschatological *meaning* of the new order. Agamben writes, "What does it mean to live in the messiah, and what is the messianic life? What is the structure of messianic time?" (*TR* 18). Service to the Messiah and the inversion signaled by Paul's adoption of a surname point us toward the question of the complexity of time become double. That is, the messianic time *unfolds* in Paul's letters as a post-messianic present that inhabits but does not change the essence of world-time. The Messiah has come; his quality as "*christos*" is demonstrated by his resurrection. What remains is the "time-between," that is, between a de facto death and the awaiting of the return. This messianic present corresponds to what Levinas calls the "adverbial modification" of being, which carries on like a dynamism or a verb and is not substantially altered by messianism.

In respect of its fragility, Levinas and Agamben are in agreement about messianism, Pauline or ethical. The diminution of the social significance of those who have been called is one effect of the messianic inflection of time. This diminution, signaled by Paul's and others' choice of surnames, is related to the personal responsibility that Levinas insists is the most particular *and* universal dimension of the messianic calling. There, where factual history is doubled by a new "counter-history," personal responsibility becomes the affective correlate (Levinas) of the time of awaiting (Paul).

THE MESSIANIC LOGIC OF THE AS-NOT: THE NAME AND THE CALL

In the messianic time that Paul expatiates, the proper name ceases to function as a mode of individuation and social value. Many adopted "those non-names . . . of mere slaves . . . [thus] we often find . . . nicknames that describe a physical quality, such as *micos, micros, micrine* (little, tiny). . . . The apostle must, like a slave, lose his name, whether it be Roman or Jewish" (*TR* 11). The "principle of a particular transformation," due to the "messianic condition," meant that "all juridical conditions" are not "simply abolished"—but certainly suspended (*TR* 13).[4] This is the famous antinomianism attaching to all messianic movements. In Paul, this transformation will be denoted "*klēsis*"—a word translated too simply as "call," issued to those, the "*klēseis*," who form a *messianic community:* the *ekklēsia* (*TR* 22). If these terms bring unfailingly to mind all those concepts formed around "eccles-," this is only the sign of a singular *forgetting:* the central, *messianic* sense of an event whose implications defy the logic of the everyday, including that of simple linear temporality.

In Paul's logic, the call comes to pass within everyday facticity but does not change it. We are summoned precisely "in or as [that] which we are called" (*TR* 23). The call applies indifferently to all, independently of their station. Agamben takes pains to show that the call need not lead to Max Weber's socioeconomic interpretation of quietism (remain as you are, though you are but a slave, etc.). The point is that Nietzsche, Weber, Benjamin, and Taubes are *all* reading Paul—differently—and they are doing so through Luther's translation. The upshot of this is a number of philosophical thematics whose dissimilarity belies a shared messianic core.

Like Heidegger's ontology, Levinas' ethics turns on a messianic call that is without specific content—or whose content combines injunction and exhortation. This is why Derrida aptly called it an "Ethics of Ethics" in 1967.[5] As Agamben puts it, the messianic call is "essentially and foremost *a calling of the calling*" (*TR* 23). That makes it the concrete condition of possibility of any summons to surpass our factical condition *without changing our perceptible status or way of living* (*TR* 23).

While this tautological structure (that is, a "call of the call") also reminds us of Heidegger's *Dasein* and its indifference to its worldly status, the key to this tautological structure is this: it is a lexical "tensor" of a "special type." Expressed in the Greek as *hōs mē* or "as not,"[6] Paul borrows this "tensor" from prophets like Ezra (*TR* 25). A tensor is a periphrasis that functions, not to move the field of meanings within a specific discourse from one concept to the next, but rather to set the first field into a tension specific to itself—"in the form of the *as not:* weeping, [for instance] as not weeping" (*TR* 25).

Agamben explains this in the following way: "According to the principle of the messianic *klēsis,* one determinate factical condition is set in relation to itself—the weeping is pushed toward the weeping, the rejoicing toward the rejoicing. In this manner, it revokes the factical condition and undermines it without altering its form" (*TR* 24). Thus the messianic changes the world without altering any factual, *phenomenologically describable* dimension of it. The messianic "is not another figure or another world: it is the passing of the figure of *this* world" (*TR* 25; emphasis added). We find a similar tensor in Levinas' examination of the adverbial in *Otherwise than Being or Beyond Essence.* There the adverb, in its relation to the verb, inflects the active quality of being; but rather than durably changing it, it leaves a trace: the disinterestedness found in justice. Thus messianism in Levinas' late philosophy functions surreptitiously as the modalization of being analogous to the relation of the adverb to the verb.

Paul's *hōs mē,* or as-not, ultimately points out the fragility—or finitude, as Levinas called it—of existence, *and* makes what is unlike it into a question. "The Pauline passage on the *hōs mē* . . . may thus conclude with the phrase . . . 'for passing away is the figure, the way of being of this world'" (1 Corinthians 7:31; *TR* 24). This notion of radical finitude is brought to light by a messianic consciousness whose principal distinction is that *in Paul's case,* which is one of an apocalyptic messianism not unfamiliar to the Jewish tradition, *the messiah has already come.* Because the messiah has already come, the passage from Corinthians can be opposed to the more fatalistic vision of the mysterious *Qoheleth,* supposed to have been the wizened Solomon ('Ecclesiastes'): "A time [*kairos,* in the Septuagint] to weep and a time to laugh, a time to mourn and a time to dance . . . a time to seek and a time to lose . . . a time for war and a time for peace" (*TR* 25–26). *Qoheleth* separates these times—which Paul assembles in the indifference to and of a world and its temporality, standing under the sign of the Messiah's passage and the promise of his return—because for the older text, the question of the Messiah cannot be compared to Paul's understanding of it here.

In that most peculiar perspective, in which mundane particularity—of social station, everyday pursuits, accomplishments, expectations—has been preserved and "sublimated" *messianically,* the world and its objects are for our use. And we cannot fail to note Heidegger's appropriation of Paul, here, in his depiction of entities as if *Zuhanden* or "ready-to-hand." A similar notice is taken of the world, under a more positive light, by Levinas when he speaks of "living from good soup, air, light, spectacles, work, ideas, sleep" (*TI* 110). The messianic modification—a *supplement* that defers meaning toward an indeterminate future into which it slices—means that there is no further reason to focus on domination over things or persons. "To be messianic, to live in the Messiah, signifies the expropriation of each and every juridico-factical property (circumcised/noncircumcised; free/slave; man/woman) under the form of the as not. *This expropriation does not, however, found a new identity;* the 'new creature' is none other than the use [above all, the peaceable use of the world] and the messianic vocation of the old" (2 Corinthians 5:17; *TR* 26, emphasis added).[7]

This "pure praxis," in which one lives just as one was yet has become as if new, is not simple quietism (Weber). But the *manner of its modification of traditional practice remains invisible to the unbelieving eye.* Is this comparable to Levinas' insistence that one can choose "to be otherwise," but one "cannot otherwise than be"? The claim is similar in its insistence on the non-phenomenality of responsibility and fraternity. Of course, Levinas' claim is entrenched in more sophisticated debates about the grounds of phenomenology and with Heidegger's hermeneutic ontology. Nevertheless, the similarity of spirit between Paul and Levinas here, leads me to find, in Levinas' last great work, a distinct *messianism.* The image of that messianism will be completed at the end of this essay. It is enough to emphasize, for now, that this is the messianism in which, in the midst of real or anticipated political disorder, "my responsibility is the more irreplaceable" (*DF* 95). I recall this remark because when Levinas first presents his interpretations of messianism in 1961, he runs up against the meaning, simultaneously regulative and pragmatic, of the State of Israel. His philosophical answer to this will be that authentic messianic light shines through personal responsibility. In addition, he will fuse the contradictory positions of the rabbis into a single messianic lesson: we are both free to be ethical, and redemption comes from the other. In that way, being ethical does not foreclose the possibility of evil, and redemption from the other translates into subjective responsibility. The "Messianic Text" is a complex document that we cannot examine here. Let us retain Rabbi Abbahu's response to a heretic who asks him "When will the Messiah come?" His answer, "When darkness covers those people who are with you" (*DF* 93). The *Min* (heretic) is devastated: "'You have condemned me!' exclaims the *Min.* Or . . . your messianism is not universalist . . . you are a man of closed morality" (*DF* 93).

In Levinas' reading, R. Abbahu's darkness is the condition of a new light. The new light brings the rabbinic text around to Levinas' philosophical position. There is a universalism in Judaism that the *Min* has not seen in it. Levinas sees it, as does Paul. Rather, Paul extends it. The light can only be seen—against the glare of philosophy and politics' indefatigable *pretense* to light and truth—when, in the darkness that besets those "who have lost the meaning of the political and the consciousness of its grandeur" and who find themselves "outside, alone and abandoned" (*DF* 94), one recognizes, in responsibility, a different light and a different call. That call concerns everyone, but it changes nothing in the world. It is a call to responsibility that we do not choose but that chooses us.

Here is a distinct parallel between Levinas' "messianism" and Agamben's reading of Paul, which proceeds in the world under the logic of the as-not or the *hōs mē*. The only thing lacking in Paul is the restorative messianic dimension (the reestablishment of the temple or a home for the Jews), which is abrogated by contraction of time measured on the imminence of the Messiah's return. That is consonant, too, with Levinas' reminder that there is a difference between the messianic world and time, and the world to come.

UNIVERSALISM, PARTICULARITY, AND UNIVERSAL PARTICULARITY

The dual status of universalism, such that a community lives out its calling for and on the stage of world history; or again, the universal message of a messianic call is offered to everyone and no one in particular: this duality cuts across Levinas' Jewish writings and his philosophy. It is likewise the great question in the messianic Paul. Did he not destroy the very ground from which he drew his call, abrogating both the sign of the pact and the letter of the Law? Are not the new "particulars" the "*klēseis*," those proto-Christians? Under the logic of the *hōs mē*, neither universalism nor particularism is to predominate. These categories are bracketed by Paul, although such an *épochè* as this could hardly extend indefinitely in historical time.

We must understand universalism and particularism in their relation to the themes of uncoerced, repentance versus the acknowledgment of some salvation from without. When Levinas cites the extended debate between R. Eliezer and R. Joshua, the two above-mentioned *Tannaïm*, concerning *when* the messiah would come, this was really a question about two core values in the scheme of redemption: freedom and choice versus "paternal" intervention. Levinas does not decide these positions, as though both were necessary. But in Paul, the messianic event has sublimated human freedom in such a way that it too is transformed by the as-not. Clearly, for Paul, if this were not the case, and freedom opened to the possibility of evil while the Messiah's return stood in doubt, moral Manichaeism would be unavoidable. Paul thus opens an exit door in the midst of these dilemmas precisely in his capacity of a messianic thinker.

Because a trace of difference remains between Levinas' philosophy and his Talmudic readings, we must insist that in the secular reflection messianism enters through the face of the Other. Freedom is neither sidestepped nor abrogated. The face remains "the only being I can wish to kill" (*TI* 198), and murder is the annihilation of what is least protected yet most ethically powerful—the simple interruption of alterity. Even if we do not murder the other because of their freedom (which also seeks recognition as nonrelative), murder is a matter of my freely struggling *to twist free of responsibility*. I try this without God or state hindering my élan. This constitutes the essential difference between Levinas' messianic thematic (in his philosophy) and his avowed agnosticism in rabbinical debates.

I believe this tension is why Levinas explores messianic *sensibility* in 1974, appearing to make the other into pure immanence. He has understood R. Nachman's musing, already in 1961, and adapts it: "The Messiah is myself " (*DF* 89). As an interruption of flowing time, as a responsibility I cannot elude, the sensuous equivalent of a messianic intervention is the short-circuiting of freedom by suffering for-the-other. In this way, Levinas also sublates the freedom–external salvation debate. Moreover, he implies universalism in the hermeneutic reduction of dialogue and social commitment to their sensuous conditions of possibility. He would thus say, as he did already in 1961, that it is a secondary matter whether or not "the world is wholly guilty" (*DF* 77). Guilty or not, by this logic, the Messiah will come in the sense that the other carries more eschatological weight than human freedom carries ontological significance.

A strange logic. But we find aspects of it in Paul as well. The Messiah came "when evil [was] triumphant in the world," at least for and among Jews. And his resurrection, whatever the transformation it effects in the world, subjects the community of the called to the neutralization of every worldly value. The *hōs mē* effect produces a simple if perplexing equivalence, rather a pneumatized inclusive disjunction: "weeping as if not weeping," is the ultimate intensification that changes identity and passions into the indifference of awaiting. We might go so far as to say that a comparable hope glimmered in Heidegger's attempt to adumbrate Dasein's authenticity, thanks to anxiety, which functions analogously. Be that as it may, the difficulty of Paul's text, as Agamben reads him, is that it is the first *Jewish* text to inquire into the time and circumstances *after* the passing of the Messiah. It concerns messianic time, but in a way that exceeds the messianic hope of R. Joshua, for whom the Messiah must surely come, because without him, human freedom points to perdition.

WEAK MESSIANISM

The question for us remains the same: Is there a way of articulating the restorative messianism that, in Levinas at least, praises and underscores the necessity of a site for the community, with the philosophical messianism in which the site has become a self bearing what it cannot contain? If Levinas and Heidegger resemble each other in their attention to a personal site (the "me" and Dasein, respectively) that contains that which it cannot think (the Other for Levinas, the call of Being for Heidegger), the meaning of history is utterly different for them. In this, Levinas is closer to Paul, for whom history had become the *hope* of a community facing an imminent return. Heidegger, by contrast, approached authentic history, in 1927, according to a structure of repetition, not hope. A people constructs a destiny for itself in confronting collectively its abandonment and repeating historic possibilities; only thus can it acquire "its own superior power" which is to be "free for death" (*BT* 436).

Yet even in Paul, the messianic future implies the repetition of an indescribable event (the resurrection). And this poses the question of the relationship between the messianic present and the Jewish past. If this relationship has become that of the present and the past of all those "nations" who would hear the call, the hiatus created by the messianic logic leaves the connection to Judaism difficult. The *hōs mē* logic spares Paul the lion's share of this difficulty, but it enters into secular messianism most poetically with Walter Benjamin. Indeed, Levinas scarcely does better, in 1974, when he writes about the need for a "relaxation of essence" and war. Benjamin too argued for a weak messianism:

> The image [*das Bild*] of happiness, which we cherish, [is] tinged through and through by time, to which the course of our own existence has simply referred us. Happiness, which can awaken envy in us, is only in the air, which we have breathed, with people, to whom we could have spoken. . . . It oscillates, in other words, in the representation of happiness together, inalienably, with that of redemption [*die Erlösung*]. Things are likewise with the representation of the past. The past carries with it a surreptitious link [*heimlichen Index*], through which redemption is indicated . . . [thus] there consists a secret appointment [*Verabredung*] between the generations that were and our own. In that case we are anticipated on earth. In that case, a *weak* messianic force is co-given to us, as to every generation [*wie jedem Geschlecht*], to which the past has a claim.[8]

Benjamin dramatizes our relation to the past, providing glimpses of public places, air breathed and savored, as though the formal repetition of something like Heidegger's resoluteness scarcely convinced him. This *geheime Verabredung* recalls the vividness of Paul's *klēsis*. Both confer a weak messianic force. That is not to say that Benjamin's and Paul's messianism are the same thing. It has to do with the options for *figuring* the lived senses of an intensification (of time and space) that is affective and transformative. Whether we insist on its secularization or not, this temporalized intensity called messianism carries a peculiar historicity. It is *not* that of historical materialism, according to Benjamin. It is *not* that of the history of the Jewish community, according to Paul. Is it sufficient, as a mapping of the relationship between the historic past and the present, to assure us of the ultimate triumph of good in the wake of freedom? Given the impact of the *hōs mē* on freedom, the question remains open. Nevertheless, the central characteristic we find in Paul's conception of messianic time as contracture is that we now bear with us a secret appointment and a weak force. For Benjamin, as for Paul, the upshot is the transformation of language, requiring a new emphasis on the performative over the denotative, an attention to detail, and a renewed understanding of the *Bild* and the symbol.

LANGUAGE AND MESSIANISM: THE NOMINAL PHRASE

Since his earliest original writings (1935), Levinas maintained an ontological distinction between the embodied self and the "I" of intentionality. The latter was concerned with and given to reflection on itself and its world, while the former was sensible-affective. If Idealist philosophy conceived the I as a pure activity of positing, or as the always accompanying awareness of itself (apperception), Levinas will make two significant shifts in this concept of the I. First, he holds the embodied self and the I *together*, but without synthesis or positing, such that the I can feel itself hindered by its "self," sometimes yearning to escape the heavy materiality of that self. Second, the close bond between the two implies that the I of intentionality and reflection may project itself forward and appear to itself to live "in time" as though through repeated out-stancings or ec-stases (Heidegger's understanding of lived time). However, the bonding of the pair—that is, the incarnate, affective self and the I as formal, cognitive movement—implies that human consciousness is grounded in a progressive *present time,* not firstly in futural projections. This dual subject awakens out of itself and falls to sleep "into itself," curled up under a blanket, on a daily basis: the present is thus the ineluctable *stance* taken by the self-I dyad.

The priority of the present, which Levinas takes from Husserl's phenomenology, appears anything but messianic at first glance. Is messianism not the *contraction* of time become end-time, that hiatus of which Paul speaks repeatedly, anticipating not the *coming* of the Messiah, but his *return?* Nevertheless, if we read Levinas and Paul together, we find a contraction of time in both of them. This contraction-intensification arises from two sources. For Paul, it is the affective intensification of being-called or *klēsis,* with all that this entails of transformations of self and community. For Levinas, a similar intensification of time—likewise comparable to contraction into an instant—comes to pass in the face-to-face encounter with the other person. Moreover, by the time he writes *Otherwise than Being,* Levinas will have sketched this contraction as a permanent, albeit fragile, dimension of subjectivity itself—like the *hōs mē* overlay of Paul's messianic logic. This rethought subjectivity is still understood as responsible, because it is inhabited by alterity prior even to becoming self-aware. I can only be I insofar as I discover that something elects me and, in so doing, disempowers or "disappropriates" me such that I am both unique and, in a sense, nothing. But that is the logic of Agamben's remnant. The later Levinas thus presents us with a subject repeatedly experiencing itself as "too tight in its skin" (*mal dans sa peau*), in the contracture of an instant (*OB* 104). Messianic time, no matter how much it anticipates end-time, is *lived* in the intensification of the moment. And the theme of the moment structures Levinas' phenomenology of ethical investiture, whether that investiture comes to pass from without or from within the I-self. To be sure, focusing emphasis on the lived immediacy of (messianic) time, in preference to a time given over to projection or ecstasis, does not tell us what "time" itself is. It simply elucidates the modality by which time, if it "is" at all, is lived experience.

A fundamental insight about time in *Otherwise than Being* came to Levinas through Heidegger, who took it from his reading of Paul. In that work, Levinas argues that philosophy is a discourse on, or disclosure of, what-is: philosophy is ontology. But what-is, or Being, is that which concerns only an entity, the human being, who is concerned with its own existence. From Husserl's phenomenology we know that the human being experiences itself as if living in a time that is continuous, comparable to Penelope's tapestry. "Being's essence is the temporalization of time, the diastasis [stretching out] of the identical and its recapture or reminiscence, the unity of apperception [of self by the I]," writes Levinas (*OB* 29). In this phenomenological time, whether we project ourselves into the future or restore what we can of the past, an identical whole maintains the unity of the existent that is us. Yet another time, the passive, unremarked time, say, of aging, unfolds "behind our backs." It poses the question of an *other* time—a time that did not happen to an ego holding sway in its world and over the consciousness that it is.

"This modification by which the same comes unstuck or parts with itself, undoes itself into this and that, no longer covers itself over and thus is disclosed," writes Levinas (*OB* 30). This "is the *esse* [the verb-like way of being] of every being," he insists. In the host of intentional modifications, all of them tied simply to the fact of our concrete embodiment, the unsticking of the whole takes place in us while we are unaware. It "does not await, in addition, an illumination that would allow for an 'act of consciousness'" (*OB* 30).

The modification occurs passively. Like aging, it proceeds with or without consciousness, only to be remarked on *post facto*, which proves that the lapse between one moment represented by consciousness and another is irrecoverable *but is nevertheless a paradoxical, passive effectivity*. How can effectivity be passive? What happens in aging is a fact, but it happens *to us*. We cannot blame our bodies for aging. In this respect, Levinas asks, "Does temporality go beyond essence?" (*OB* 30).

So far as it may do so, it changes nothing about Being, understood in its verb-like quality. Instead, the modifications by which the whole becomes "unstuck" or older than itself, or affected by a sensation it is half conscious of—all these modifications would amount to the signs of a metaphoric "lining" that doubles the coat called representable existence. The "locus" of this lining, if it is not unconsciousness or pre-consciousness, is sensibility. Writes Levinas: "There is consciousness [as representation, only] insofar as the sensible impression differs from itself without differing; it differs without differing, other within identity. The impression, as though it had blocked itself up, clarifies itself in 'unblocking itself'; it undoes that coincidence of self with self in which the 'same' smothers beneath itself, as under a candle snuffer. It is not in phase with itself; *just* past, *just about to* come" (*OB* 32).

This "differing without differing"—illustrated by the examples of extreme passivity *in which the self gets out of phase with itself* in the fact of aging and in the continuous modifications of sensibility—expresses in a secularized way the as-not logic with which Paul worked to bring to light the "lining" that messianic time represents vis-à-vis the time of the world. This strange temporality—which cuts across the *just* past that we cannot recover, and into the *about to* come, which we cannot foresee—resembles Benjamin's minute "*Apellnischer Schnitt,*" which doubles ordinary time with messianic time, modifying the just past and the uncertainty to come.

How to express such a temporality? Recourse to tropes is a necessity, especially insofar as they disrupt the hierarchy of parts to whole by which time is given its everyday "logical form." Levinas resorts to metaphors and metonymy. He "invents" catachreses by insisting, for example, that "fraternity" precedes biological brotherhood *but also* consciousness of "kinships" of *any* kind. He resorts to parataxis and performative speech, eliminating (in the French) recourse to the verb "to be." What is the purpose of his stylizations? Paul, Agamben recalls, resorts to the "nominal sentence" (*TR* 127–28). When Paul speaks of believing in Jesus the Messiah, he precisely avoids writing "Jesus the messiah" or worse, "Jesus *who is* the messiah." "It is as if, for Paul, there were no space, between *Jesus* and *messiah,* for the copulative *is* . . . [Paul] only knows *Jesus messiah*" (*TR* 127). Using the linguistic discoveries of Émile Benvéniste, Agamben argues that the nominal phrase differs from the predicative phrase that has recourse to "to be," in that the nominal phrase *refuses predication* and, with predication, it also refuses to posit existence or to attribute qualities. "The nominal sentence escapes this distinction [that is, the fundamental division of ontology: the ontology of existence and the ontology of essence], presenting a *third type,* irreducible to the two other types" (*TR* 128; emphasis added). The novelty of the nominal phrase lies in its holding together—in the tension created when an entity is grasped spontaneously in its multiple nature, without positing a subject and "its" accidents—two or more states or qualities without attributing them to some fundamental "ground." Agamben writes:

> I love beautiful, brunette, tender Mary; 'I love Mary' not because she is 'beautiful, brunette, tender,' in the sense of possessing such and such an attribute. The moment when I realize that my beloved has such and such a quality . . . then I have irrevocably stepped out of love, even if . . . I continue to believe that I love her. . . . Love has no reason, and this is why, in Paul, it is tightly interwoven with faith . . . [faith thus presents us with] a world of indivisible events, in which I do not judge, nor do I believe that the snow is white and the sun is warm, but in which I am transported and displaced in the snow's-being-white and the sun's-being-warm. In the end, it is a world in which I do not believe that Jesus, such and such a man, is the Messiah. . . . I only believe in Jesus-Messiah; I am carried away and encaptured in him, in such a way that "I do not live, but the Messiah lives in me." (*TR* 128–29)

The nominal phrase thus strives for and suggests a situation of alterity-in-the-same—better, alterities *as* the same. As a faith that Agamben argues is closer to the Hebrew *emunah*, or confidence, than scholars have insisted, Paul's messianic promise sets us outside the "work" of the verb "to be" as copula or illumination of qualities. So far as it succeeds, it carries us into a complex moment in which neither qualities and substance nor subject and object have yet been distinguished. This attempt at expressing what is pre-reflective or pre-predicative is also the stuff of lived experience. It is complicated, because it "folds together" what grammar sets apart for the purposes of denotation and predication.

This is very close to Levinas' work with parataxis, not to mention the astonishing way he inundates us with figures drawn from distinct registers. Speaking of the other-in-the-same, he will also speak of "kenosis," "recurrence," "obsession," "substitution," even "psychosis"—never intending to tie us to a unique level of discourse that might claim the "experience" originally called responsibility for a single "discipline" that would master it. But does the nominal phrase follow as radical a tack as Levinas takes when he insists that it is the verb that brings Being to light, and therefore any event that took place "beneath the notice or threshold" of Being would have to be expressed differently, nonverbally? We know that Levinas tried several experiments to that end. He speaks of the ad-verbial, inflecting or modifying be*ing* imperceptibly—his first paradox. He speaks of words said that must then be un-said, that is, stated and then disclaimed for the predicative, ontologizing gestures they contain. Whatever the success of his wager, the end is comparable to Paul's nominal phrases.

To express that which has seized hold of us and intensified our experience of time, space, and our very relations with others—and to state this as experience in its immediacy—a (para-)language must be conceived, in which "I am transported and

displaced into the being-the-white-snow," and so forth. These extraordinary experiments in conceptual and predicative collapse are widespread in literature. Here,
however, they would take on an almost mystical strangeness were it not for the signal insight, resurrected in the twentieth century by thinkers as different as Heidegger and Walter Benjamin, that *language fashions existence,* language brings Being to
light for and as what it is. Arguing against Buber, Benjamin put this succinctly by
equating speaking and acting. "I do not believe that the word stands somewhere
farther away from the divine [*göttlichen*] than does 'real' action," he wrote to Buber.
The task of language amounts to "the crystal-clear elimination of the unsayable in
language. . . . Only the intensive directing of words into the kernel of the innermost silence will achieve true action," he concluded.[9]

To my eyes, this is Levinas' intent in his late work. It is the unheard-of messianic action Paul is attempting, as well, in his nominal phrases and his performative expressions. At the beginning of his philosophical career, in the *Logical
Investigations,* Husserl acknowledged that the entire sphere of intentionality—the
whole life of human consciousness—was doubled or encompassed by linguistic signification. Heidegger took a step further: language is the house of Being. Being
comes to be in certain modalities of expression, most notably the poetic. Language,
or *logos,* gathers Being and illumines it. For finite beings, language gives rise to
what we experience as existence. This is very far from disputes about the status of a
"copula"; rather, those disputes proceed from an unstated supposition: what is
"there" *is* there as it is, only to appear to us who are disposed to repeat it linguisti-
cally and in conceptual representation. But that presupposition is unprovable. If it
maintains that our task is simply to mirror what-is with our concepts, then it remains undeniable that there is no stance (other than our plurality of perspectives)
from which we could insist that we are approximating "what-is" independent of us.
That is why messianic language is more than "simply" poetic; it enacts and deploys
other relations, as if recognizing that words and concepts do not match up with
naively pre-given objects "out there." Messianic language plunges us instead into
what is not us, filling us with what is other than us, shaping our experience of time
and affectivity—even as it evaporates like the air and breath Benjamin describes in
his aphorism—outside the consolidation that accompanies conceptualization obe-
dient to its grammatical temporalities.

BY WAY OF CONCLUSION:
DISCOURSE *IN ACTION* AND CHRONOGENESIS

The difficulties of messianic time, that time of passivity, awaiting, and intensive
contraction, were examined by Franz Rosenzweig and Levinas as well as by Heidegger, all of whom were aware of the challenge of expressing it in a denotative

and constative language that posits: "that stands over there," "this is that," "this is unlike *x*," and so on. The bond between temporalization and language thus proves reciprocally generative. But it must also be restrictive, insofar as attempted breaches of grammatical propriety invite a skepticism that is always fundamentally naïve in its belief in adequation. The specificity of the "messianic" moment amounts to expressing a now that is neither punctual nor set in a linear succession. This now was grasped by the linguist Gustave Guillaume before World War I. Guillaume investigated the "operational time" [*temps opératif*] that elapsed in the process of consciousness constituting an image of an experience undergone just before consciousness identified it. While this operational time remained a time invisible in the apparent spontaneity of representation's activity, it was nevertheless representation's constitutive moment. Language, to Guillaume, was unconsciously aware of the "lapsed," constitutive mind-time. For the "operational time" required to form a thought-image figures in many languages as the modalization of verbs' potentialities. Agamben recalls, in this regard:

> [Guillaume's] "operational time" [*temps opératif*] is the time "that the mind takes to realize a time-image [*une image-temps*]. An astute study of linguistic phenomena shows that languages do not organize their verbal systems according to . . . the linear schema . . . but rather by referring the constructed image back to the operational time in which it is constructed. In this way, Guillaume is able to complicate the chronological representation of time by adding a projection in which the process of forming the time-image is cast back onto the time-image itself. In so doing, he comes up with a chronogenetic time, which is no longer linear but three dimensional. The schema of chronogenesis thus allows us to grasp the time-image [or time represented] in its pure state of potentiality (time *in posse*), in its very process of formation (time *in fieri*), and, finally, in the state of having been constructed (time *in esse*), taking into account all of the verb forms of language (aspects, modalities, and tenses) according to a unitary model. (*TR* 66)

Guillaume's reintegration of "operational time" not only expanded linguistics' possibilities for approaching time in its modes and aspects, but it opened the approach to "a pure instance of discourse *in action*" (*TR* 66), which entails a present that carries in itself what is not itself. This present—potentially constituted, in the process of being constituted, and then reviewed as a construction or completed representation—makes us aware of the lag, or lapse, already noted by Levinas between the life of the embodied self and the I of intentionality. The lag is close to what Guillaume calls "chronogenesis": the dynamic coming to pass of lived time as "lost" but nevertheless diversely reconstitutable. Guillaume's enlargement of our understanding of verb functions rejoins Levinas' 1974 extension of the meaning of the adverbial in human experience. It joins Benjamin's insistence that language, as "the crystal-clear elimination of the unsayable [through] the intensive directing of words into the kernel of silence," is true action. But none of these insights are possible without an understanding of the creative "ontological" force of language.

So far as language reaches toward the very lapse of time implicit in its own reflective and enunciative operations, it has expanded to include—to bring to light—that delay in the presence of the utterance or enunciation itself. To this Agamben adds, "since Benvéniste makes enunciation [*énonciation*] the very foundation of subjectivity and consciousness"—as Levinas also does, though Levinas calls it "responding-to"—"this lapse and delay would then be a part of the structure of the subject" itself (*TR* 66–67). It is precisely this lapse, expressed and conceived perspectively as passivity, lost "time," aging, a pre-thetic sensibility *qua* being-affected that Levinas is expressing when he explores the metaphoric "site" in which the subject comes to be, always "carrying" within it what it could not cognize *as* itself: the other-in-the-same.

We have now had about a century of philosophical and linguistic work adumbrating the subject, non-idealistically, as dialogical in its origin, as coming to be through its openness to what is not itself and to what calls it out of itself. Because such an approach to the heteronomous subject can be described, it finds its way into ordinary predication, albeit always under threat by skepticism. Yet when the modalities and aspects of temporality, which Guillaume studied, are set into language *in something like a simultaneity* (that is, expression of the lived simultaneity of the gap called "operational time" *plus* the representation it made possible), more experimental modes of expression—like recourse to performative language—become necessary.

There is not enough space here to discuss the performative in Levinas or that discerned by Agamben in Paul's letters. What we can say is that much of this "dialogical" thinking about time and subjectivity has no messianic aspirations. Agamben's argument turns in large part on the definition of Paul as a radical messianic thinker who started from the perspective of time's lining as the "time which remains." Up to now, we have been led to believe that this time was basically linear: starting from the death of the Messiah and extending until his return. This is why insisting on the contraction of time, or making the claim that this time-intensity "cuts into" the past while overhanging the future, appeared implausible. Using Guillaume, Agamben explains this time-intensity as infra-temporal, because for Paul, it is "the time that time takes to come to an end" (*TR* 67). In other words:

> This is not the line of chronological time (which was representable but not thinkable), nor is it the instant of its end (which was just as unthinkable), nor is it a segment cut from chronological time [which would run from the resurrection to the end of time]; rather, it is operational time pressing within the chronological time,

working and transforming it from within; it is the time we need to make time end, and in this sense: *the time that is left to us* [*il tempo che ci resta*]. . . . (*TR* 67–68)

This "time that remains" does *not* require that chronological time come to an end. What it requires is that thetic acts, acts of positing and representation of lived events, come to rest with the completion of a viable representation. In that moment of resting or constructive completion, we find that the infra-temporal *effort* of Guillaume's "operational time" has been at work, as an irrecoverable lapse. Reaching that lapse means moving back through the in-credible (the messianic, for Paul) that has seized hold of us. Or it requires an effort at uncovering the significance of sensibility, which was Levinas' project in *Otherwise than Being*. Thus, to the question of whether Levinas, the philosopher, was also a messianic thinker, we may answer in the affirmative—understanding that the time that remains, in the "operational time" of sensibility, is a time in which, for him, the "Good" comes to pass. But now the messianic question gives rise to another one. For his extraordinary effort to portray Paul as the first radical Jewish messianist, has Agamben convinced us that *this* difficult messianism, founded as it was on the having-come of the messiah and *not* on his older more prophetic quality as one who is to-come, is Jewish and not apostasy, not "Christ-ian"? The answer to these questions exceeds the limits of this essay.

NOTES

1. Jacob Taubes, *Paul's Letter to the Romans: A Socio-Rhetorical Commentary,* trans. Ben Witherington III and Darlene Hyatt (Grand Rapids, Mich.: Eerdmans, 2004).
2. Giorgio Agamben, *The Time that Remains: A Commentary on the Letter to the Romans,* trans. Patricia Dailey (Stanford: Stanford University Press, 2005). Hereafter abbreviated *TR*. Where the French linguists G. Guillaume and E. Benvéniste are cited, French expressions are preserved in brackets.
3. Martin Heidegger, *Being and Time,* trans. John Macquarrie and Edward Robinson (New York: Harper and Row, 1962), 402. Hereafter abbreviated *BT*.
4. Elsewhere in the text the claim is made still more forcefully: "It may apply to any condition; but for that reason, it revokes the condition and puts it radically into question in the very act of adhering to it." *TR* 23.
5. Jacques Derrida, "Violence and Metaphysics," trans. Alan Bass (Chicago: University of Chicago Press, 1978), 111.
6. The *hōs mē* could also be translated as "as-if-not," because it expresses a logic that blurs distinctions of name, status, and existential condition. As such, it is not real in a positivistic sense, but it is in no way a simple fantasy time.
7. 2 Corinthians 5:17: "So if anyone is in the messiah, the new creature [*kainē ktisis*]: everything old has passed away; see, everything has become new." Cf. *TR* 27.

8. Walter Benjamin, "Über den Begriff der Geschichte [Of the Concept of History]," in *Gesammelte Schriften,* vol. 1, no. 2, ed. Rolf Tiedemann and Hermann Schweppenhäuser (Frankfurt am Main: Suhrkamp Verlag, 1980), 694.

9. Cited in David Biale, *Gershom Scholem: Kabbalah and Counter-History* (Cambridge, Mass.: Harvard University Press, 1979), 104.

PROXIMITY IN DISTANCE:

LEVINAS AND PLOTINUS

John Izzi

11

It may appear strange to find the name of Emmanuel Levinas, a phenomenologist and an advocate of alterity, beside that of Plotinus, who (from Levinas' perspective) would be considered a metaphysician of identity. My intention is not to dismiss the differences between them but to show that a close reading of their philosophies, at least according to some decisive texts, helps us to understand how the same has a relation with the other that preserves both the identity of the same and the alterity of the other. The other here refers to what Vladimir Jankélévitch calls the "absolutely other, always-wholly-other" (*absolument autre, toujours-tout-autre*).[1] I want to show that the same's relation to the other consists of proximity in distance.

TRANSCENDENCE AND THE OTHER

The principal danger to avoid when describing the relation between the same and the other, one that Levinas believes is often disregarded, is the theoretical construction of an all-encompassing totality. Levinas is opposed to the philosophical tradition started by Parmenides and continued by Spinoza and Hegel, in which he would situate the thought of Plotinus (*TI* 102–104). These philosophies are interpreted by him as misguided attempts to reconcile the same and the other by incorporating them into a larger whole (*TI* 104). Levinas objects to totalization because he believes that it excludes the transcendental relation, which alone preserves the *identity* of the same and the alterity of the other.

It will here be helpful to recall the opening section of *Totality and Infinity*, where Levinas establishes the framework for the essay on exteriority that follows.

Taking his point of departure from the distinction between need and desire, he describes the relation between the same and the other as transcendence. Needs can be satisfied. They complete me by filling a lack, by being "reabsorbed into my own identity as thinker or possessor" (*TI* 33). Objects of need do not transcend my being because they are eventually assimilated by me. In need, I ultimately long to belong to myself. My search for self-completion ends in self-possession, whereby the other gets reduced to the same.

Desire tends toward a term that is other than anything I can think or possess. The term of desire neither fills a lack nor completes my being; rather, it expresses itself in and through distance. The desired is not comprehended by a concept; it is known or understood (*entendu*) by its alterity (*TI* 34). This alterity is irreducible to a concept because it transcends my grasp. Unlike need, desire is set in motion by an alterity that "overflows" all my efforts at conceptualization, that eludes all my attempts to possess it. The term of desire and I cannot merge into a totality because the alterity of the other and the identity of the same would be abolished. The transcendence that permits their relation would thereby be *eliminated*.

Positioning himself in the tradition founded by Plato (*Republic* 509b9), Levinas places the term of desire, the Good, beyond being. "The Good is good *in itself* and not by relation to the need of which it is wanting; it is a luxury with respect to needs. It is precisely in this that it is beyond being" (*TI* 103). For Levinas the Good transcends the totality of being because desire for it does not result from a lack but occurs in one whose essential being is already complete. As the title of his second major work suggests, the Good is "*autrement qu'être ou au-delà de l'essence*" (otherwise than being or beyond essence).

Not surprisingly, Plotinus develops the Platonic tradition of placing the Good beyond being. The life and term of desire are as boundless for him as they are for Levinas. In the treatise entitled "How the Multitude of the Forms Came into Being and on the Good," Plotinus writes: "When you cannot grasp the form or shape of what is longed for, it would be most longed for and most lovable, and love for it would be immeasurable. For love is not limited here, because neither is the beloved, but the love of this would be unbounded" (VI.17.32).[2] Desire for the One is boundless because the One, unlimited by form (*eidos*), is beyond being (*epêkeina ontos*) and substance (*ousia*):

> Since the substance [Intellect] which is generated [from the One] is form . . . the One must be without form. But if it is without form it is not a substance; for a substance must be some one particular thing, something, that is, defined and limited; but it is impossible to apprehend the One as a particular thing, for then it would not be the principle, but only that particular thing which you said it was. But if all things are in that which is generated [from the One], which of the things in it are you going to say that the One is? Since it is none of them, it can only be said to be beyond them. But these things are beings and being: so it is "beyond being." (V.5.6)

Plotinus distinguishes the One (*to hen*) from the totality of being, which he attributes to Intellect (*nous*). It is in Intellect that we find being and substance. For Plotinus, being and substance can only be predicated of something, of what is limited by particular shape and form. Each object perceived by our senses reflects its corresponding form in Intellect. Intellect, the seat of intelligible forms and the site where archetypes of sense-objects reside, contains every possible being and substance. In this capacity it comprises a totality.

The One is not a totality because, as principle (*archê*) of Intellect, it is beyond being, substance, and intelligibility. We can conceptualize only what has form, what is found in Intellect. Referring to the One, Plotinus says that "it would be absurd to seek to comprehend that boundless nature" (V.5.6). The Plotinian One is incomprehensible because, as principle of form, it is without form. The absolute formlessness of the One results in its distance from the same. Similar to the Levinasian term of desire, it transcends anything I can think or possess. I do not relate to the One as I do to an object, because in itself it is nothing (*mê on*).

This approach to Plotinus is followed by Reiner Schürmann, who describes the One as a verb rather than as a noun.[3] We cannot say that the One does something, that it is the agent of an activity. The Plotinian One must not be understood as a being because it is irreducible to the idea of substance. It is not a being that unifies but the "event" (*événement*) of unification (*henôsis*). "The One will not be the most exalted noumenon. Rather, its 'nature' must be discovered in the way it operates at the heart of phenomenon." As principle, it is not a foundation, which Schürmann correctly locates in Intellect: "It will be 'first' only as factor of order among beings and their constellations."[4] The One is the process by which the various configurations of historical meaning are given. "It is the very movement of coming to presence in all that is."[5] It is precisely the non-substantiality of the One that, by allowing free play of difference, liberates it from ontotheological domination by the same.

Like Levinas, Plotinus recognizes the necessity for transcendence with respect to the life and term of desire. The totality of being of which Levinas is critical is found in Intellect, not in the One. Plotinus is as unyielding as Levinas in his insistence on not reducing the alterity of the other to the identity of the same. Both philosophers understand the alterity of the other as transcendence insofar as they both maintain that the other's alterity consists of non-being. But to what do they attribute the identity of the same, whereby the same is distinguished from the other and therefore able to have a relation with it?

DIFFERENTIATION AND THE SAME

Levinas refers to the process whereby the same establishes its own proper identity as the egoism of separation. For him separation of the same from the other must be "so complete that the separated being maintains itself in existence all by itself, without participating in the Being from which it is separated" (*TI* 58). We do not participate in the other because it is neither a being nor a totality.

Levinas names this separation "atheism." Atheism here refers to a position that is "prior to both the negation and the affirmation of the divine . . . [and it is] the breaking with participation by which the I posits itself as the same and as I" (*TI* 58). My soul or psychic being is by nature atheistic because it is produced by separation from God. As an I, an egoism, I dwell outside the other insofar as I am at home with myself (*chez moi*).

My capacity for atheism, or my ability to be at home with myself, testifies, according to Levinas, to the glory of God. It is only because I am naturally atheistic that I may choose to believe in God and thereby willfully to relate the identity of the same, my I, to the alterity of the other (*TI* 58–59). Levinas understands the egoism of separation as providing the necessary condition for the same to have a relation with the other because it does not reduce the identity of the same to the alterity of the other.

Plotinus takes a different approach to the idea of differentiation. The fifth *Ennead* opens with a description of the origin of evil:

> The beginning of evil for them [souls] was audacity and coming to birth and the first otherness and the wishing to belong to themselves. . . . Since they do not anymore see their father [Divine Intellect] or themselves, they despise themselves through ignorance of their birth and honor other things, admiring everything rather than themselves, and, astonished and delighted by and dependent on these [earthly] things, they broke themselves loose as far as they could in contempt of that from which they turned away; so that their honor for these things here and their contempt for themselves is the cause of their utter ignorance of God. (V.1.1)

If we work past the anthropomorphic language of Plotinus, we shall see the complexity of differentiation in his philosophy. Plotinus distinguishes between two moments of differentiation: the estrangement of souls from Intellect, which he discusses in the above citation, and the otherness of Intellect with respect to the One, which he describes in subsequent sections of the same *Ennead*.

When he speaks of the former, Plotinus equates ignorance of self with ignorance of God, here understood as Divine Intellect. Self-knowledge requires concomitant knowledge of God because, as foundation of my soul, Divine Intellect constitutes my home. Like Levinas, Plotinus believes that, to be at home with myself, I must realize my identity, whereby I become complete. The difference between them lies in the fact that for Plotinus self-identity is found by participating in a totality. My essential being is found in Divine Intellect, the site of every form and the seat of Universal Soul.

Evil, which Plotinus attributes to ignorance of myself and my foundation, re-sults from the first moment of differentiation, estrangement of souls from Intellect. Estrangement arises from the longing for independence, the wish of the same to belong to itself. This yearning for self-assertion and for life independent from my foundation leads to dependence on "earthly things" because it is toward them that I turn for completion.

When estranged from Intellect, when ignorant of my foundation and identity, I value things only in their capacity to fill a lack within me and therefore to be as-similated by me. Similar to Levinasian need, estrangement of souls from Intellect leads to the reduction of things to myself because the wish for independence re-quires the satisfaction and eventual elimination of this lack within me. Independ-ence is fully realized only when I am complete, when I do not need or depend on other things.

Self-love here results in self-contempt. *Enneads* V.1.1 continues: "For what pursues and admires something else admits at the same time its own inferiority; but by making itself inferior to things which come into being and perish and consider-ing itself the most contemptible and the most liable to death of all the things which it admires, it could not possibly have any idea of the nature and power of God." The soul needs Intellect in order to realize its essential being. But its quest for completion will not be dissatisfied if it turns its gaze inward to Intellect, be-cause the being found there is imperishable and the soul's dependence is on its own identity as part of Universal Soul.

Self-assertion and estrangement of souls from Intellect end in alienation from self because self-identity is found in Intellect. At the same time, since Intellect is divine for Plotinus, separation from it results in alienation from God. Like Levinas, Plotinus sees differentiation as providing the necessary condition for the relation between the same and the other. But he understands the first moment of differen-tiation, the estrangement of souls from Intellect, to prevent this relation because it does not establish self-identity of the same.

Both Levinas and Plotinus agree that I have a relation with the term of desire only after I have been differentiated from it. For Levinas, this process occurs in the egoism of the same; for Plotinus, it takes place in the return of souls to Intellect. Does Plotinian self-identity truly lead to differentiation of the same since it results from participation in a totality? My primary concern is to establish the identity of the same in regard to the other, the One, which transcends Intellect. The second moment of differentiation, which alone provides the necessary condition for a relation between the same and the other, is found in Intellect's otherness with respect to the One.

Unlike the estrangement of souls from Intellect, the otherness of Intellect in relation to the One does not lead to alienation. Rather, it establishes the identity of the same as other.

This [Intellect], when it has come into being, turns back upon the One and is filled, and becomes Intellect by looking towards it. Its halt and turning towards the One constitutes being, its gaze upon the One, Intellect. Since it halts and turns towards the One that it may see, it becomes at once Intellect and being. (V.2.1)

[B]ut it sees him, not as separated from him . . . the offspring [of the One] is necessarily with him and separate from him only in otherness. (V.1.6)

What does Intellect see when it looks at the One? It sees the alterity of the other. The One fills Intellect with vision of itself, of otherness. Intellect, though inseparable from the One, is nevertheless other than the One. It is inseparable from the One because the being of Intellect depends on vision of the One; it needs the One. Intellect is other than the One insofar as this vision brings to light the alterity of the One as transcending being and therefore as other than Intellect. Here we find the second moment of differentiation, the otherness of Intellect with respect to the One, which provides the necessary condition for Intellect to desire the One because it maintains distance between them. We also find an essential difference between Levinas and Plotinus. For Plotinus, it is possible for need and desire to coexist.

Vision of the One fills a lack within Intellect. But since this lack is filled by vision of the One's alterity as transcending being, the identity of the same is not reduced to the other. As being, the identity of Intellect is other than the One. At the same time, since the being of Intellect is inseparable from vision of the One's alterity, and since the content of this vision consists of non-being or formlessness, the form of Intellect's being becomes itself formless, whereby the identity of the same, of Intellect, becomes other to itself. Plotinus is right to point out that this vision is "hard to put into words. For how could one announce that as another when he did not see, there when he had the vision, another, but one with himself?" (VI.9.10).

THE SAME AS OTHER

Both Levinas and Plotinus describe the relation between the same and the other as distance. They also agree that there must be proximity between the same and the other in order to realize the relation that the experience of distance implies. Levinas locates this proximity in an interior act that opens onto the exterior, in an idea whose content overflows the capacity of thought. He refers to Descartes, whose *Meditations* describe a situation in which the knowing being remains separated from the known (*TI* 48). The *Cogito*, the *I think*, has a relation with the infinite in which the same does not contain the other but remains separated from it. This relation neither unites the same and the other into a whole nor prevents the proximity that relation implies. Descartes calls this relation the "idea of infinity."

Unlike ideas accounted for by the coincidence of objective and formal realities in my mind, the idea of infinity is unique among ideas because the infinity of which I have an idea surpasses my idea of it. The distance that separates infinity from its idea constitutes the content of infinity itself. For Levinas, infinity best expresses the transcendence of the other because "the infinite is the absolutely other" (*TI* 49). It is infinitely removed from the idea that I have of it. The idea of infinity presents to my mind an idea whose content overflows my capacity to contain it. In Descartes' notion of the idea of infinity, Levinas finds the possibility of a relation with the other that guards the other's alterity from possession by the I who thinks it. It signifies "contact with the intangible, a contact that does not compromise the integrity of what is touched" (*TI* 50).

Infinity is not an object of cognition because it cannot be reduced to the measure of the regard that contemplates it. Thought can approach infinity only if it "thinks more than it thinks." Infinity arouses desire. Desire, not cognition, measures the infinity of the infinite because infinity's measure resides in "the very impossibility of measure" (*TI* 62). Desire is not fulfilled by the desired; it is deepened by it. "It nourishes itself, one might say, with its own hunger" (*TI* 34). Continual longing for the other maintains the distance that, by separating me from it, renews my relation to it.

By alluding to Plato's notion of "winged thought" or delirium, Levinas suggests the manner in which the same's proximity to the other comes to pass (*TI* 50). In the *Phaedrus*, Plato distinguishes between thought that proceeds from one who "has his own head to himself" and inspired thought that "comes from a god" (244a).[6] The latter arises from "divine release of the soul from custom and convention" (265a). It marks the end of solitary existence because it consists of being possessed by another. The notion of the same's possession by the other, not of the other, is vital for understanding the relation between them.

Although Levinas' allusion to the Cartesian idea of infinity and to the Platonic notion of divine possession helps him to account for proximity between the same and the other, in my view he falls short of seeing the consequences regarding the same's identity. His concern to preserve the alterity of the other and the identity of the same curtails the significance of the alterity of the same when possessed by the other.

Plotinus provides us with a more thorough treatment of divine possession. Possession of the same by the other, by what overflows the same's identity, calls into question, as Levinas also recognizes, the very identity of the same. It disturbs my being at home with myself. When the familiarity of the same vanishes, I become a stranger to myself; my I becomes unknown by me. Plotinus takes this idea one step farther than Levinas. For Plotinus, the strangeness of my I permits my coming to presence in the other, whereby I become other to myself:

And we shall no longer be surprised if that [the One] which produces these strangely powerful longings is altogether free of intelligible shape; since the soul also, when it gets an intense love of it, puts away all the shape which it has, even whatever shape of the intelligible there may be in it. For it is not possible for one who has anything else and is actively occupied about it to see or to be fitted in. (VI.7.34)

The One, whose alterity overflows all my attempts to possess it, arouses desire. Pursuit of this desire demands that I strip myself of whatever form I contain, because the One as other is unlimited by form. In order to be possessed by it, I must rid myself of all the forms and meaning that I find upon my return to Intellect. This dispossession of the same or deconstruction of self requires that I abandon even my own identity and foundation in Divine Intellect. I must allow myself to be drawn outside the confines of any totality, divine or otherwise, if I wish to be possessed by the other. In short, I must be entirely empty, even of God.

Possession by the One leads to *"God without God"* (*Dieu sans Dieu*), of which Pierre-Jean Labarrière speaks.[7] This God is "truly God" (*Dieu véritable*) because it is other than all divinity that is merely objective. Similar to the idea of infinity in Levinas and to the One in Plotinus, *God without God* is not an object of thought that can be comprehended by the same. This God can only be experienced in and through its alterity, an alterity that nonetheless constitutes my identity: *God without God*, "escaping possession in the very act by which it gives itself."[8] The movement of the same's coming to presence in the alterity of the other occurs in what Labarrière calls "the play of this paradox." Self-identity is found by surpassing the self-established identity of the same. I am truly myself only when I enter the abyss of *God without God* and become other to myself.

As we can intimate the Plotinian One by the expression *God without God,* so we can describe the same, when possessed by the other, as the abyss of *self without self*:

But if it [self] runs the opposite way [toward the One], it will arrive, not at something else but at itself, and in this way since it is not in something else it will not be in nothing, but in itself; but when it is in itself alone and not in being, it is in that; for one becomes, not substance, but "beyond substance" by this converse. If then one sees that oneself has become this, one has oneself as a likeness of that, and if one goes on from oneself, as image to the original, one has reached "the end of the journey." (VI.9.11)

At first, entrance into the abyss of the One does not lead to another but to the strangeness of myself. Still in myself, I am not in nothing. Plotinus distinguishes arriving at myself or *being in myself* from *myself alone*. In the former I have not been moved into the alterity of the other, into the One beyond being and substance, because I am a stranger to myself. Although I experience the alterity of the same, I have not been entirely drawn into the abyss of nothing. My identity as other may be unknown by me, but I remain within the identity of the same. I approach nothing only when I am in *myself alone.*

This latter aspect of self arises from "converse" with the One, whereby I experience myself no longer separated from it, and therefore separated from being and substance. The identity of *myself alone* is what remains when the movement of coming to presence in the One takes another step. But vision of *myself alone* in the One as other is not vision of the One. It is still vision of myself. I have not reached the "end of the journey" because what I see is myself as a "likeness" or an "image" of the One. "But that other [vision of the One], perhaps, was not a contemplation but another kind of seeing, a being out of oneself and simplifying and giving oneself over and pressing towards contact and rest and a sustained thought leading to adaptation" (VI.9.11).

What is this other "kind of seeing" which, though "not a contemplation," describes vision of the One? It is *self without self,* where the movement of coming to presence in the One is accomplished. I must abandon even vision of *myself alone* in the One as other in order to have, or rather to become, vision of the One. I must be "out of" myself because any remnant of self would permit reduction of either the One to myself or myself to the One. *Self without self.* Dispossession of self for possession by the One. Donation of the same to the other. This is "adaptation" or alteration of self into the alterity of the other, where *self without self* sees, where "he himself was not there, if we must even say this: but he was as if carried away or possessed by a god, in a quiet solitude and a state of calm" (VI.9.11).

EXCESS

How does the same have a relation with the other that preserves the same's identity and the other's alterity? The notion of *self without self* points us toward a response to this question because it reduces neither the identity of the same to the alterity of the other nor the alterity of the other to the identity of the same. Rather, it establishes a relation of proximity in distance. *Self without self* is distant from the other. It is not the other but vision of the other's alterity. At the same time, since it is the other's vision of itself, *self without self* is in proximity of the other. Proximity occurs *in* distance. Seer and seen are not fused into a totality; they are, in the words of Plotinus, "separate only in otherness." The alterity of the other, though inseparable from the same, remains absolutely other, always-wholly-other than the other (*toujours-tout-autre que l'autre*).[9] Its alterity surpasses even the same as other.

Does Plotinian alterity, understood in terms of *self without self* and vision of the One, truly make a break with the specular framework that is at the core of the Levinasian critique of totality? For Levinas, alterity is first and foremost deonticmoral; his philosophy privileges practical reason over theoretical reason. The root-cause of Levinas' problem with Plotinus is that he would view Plotinian alterity as primarily apophatic-epistemological and therefore as remaining within the confines of a theoretical totality.

It is precisely at the place where Levinas would take issue with Plotinus, namely, in his categorization of the latter's philosophy as totalization, as irretrievable loss and suppression of distance, that, in my view, their philosophies intersect. Plotinus avoids totalization because for him, as for Levinas, practical reason is not derived from theoretical reason. Both philosophers emphasize the primacy of ethics over speculative metaphysics. Plotinus tells us that vision of the One is "not a contemplation but another kind of seeing," namely, a "giving oneself over" and an "adaptation." Plotinian apophaticism arises from and leads back to *praxis* or doing. It requires the free donation of the same to the other, which overflows theoretical reason and the being it wishes to know. The "seeing" that constitutes *self without self* is not specular; *self without self* is an ethical relation. This relation is perplexing in that it exceeds customary categories of thought.

As Levinas indicates, "If the same would establish its identity by simple (either/or) opposition to the other, it would already be part of a totality encompassing the same and the other" (*TI* 38). Distance between the same and the other would be more than just compromised; it would be abolished. The same and the other would belong to an all-encompassing unity of both/and that would eliminate the distance that permits their relation.

Plotinus agrees. "All these things are the One and not the One: they are he because they come from him; they are not he because it is in abiding by himself that he gives them" (V.2.2). The identity of the same is not opposed to the alterity of the other, nor are the same and the other synthesized into a third element. *Self without self* does not comprise a totality, because it is not the other but the other's vision of itself. The identity of the same and the alterity of the other remain intact, as does the possibility of desire.

The movement by which *self without self* comes to presence in the other is unique in that it alone is occasioned exclusively by desire. Even *being in myself* and *myself alone* both need and desire the other. As *being in myself*, I need the other because my completion depends on vision of the other's alterity in me. I also desire the other since, insofar as this vision occurs in me (someone who is established in rather than beyond being), distance between myself and the other still remains. As *myself alone*, I need the other because my completion rests on vision of my alterity in the other. The move beyond being has been made, but desire is operative here as well, since *myself alone* is not the other; it is a likeness of the other.

Self without self does not need the other because it does not lack anything. Self-completion is realized on the levels of *being in myself* and *myself alone*. Myself complete, I am free simply to desire. The movement whereby *self without self* comes to presence arises from an excess that surpasses myself, from an alterity that overflows the identity of the same as self. Only because I am complete in myself and do not need the other can I, in a Levinasian sense, "willfully relate" the identity of the same, my I, to the alterity of the other. The Plotinian notions of "giving oneself over" and "adaptation" also apply here. Donation of the same to the other and alteration of self into the alterity of the other occur in one whose being is already complete. I truly offer only what I do not need to give. Completion allows desire to flow freely.

Self without self is differentiated from the other in the very act by which it is possessed by the other. It is not the other but the other's vision of itself as overflowing. In its capacity as principle, the Plotinian One, "perfect because it seeks nothing, has nothing, and needs nothing, overflows, as it were, and its superabundance makes something else" (V.2.1). Strictly speaking, the One does not overflow, because it is not a being that acts. Rather, as Reiner Schürmann points out, it is the "event" of overflowing. The identity of the One, its "sameness" with respect to itself, is exorbitant. The One is out of itself in the very act by which it is itself. It is the simplicity of selfless giving. What it gives is vision of itself as pure excess.

Levinas differs significantly from Plotinus in that he finds excess in an alterity that is exterior rather than interior to the same. For him "the absolutely other is the personal other" (*l'absolument Autre, c'est Autrui*) (*TI* 39). His choice of the term "face" (*le visage*) to describe "the presentation of the other that surpasses *the idea of the other in me*" is noteworthy (*TI* 50). The face of the personal other does not present itself as a set of qualities forming an image to be thematized by my regard; it overflows the image that it leaves me. It does not manifest itself but expresses itself when thematization is turned into conversation (*discours*). Only when I approach the personal other in conversation do I welcome the other's expression, which continually overflows the idea I have of it. In conversation I "receive from the Other beyond the capacity of the I, which means exactly: to have the idea of infinity" (*TI* 51).

The critical nature of conversation welcomes the personal other as the calling into question of my world. Unlike dogmatism, which appropriates the other by constructing theoretical totalities, the critique of conversation deconstructs these totalities in order to uncover the arbitrary grounding of their foundation in the same. The irreducibility of the other to the same challenges the same's identity.

Although Levinas and Plotinus differ regarding where they find the alterity of the other, they both stress the importance of non-thematization for the same to be present to the other. Like the face of the personal other and the idea of infinity in Levinas, the Plotinian One escapes my grasp. I cannot thematize Plotinus's One because "converse" with it transcends intelligibility. Contact with the One disrupts my being at home with myself by defying the intelligibility of my world.

What, then, becomes of the world? Does Plotinus, by privileging the alterity found within, compromise the integrity of the world? In *Enneads* V.5.9 he discusses the world's relation to the One: "But Soul is not in the universe, but the universe in it: for body is not the soul's place, but Soul is in Intellect and body in Soul, and Intellect in something else; but there is nothing other than this for it to be in: it is not, then, in anything; in this way, therefore, it is nowhere." The world is in Soul, and Soul is in Intellect. But where is the "something else" in which Intellect is? Intellect, as the totality of being, contains all that is. It cannot reside in anything because there is nothing else in which it can be. It is nowhere in nothing, in the abyss of the One. We will not find the One by looking for it in the world, because the One is not in the world. Rather, we dis-cover the world by seeing it in the One.

"As he [the One] does not abide in place he is contemplated in many beings, in each and every one of those capable of receiving him as another self" (V.I.11). Contrary to compromising the integrity of the world, vision of the world in the One allows it to appear in its principal dis-position, in its principle's ex-orbitance. Seen in the One, the world's identity becomes unknown. The movement of the world's coming to presence in the One is experienced as question-able, as wonder-ful, in a word, as mysterious. Viewed in the One, the identity of the world becomes other because our customary understanding of it is displaced. Rather than impose our self-constructed meaning onto the world, vision of the world in the One lets the world present itself to us. Although Plotinus privileges interiority, he does not disregard exteriority since the world is perceived, when seen in the One, as the overflowing of the One's unintelligible excess.

The identity of the same does not here get reduced to the alterity of the other because the world, as being, is not the One. Vision of the world in the One comes to light in the darkness of the One, which is beyond being. The world still has form, but its form is seen as the overflowing of the One's formlessness, as the donation of the other. Stripped of its solidity, the world is free to enter the abyss of *world without world*.

Levinas also regards the other as placeless. The other is not there rather than here. Its distance from me is not determined by a frontier that I can cross. All attempts "imperialistically to conquer" the other's alterity by dominating it with the identity of the same end in defeat. These acts of aggression would deny the transcendence of the other, they would limit the alterity of the other by confining it to the other side of a common frontier. A shared frontier would incorporate the other into a larger whole and allow assimilation by the same (*TI* 39).

World without world. Self without self. God without God. Is the final word concerning the relation between the same and the other *nihilism*? This conclusion would be unjustified. First, the other is beyond being; it is not beyond the Good. Second, the stature of the world is not diminished but enhanced. Third, the other's nothingness does not result from privation. Possession of the same by the other neither fills a lack within the other nor absorbs the same into itself; the other is entirely without need. And last, the alterity of the other is not negative, since it is not opposed to the same. The same's identity and the other's alterity cannot be consolidated into the sovereign sameness of an all-encompassing totality. The alterity of the other escapes confinement by any same, supreme or otherwise. It is the other that possesses the same; the same does not possess it. The other is not in the world, not in self, not in God (if God exists). They are in the other, in the nothingness of pure excess. Herein lies a fundamental difference between Levinas and Plotinus.

Levinas views movement toward the other as linear, as departure from our home in the familiar present toward the unknown future. The other, which exceeds the same, is always one step ahead of us; we never arrive at the other. For Plotinus, movement toward the One consists of two movements. The first movement is circular; it leads toward our home, toward our foundation in Intellect. Only after we have realized self-completion and have returned to Intellect are we able to make the second movement, the spiral movement of excess whereby we arrive at the One, our *home without home.* Arrival at the One entails not re-settlement in the remembered past but movement in and through the unknown present. It marks not the termination of movement but the process by which movement is repeatedly initiated. Levinas and Plotinus agree that there is distance between ourself and the other, for they both maintain that we are not the other. But Plotinus differs from Levinas insofar as he claims that we are also in the other.

Where are we, then? We are nowhere in nothing, in this place that is not a place but the beginning of the abyss, where we meet both ourself and each other in the other as other. We are in our home without home, where we wander across the desert of desire on the way toward the place where we already are and always have been.

Proximity in distance. The same in the other as other. Proximity as reciprocity of donation. Distance as acceptance of excess. The proximity described here is "other" than the nearness sought by philosophies of totalization because it does not stand on the *terra firma* of self-identity. Rather, it moves along the uncertain terrain of self-absence. This approach to proximity guards the other's distance from the same. The alterity of the other is not reduced to the same's identity, including the "identity" of the same as self-absence. Nor is the identity of the same assimilated by the other. The other's alterity transcends even the same as other. To return to the expression introduced by Jankélévitch, it is "absolutely other, always wholly other than the other."

Despite their differences, Levinas and Plotinus recognize excess as central for understanding the relation between the same and the other. Levinas, a phenomenologist and an advocate of alterity, while he acknowledges the part played by interiority with respect to the idea of infinity, finds excess in what overflows the identity of the same, in what constitutes the life of exteriority. Plotinus, although he maintains the integrity of the world seen in the One, emphasizes the alterity found in interior life. For this reason, Levinas would interpret his philosophy as a misguided attempt to reconcile the same and the other by incorporating them into a larger whole or totality. But to readers of Plotinus, who (like Levinas) would consider him a metaphysician of identity, I respond: What is the One? Who are we?

NOTES

This essay was originally published in *International Philosophical Quarterly* 38, 149 (March 1998): 5–16, and is reprinted here with permission of the publisher.

    1. Like Levinas, I borrow these terms from Vladimir Jankélévitch, *Philosophic premiere: Introduction a une philosophic du 'presque'* (Paris: PUF, 1953). He uses the expressions *absolument/autre* and *toujours-tout-autre* to indicate the Neoplatonic One.

    2. Plotinus, *Enneads,* 7 vols., trans. A. H. Armstrong (Cambridge: Harvard University Press, 1981). All subsequent references to Plotinus's writings will be taken from this edition and noted parenthetically without an abbreviation of the title.

    3. Reiner Schürmann, "L'Hénologie comme dépassement de la métaphysique," *Les Etudes Philosophiques* (July–September 1982): 331–50. The translation is my own.

    4. Ibid., 331.

    5. Ibid., 337.

    6. Plato, *Phaedrus,* in *Plato's Erotic Dialogues,* trans. with introduction and commentaries William S. Cobb (Albany: State University of New York Press, 1993).

    7. Pierre-Jean Labarrière, *"Dieu sans Dieu"* in *Penser la Foi. Recherches en théologie aujourd'hui: Mélanges offerts à Joseph Moingt* (Paris: Cerf, 1993). The translation is my own.

    8. Ibid., 918.

    9. Jankélévitch, *Philosophie première,* 123.

A TRACE OF THE ETERNAL RETURN?

LEVINAS AND NEOPLATONISM

Brian Schroeder

12

> Peace as the return of the multiple to unity, in conformity
> with the Platonic or Neoplatonic idea of the One.
>
> —Levinas, "Peace and Proximity"

Despite the predominantly materialist turn of late modern philosophy, the "death of God," the deconstruction of metaphysics, and the poststructuralist critique of philosophies of identity, one still finds vestiges of Neoplatonism in contemporary philosophy and theology. Even Heidegger, at least in his early thought, is unable to vanquish completely the specter of this ancient though potent philosophy;[1] and although he ultimately abandons his attempt to develop a fundamental ontology, the impact of that project, and with it that of Neoplatonism, continues to reverberate throughout much subsequent thinking. One who reveals the abiding influence of Neoplatonism is Heidegger's former student and later critic Emmanuel Levinas, whose philosophy signals a marked retrieval of specific Plotinian themes, reinterpreting and appropriating them in the development of his ethical metaphysics.

Levinas has, to be sure, a decidedly ambiguous relation to Neoplatonism, retaining some of its fundamental insights while rejecting its gnostic overtones and its totalizing idealist objectives. Does his Jewish-influenced philosophy truly mark a significant departure, however, from the idealism of Plotinus and later variants of Neoplatonist theology, expressions of the very ontology that he claims is implicated in the originary violence of absolutely conceptualizing, that is to say, of totalizing the other? While taking recourse to a preoriginary difference that ostensibly frees thought itself from the "imperialism of the same" (*TI* 38–39; cf. *OB* 92), does the thinking of Levinas nevertheless signal a return to a primordial transcendent plenum, one that is barely distinguishable in the end from the primordial myth of the eternal return,[2] the very myth that captivated preexilic Israel along with the rest of the ancient world and that ultimately found a deep philosophical expression in Plotinian metaphysics and a theological one in orthodox Christianity? But then, could anything be more different than the philosophies of an ancient Greek and a modern Jew? Although Plotinus and Levinas may initially appear to be literally worlds apart in terms of both ground and history, they are brought into a remarkable proximity through their mutual affirmation and retention of the notion of transcendence and also their radical perspectives on the One (*to hen*).

How should this proximity be interpreted? In what ways does the thought of transcendence, of the beyond, condition not only a response to evil and violence but the very concept of identity itself? Does Levinas' insistence on the "excess of evil"[3] actually effect a radical departure from Plotinus on evil as privation? Or do their seemingly polar positions amount to what may be effectively termed the same difference? In taking up these guiding questions, I will focus on three main points wherein Levinas and Plotinus are brought into proximity: the transcendence of the One, the status of the trace, and the problem of evil. In conclusion, I will consider whether Levinas' philosophy breaks away from the archaic notion of eternal return that characterizes Plotinian and Neoplatonist thought in general.

THE ONE OR THE OTHER?

Who are we? And what—or who—is the One that draws us, as Levinas frames it, to the "hither side," the "other shore," in postulating this question?[4] Plotinus, for one, provides an answer to these queries. In his famous tractate "On the Beautiful,"[5] he invokes the Homeric character Odysseus as his proper human archetype. The Greek hero's flight from the bewitching pleasures of Circe and Calypso to his "beloved country" serves here as an analogy for the soul's ascent from the corrupting, material, "evil" lure of perceptual vision, to the higher, spiritual "inner vision" drawn forth in its desire for the One—in other words, for rest. Levinas, however, draws his inspiration from the biblical figure of the first Hebrew patriarch, going so far as to state that "any man truly man [*sic*] is no doubt of the line of Abraham" (*NTR* 99). Emulating the desert nomad, Levinas characterizes his philosophy as a "movement going forth from a world that is familiar to us, whatever be the yet unknown lands that bound it or that it hides from view, from an 'at home' which we inhabit, toward an alien outside-of-oneself, toward a yonder" (*TI* 33).

Two movements toward the beyond, one Greek, the other Hebraic—what is the difference? More importantly, what difference does this difference make?

"Jewgreek is Greekjew."[6] These are fitting words to open an encounter between one (Plotinus) who closes the ancient world of thought while opening its next phase,[7] namely, the birth of the subject, and another (Levinas) who pushes modernity to the brink of its horizon while signaling to its beyond from the standpoint of the beyond, that is to say, from "outside the subject."[8] Athens and Jerusalem, Odysseus and Abraham, the Mediterranean and the Mesopotamian—the identity of the West falls somewhere in between. How better to address that which is without a site—the One—than by returning to the common backyard, as it were, of both the Greek and the Jew, one of the oldest sites of known human civilization: Egypt, the native soil of the non-Greek Greek Plotinus? Indeed, the very notion of "return," of its possibility *or* impossibility, constitutes not only the trajectory of this meditation but also the point of departure between Hellenism and Hebraism.

The longing, the desire, for the beyond unifies Plotinus and Levinas as much as it separates them. Surely the same can be said also of Odysseus and Abraham: both are wanderers continually in search of the welcome, strangers who come unbidden and disturb the present order of things; both signify the plight and desire of all human beings—to establish a dwelling. The difference lies in the knowledge, or lack of it, regarding the *telos* of this sojourn. Unlike the knowability that subtends the Odyssean figure admired by Plotinus, the indeterminacy of Abrahamic subjectivity is what proves decisive for Levinas: the promise and perpetual postponement of eschatological desire, the orientation of consciousness that both conjoins and separates religion and philosophy, and likewise action and intention.

According to Levinas, the nonteleological desire for the absolutely other, for the Invisible,[9] inaugurates and sustains the ethical relation and refuses the longing or need (*besoin*) that characterizes the Neoplatonist and later Christian scholastic emphasis on the knowledge of the transcendentals as the highest good on the grounds that it is a movement of time outside of itself. Nevertheless, "the knowledge of the world—thematization—attempts to reduce, and succeeds in reducing, the disturbance of the Same by the Other" (TE 134). Yet it is precisely this disturbance that Levinas wants to retain in the fullness of its expression, a disturbance signifying the priority of ethics over knowledge, of *praxis* over *theōria*. Contrary to Plotinus, for Levinas time is not coextensive with eternity in the sense of Being rejoining the One[10] in a movement of perpetual return from diremption; rather, time is alternation without synthesis—diachrony—a noncoincidental movement, a tendency or intending toward the beyond, the other, the Good, the One. "As if," Levinas sardonically states, "knowledge, concreteness of presence, were the psychism of all thought. . . . As if time, in its diachrony, came down to a failed eternity, to 'the moving image of an immobile eternity,' or of the consummate One" (*AT* 13).

The other (*to heteron; l'autre*) "possesses" the same (*to auton; le même*) in the formless structure of its command, its incessant call to responsibility, claims Levinas. This does not, however, reveal alterity in the same, as it does for Plotinus; rather, it indicates the radical exteriority of the absolutely or wholly other (*tout autre*). "It would signify the ambiguity of an incessant adjournment or the progression of holding and possession. But it also signifies the approach of an infinite God, an approach that is His proximity" (TE 134). While contesting the primacy of the nominative case, the irruption or breaking-through of the absolutely other into the totality[11] (into the various hypostases of being, to use Plotinus's language) nonetheless does not diminish the force of the accusative case, that of the ethical imperative, even though the accusative is predicated on the nominative.

Levinas recognizes within his own thinking a deep tension between the nontheoretical desire for the other and the need that attends knowledge of the other. On the one hand, he asks, "Cannot thought approach the absolute otherwise than by knowledge and in knowledge and excel by that approach, better than the return to the One and coincidence with unity?" (*AT* 16). Yet on the other hand, he queries, "Must we with the—from the first unthinkable—contact with transcendence and alterity renounce philosophy?" (TrO 347). This very oscillation between the desire to "approach" that which is "otherwise than being" non-philosophically and the need to preserve philosophy's integrity in fact conditions his philosophical project as a whole and characterizes the perpetual quandary of ethical existence. Philosophy invariably privileges the standpoint of the selfsame. This is unavoidable. It is also necessary for the politically and epistemologically instrumental extension of thought into the concrete everyday life. From this ground, however, philosophy slides into violence as the "imperialism" of theory, the moment it unavoidably includes alterity as part of that extension.

The question raised by and within this tension is whether the ethical comportment can flourish whereby all actions undertaken for the sake of the other are, in the end, also actions oriented toward the self. In the case of the mythical Odysseus, there is no doubt about this. He is fully aware of his destination and fate, both provisional (Ithaca) and final (Hades), and consequently his decisions and actions are made in the fullness of conscious choice. Through his own connivance and the continual assistance he receives from the goddess Athena because of his unfailing *gratitude* to her, Odysseus prevails against the will of Poseidon and is able to return to his beloved Penelope, kingdom, and homeland. Similarly, for Plotinus the soul's ascent toward the One is bound to its very self-interest to return home, an interest that lamentably, according to Levinas, ultimately characterizes the basic movement of philosophy itself:

> Philosophy, always dissatisfied with being only philosophy! The return to the One from which it had emanated without diminishing it—the coincidence with the source of "beyond being"—was to be the main thing, in separation, of the

intelligence from the One, for the philosophy that emerged from it. The aspiration *for the return* is the very breath of the Spirit; but the consummate unity of
the One is better than the Spirit and philosophy. The best is the indivisibility of
the One, a pure identity in which all multiplicity and all number are abolished at
rare "instants" that Plotinus attests to, when the distance, or even the distinction
of knowing—even if it is only the distinction between knowing and the known
in consciousness of Self—disappears without a trace. The One to which intelligence piously aspires, beyond the ideas it attains and grasps in their multiplicity
(in which, however, it is completed, realized, in act, satisfied)—the One beyond
the noema that is equaled by the noesis of intelligence—would be, according to
the neo-platonic schema, better than that aspiration and that approach from
which the One is still absent. (*EN* 135; see also *AT* 9–10)

However, this pious aspiration is not the case for Levinas, who conjoins the movements of *ingratitude* and *irreversibility,* eschewing the sense of reciprocal movement that is occasionally portrayed between the Greek heroes and gods, and later
between the theologically knowing faithful and the divinity.

A work conceived in its ultimate nature requires a radical generosity of the same
who in the work goes unto the other. It then requires an *ingratitude* of the other.
Gratitude would in fact be the *return* of the movement to its origin. . . . The departure without return, which does not go forth into the void, would also lose its
absolute goodness if the work sought for its recompense in the immediacy of its
triumph, if it impatiently awaited the triumph of its cause. The one-way movement would be inverted into a reciprocity. (TrO 349)[12]

Unlike the Greeks, bound by the necessity (*anankē*) of fate (*moira*), for Levinas
there is only the endless tarriance, and the continual questioning and wondering.
There is no question of a return, or of an absolute revelation of evidence:

But the manifestation of the invisible cannot mean the passage of the invisible to
the status of the visible; it does not lead back to evidence. It is produced in the
goodness reserved to subjectivity, which thus is subject not simply to the truth of
judgment, but to the source of this truth. The truth of the invisible is ontologically
produced by the subjectivity which states it. (*TI* 243)

Abraham is the model of subjectivity that Levinas has in mind here. Abraham's actions are dictated by an eschatological undecidability; his fate and destination are
not predetermined, they are only aspired to, and the invisible power also at play besides his own will leaves him bereft of the consolation of knowledge of their in-
evitability. In his freedom to choose the good, the truth of the invisible is
ontological, produced in Abraham, establishing a certain unity between the One
and the other that does not negate the absolute separation between the terms that
makes freedom and responsibility simultaneously possible.

THE ONE OR THE GOOD?

Levinas qualifies his philosophy as a "return to Platonism in a new way" ("Meaning and Sense," *BPW* 58), and it is altogether significant that despite his Jewish background he declares, "The Place of the Good above every essence is the most profound teaching, the definitive teaching, not of theology, but of philosophy" (*TI* 103). Moreover, he asks: "In agreement with Plato and Plotinus, who dared to pose, against all good sense, something beyond being, is not the idea of being younger than the idea of the infinite?" ("Transcendence and Height," *BPW* 21). If this teaching of transcendence remains somewhat obscure in the Platonic corpus, appearing only inconsistently, and increasingly less so later on, it clearly occupies a central role in the philosophies of Plotinus and Levinas. Plotinus adheres to Plato's famous contention that the Good is "beyond being" (*ouk ousias ontos tou agathou, all eti epekeina tēs ousias*) (*Republic* 509b) while discarding the inconsistencies of Platonic metaphysics (in part through an appropriation of certain Aristotelian concepts), and in doing so establishes a hierarchical order of being while insisting upon the utter transcendence of the One.[13] Like Plato, Plotinus considers philosophy and religion mutually informative, as does Levinas, who deftly conjoins the insights of phenomenology with ancient Greek philosophy and Judaic Talmud. Nevertheless, despite their connections to traditions that made possible postclassical-era monotheistic theologies, both Levinas and Plotinus advance fundamentally religious philosophies that refuse traditional interpretations of monotheism,[14] though with the critical difference that Levinas retains the notion of creationism, whereas, according to most interpretations, Plotinus does not.[15]

Though bordering on pantheism, Plotinus's philosophy is, on the one hand, despite his periodic employment of the masculine pronoun to describe the One, essentially nontheistic. Levinas, on the other hand, characterizes his religious position as "atheism" (a point that we shall revisit later). According to Plotinus, the Intelligence (*nous*) and the One do not form a totality; they are absolutely separate from each other though connected. Similarly in Plato, the relation between the Good and the One is for the most part left ambiguous—as is so often the case with his thinking. Plotinus addresses this ambiguity. Though he links the One of Plato's *Parmenides*[16] with the Good of *Republic*, he expressly distinguishes between the two terms: "The One cannot aim at any good or desire anything, it is superior to the Good; it is the Good, not for itself, but for other things to the extent to which they can share in it" (VI.9.6). The Good and the One are both the same and different. There is an essential paradox within the One/Good itself: "Because it is the cause of good it cannot, then, be called the Good; yet in another sense it is the Good above all" (VI.9.6).[17] This difference in the same is crucial as it signifies the inability of purely rational thought to totally grasp the nature of the Absolute. Both Plotinus and Levinas hold the power of reason in highest esteem, yet both abandon that power at decisive moments in their respective philosophies. The union with the One, the *telos* of the Plotinian soul, or self, is, in the end, for lack of a better term, mystically, which is also to say ecstatically, achieved. Knowledge of the order of existence, of its emanational construction and adherence to the movement inherent in that order, brings the rational soul into contact with *nous*, from which it is able to finally liberate itself from the fetters of composite existence and attain the motionless rest of the One.

"The complicity of theoretical objectivity and mystical communion," as Derrida incisively frames the issue at hand, thus "will be Levinas' true target. The premetaphysical unity of one and the same violence. An alternation which always modifies the same confinement of the other."[18] This alternation signifies neither reciprocity of donation, nor symmetry of the same and other, nor reversibility of movement. In Plotinus, the One is prior to, higher than, God, or the divine Intelligence. The One is complete, totally in itself, without desire or need. Perhaps more accurately put, the One is neither at rest nor in motion (since to be either is to imply a duality) and unable to be affected or to affect (since that would presume a will and only a being can possess a will). Levinas' fundamental point of departure from Neoplatonism is that the other as Other,[19] while not another ego or even an alter ego, both affects and is affected by the same, while simultaneously refusing any reciprocity of responsibility or generosity.[20] Thus can Levinas state that the other is a "passivity beyond all passivity" that disrupts the pretended domesticity, the quietude, of the same precisely because of its passivity.

To the notion of union with the One, Levinas opposes that of radical irreversible separation. What is a lack, an evil, in Plotinus is a "glory" for Levinas. In short, the separation that is overcome in Neoplatonism is maintained in Levinasian metaphysics. Ironically, both Plotinus and Levinas find their source of inspiration in Plato's construal of the transcendence of the Good and the One. Like the Platonic Good, the Plotinian One engenders being. The One is neither the totality of being nor is it the Being of beings. It is not possible to speak of the One in any positive or negative sense, Plotinus avers, since "it is a measure and not measured [*metron gar auto kai ou metroumenon*]" (V.5.4; cf. I.8.3; VI.5.11; VI.6.18). Similarly, Levinas writes:

> [The One] is the Unrevealed, but not unrevealed because all knowledge would be too limited or too narrow to receive its light. It is unrevealed because it is *One*, and because making oneself known implies a duality which already clashes with the unity of the One. The One is not beyond being because it is buried and hidden; it is buried because it is beyond being, wholly other than being. (TrO 347)

But if Plotinus seems at times to separate cognitively the One and the Good, Levinas does not follow suit. Goodness is "not an attribute that would multiply the One, for if it were to multiply, if the One could be distinguished from the Goodness that sustains it, the One could take up a position with regard to its goodness, know itself to be good, and thus lose its goodness" (*OB* 57). Levinas equates the absolutely other with the One; and like the One, the absolutely other is ineffable. Beyond all differentiation and plurality, the One is the absolute source of the multiple. It neither denies nor negates the plural; rather, its transcendence signifies distance, separation, absolute alterity, pure difference—infinity.

The radical hermeneutical move that Levinas makes is the equation of the Infinite, the One, with social multiplicity, stipulating that his philosophical project is an attempt at "a 'phenomenology' of sociality starting from the face of the other person—from proximity" (*TO* 109). In other words, for Levinas, transcendence *is* sociality. Yet sociality is also the convergence of ethics and politics, of asymmetry and symmetry, of nonreciprocity and reciprocity. This double aspect of Levinasian metaphysics parallels the Plotinian insistence that the One both is and is not, although it differs significantly from Neoplatonism in being closer to a "logic" of neither/nor. More importantly, Levinas points to a radical difference in the meaning of transcendence. In a direct reference to Plotinus, Levinas writes, "Contrary to the philosophy that makes of itself the entry into the kingdom of the absolute . . . Judaism teaches us a real transcendence, a relation with Him Whom the soul cannot concern and without Whom the soul cannot, in some sense, hold itself together" (*DF* 16). It is at this point that Levinasian metaphysics breaks with Neoplatonist metaphysics, the latter lending itself to what its commentators termed "mysticism," a position adamantly rejected by Levinas as applicable to his own philosophy.

THE VISIBLE OR THE INVISIBLE?

Despite this seemingly critical difference with respect to the concept of transcendence, Levinas is indebted to Plotinus's philosophy on a very important point—interestingly, one rarely mentioned by the latter's commentators—namely, the concept of the trace (*to ichnos; la trace*). While acknowledging that "Plotinus conceived the procession from the One as compromising neither the immutability nor the absolute separation of the One" ("Meaning and Sense," *CPP* 105),[21] Levinas nevertheless distances himself from the Neoplatonist with regard to the nature of the other's "presence" within the same, the other's "possession" of the same. "The marvel of infinity in the finite" is the great metaphysical wonder for Levinas, the full significance of the trace, "the overwhelming of intentionality, the overwhelming of this appetite for light" (TrO 354). This thought also finds expression in Plotinus when he addresses the essence of primary beauty in bodies, a position that runs counter to Platonist and Greek philosophy as a whole.[22] Furthermore, Plotinus stipulates, "the soul, since it is by nature what it is and is related to the higher kind of reality in the realm of being, when it sees something akin to it or a trace of its kindred reality [*ē ichnos tou suggenous*], is delighted and thrilled and returns to itself [*anapherei pros heautēn*] and remembers itself and its own possessions" (I.6.2). Extending the notion of the trace, the Plotinian One is "seen" (though neither perceptually nor even cognitively, but rather ecstatically) in the clarity of "vision" emanating from the Intelligence.

Levinas incorporates the concept of the trace into his philosophy as the epiphanic vision of the Other's face. However, whereas in Plotinus the trace of the One is disseminated via the manifold ideas of *nous* and grasped cognitively by the higher aspect of the soul, closer to Intelligence than to matter, in Levinas' hermeneutic, the trace is a disturbance, a disruption that produces interiority by causing the same to recognize the exteriority of the other. The separation of the same from the other is not the locus of evil for Levinas though, as is apparently the case with Plotinus. Levinas refers to this separation as *atheism*, "a position prior to both the negation and the affirmation of the divine, the breaking with participation by which the I posits itself as the same and as I" (*TI* 58). Rather than constituting the source of evil, this is testament or witness to the "glory of the Infinite."[23] Construed in this sense, separation enables the same to be grasped as the subjective self or I. Radical separation is produced as a "psychism," as the "idea" of infinity whose content "overflows the thought that thinks it" (*TI* 25). Expressed differently and more concretely, the trace of the absolutely other, revealed in and as the face (*visage*) of the other person, exposes the meaning of transcendence as sociality, as the relationship with the Other—not as alterity, the One alone, or as Plotinus claims, as "escape in solitude to the solitary [*phugē monou pros monon*]" (VI.9.11). Levinasian transcendence is ethical because it *is* ethics.

The trace signifies that which is beyond being, or essence. In a teaching that Levinas incorporates into the very heart of his philosophy, Plotinus declares that

> being is a trace of the One [*to einai ichnos tou henos*]. And if someone says that this word *einai* (being)—which is the term that signifies substantial existence—has been derived from the word *hen* (one), he might have hit upon the truth. For this which we call primary being proceeded, so to speak, a little way from the One, but did not wish to go still further, but turned inwards and took its stand (*estē*) there, and became substance (*ousia*) and hearth (*hestia*) of all things; it is like what happens in the utterance of the sound: when the utterer presses on it *hen* is produced which manifests the origin of the One and *on* (being) signifying that which uttered, as best it can. Thus that which came to exist, substance and being, has an image of the One since it flows from its power [*mimēsin echonta ek tēs dunameōs autou hruenta*]; and the (soul) which sees it and is moved to speech by the sight, imaging [*mimoumenē*] what it saw, cried out "*on*" and "*einai*," and "*ousia*" and "*hes-*

tia." For these sounds intend to signify the real nature of that produced by the birth-pangs of the utterer, imitating, as far as they are able, the generation of real being. (V.5.5)

This passage is important for Levinas on at least two points: first, it formulates a conception of being as *a* trace (it is interesting to note that Plotinus does not here write "the" trace, omitting the definite article *to*) of the One (what Levinas will reframe as the absolutely other); second, it points to the fundamental role performed by speech as that which grasps "the generation of real being," to use Plotinus's phrase. Ethics, for Levinas, is predicated on the primacy of speech over the image as the proper signifying power of the heterogeneous ethical command.[24] Retaining the sense of the *epekeina tēs ousias* implied in Plotinus's formulation of the trace, Levinas reconceives the unity beyond essence and extends its application to social plurality. "*Beyond being is a third person,*" he claims, emphasizing these words, "which is not definable by the oneself, by ipseity. . . . The *illeity* of the third person is the condition for the irreversibility" (TrO 356). The face of the Other is the trace of the absolute other: "The presence of the face—the infinity of the other—is destitution, presence of the third party, that is, of the whole of humanity that looks at us" (*TI* 188). The meaning of the trace, in Levinas' reformulation of it, is ethical, and ethics is transcendence actualized. Transcendence is neither alterity per se nor the One and therein is absolved from any prior intimacy with knowledge. This intimacy is the hallmark of traditional philosophy, which Levinas describes thus:

> This nostalgia, or this piety or gathering of oneself, going beyond and above the intelligible that is present in the intelligence—is philosophy, aspiration to a wisdom that is not knowledge, that is not representation, that is not love. Love of a wisdom other than the intelligible giving itself to knowledge. Philosophy that would thus be transcendence itself. Philosophy as union with the One or fusion with it. (*AT* 8; *EN* 134)

Modern philosophy is the direct descendant of Greek thinking, and nowhere is this lineage more pronounced than in its emphasis on epistemology as the proper mode of philosophy. Levinas' break from the climate of Greek philosophy hinges on radically reconceiving the meaning of transcendence, breaking with the Parmenidean unity that culminates in Neoplatonism, wherein "the union with the One is not a utopian ideal. It is not love as aspiration that is triumphant transcendence, but love as union. *The idea of an effective transcendence in sociality itself, in proximity rather than in ecstasy, will remain foreign to Greek thought*" (*AT* 9; emphasis added). For Levinas, what marks the decisive difference with the Greek Neoplatonism is that the transcendence of ethics, while oriented toward the invisible, is a movement that occurs within the visible, not as the freeing of the soul from the fetters of the material body as in Plotinus, but as actualized concretely though imperfectly in the relation with the third (*le tiers*). In the metaphysics of Plotinus, there is no place, or need, for a conception of the third, because the interest is solely that of the same and not of the other. Hence, ethics is essentially a means to an end in Neoplatonism—the return to unity with the One—rather than the end itself. Indeed, Levinas writes, "The eternal return of idealism does not result from a capricious preference for the theory of knowledge on the part of philosophers. It rests upon solid reasons which found the privilege of the Same in comparison with the Other" ("Transcendence and Height," *BPW* 12).

GOOD OR EVIL?

According to Levinas, the error and danger of modern through contemporary ontology is its tendency to neutralize the question of being, a position that clearly distances him from Hegel and, interestingly, draws him into closer proximity with Nietzsche, although further away from Heidegger.[25] But it is against another German philosopher that Levinas succinctly frames his position:

> The first metaphysical question is no longer Leibniz's question "why is there something rather than nothing?" but "why is there evil rather than good?" It is the de-neutralization of being, or the beyond being. The ontological difference is preceded by the difference between good and evil. Difference itself is this latter; it is the origin of the meaningful. . . . Meaning implies this transcendent relation, "the alterity of the other scene," which is no longer a negative concept. (TE 182)

In reformulating Leibniz's famous query, Levinas is revaluating the entire Western metaphysical tradition: first, by inverting the Neoplatonist and Augustinian positions of evil as privation or lack; and second, by casting metaphysics primarily as a concern with valuation rather than with ontology, and moreover as a matter of *desire*. Plotinus also took up these very concerns and asked: "But how can evil have a desire of the good?" (VI.7.28). Almost as if in response, Levinas proffers a possible answer in the form of a surprising, indeed, shocking, question: "Is the horror of evil—in which, paradoxically, evil is given—the Good?" (TE 131).

As is well known, Plotinus correlates matter (*hulē*) with "evil itself" (I.8.8, 13).[26] Moreover, drawing on Plato's *Sophist*, he identifies matter with "non-being" (*mē on*) (II.4.16; II.5.4–5; III.6.7). Evil, he writes,

> cannot be included in what really exists or in what is beyond existence; for these are good. So it remains that if evil exists, it must be among non-existent things, as a sort of form of non-existence, and pertain to one of the things that are mingled with nonbeing or somehow share in non-being. Non-being here does not mean absolute nonbeing but only something other than being; not non-being in the

same way as the movement and rest which affect being, but like an image of being or something still more non-existent. (I.8.3)

Yet evil or matter does not exist independently (I.8.11). Matter here does not refer to that which merely has a corporeal component. Evil is privation (*sterēsis*), that is, where the *archē* is not. Evil is formless. "How could anyone imagine," asks Plotinus, "that evil is a form when it appears in the absence of every sort of good?" (I.8.1). But like all else, matter derives its existence from the One. Is it the case, then, that the One, the highest good, is the cause of evil? In a sense it is; in fact, Plotinus cannot maintain otherwise lest he fall prey to the ontological dualism that his philosophy is so attentive to avoid.

Even though the One is the *archē* of the All (*to pan*), the One is formally that which gives birth to the Intelligence, which in turn generates the soul, divided into higher and lower aspects, and from the soul, matter, in turn also divided into that which is intelligible and that which is sensible. The difference between the generative power of the One and that of the lower hypostases is that the One engenders out of necessity but without need. The soul, on the other hand, generates matter because it needs the corporeal in order to enter the sensible world (IV.3.9). The evil that is identified with matter is specifically sensible—that is, formless—matter. Lacking form, sensible matter is unable to return of its own accord toward the One. This is precisely what constitutes its evil.

The deeper concern is how the soul, or self, becomes evil. Evil is both physical and moral, but moral evil is only the result of a prior physical evil, according to Plotinus, who likens the evil of matter to a soul covered by phlegm or bile that, while not penetrating the soul, nevertheless darkens its luminosity (I.8.14). Moreover, evil is not uniform; there is primary or pure evil, that is, matter without form. "Just as there is absolute good and good as a quality, so there must be absolute evil and the evil derived from it which inheres in something else" (I.8.3). There is also relative evil, that is, particular kinds of evil (I.8.5), which arise when a form that should be present is not, for example, the absence of a virtue when such a presence is required. This is the locus of moral evil that affects the soul.

Plotinus maintains that all bodily existence is inherently evil. To be human is to be a composite being. The body is merely an occasion, a sufficient condition, for evil, and not a sufficient cause. Thus, it is matter that "is the cause of the soul's weakness and vice; it is then itself evil before soul and is primary evil. Even if soul had produced matter, being affected in some way, and had become evil by communicating with, matter would have been the cause of its presence: soul would not have come to it unless its presence had given soul the occasion of coming to birth" (I.8.14). The danger to the soul of becoming evil is the turning of desire downward, so to speak; in other words, of perceiving matter as capable of filling a lack in the soul. This is an error of judgment on the soul's part, since sensible matter, being formless, does not inspire one toward otherness but encloses one in a totality that excludes exteriority. One could well ask with Plotinus here, who answers his own question:

> Is matter, then, the same thing as otherness? No, rather it is the same thing as the part of otherness that is opposed to the things which in the full and proper sense exist, that is to say rational formative principles. Therefore, though it is non-existent, it has a certain sort of existence in this way, and is the same thing as privation, if privation is opposition to the things that exist in rational form. (II.4.16)

In this sense, matter is practically nothingness. That is to say, matter does not lead anywhere except to degeneration and death. When the soul becomes evil, it becomes removed from the ascent toward the One and no longer participates in the return to its origin.[27] Cut off, isolated, it becomes "lifeless" as the sensible matter to which it attaches itself. In its lack of participation (*methexis*), it is alone; its solitude, its "nonbeing," is that of privation. In this sense it is the opposite of the solitary aloneness desired by the higher soul's mystical ascent, a communion with the One that is only finally realized in the goodness of death itself. This death "is the separation of the body and the soul; and [one] does not fear this if [one] welcomes the prospect of being alone" (I.6.6).

To the notion that evil is a privation, Levinas counters the surprising thesis that evil is an "excess." Like Plotinus, for Levinas, evil is also bound to matter, insofar as violence is always found in the totality, in being, and not in the beyond or that which is "otherwise than being." Levinas postulates that evil "signifies excess, refusing any synthesis in which the wholly-otherness of God would become visible" (TE 183). As excess, evil "leads beyond; elsewhere than to being. . . . Evil is neither a world nor a species, not some sort of perfection of negation" (TE 127). But if it is none of these, then what is it? For Levinas, evil is always moral evil; it is not brute matter or formlessness. The evil that results in intersubjective violence is, rather, the result of conceptualization or intellection, of theory's self-proclaimed sovereignty. Evil is always social, and since sociality is transcendence—the overflowing of the Good, the Infinite in the finite, the "possession" of the same by the other—it follows that the reality of evil (and for Levinas evil *is* real) is, like the Good, the One, an excess. "Sociality," writes Levinas, is "not to be confused with some weakness or privation in the unity of the One" (*AT* 30). Evil is not merely a lack or absence of the Good, the absence of awareness or cognition. On the contrary, evil is fully conscious in its refusal of the Good and ignoring of the pleas of the Other to respond.

The Plotinian One is absolutely remote and removed from any volition, feeling, or intelligible interaction with being. As a result, the question of ethics is never fully resolved by Plotinus. For Levinas, the infinitely other, while beyond essence, is not beyond experience. The alterity of the absolutely other is experienced as the trace in the face of the other person: "The absolutely other is the Other" (*TI* 39). As the face, as the *socius* itself, the Other suffers, is affected. Evil is thus not so much a personal as it is an interpersonal matter:

> The exteriority or transcendence in evil does not receive its meaning in opposition to psychic "interiority." It does not borrow its meaning from some sort of prior correlation between the illusion of multiple worlds behind the world, accumulating nevertheless in the same space. It is in the *excess* of *evil* that the prefix *ex-* signifies in its original sense, as exceeding [*excession*] itself, as the *ex-* of all exteriority. No categorical *form* could invest it, none could hold it in within its framework. The "wholly other," beyond the community of the common, is no longer a simple term! It is the *other*. (TE 128–29)

Are Levinas and Plotinus so far apart on the question of the status of evil? They seem to converge on the point that evil is evil because, as Levinas states, its "'quality' is *non-integratableness* itself. . . . The concrete quality is defined by this abstract notion of evil. Evil is not only the non-integratable, it is also the non-integratableness of the non-integratable" (TE 128).[28] Evil is *more* than lack or absence of the Good. While in Plotinus it takes form as matter (or nonbeing), in Levinas evil is coextensive with being, which is also to say, with history. But the "excess" of evil, its "transcendence," is not of the same order as the plenitude of goodness.

Levinas indicates that his philosophy does not affirm the equiprimordiality of good and evil, a point shared by Plotinus. The asymmetry of the metaphysical relation, wherein responsibility for the Other precedes the freedom of the self, is also present in the relation between good and evil. Ironically, though, the very asymmetry of the ethical relationship lies at the base of the "insurmountable ambiguity of evil."

> Thus there is, in the midst of the submission to the Good, the seduction of irresponsibility, the probability of egoism in the subject responsible for his responsibility, that is, the very birth of the ego in the obeying will. This temptation to separate oneself from the Good is the very incarnation of the subject or his presence in being. . . . Evil shows itself to be sin, that is, a responsibility, despite itself, for the refusal of responsibilities. It is neither alongside of nor in front of the Good, but in the second place, beneath, lower than, the Good. The being that perseveres in being, egoism or Evil, thus outlines the dimension of baseness itself, and the birth of hierarchy. Here begins the axiological polarity. ("Humanism and Anarchy," *CPP* 137–38)

In opting for the hierarchy of good over evil, Levinas is not reverting to some modified version of the Augustinian position that maintains evil is the privation of goodness, that is, arguably of a lesser ontological status than the goodness of God; the reality of evil is not questioned by Levinas, only the thesis of its equiprimordiality with goodness.

Evil is not, however, the final word of being, or history. The transcendence of evil points toward the beyond, to the goodness of alterity, in relation to which evil is defined but never identified. In this sense, evil is "abstract," as is, interestingly enough, the face, for Levinas:

> A face is abstract. This abstractness is not, to be sure, like the brute sensible datum of the empiricists. . . . the abstractness of the face is a visitation and a coming. It disturbs immanence without settling into the horizons of the world. Its abstractness is not obtained by a logical process starting from the substance of beings and going forth from the particular to the general. On the contrary, it goes toward those beings, but does not compromise itself with them, withdraws from them, ab-solves itself. Its wonder is due to the elsewhere from which it comes and into which it already withdraws. (TrO 354–55)

Though Levinas is certainly employing the term "abstract" in a highly qualified sense here, the important aspect of the face and evil's mutual abstractness is that they both signify a disruption without a corresponding leveling of being's horizon. In other words, despite this disturbance, the totality of being is defined neither in terms of pure evil nor of goodness. Both evil and goodness are transcendent with regard to being in that respect. Furthermore, on the one hand, one could say that evil is the sovereign claim of the power of abstraction, that is, the power of reason or theory unchecked, that renounces any subordination to the concrete appeals of the Other, whose very passivity constitutes "the way opposed to the imperialism of consciousness open upon the world" (*OB* 92). Goodness, on the other hand, is the abstract "face" of that incessant plea, the trace of the absolutely other.

Though seemingly polar in their respective accounts of evil—for Plotinus, evil is matter and a degeneration of the One; for Levinas, evil is excess and a transcendence—Levinas is remarkably close to the Plotinian position that evil is the standpoint from which the vision of the Good demonstrates the force of its lure. In other words, the transcendence that Levinas associates with evil points to that which is beyond, that is, the Good. The absolute passive power that the Good exerts leads to a realization, or knowledge, that evil's excess is not the final word, that evil opens to another vision of existence, of possibility, that breaks through the totality of finite being onto the infinite horizon of the wholly other. This *height* that summons and commands is for both Levinas and Plotinus nothing other than divinity, the source of all signification and the locus of all ethical movement revealed in the trace.

THE RETURN OF THE ETERNAL RETURN?

The most ancient and universal myth is arguably that of the eternal return, the primordial religious worldview that extended throughout the two prongs on the fork of Western culture, the Mesopotamian and Mediterranean regions, encapsulating even the Greek philosophical world, including the thought of Plotinus. Yet it is Plotinus who marks the closure of the Greek intellectual milieu and stands at the threshold of a new era in human consciousness, one whose metaphysics was also partially influenced by late Jewish and early Christian thinking, despite the fact that Greek Neoplatonist metaphysics reverses the apocalypticism of this thinking, giving rise to orthodox or traditional Christianity's subsequent retrieval of the eternal return, even if in a unique variant. Plotinus is indeed an enigmatic figure: though born and bred on the very cultural soil that formalized religiously the myth of the eternal return perhaps more than any other civilization in history, he decisively affects the transition from Hebraism to Judaism, a transition marked by the postexilic prophetic revolution of Israel that first challenged and reversed the archaic myth of eternal return, advancing an irreversible, forward-moving conception of time and history. One can only speculate on the impact of that coincidence, although one wonders if it did not produce a tension within Plotinus's thinking that manifests itself in terms of a certain inconsistency, if not an ambiguity, with respect to the question of evil.[29]

Although remarkably close to the Plotinian position, according to Levinas, the decisive difference that ultimately distinguishes the Jewish from this late Greek understanding of goodness is that the Good is approached neither gnostically nor mystically; rather, the Good is approached directly, albeit in the enigmatic ambiguity of the oblique relationship between the self and the Other. This relationship testifies to the *uniqueness* of the trace found in the face of the Other. "The epiphany of the other involves a signifyingness of its own, independently of this signification received from the world. The other does not only come to us out of a context, but comes without mediation; he signifies by himself" (TrO 351). Succinctly stated otherwise, "Ethics is first philosophy" (*TI* 304; "Ethics as First Philosophy," *LR*).

For Levinas, ethics *is* transcendence: the approach of the self to the Other, the response to a summons from without, departure *without assurance* of return—yet nevertheless predicated and motivated by the *hope* of return. Is this the hidden *coincidentia oppositorum* in Levinas' thought, a coincidence that reveals itself in his construal of the excess found in both good and evil? Could the same be said here regarding whether evil is privation or excess? Do these two perspectives constitute a veritable coincidence of opposites? Would such an interpretation corroborate the thesis advanced by both Plotinus and Levinas, namely, that the source of evil is *beyond* being, which, though neither the One, the Good, nor the absolutely other, can nevertheless arguably be termed "the same"? Do, indeed, these "extremes meet"[30]— but only in transcendence?[31] And is this transcendence inseparable from a movement of return: an eternal return to the eternal? These are the questions that continue to return, both indicating and disturbing the proximity between Levinas and Plotinus.

NOTES

1. On the confluence between Heidegger and Plotinus, see Eugene F. Bales, "A Heideggerian Interpretation of Negative Theology in Plotinus," *The Thomist* 47 (1983): 197–208; Jean Greisch, "The Eschatology of Being and the God of Time in Heidegger," trans. Dermot Moran, *International Journal of Philosophical Studies* 4, 1 (1996): 17–42; John D. Jones, "A Non-Entitative Understanding of Be-ing and Unity: Heidegger and Neoplatonism," *Dionysius* 6 (1982): 94–110; Herve Pasqua, "'Henosis' et 'ereignis': Contribution a une interpretation plotinienne de l'Etre heideggerien," *Revue Philosophique de Louvain* 4 (2002): 681–97. For a discussion on Plotinian henology, departing from a consideration of Heidegger's relation to Plotinus with respect to Plato's influence on Neoplatonism, see John Sallis, "Platonism at the Limit of Metaphysics," *Graduate Faculty Philosophy Journal* 19/20, 1–2 (1997): 299–314.

2. I am indebted here to Thomas Altizer, whose radical theology has most forcefully articulated the distinction between the concepts of "eternal return" and "eternal recurrence." On the notion of the archaic eternal return, see Mircea Eliade, *The Myth of the Eternal Return,* trans. Willard R. Trask (Princeton, N.J.: Princeton University Press, 2005). For a historical overview of the concept of eternal recurrence, see Ned Lukacher, *Time-Fetishes: The Secret History of the Eternal Recurrence* (Durham, N.C.: Duke University Press, 1998). I discuss the difference between the archaic eternal return and Nietzsche's notion of eternal recurrence in "Blood and Stone: A Response to Altizer and Lingis," *New Nietzsche Studies* 4, 3–4 (2000–2001): 29–41; and in "Absolute Atonement," in *Thinking through the Death of God: A Critical Companion to Thomas J. J. Altizer* (Albany: State University of New York Press, 2004), 77–78.

3. See Emmanuel Levinas, "Transcendence and Evil," in Philippe Nemo and Emmanuel Levinas, *Job and the Excess of Evil,* trans. Michael Kigel (Pittsburgh: Duquesne University Press, 1998). Hereafter abbreviated TE (this essay is published also in *CPP* and *OG*).

4. John Izzi concludes his chapter in this volume, "Proximity in Distance: Levinas and Plotinus," with these questions.

5. Plotinus, *Enneads,* 7 vols., trans. A. H. Armstrong (Cambridge: Harvard University Press, 1981), I.6.1–9. Unless indicated otherwise, all subsequent references to Plotinus's writings will be taken from this edition and noted parenthetically without an abbreviation of the title.

6. Jacques Derrida uses these words from James Joyce's *Ulysses* to close his seminal essay "Violence and Metaphysics: An Essay on the Thought of Emmanuel Levinas," in *Writing and Difference,* trans. Alan Bass (Chicago: University of Chicago Press, 1978). Referring to "the thought of Being" that gave rise to Greek philosophy and to Western metaphysics and ontology in general, the radical difference signified by Joyce's words finds expression in

Levinas' construal of the Infinite or absolutely other—a thinking that "can make us tremble," writes Derrida. "In Greek, in our language, this thought [of the infinitely other] summons us," Derrida continues, "to a dislocation of the Greek *logos*, to a dislocation of our identity, and perhaps of identity in general; it summons us to depart from the Greek site and perhaps from every site in general, and to move toward what is no longer a source or site (too welcoming to the gods), but toward an *exhalation*, toward a prophetic speech already emitted not only nearer to the source than Plato or the pre-Socratic, but inside the Greek origin, close to the other of the Greek. . . . seek[ing] to liberate itself from the Greek domination of the Same and the One . . . as if from oppression itself . . . an ontological or transcendental oppression, but also the origin or alibi of all oppression in the world" (82–83).

7. See Reiner Schürmann, *Broken Hegemonies* (Bloomington: Indiana University Press, 2003), 139–88, for a radical reinterpretation of Plotinus. Although absorbing nearly intact the vocabulary of Parmenides of Elea, Plotinus departs from his metaphysics, thus marking "the closure of the Greek epoch, that is, the destitution of *hen-fantasm*" (139).

8. This phrase is taken from "Outside the Subject," *OS* 151–58.

9. "Desire is absolute if the desiring being is mortal and the Desired is invisible. Invisibility does not denote an absence of relation; it implies relations with what is not given, of which there is no idea" (*TI* 34).

10. On the return to the One, see Clyde Lee Miller, "Union with the One: *Ennead* 6, 9, 8–11," *New Scholasticism* 51 (1977): 182–95.

11. In scriptural Hebrew, the term *qadosh* signifies a breaking in or rupture of the spatiotemporal horizon by the transcendent deity.

12. On the corresponding notion of generosity in Plotinus, see Eric D. Perl, "'The Power of All Things': The One as Pure Giving in Plotinus," *American Catholic Philosophical Quarterly* 71, 3 (1997): 301–13. Perl addresses the problem of otherness in Plotinus and how it is "overcome" by assigning to the One, not the role of "producer," but rather the "power" of beings. The One generates beings by "giving" or "overflowing" itself (terms that Levinas himself uses in describing the absolutely other or the Infinite), thereby allowing the One to produce beings without enduring affection or being corrupted by means of a relationship to beings. Otherness is therefore not introduced by the One since the One itself "is" otherness itself, in distinction to which all other beings subsist, according to Perl.

13. On the philosophical and religious influences on Plotinus extending from the Presocratics to his time, see Giannis Stamatellos, *Plotinus and the Presocratics: A Philosophical Study of Presocratic Influences in Plotinus' Enneads* (Albany: State University of New York Press, 2007).

14. Nevertheless, Levinas acknowledges that Neoplatonism "offered the monotheism that conquered Europe in the first centuries of our era an itinerary and stations capable of corresponding to mystical tastes and the needs of salvation" (*AT* 10).

15. For a view that argues that Plotinus's theory of emanation is actually more creationist, see Lloyd P. Gerson, "Plotinus' Metaphysics: Emanation or Creation?" *Review of Metaphysics* 46, 3 (1993): 559–74.

16. On Plotinus's relation to the *Parmenides*, see John Fielder, "Plotinus' Reply to the Arguments of *Parmenides* 130A–131D," *Apeiron* 12 (1978): 1–5; Hans-Georg Gadamer, "Plato's *Parmenides* and its Influence," *Dionysius* 7 (1983): 3–16; Gary M. Gurtler, "Plotinus and the Platonic *Parmenides*," *International Philosophical Quarterly* 32, 4 (1992): 443–57; Darrell B. Jackson, "Plotinus and the *Parmenides*," *Journal of the History of Philosophy* 5

(1967): 315–27; F. M. Schroeder, "The Platonic *Parmenides* and Imitation in Plotinus," *Dionysius* 2 (1978): 51–73.

17. These two passages are translated by Elmer O'Brien in *The Essential Plotinus*, ed. Elmer O'Brien (Indianapolis: Hackett, 1975).

18. Derrida, "Violence and Metaphysics," 87.

19. *Autrui/autrui* and *Autre/autre* will be translated as "Other" and "other," respectively.

20. What Izzi (chapter 11 in this volume) finds lacking in Levinas is the sense of reciprocity found in Plotinus's construal of the relation between the same and the other, noting, for instance, "the otherness of the Intellect with respect to the One."

21. Elsewhere, Levinas writes: "The signifyingness of the trace places us in a lateral relationship . . . answering to an irreversible past. No memory could follow the traces of this past. . . . Eternity is the very irreversibility of time, the source and the refuge of the past" (TrO 355–56). Also, the anarchic past "signals a lapse of time that does not return, a diachrony refractory to all synchronization, a transcending dichotomy" (*OB* 9).

22. According to Gadamer, in Greek philosophy the idea of the Good and the form of the beautiful are so close as to constitute a veritable "confusion" (Hans-Georg Gadamer, *Truth and Method*, trans. Joel C. Weinsheimer and Donald G. Marshall, 2nd rev. ed. [New York: Continuum, 1993], 478). On the distinction between beauty and the beautiful in Plotinus (on which Gadamer does not comment) in relation to the Good, cf. John M. Rist, *Plotinus: The Road to Reality* (Cambridge: Cambridge University Press, 1967), 53–65.

23. Levinas writes: "It is certainly a great glory for the creator to have set up a being capable of atheism, a being which, without having been *causa sui*, has an independent view and word and is at home with itself " (*TI* 59). See also *OB* 140–52.

24. On the relation between the word and the image in Levinas, see my "The Listening Eye: Nietzsche and Levinas," *Research in Phenomenology* 31 (2001): 188–202.

25. On the notion of neutrality as it relates to the problems of being, transcendence, and Dasein, see Martin Heidegger, *The Metaphysical Foundations of Logic*, trans. Michael Heim (Bloomington: Indiana University Press, 1984), 136–40.

26. For a developed treatment of this issue, see John M. Rist, "Plotinus on Matter and Evil," *Phronesis* 6 (1961): 154–66.

27. According to O'Brien, "The soul will be contaminated by matter only if it abandons itself with too great a desire to the care of the object that it has herself brought to birth. Even so, the soul does not become evil of its own volition. Its 'sin' is not the expression of any will for evil. The soul's excessive absorption in caring for the things of this world has the tragic consequence that the soul itself becomes evil, because of the nature of the object that it cares for. The soul becomes evil, when it does so, because the object of its care is 'evil itself'" (*Essential Plotinus*, 190; translation revised slightly).

28. Commenting on the relation between the self and the other, Rist notes that Plotinus himself did not grasp the full implications of his theory. While the goal of desire is to transcend the self, insofar as the self is separated from the unity of the Intelligence and the One, "the traditional desire for independence of spirit prevents Plotinus from wholly seeing that one means of achieving precisely this end is to admit openly that all [people] are [related], all deriving from the same One, all striving for the same goal; in fact that one path to union with the One is through supporting *both* the inner and the outer [person] in his [or her] fellows. . . . In practice he has recognized that concern for others does not entail the withdrawal of the mind from the higher things and its submergence in the lower" (Rist, *Plotinus*, 168).

29. For a developed treatment of this question, see Edward B. Costello, "Is Plotinus Inconsistent on the Nature of Evil?" *International Philosophical Quarterly* 7 (1967): 483–97.

30. These words complete Derrida's above-mentioned citation from Joyce: "Jewgreek is Greekjew. Extremes meet?"

31. Though beyond the scope of inquiry here, perhaps it is apropos to suggest another closing—one that extends beyond the horizon of Western thought to a considerably different tradition to find a possible answer to the aporia left by this strange dialogue between the Greek and the Jew. While Levinas disavows any influence of "orientalism" at least with respect to the idea of the transcendence of the Good, Plotinus, it is said, was drawn toward Asian thought through his teacher Ammonius Saccas, although he never did embark on his desired quest to the East. In all likelihood, the influence in question was that of Indian thinking, and probably that of Samkya and Vedanta philosophies. The common element shared by these systems is the notion of *Brahman,* the transcendent infinite Absolute All that simultaneously includes and negates *maya* (transient phenomenal and psychological existence). In Madhyamika Buddhist philosophy, this finds expression as the difference between *sunyata* (emptiness) and *tathata* (suchness), a difference eventually recognized as being merely a matter of perspective: *sunyata* is *tathata* and *tathata* is *sunyata* (see Nagarjuna, *Mulamadhyamakakarika,* 25.18–19). Later, in the Chan and Zen traditions, this realization is reformulated, with the issue of the nature of reality articulated in terms of the difference between *samsara* (the cycle of birth and rebirth) and *nirvana* (the release from that cycle) are disclosed as both non-identical and the same. In other words, to employ a fundamental category of Buddhist thought, grasped in its initial apprehension as pertaining to sentient entities alone but later extended to embrace the totality of being, sentient and nonsentient, phenomenal and transcendental, this is but to say that everything is predicated on "dependent arising" (*pratityasamutpada*).

For a collection of perspectives on Plotinus's relation to Indian thinking, see *Neoplatonism and Indian Thought,* ed. Paulos Mar Gregarios (Albany: State University of New York Press, 1982). For a consideration of the relation between Plotinus and the Yogachara (Mind-Only) school of Buddhism, see Thomas McEvilley, "Plotinus and Vijnanavada Buddhism," *Philosophy East and West* 30, 2 (1980): 181–93. For a judicious comparison between Neoplatonism and Mahayana Buddhism, see Stanislas Breton, "L'un et l'etre," *Revue Philosophique Louvain* 83 (1985): 5–23. Breton also considers the difference between henology and ontology and why Neoplatonism opted for the former, framing the issue in terms of the relation between the "ontological difference" and the "meontological difference."

ETHICS AND PREDESTINATION

IN AUGUSTINE AND LEVINAS

Thomas J. J. Altizer

13

Emmanuel Levinas is perhaps our most purely non-apocalyptic or anti-apocalyptic thinker, one absolutely distancing his thinking from that apocalypse or new age released by the uniquely modern realization of the death of God. This is a distancing so absolute that it must go beyond any possible primordial condition to the absolutely pre-primordial, and a passivity so total as to bear no marks of passivity itself. This is as radical a project as has occurred in our world, and it inevitably evokes other horizons and other worlds. Perhaps the most revealing of these is the Augustinian revolution in the ancient world, a revolution giving birth to that center or subject of consciousness which became an ultimate ground of a uniquely Western culture and consciousness, or that very center that the thinking of Levinas so deeply intends to subvert or reverse.

The clearest dimension of Levinas' thinking is arguably its unveiling of the purely aethical condition of the world it confronts, a world that is unquestionably our world, a world that can be understood as a consequence of the death of God. While it is true that Levinas resists the language of the death of God, it is nonetheless true that, if only all too indirectly, he profoundly understands the consequences of the death of God, consequences so deeply ending ethical thinking and an ethical consciousness that only a truly revolutionary move could recover ethics, a move demanding a truly new and ultimately pure thinking. Here there is a genuine parallel between the thinking of Levinas and that of Augustine, who encountered a pagan world that he could know as the very opposite of the new world of Christianity, a pagan world that in this perspective is an absolutely aethical world, and one impelling a revolutionary new thinking. While Augustine was under the influence of the Neoplatonism of Eastern Christian thinking, he nonetheless profoundly transformed that thinking and did so as the first truly Pauline thinker, so that it is not until Augustine that a fully biblical thinking occurs theologically, and one decisively establishing a new Western consciousness, a consciousness that became the very center of a new Western world.

There has been no greater philosophical revolution than one establishing the center of consciousness as the center of thinking itself. This is the Augustinian revolution, and while unrecognized in our philosophical world, it is profoundly recognized by Hegel, who is deeply Augustinian in creating a philosophy of an absolute self-consciousness, although Hegel is deeply anti-Augustinian in knowing absolute self-consciousness as Absolute Spirit. This is possible only because Hegel is the first philosopher of the death of God, but he knows that death as an Augustinian or reverse Augustinian thinker, for he knows it as occurring in the depths of self-consciousness and as a fulfillment of that third or apocalyptic age inaugurated by the advent of Christianity. Nietzsche, too, can be understood as an Augustinian or reverse Augustinian thinker, and not only in his understanding of predestination as eternal recurrence but also in his understanding of the death of God, a death of God that is the ultimate apocalyptic event, and one bringing history to an end.

Augustine is most ambivalent or most elusive as an apocalyptic thinker, and this despite the fact that he is the most influential apocalyptic theologian in Western history. It is the concluding books of his *City of God* that have most deeply shaped Western apocalyptic theology, and just as this work inaugurates a genuine thinking that is a historical thinking, it thereby inaugurates an apocalyptic philosophy and theology of history that is consummated in Hegel and Nietzsche. Hegel and Nietzsche are our greatest historical thinkers, but each is so as an apocalyptic thinker. Here history itself is inevitably an apocalyptic history, a history not only culminating in the death of God but ultimately grounded in that absolute kenosis or absolute self-negation or absolutely reverse or inverted will to power that are the very opposites of everything Levinas understands as passivity.

If Augustine is the philosophical discoverer of the will, then it is Levinas who most purely unthinks the will, an unthinking that is simultaneously the unthinking of apocalypse, or the unthinking of that apocalypse released by the death of God. It is all too significant that the theological orthodoxies of Judaism, Christianity, and Islam alike arose in a negation or reversal of apocalypticism, an apocalypticism whose absolute negation issues in the advent of the absolutely sovereign and absolutely transcendent God. Thus, only the death of this God makes possible a genuine or full or absolute renewal of apocalypticism; and just as that apocalypticism is inevitably an atheistic apocalypticism, full or genuine modern atheism is inevitably an apocalyptic atheism.

Eastern Christian thinkers and visionaries are wholly free of the impact of Augustine, and they can respond to Western Christianity as being genuinely atheistic, as witness Dostoevsky. But the uniquely Western Christian God is an Augustinian God, being not only the God of an absolute predestination, a predestination wholly unknown in Eastern Christianity, but precisely thereby a *horror religiosus* known nowhere else in the world. Augustine created the doctrine of predestination as a deeply Pauline thinker, and it became a primal center of every genuinely Western theology. In its origin and its deeper ground, predestination is, however, deeply and profoundly dialectical, for not only does it know a total sin and a total grace that are inseparable, but that original sin which is the source of eternal death is a consequence of predestination, just as that absolute grace which is the sole source of eternal life is unknowable apart from the eternal death of damnation. Accordingly, Augustine can conclude the *City of God* with the affirmation that the eternal misery of the damned does not disappear in the blessed redemption of the saints, for only an awareness of that misery makes possible a knowledge of the absolute grace of forgiveness.

Predestination is also deeply dialectical in knowing an absolute predestination that is inseparable from a full and actual freedom. Indeed, Augustine as the first philosopher of the will is the first philosopher of the freedom of the will, but that freedom is inseparable from the impotence or slavery of the will, and it is the discovery of that impotence that made possible Augustine's conversion, as recorded in the *Confessions*. The *Confessions* is the first autobiography, and the creation of this genre is inseparable from the advent of what we have known as self-consciousness, but a self-consciousness that is wholly free and wholly impotent at once. For a uniquely Western freedom is inseparable from a uniquely Western impotence or repression, one inevitably generating self-laceration in its own willing or self-willing, so that this center of consciousness could only be a dichotomous center; and in discovering this center, Augustine discovered a purely dichotomous thinking.

Only this thinking could discover predestination, apart from which we are wholly without hope, being absolutely enslaved at our very center, but a predestination that is the source of every possible freedom. For freedom is wholly illusory apart from grace, and it is only actually realized with the actualization of grace and with the actualization of that grace which is absolutely prior to the creation. Nothing could be further from our common understanding of freedom than an Augustinian understanding, yet Augustine is the father of our Western freedom and is so as the first theologian of predestination. Nothing else so purely unveils that pure dichotomy which is the dichotomy of a uniquely Western subject, and nothing else so fully calls forth an absolute responsibility. It is a responsibility that can only ultimately issue in either redemption or damnation, and if the great mass of humanity is eternally predestined to damnation, that predestination is inseparable from the predestination of the saints, who are in no way whatsoever responsible for their own election, but who are nonetheless absolutely responsible, a responsibility that they share with the damned.

It is damnation itself that most purely unveils our absolute responsibility, a damnation that is not only an eternal damnation, but an eternity of the most horrible suffering, and even a bodily suffering, as Augustine attempts to demonstrate in the *City of God*. This is the damnation which is the most ultimate threat throughout the greater course of Christian history, one that has been the most ultimate sanction of justice itself, if not the most ultimate sanction ever actualized in our history. Perhaps Levinas is above all a philosopher of absolute responsibility; but as opposed to Augustine, this is not an actual responsibility in the Augustinian sense: not only is there no damnation within this horizon, but nothing that the Augustinian can know as either an actual history or an actual consciousness, and therewith there is here missing everything that we have known as world itself. Levinas may well be our most otherworldly philosopher, and most so as the philosopher of an absolute responsibility, and an absolute responsibility that here can only be an absolutely pre-primordial responsibility.

It is the pre-primordial that makes this thinking most purely ahistorical, but therewith it wholly dissolves or reverses also what we have known as the subject or center of consciousness. As opposed to all Eastern thinking, however, it does not know the absence or illusion of that subject, but far rather its actual dissolution, and its actual dissolution in the abyss or chaos of a uniquely modern world. Perhaps Levinas is the thinker who most purely reflects or gives witness to the Holocaust and to the absolutely catastrophic consequences of the Holocaust. In one sense, here Levinas is more Augustinian than Augustine himself, or more decisively aware of an absolute horror, and an absolute horror that is absolutely real. So it is that Levinas is our only twentieth-century philosopher who can actually think about evil; and while Augustine could not escape a Neoplatonic understanding of evil as privation, Levinas is not even tempted by such thinking, even if he is tempted by Neoplatonism, and above all by the purely primordial ground of Neoplatonism.

It is noteworthy that Levinas seldom if ever evokes the Name of God; rather, he speaks of the Infinite—moreover, of the absolutely pre-primordial Infinite—thereby distancing himself from what we have known as God and even perhaps distancing himself from the theologies of Judaism. This would be perfectly consistent with an unthinking of the death of God; it would be an unthinking of the God who dies in that death, or of the uniquely Western God, who is first purely thought by Augustine, and thought in a theological thinking first conceptually enacting that subject that is now realized as the center of consciousness. Levinas can be understood as most purely unthinking the death of God in his unthinking of the subject of consciousness, that very subject in which this death is first historically realized, and a subject apart from which this God would be wholly unmanifest. All too significantly, Levinas is thereby allied with his great predecessor Spinoza, who was a revolutionary thinker in first unthinking that subject, an unthinking making possible a radically new thinking of the totality of God.

Levinas is disguised for us if only because his theological identity is disguised. If a thinking of Levinas and Augustine at once is a way of dissolving this disguise, then Levinas would appear as an anti-Augustinian thinker, one not only unthinking that subject established by Augustine, but unthinking an Augustinian grace that is the grace of predestination. Indeed, this grace and this subject are inseparable from one another, which perhaps we can only decisively understand by relating Augustine and Levinas to each other, and even doing so on the basis of their understanding of an absolute responsibility. Here, Nietzsche's enactment of eternal recurrence is truly relevant, one that can be understood as a reverse Augustinian enactment of predestination, calling forth an absolute yes-saying to every event whatsoever; and thereby every event whatsoever is absolutely willed, and absolutely willed by that absolute will to power that Augustine knows as the Will of God.

This is a revealing perspective through which to understand the uniquely Western God, whom perhaps Nietzsche understood most purely, and did so by enacting an absolute Will to Power. And if thereby Nietzsche is the last philosopher of the will, he is just thereby a fulfillment of the first philosopher of the will, Augustine. Now if it is Augustine who inaugurates a uniquely Western thinking of God, then this is the God who dies in the uniquely modern realization of the death of God, one at the very center of the thinking of both Hegel and Nietzsche; and this is the thinking that Levinas most deeply negates. No other contemporary thinker is as deeply anti-Hegelian as is Levinas, nor so purely turned away from Nietzsche; only this makes possible the unthinking of the death of God in Levinas, and one inseparable from a pure negation of the uniquely Western subject. But this can occur only by way of an anti-Augustinian thinking. Only in this perspective can we understand how profoundly Augustinian both Hegel and Nietzsche are, and perhaps most manifestly Augustinian in their understanding of an absolute responsibility, an Augustinian absolute responsibility that is so purely reversed by Levinas.

If it is predestination that most openly draws forth the absolute responsibility of God, or the absolute responsibility of the Augustinian God, then the absolute responsibility of Levinas is clearly an opposite of this responsibility, and is so in its pure or absolute passivity that is will-lessness itself and therefore the very opposite of an absolute will to power. Nothing more decisively unveils that will to power than does an absolute predestination; and if absolute predestination is the ultimate *horror religiosus*, it is wholly reversed by Levinas, but only by a reversal of a uniquely

Augustinian grace. While this is the only grace that can actually be known in the Western Christian world, or known in that world centered in the subject of consciousness, it is a grace inseparable from the fallen will, or that will that wills only itself, and therefore a will that is the source of eternal death. This is a will that is reversed by an Augustinian grace, but this grace itself is possible only in and for the fallen will, an absolutely impotent or imprisoned will, and this is just the impotence or imprisonment that can only be liberated by an absolute predestination.

There is a fascinating parallel between an Augustinian understanding of the impotence of the will and the understanding of a pure passivity in Levinas. For Augustine, impotence is a wholly self-enclosed and self-imprisoning condition, whereas what Levinas understands as an anarchical passivity in *Otherwise than Being* is a passivity-for-the-other, more passive than the passivity of matter, answering for everything and everyone, a sacrifice without reserve. While an Augustinian understanding of the impotence of the will is immediately meaningful to us, and meaningful if only because of our fallen condition, the anarchical passivity of Levinas is one beyond all possibility of actual understanding, or one that could only be understood by a saint. Such a passivity for Augustine could only be a consequence of grace and of grace alone, a grace absolutely transfiguring the fallen and the impotent will, and a grace wholly silent and invisible to the impotent will. But is not the pure passivity of Levinas wholly silent and invisible, or invisible and silent to the will itself, or to everything that is actual as the will?

Could such a passivity possibly be understood as occurring in anything that we can actually know as consciousness or history? Even if it occurs in what Levinas speaks of as the incarnate subject, is that a subject that has anything but a wholly negative relationship to what we have known as the subject of consciousness? An Augustinian grace has meaning for us if only because it is the very opposite of our wholly fallen condition; it is just in knowing an absolute fall that we can become open to an absolute grace. Hence, the Augustinian places an overwhelming emphasis on the Fall, drawing forth the absolute negativity of the fallen will, for it is the very evocation of that negativity that awakens us to the necessity of a grace that would reverse it. The very opposite of this is true in Levinas, who places an overwhelming emphasis on an absolute responsibility as an absolute passivity, but who can never actually speak of its opposite, or of what the Augustinian so deeply knows as sin, and an absolute sin realizing an eternal death or damnation.

While it is true that damnation is primal in Christianity and peripheral in Judaism, nevertheless primal modern Jewish visionaries such as Proust and Kafka can enact an absolute judgment that is absolutely real, and absolutely real to the subject of consciousness; and all too ironically, that subject is here more actually real than anywhere else. This is an actuality truly missing in Levinas, or present only insofar as his thinking enacts the absolute horror of the Holocaust, but this is always an indirect enactment even if it profoundly affects this thinking. At no other point is Levinas so distant from Augustine, but this is an ironical distance, for Levinas is more profoundly opposed to a uniquely modern subject of consciousness than is any other contemporary thinker. Levinas thinks most purely by thinking against that subject, thus thinking the very opposite of that subject in thinking an absolute responsibility; and yet, it is this very dialectical ground that most establishes the thinking of Levinas as an actual thinking for us. So perhaps Levinas does know damnation, and knows it as being fully actual for us and most actual in our very irresponsibility, an irresponsibility that in our world has become all in all.

If it is in knowing the totality of sin that Augustine could know the totality of grace, a totality of grace that is predestination itself, then does Levinas actually know an absolute responsibility by knowing and reversing a uniquely modern subject of consciousness, a subject of consciousness that ultimately enacts the death of God? Augustine is the only ancient thinker who has truly been renewed in full modernity, but is he renewed by Levinas and renewed by effecting a full reversal of the Augustinian subject? Just as Augustine is the most influential of all ancient Christian thinkers, and so influential that Western Christianity simply is Augustinian Christianity and this in both its Catholic and its Protestant expressions, is an Augustinian presence a universal presence in our world, even if only influencing what we have come to know as an eternal death? Is Levinas that contemporary thinker who most decisively knows an eternal death, and as one who was most deeply initiated into philosophy by Heidegger himself? Is Levinas now the most influential of all philosophical theologians—or all apart from Heidegger—and like Heidegger is this an impact that occurs apart from a speaking of God?

The only glory that Levinas evokes is the glory of the Infinite, once again reminding one of Spinoza. But for Spinoza, finitude and infinitude are identical, whereas for Levinas the Infinite evokes the uniquely biblical God. At this crucial point, Levinas is truly alone among major twentieth-century philosophers, thus once again giving him a unique relationship to Augustine, who is the most biblical of all ancient theologians. While Augustine knows a biblical God who is simultaneously immanent and transcendent, and even absolutely immanent while being absolutely transcendent, Levinas knows that transcendent Infinite who is immanent only as an absolute call, and an absolute call to absolute passivity. Here there is another gulf between Augustine and Levinas—Augustine could found a uniquely Western Christian mysticism, one revolving about a genuine intimacy between the individual and God, and an intimacy that is a truly personal intimacy. Nothing like this is present in Levinas or in any other modern philosopher, yet it is precisely in hearing a pre-primordial call that Levinas hears an ultimate call to the other, an other to whom we must give ourselves without reserve, and for whom we must be absolutely responsible.

There are those for whom Levinas wholly reduces philosophy to ethics, and even to a theological ethics; and it is true that ethics is more primal for Levinas than for any other thinker. Or is this true? All too ironically, is this not also true of Nietzsche, that thinker who is most other than Levinas and with whom Levinas engages in a continual although commonly silent conflict, a conflict most deeply over Nietzsche's enactment of the death of God? Surely Nietzsche is the most revolutionary of all of our ethical thinkers and the only one seemingly effecting an absolute reversal of all given or manifest ethics and enacting an absolute engagement that is an inversion or reversal of all passivity, so that Nietzsche is the very opposite of Levinas as an ethical thinker.

Yet here too, Nietzsche is a reverse Augustinian thinker, one truly inverting that subject which Augustine established, and doing so by reversing a uniquely Augustinian predestination, a predestination that now becomes an absolutely immanent eternal recurrence, and an eternal recurrence that is the very reversal of the Augustinian God. This goes far beyond Levinas in its reversal of Augustinian thinking, thereby raising the possibility that Levinas is deeply in continuity with Augustine, and perhaps most so in his intended dissolution of the apocalyptic consequences of the death of God. Despite the fact that Augustine is a deeply Neoplatonic thinker, he nevertheless profoundly assaults the classical world, and above all, the ethical ground of that world. Only Augustine among our genuine thinkers has a deep hostility toward the imagination, although here he has a partial counterpart in his beloved Plato; but Augustine's hostility was inspired by his original love of classical art and literature, an art and literature that he comes to identify as purely pagan and therefore deeply sinful, and thus ancient Christianity goes beyond even Islam in its assault upon the pagan world. Of course, there is nothing like this in Levinas, but is there a deep opposition to modern secularism or modern atheism, which is its counterpart?

Such an opposition could be understood as occurring in Levinas' deconstruction of a contemporary selfhood or subject. Only this deconstruction makes possible an opening to a subjectivity before consciousness, or beyond consciousness, and one that is indeed the very inversion of a truly modern consciousness. Levinas engages in a radical rejection of the will, that is, a rejection of a uniquely modern will, a will that is the will of the will to power, and a will finally realizing a pure or absolute nothingness. This is a nothingness that is most purely understood by Nietzsche, and this is a nothingness that Levinas purely reverses, but only this inversion or reversal makes possible an opening to the absolutely pre-primordial. Augustine also discovers a pure nothingness in consciousness, a nothingness that is the nothingness of sin itself. A reversal of this nothingness occurs in the realization of grace, and it is just because of this nothingness that this grace could only be the grace of predestination.

For Augustine, pride is the beginning of all sin; but if it is the source of sin or evil, it is not its cause, for nothing causes an evil will, since it is the evil will itself that causes the evil act, and an evil choice proceeds, not from a nature or being, but rather from a deficiency of being deriving from our being created out of nothing (*City of God*, XII, 6). An evil choice never consists in a defection to things that are evil in themselves; it is the defection in itself that is evil, for there is nothing whose existence or nature is evil. Evil choice and evil itself consist solely in falling away from and deserting God. Although evil diminishes or corrupts the goodness of nature or being, it does so only in the consequent deficiency of its own will, a deficiency that is itself an absence or privation of goodness or being, so that sin or evil in itself gives witness to the goodness of existence. That goodness is not even compromised by the birth of "flesh," and for Augustine, flesh is that lust of the body which is in opposition to spirit, a lust that is born with original sin, whereby and wherein the original disobedience of the will fulfills itself in the body's disobedience of the soul.

So it is that the first act of Adam and Eve after the fall is to cover their *pudenta*, their organs of shame, for while these organs remain physically the same, now for the first time they become shameful. This is a shame reflecting the disobedience of the "flesh," a disobedience that immediately seizes power over the whole man. And the most decisive sign of this ultimately and fatally pathological condition is the advent of sexual orgasm, one that could not exist before the fall, for orgasm is the consequence of a new dichotomy between the body and the soul. This is a violently discordant state in which passion and mind are wholly unlike but wholly commingled, thus making possible a climax in which the mind is overwhelmed (*City of God*, XIV, 6). This is the very moment and condition that makes possible the transmission of original sin, the one moment in which the mind is wholly absent, a moment of lust in its purest form and also the moment in which the will is least free. Each of us has our origin in this moment of pure lust, and our actual origin therefore becomes the very opposite of our origin in the Creation.

Nothing more purely embodies Augustine's understanding of the radical deficiency of evil or the sinful will than his conception of orgasm. Here his theological genius is at its height, for not only does he fully conjoin his Plotinian and his Pauline roots in this conception, but precisely thereby he fully brings together an interior and psychological understanding with an ontological and theological understanding. Not until Augustine is sexual passion or lust realized and portrayed as being simultaneously an exterior and an interior bondage. At no other point is Augustine further from his great classical predecessor Euripides. Moreover, it is in his understanding of lust or concupiscence that Augustine most clearly and most decisively realizes his revolutionary psychological understanding; here he makes fully concrete his conception of the will as being wholly enslaved yet nevertheless free.

And he incorporates this understanding not only in his self-portrait in the *Confessions*, but again and again throughout his work, just as this understanding becomes a dominant power in a uniquely Western civilization.

For Augustine the most remarkable feature of the sexual sphere is its involuntariness. Nonetheless, we know from within that we will concupiscence with our own free will. So far from simply happening to us as though it visited us from without, it is present at the very center of the activity of the will and is so most firmly when it occurs most involuntarily. This is precisely the point at which Augustine realizes the overwhelming actuality of original sin and its consequence, that *massa perditonis,* which is sin and judgment at once. It is the judgment of sin that we do the evil that we would not. This is the judgment that is eternal death, and it is a judgment that we enact within ourselves in every moment of concupiscence. Each such moment is at once an involuntary and a freely willed moment, a moment in which our own will is unquestionably present, as witness that unique delight released by lust, a delight that is so fully our own. And yet the very power of that lust is wholly beyond us even if wholly within us, and this beyondness of lust is what most enslaves us, and does so even if it is our own immediate ground and source.

We can fully recognize that we are born of lust, a lust that we most passionately will, and that such a will is in its innermost center a deeply divided or self-divided will. It is a will that can never will concupiscence without willing against itself and therefore can never will concupiscence without internally realizing its own ultimate guilt; yet it can never will not to lust, or not do so fully and decisively, and this is because the divided will is by necessity an incomplete or partial will and therefore can never fully and wholly will. This divided will is that will which is most interiorly our own, a will that is at once free and impotent, free insofar as it is and exists as will, impotent insofar as it wills to be itself or to be autonomously. So it is that the fallen and rebellious will is an impotent will, an impotence born with original sin, and an impotence that can only be reversed by grace and by grace alone. Hence it is the grace of predestination, a predestination whose absolute necessity is most concretely demonstrated by our sexual lust and bondage. This is a predestination whose necessity each of us can interiorly know, and interiorly know in our all-too-intimate experience of an ultimate bondage, which is most concretely manifest in lust itself.

Never has any thinker been more concrete than this, nor has any other thinker had so universal an impact in such thinking. And if it could be said that each of us knows both the freedom and the impotence of the will, one must inevitably question whether Levinas could reverse such an understanding. Or is this a misunderstanding of Levinas? Is it not an Augustinian will but a uniquely modern will that Levinas intends to reverse, a will that is a will to nothingness itself, and one only released or embodied as a consequence of a uniquely modern realization of the death of God? Yet Augustine knows the will as a will to nothingness, which is precisely why our will is an impotent will; and yet, that is a will inseparable from everything that we actually know as freedom, and the freedom of our will is the freedom of the fallen will, hence it is inevitably inseparable from bondage. Nonetheless, this is an extraordinary freedom, one not realized until Augustine, and one overwhelming in a uniquely Western subject. Is this the subject that Levinas must reverse, and must reverse to realize an absolute responsibility, a responsibility that is the call of the Infinite, and one alone making possible a real and actual ethics?

Yet the absolute responsibility of Levinas is an extraordinarily abstract one, as is most ironically clear in everything that he writes about the face and the face-to-face encounter when we experience the absolute alterity of others. All of this under-standing is wholly closed to the actuality of face or to its rich historical diversity as manifest in the visual arts and in literature, wherein face is manifest in innumerable forms throughout the world, forms that can be truly distant from each other. This is the context in which we can most decisively see that Levinas never thinks concretely about face, or thinks so as to make possible an actual envisionment of face, and this despite the fact that he is thinking in a truly new world, a truly anonymous world in which face as face can only be a mask. Has the Holocaust had no effect upon the face? Has that absolute horror affected every domain but this one? And is that be-cause Levinas has a wholly abstract understanding of face and can only know face as a universal face that is always and everywhere the same, so that even its alterity can only be a wholly abstract alterity?

Whereas Augustine can write about sin and concupiscence and freedom in such a way as to evoke their full actuality for the reader, this never happens with Levinas, whose absolute responsibility is just as abstract as Kant's categorical im-perative and hence fully removed from the whole realm of actuality. Now this is just the charge that is commonly made against philosophical ethics, and above all against our deeper philosophical ethics. Only Nietzsche in the modern world and those thinkers who have been most affected by Nietzsche, such as Heidegger and Sartre, can fully meet this charge. Is it the profound turn of Levinas against Nietz-sche that has driven him to such an abstract understanding, thereby closing him to every actuality that is a consequence of the death of God, or the consequence of the realization of an absolute immanence? No thinker in our world is more ahistor-ical than Levinas, and this may be absolutely essential to make possible his ethics. And if, thereby, it is the very opposite of Nietzsche's ethics, in that perspective we can see that it is likewise the opposite of Augustine's ethics.

Nonetheless, it is possible that the face that Levinas most deeply knows is in-deed a truly and finally concrete face, and is that unique face which is the conse-quence of the Holocaust, the face of a sacrificial victim who is a vicarious victim, one bearing the pain and suffering of all humanity. Then we could know that face as being the face of everyone, but only in that unique world realized by the Holocaust itself, a face in which everyone is no one, but only insofar as an absolute catastrophe has occurred. If that is an apocalyptic catastrophe ending humanity itself, then every manifest humanity is an illusory or unreal humanity—or unreal insofar as it is not an ultimate victim—just as every face is now illusory or a mask insofar as it is not the face of an ultimate victim. Such an understanding would be fully coincident with an Augustinian understanding and would even be coincident with an Augustinian understanding of predestination, for therein every given humanity is a wholly sinful or impotent humanity, and precisely thereby is a pure and actual nothingness. That is a nothingness only made manifest, however, in the grace of predestination, a grace actually realized only by the vicarious suffering of Christ, or only by that victim who is the absolute victim, and one embodying in this suffering the suffering of all and everyone. Only that suffering finally actualizes an absolute grace, and the absolute grace of predestination.

The grace of predestination is wholly independent of all of us; it just thereby makes manifest our ultimate emptiness or nothingness, in which we are wholly incapable of any and every ethics—and that is our actual condition, and the only condition open to the grace of predestination. Predestination is also absolutely pre-primordial, occurring before the creation of the world, and only thereby is it an absolute or a total grace. Perhaps it is Levinas who knows predestination most deeply in our world, and knows it by knowing the absolutely pre-primordial, an absolutely pre-primordial issuing in the call to an absolute responsibility, hence his creation of an absolutely impossible ethics, or an absolutely impossible ethics apart from this absolutely pre-primordial ground, a pre-primordial ground fully coinciding with an absolute predestination. In this perspective, Levinas could finally be profoundly Augustinian, and even our purest Augustinian apart from Beckett and Nietzsche. Thereby an absolute guilt becomes a way to an absolute grace, and one only possible in the depths of emptiness or nothingness itself, or in the depths of that very world released by the Holocaust, which is impossible apart from a full and actual realization of the death of God.

Contributors

Thomas J. J. Altizer is Professor Emeritus of Religious Studies at Stony Brook University. He is the author of fifteen books, including *The Self-Identity of God, Genesis and Apocalypse, The Genesis of God,* and mostly recently, *Godhead and the Nothing* and *Living the Death of God.*

Deborah Achtenberg is Associate Professor of Philosophy at the University of Nevada, Reno. Her previous work, centering on the relation between ethics and metaphysics for Aristotle, includes *Cognition of Value in Aristotle's Ethics: Promise of Enrichment, Threat of Destruction.* In her current work, a book in progress on Levinas and Plato, she continues to pursue her interest in the relation between ethics and metaphysics.

Claudia Baracchi is Associate Professor of Philosophy at the New School for Social Research. Her research interests include ancient philosophy, nineteenth- and twentieth-century Continental philosophy, philosophy of history, feminist thought, philosophy of art, political philosophy, and ethics. She is the author of various articles on these areas and of the books *Of Myth, Life and War in Plato's Republic* and *Aristotle's Ethics as First Philosophy.* She is currently working on two book-length projects, one on the question of nature and one on war from a philosophical as well as psychoanalytical perspective.

Silvia Benso is Professor of Philosophy at Rochester Institute of Technology. In addition to several articles on Levinas, especially in his relation to various philosophers such as Plato, Nietzsche, and Heidegger, she is author of *Pensare dopo Auschwitz: Etica filosofica e teodicea ebraica; The Face of Things: A Different Side of Ethics;* and *Pensare ambientalista. Tra filosofia e ecologia,* with Brian Schroeder, with whom she is also co-editor of *Contemporary Italian Philosophy: Crossing the Borders of Ethics, Politics, and Religion.*

Bettina Bergo is Associate Professor of Philosophy at the Université de Montreal. She is author of *Levinas Between Ethics and Politics* and co-editor of an anthology of Levinas' work entitled *Levinas' Contribution to Contemporary Thought* (*Graduate Faculty Philosophy Journal* 1998). She has translated three works of Levinas and

M. Zarader's *The Unthought Debt: Heidegger and the Hebraic Heritage,* and she is co-translator of *Judéités: Questions à Jacques Derrida.* The author of articles on Levinas, Merleau-Ponty, feminism, and psychoanalysis, she is currently working on a history of anxiety in nineteenth-century philosophy and psychoanalysis.

Francisco J. Gonzalez is Associate Professor of Philosophy and Department Chair at Skidmore College. He is author of *Dialectic and Dialogue: Plato's Practice of Philosophical Inquiry* and editor of *The Third Way: New Directions in Platonic Studies.* His publications also include a wide variety of articles on Plato, Aristotle, Heidegger, and contemporary hermeneutics. He recently completed a book entitled *Plato and Heidegger: A Question of Dialogue.*

Catriona Hanley is Associate Professor of Philosophy at Loyola College in Maryland. She is author of *Being and God in Aristotle and Heidegger: The Role of Method in Thinking the Infinite.* Her primary interests are metaphysics and epistemology in the Greek and Continental traditions. She is the author of various articles on the confluence of Greek and German thought, with a special interest in the relationship between Levinas and Heidegger. More recently, she has become interested in using classical thinkers to enlighten current political events. Currently she is working on a book on the concept of panic.

John Izzi is Chair and Professor of Philosophy at Saint Michael's College in Vermont. His interests include, in addition to contemporary French thought and Neoplatonism, Spinoza and Nietzsche. He received the doctorate in philosophy at the University of Paris–Sorbonne.

Pierre Lamarche is Associate Professor of Philosophy at Utah Valley University. He has published broadly on the work of Heidegger, Benjamin, Kofman, Derrida, Blanchot, Proust, Bataille, and Hellenistic Skepticism. He is co-editor of a forthcoming volume on Antonio Negri, and is currently completing a manuscript on Heidegger and Benjamin.

Michael Naas is Professor of Philosophy at DePaul University. He is author of *Turning: From Persuasion to Philosophy* and *Taking on the Tradition: Jacques Derrida and the Legacies of Deconstruction.* He is the co-translator or co-editor of seven books by Jacques Derrida, including *Adieu: To Emmanuel Levinas; Chaque fois unique, la fin du monde;* and *Rogues: two essays on reason.*

Adriaan Peperzak is the Arthur J. Schmitt Professor of Philosophy at Loyola University Chicago. He is the author of numerous works, including *To the Other; Be-*

yond; Before Ethics; Modern Freedom: Hegel's Legal, Moral, and Political Philosophy; Elements of Ethics; Philosophy Between Faith and Theology; and *Thinking: From Solitude to Dialogue and Contemplation.*

Julie Piering is the Richard Wood Professor for the Teaching of Philosophy at Northern Arizona University. Her main fields of study are ancient Greek and contemporary French thought. She has published articles engaging the Cynics as well as their importance for contemporary thinkers such as Foucault and is currently at work on two projects—a study of the relation between shame and irony in the Platonic corpus, and the problem of writing in antiquity.

Brian Schroeder is Professor of Philosophy, Department Chair, and Director of Religious Studies at Rochester Institute of Technology. He is author of *Altared Ground: Levinas, History and Violence,* and, with Silvia Benso, of *Pensare ambientalista. Tra filosofia e ecologia.* He is co-editor of *Thinking Through the Death of God: A Critical Companion to Thomas J. J. Altizer* and, with Silvia Benso, of *Contemporary Italian Philosophy: Crossing the Borders of Ethics, Politics, and Religion.*

Tanja Stähler is Lecturer in Philosophy at the University of Sussex, United Kingdom. Her publications include a book on Hegel and Husserl entitled *Die Unruhe des Anfangs: Hegel und Husserl über den Weg in die Phänomenologie* as well as articles on Plato, Hegel, Husserl, Heidegger, Merleau-Ponty, Levinas, and Derrida. She is currently writing a book titled *Plato and Levinas: The Ambiguous Out-Side of Ethics.*

Index

Abbahu (Rabbi), 183
ability, 25, 26, 28, 30
Abraham, 211, 212, 214
Absolute, the, 216, 217
abstract, xi, 17, 56, 109, 114, 119, 140, 145, 149, 159, 223, 224, 240
abyss, 115, 203, 204, 207, 208, 233
Aenesidemus, 167
aer, 13–16, 19–22
affirmation, 2, 95, 101n19, 170, 176n10; of the divine, 199, 218, 232
Agamben, Giorgio, 7, 179–185, 188–190, 192–194
Agathon, 25–27, 29, 30, 50
agent intellect, 88, 104, 115
agogē, 167, 169
air, 4, 9, 11–22, 183, 186
aisthēsis, 106, 110, 115–117, 119, 120
akin (*oikeion*), 47, 48, 58
aletheuein, 113
Alexander of Aphrodisias, 123, 124n6, 161n9
All, the (*to pan*), 125, 221
alterity, 6, 10, 12, 20, 58, 59, 64, 68, 99, 144, 145, 148–150, 155–157, 159, 174, 185, 187, 190, 196–199, 201–209, 213, 217, 218–220, 223, 224, 240
Altizer, Thomas J. J., 226n2
ambiguity, 16, 21, 40, 50, 52, 56, 78, 90, 92, 213, 215, 223, 225
Ammonius Saccas, 229n31
Amos, 178
analogy, 14, 46, 56, 70, 75, 81, 95, 100, 102, 145–147, 151, 211
anamnesis, 60, 61, 83, 100
Anaxarchus, 175
Anaximander, 11, 13, 18
Anaximenes, 4, 9, 11, 13–16, 18–22
animality, 18, 20, 21
animation, 15, 19–21
Annas, Julia, 151, 163n29
Antipater, 161n10
apatheia, 144, 150, 160n1, 168
apeiron, 11, 32
apocalypse (apocalyptic), 178, 183, 225, 230, 231, 237, 241; anti-, 230; non-, 230
Apollodorous, 26, 27
apperception, 187, 188

Arcesilaus, 167, 170
Aristo, 150, 162n23
Aristodemus, 26
Aristophanes, 24, 26, 28–32, 50, 51, 63, 87
Aristotle, xi, 4–6, 8, 13, 23n2, 36, 82, 83, 88, 99, 103–143, 162n16, 163n31, 167; works: *De Anima*, 120–122, 124n6, 125nn11,13,15; *Metaphysics*, 5, 105, 111, 114, 119, 123, 124nn4,16, 130–132; *Nicomachean Ethics*, 115–118, 120, 123, 124n4, 125nn9,14, 130–135; *On the Generation of the Animals*, 104; *Organon*, 5, 105; *Physics*, 105, 119, 124n4, 125n8; *Posterior Analytics*, 105–114, 124
arkhe (*arche*), 4, 9, 13, 18, 23n2, 103, 107, 108, 111, 112, 121, 198, 221
ascent, 97, 211, 213, 222
askēsis, 145, 161n4
asymmetry, 3, 61n19, 63, 88, 95, 175, 175n2, 217, 223
asynchrony, 3
ataraxia, 162, 168, 169
atheism, 31, 53–56, 66, 199, 215, 218, 228, 231, 237
Athens, 25, 26, 39n8, 128–130, 140–142, 212
Augustine (Augustinian), 7, 8, 23n9, 220, 223, 230–241
autochthonous, 55
autonomy (autonomous), xii, 12, 17, 33, 53, 57, 67, 68, 103, 106, 109, 122, 239

bad conscience, 71
Bales, Eugene F., 226n1
Bataille, Georges, 97
beautiful, 25, 26, 28–30, 36–38, 46, 50, 228n22
Beckett, Samuel, 241
being-toward-death, 33, 34
belief, 107, 115, 128, 166–170, 173, 175, 176
Benjamin, Walter, 8, 180, 186, 189, 191, 192, 195
Benveniste, Émile, 189, 193
Bergson, Henri, xi, 83, 99
Bernasconi, Robert, 78nn10,11, 165, 166, 172, 173, 175n1, 176nn9,10, 177n14
Bernet, Rudolf, 78n15
beyond being, 4, 8, 12, 22, 25, 35–38, 40, 41, 51, 63, 72, 78, 82, 83, 99, 104, 147, 197, 203, 205, 207, 213, 215, 216, 218–220

247

Bible (the Book), xii, 1, 9, 22, 97, 98
Bild, das (the image, in Benjamin), 186, 187
Blanchot, Maurice, 5, 80–82, 84–87, 89–98,
    100nn9,11, 101n19, 177n11
body, 4, 13–22, 30, 67, 70, 72, 73, 76, 78, 118,
    125n16, 135, 152–154, 207, 219, 221,
    222, 238
Boreas, 26
breath (breathing), 14–17, 19–23, 186, 191,
    214
Brentano, Franz, 125n11
Breton, Stanislas, 229n31
Buber, Martin, 191
Burggraeve, Roger, 139, 143n12

Callicles, 26, 27, 69
Cantarella, Eva, 39n8
Carneades, 167
cave (Platonic), 63, 71, 77nn3,7, 96
chaos, 54, 70, 71, 233
Char, René, 84, 86, 87, 96, 97, 100
charadrios, 27
Christ (*christos*), 180, 241
Christianity (Christian), 1, 4, 7, 8, 22, 124, 128,
    161, 163, 178, 180, 184, 194, 211, 212,
    225, 230–233, 235–237
chronogenesis, 192, 193
Chrysippus, 151, 152, 161n10, 162nn13,15,
    163n31
Cicero, 150, 161n11, 163nn25,28, 170, 176n8
circle: closed, 32, 77n7; people, 29; of the Same,
    83
cogito, 201
coincidentia oppositorum, 225
Collin, Françoise, 100n9
comedy (comic), 26, 27, 29, 30
community, 18, 61, 73, 98, 133, 160, 181, 184,
    186, 187, 223
conscience, 18, 71, 141
consciousness, 7, 15–18, 31, 32, 83, 84, 103, 106,
    129, 137, 140, 158, 182, 187–189,
    191–193, 212, 214, 224, 225, 230–237
contemplation, 6, 43, 114, 120, 132–135, 142,
    204, 205
contraction, 35, 187, 191, 193
conversation, 5, 35, 45, 79–81, 85, 89–93, 96–99,
    101, 206
Corinthians (Letter to the), 180–183, 193, 194
cosmopolitanism, 6, 160
Costello, Edward B., 229n29
counter-history, 181, 195n9
Crates, 161n3
creation, 232, 238, 241; as opposed to emana-
    tion, 227n15; *ex nihilo*, 24, 25, 33–35, 54;
    of duty, 145; self-, 159
Critchley, Simon, 78n10
critique, knowledge as, 44

Cronos, 72
Cynic (Cynics), 144, 145, 160, 161nn2,3

daimon, 29, 51, 104, 115
damnation, 232, 233, 235, 236
Davidson, James, 39n8
Davies, Paul, 175, 175n2, 176n16
death of God. *See* God
death, 33, 62, 71, 74
deconstruction, 203, 210, 237
demiurgic, 24
Demos, R., 77n3
Depew, David, 134, 142n5
Derrida, Jacques, 5, 46, 59–61, 77–82, 84, 85, 90,
    91, 93–95, 99–101, 143, 166, 172, 174,
    175, 177, 181, 194, 226, 227, 228, 229
Descartes, René (Cartesian), xi, 10, 20, 40, 83,
    88, 89, 164, 166, 176, 201, 202
desire, 4, 24, 25, 29–36, 38, 39n12, 45, 47, 48,
    50–52, 54, 56–59, 70, 75, 87–89, 127,
    132, 133, 135, 140, 142, 150, 151, 153,
    154, 163, 197, 198, 200–203, 205, 206,
    208, 211–213, 215, 216, 220–222,
    227–229
dialogue, 42–44, 49, 59, 98, 101, 115, 171,
    185
dianoia, 37, 113, 124
dichotomy, 56, 117, 228, 232, 238
Diogenes Laertius, 13, 23n4, 152, 161, 162, 167,
    176n7
Diotima, 25, 26, 29, 30, 35, 36, 39n8, 50, 51
disclosure, 32, 87, 89, 95, 101n15, 124n2, 188
discourse, 43, 46, 82, 85, 92, 94, 98, 101n17,
    102n21, 105, 106, 111, 114, 123, 137,
    138, 162, 173, 182, 188, 191, 192
disinterestedness, 20, 88, 137, 182
distance, 3, 18, 21, 23, 32, 85, 88, 89, 196, 197,
    198, 201, 202, 204, 205, 207, 208, 214,
    217, 236
divinity, 120, 203, 214, 224
donation, 19–21, 204, 207, 208
Dostoyevsky, Fyodor, 63, 77n1, 232
Dover, K. J., 39n8
dunamis, 111, 117, 130
Düring, Ingemar, 125n11
duty, 6, 142, 145, 149, 150, 152–154, 158–160,
    161n5, 163n33

Ebreo, Leone (Judah Abravanel), 39n12
Ecclesiastes, 182
Ecriture, 97, 98
ec-stases (temporality), 187
ecstasy, 218, 219
egoism (egoist), 13, 17, 19, 22, 24, 31, 47, 52, 54,
    55, 57, 58, 64–66, 68, 75, 101, 138, 151,
    157, 173, 174, 198, 199, 200, 223
Egypt, 212

ekklēsia, 181
elemental, 12, 13, 18, 21
Eliade, Mircea, 226n2
Eliezer (Rabbi), 179, 184
emanation, 54, 213, 216, 227
Empedocles, 11
emunah (confidence), 190
epagoge, 108, 109, 115, 124n3
epekeina tēs ousias, 82, 215, 219
Epictetus, 4, 146, 152–155, 162n14, 163nn26,36, 164n41
episteme, 105, 107, 108, 110, 113, 122
epochē, 168, 169, 184
eros (erotic), 4, 24–26, 28, 29, 36, 40, 46–52, 56, 70, 99; *ta erotika,* 26, 35
Eryximachus, 26, 28
eschatology (eschatological), 6, 10, 128, 141, 185, 212, 214, 226n1
essence, 15, 20, 41, 54, 82, 83, 169, 186, 188, 189, 215, 218, 219, 223; non-, 16
eternal, 24, 34–36, 120, 122, 123, 125, 126, 161n9; death, 232, 235, 236, 239; forms, 30, 35, 147; life, 232; of skepticism, 165, 166, 172; recurrence (as opposed to return), 226n2, 231, 237; return, 7, 210, 211, 213, 215, 217, 219–221, 223, 225, 226, 226n2
ethics, 2, 4, 6–8, 21, 25, 38, 41, 55, 56, 59, 61, 66, 68, 70–72, 75, 78, 80–82, 98, 106, 128, 135–137, 139–141, 143, 170, 173, 174, 205, 212, 217–220, 222, 225, 230, 237, 240, 241, 243, 245; as first philosophy, 5, 103, 105–107, 109, 111, 113, 115, 117, 119, 121, 123, 125, 170, 172–175, 225, 243; of ethics, 181; Stoic, 144, 145, 147–151, 153, 155–157, 159, 161, 163
ethos, 5, 61, 105
eudaimonia, 8, 18, 70, 132, 150, 162n22
eupatheiai, 152, 160n1
Euripedes, 238
Eusebius, 162n13
evil, 7, 153, 179, 183–185, 199, 200, 211, 216, 218, 220–225, 226n3, 228nn26,27, 229nn29,31, 233, 238, 239
excess, 41, 43, 82, 103, 106, 116, 150–152, 162, 206–209; of evil, 211, 222–225, 226n3, 228n27
expiration, 14, 20, 21
exteriority, 4, 5, 12, 31, 42, 49, 50, 52, 56, 57, 59, 64, 68, 75, 101, 104, 196, 207, 209, 213, 218, 222, 223

face (*visage*), xi, 3, 5, 13, 41–43, 45, 46, 49, 52, 53, 57, 58, 60n6, 67, 68, 71, 76, 81, 82, 85, 89–91, 92–95, 97, 100, 102, 138–140, 143, 157, 162, 185, 206, 217–219, 223–225, 240, 241

face to face (face-to-face), 5, 32, 35, 44, 74–76, 92, 93, 98, 101, 148, 149, 156, 157, 159, 187, 240
faith, 128, 138, 190, 214
fate, 136, 146, 161n9, 162n13, 213, 214
fecund (fecundity), 24, 32–35
Fielder, John, 227n16
finitude, 44, 95, 122, 179, 182, 236
first philosophy. *See* ethics, as first philosophy
fitting, 37, 38
flesh, 20, 22, 30, 145, 238
for itself, 19, 53, 54, 215
form (forms), 35, 38, 228n22; in Aristotle, 126n16, 131, 132, 142n2; Platonic, 39n13, 45, 46, 60n5, 63, 70, 147, 148; in Plotinus, 197–199, 201, 203, 207, 220–223
Frederikse, T. C., 162n20
freedom, 16, 31, 33, 53, 94, 98, 100, 104, 150, 154, 157, 159, 168, 169, 180, 187, 214, 223, 232, 239, 240; human, 141, 142, 179, 184, 185
friendship, 80, 82, 91, 93, 98, 100n11, 153

Gadamer, Hans-Georg, 227n16, 228n22
Galen, 151, 152
Gerson, Lloyd P., 124n4, 176n7, 227n15
glory, 199, 216, 218, 228n23, 236
gnosis, 107, 108
gnosticism (gnostic), 7, 179, 185, 210, 225
God, 7, 13, 15, 39n12, 42, 81–83, 94, 95, 97, 100, 102, 104, 124n2, 125, 128, 143n9, 146, 164n42, 185, 199, 200, 203, 207, 208, 213, 216, 222, 224, 226n1, 231–234, 236–238; death of, 7, 210, 226, 230, 231, 233, 234, 236, 237, 240, 241
grace, 232, 234–237, 239, 241
gratitude, 213, 214
Grebowicz, Margret, 166, 172, 173, 175n2, 177nn12,14
Gregarios, Paulos Mar, 229n31
Greisch, Jean, 226n1
Guillaume, Gustave, 192, 193, 194
guilt, 77, 185, 239, 241; -free, 18
Gurtler, Gary M., 227n16
Güven, Ferit, 77n6
Gyges, 5, 55, 63–68, 73–75, 77, 88

Hades, 72, 213
Halperin, David M., 39nn5,8
happiness, 17, 18, 28, 47, 48, 68–71, 106, 132–134, 138–139, 142, 146, 150, 153, 162, 163, 186
harmony (harmonize), 1–3, 18, 28, 69–72, 163n25
healing, 29
hearing, 74, 109, 236

Hebraism (Hebraic), 94, 211, 212, 225
Hegel, G. W. F. (Hegelian), xi, xii, 10, 15, 16, 22, 23n10, 60nn1,6, 99n5, 136, 144, 196, 220, 231, 234
Heidegger, Martin (Heideggerian), 2, 10, 13, 18, 33, 34, 60nn1,6, 77n4, 78n9, 82, 85, 87, 99nn3,5, 100nn8,11, 103, 125n7, 129, 131, 142n1, 144, 156, 180–183, 185–188, 191, 194n3, 210, 220, 226n1, 228n25, 236, 240
height, 32, 63, 87, 94, 104, 138–141, 143, 156, 224, 238
helmsman, 35
Heraclitus (Heraclitean), 4, 10, 11, 28, 54, 55, 86, 87, 93, 97, 100
Herillus, 162n23
heroic, 25, 26, 29, 30, 32, 34–36
hiccups, 28
Hierocles, 153, 163n34
history, xi, 2, 15–17, 22, 33, 104, 181, 186, 195nn8,9, 223, 224, 225, 233, 235; apoc-alyptic, 231; of ontology, 40, 129; of phi-losophy, 15, 22, 83, 93, 147
Holocaust, 233, 235, 240, 241
homosexuality, 26, 39nn5,8
hope, 6, 35, 136, 137, 140, 143, 185, 186, 225, 232
hormē, 150, 162n24
horror religiosus, 232, 234
horror, 220; absolute, 233, 235, 240
hos mè (as not), 179, 182–184, 186, 187, 194
hubris, 26, 29
humanism, xi, 5, 81, 84, 85, 87, 95, 96, 101
Hume, David, 166
Husserl, Edmund, 61n19, 187, 191
hypostasis, 12, 13, 22, 92, 176, 213, 221

idealism, 7, 83, 84, 136, 137, 139, 140, 210, 220
ideology, 130, 136–137, 139–140
il y a, 11–13, 16, 19, 21
illeity, 219
immortality, 24, 30, 33, 47, 120, 123
in itself, 52, 94, 161n9, 192; good, 41, 51, 197; evil, 238
incest, 31, 48
indefinite, 11, 32, 112
infinite, the, 10, 32, 57, 58, 88, 89, 106, 122, 201, 202, 227nn7,12, 233, 240; glory of, 218, 236; idea of, 156, 215; in the finite, 222
infinity, 52, 57, 60, 88, 89, 122, 126, 144, 156, 157, 164n42, 201–203, 206, 209, 217–219
ingratitude, 214
insatiability, 26
inspiration, xi, 9, 20–22; and expiration, 14
interiority, 5, 17–19, 49, 50, 56, 61, 62, 64–68, 70, 75, 77, 88, 104, 207, 209, 218, 223
intuition, 37, 42, 46, 104, 105, 109, 110–114, 116, 117, 158

invisible (invisibility), 5, 14, 45, 55, 63, 65, 66, 73, 76, 77, 95, 183, 192, 212, 214, 217, 219, 227, 235
Inwood, Brad, 163n31
Irigaray, Luce, 16, 23n11
irreversibility, 214, 219, 225, 228
Isaiah, 178
Islam, 7, 231
isostheneia, 168
Israel: preexilic, 7, 211; prophetic revolution of, 225; state of, 183
Isaacs, Marie, 23n9

Jackson, Darrell B., 227n16
Jankélévitch, Vladimir, 7, 196, 208, 209nn1,9
Jerusalem, 128–130, 139–142, 212
Jesus, 180, 189, 190
Jew (Jewish), 1, 3, 7, 22, 73, 178–182, 184–186, 194, 210, 211, 212, 215, 225, 229, 235
Jones, John D., 226n1
Joshua (Rabbi), 179, 184, 185
jouissance, 4, 48, 56, 57, 59
Joyce, James, 226n6, 229n30
Judaism (Judaic), 2, 100, 128, 183, 186, 215, 225, 231, 233
justice, 2, 6, 36, 37, 47, 54–56, 63, 65, 69, 71, 72, 77, 78n10, 83, 101n18, 104, 136, 137, 140, 142, 155, 182, 233

Kafka, Franz, 235
kairos, 182
Kant, Immanuel (Kantian), 6, 10, 68, 72, 99, 104, 131, 142n7, 240
kataleptic impressions (*katalēpseis*), 163n28
kath'auto, 45, 46, 94
kathēkonta, 151, 152, 161n5, 163n33
Kearney, Richard, 23n13, 59, 61nn18,19
Kierkegaard, Søren (Kierkegaardian), 60n8, 166
klēseis (the called), 181, 184
klēsis (call), 181, 186, 187
knowledge, 5, 11, 30, 32, 36, 43, 44, 51, 52, 63, 67, 68, 73, 76, 78, 80, 81, 83, 84, 86, 88, 90, 91, 93, 94, 100, 103–111, 113–117, 120, 122, 125n14, 132, 133, 144, 148, 165–167, 169, 191, 199, 209, 212–214, 216, 219, 220, 224, 227, 232
koinē, 180
kosmos, 6, 108, 144, 146, 157, 158, 160, 161nn11,12, 162n13

Labarrière, Pierre-Jean, 203, 209nn7,8
lack, 4, 25, 29, 30, 33, 38n1, 39n12, 41, 47, 48, 50–52, 55, 56, 59, 65–68, 109, 110, 118, 138, 160n1, 197, 200, 201, 205, 208, 212, 216, 220–223

language, 2, 3, 6, 32, 43, 48, 74, 76, 84–87,
    90–98, 122, 146, 157, 160, 162n19, 187,
    190–193, 227n6
law, 30, 61n14, 65, 141, 142, 184
Leibniz, Gottfried, 220
Leroi-Gourhan, André, 85
light, 12, 32, 63, 66, 68, 82, 109, 100, 116, 121,
    183, 184, 207, 216, 217
listening eye, 3, 228n24
logos, xii, 2, 42, 59, 61, 63, 74, 105–107, 109,
    111, 113, 114, 116, 117, 119, 122–124,
    146, 149, 160, 165, 191, 227n6
Long, Christopher, 8, 124n1
love, xi, 17, 23–38, 48, 50–52, 62, 67, 87, 99,
    129–130, 137, 139, 142–143, 151–154,
    163, 190, 197, 200, 203, 219
Lukacher, Ned, 226n2
lust, 238, 239
Luther, Martin, 181

madness, 26, 70, 77, 89, 97
male (masculine), 24–27, 30, 34, 36, 215
Mantineia, 25
Marcus Aurelius, 154, 155, 163n40
materialism, historical, 186
materiality, 4, 12–16, 20–22, 121, 187
maternal, 20, 22
maternity, 75
Mattéi, Jean-François, 8, 59, 60nn1,9, 61n17
matter (*hule*), 13–18, 21, 24–26, 36, 38n3, 121,
    125, 126, 218, 220–224, 228nn26,27, 235
McEvilley, Thomas, 229n31
me voici, 170, 176n10
measure, 10, 55, 202, 216
meontological difference, 229n31
messiah, 178, 180, 182–187, 189, 190, 193, 194
messianic: era, 178, 186; language, 191; principle,
    180; texts, 6, 183; time, 188, 189,
    192–194
messianism, 178–194; apocalyptic, 178, 182;
    Levinas and, 179, 193, 194; restorative,
    178; weak, 186
metaphysics, 2, 7, 22, 31, 43, 101, 104, 118, 132,
    143n14, 145, 148, 161, 210, 215–217,
    220, 225, 226n6, 227n7
Metrodorus (of Chios), 176n10
Miller, Clyde Lee, 227n10
multiplicity, 11, 54, 82, 113, 139, 214, 217
mysticism (mystical), 10, 178, 191, 216, 217,
    222, 225, 227n14, 236
myth (*muthos*), 62–64, 67, 72, 74, 75

Nachman (Rabbi), 185
Nagel, Thomas, 142n2, 143n11
naked (nakedness), 5, 11, 20, 46, 62, 63, 72, 74,
    83, 93, 116, 138
Narbonne, Jean-Marc, 8

nature, 3–5, 12, 13, 16, 18, 21, 22, 29, 238; in
    Aristotle, 105, 106, 119, 121, 132; in
    Pyrrhonism, 172; in Stoicism, 146, 150,
    153, 154, 161n9, 163nn28,30
necessity, 108, 110, 112, 132, 146, 185, 189, 198,
    214, 221, 235, 239
need, 4, 16, 17, 20, 24, 25, 28–31, 33, 38n2, 41,
    42, 45, 47, 48, 51–57, 59, 65, 67, 75–78,
    90, 99, 100, 114, 131–138, 140–142, 153,
    197, 200, 201, 205, 206, 208, 212, 213,
    216, 220, 221, 227
negative dogmatism, 166, 169, 172
negative theology, 226n1
Nemo, Philippe, 62
Neoplatonism, 7, 23n8, 120, 209, 210, 216, 217,
    219, 220, 226, 227, 229, 231, 233
New Testament, 178
New Thinking, the, 179
new, 24, 34–36, 38
Nietzsche, Friedrich, 10, 13, 23n1, 97, 136, 166,
    173, 181, 220, 226n2, 228n24, 231, 234,
    237, 240, 241
nihilism, 207
nominal phrase, 189–191
nonbeing (non-being), 11, 20, 37, 59, 83, 198,
    201, 220, 222, 223
non-integratable, 223
nothingness, 11, 44, 162n20, 208, 222, 237,
    239–241; will to, 239, 240
nous, 35, 37, 104–107, 109, 110, 113, 115–125,
    146, 161nn8,11,12, 198, 215, 216, 218
nudity, 46, 60n7, 100

O'Brien, Elmer, 228nn17,27
Odysseus, 211–213
oikeiōsis, 150, 151, 153, 161n5, 163n27
Old Testament, 178
One, the (*to hen*), 7, 10, 59, 83, 139, 148,
    197–201, 203–219, 221, 222, 224, 226,
    227nn6,10,12, 228nn10,28
ontology, 4, 7, 10, 21, 30, 31, 40–42, 56, 59, 61,
    82, 83, 87, 101, 103, 106, 124nn1,2,
    128–130, 135–140, 142–145, 147–149,
    156, 157, 159, 162, 181, 189, 210, 220,
    226
open responsiveness, 4, 25
operational time (Guillaume), 192–194
opposites, 2, 28, 231
oral discourse, 43
Oreithyia, 26
orgasm, 238
other: absolutely or wholly, 4, 24, 34, 35, 48, 53,
    56, 59, 138, 202, 204, 206, 208, 212, 213,
    216–219, 223, 224, 226, 227nn6,12; the,
    24, 25, 31–33, 104, 125n12, 127–128,
    130, 132, 135–143
ousia, 121, 131–132, 197, 218

Index

pagan, 13, 15, 230, 237
paideia, 77n7
Pappas, Nickolas, 78n13
Parmenides (of Elea), 10, 11, 196, 227n7
participation (*methexis*), 53, 54, 56, 64, 75, 99n5, 146, 158, 199, 200, 218, 222
Pascal, Blaise, 97
Pasqua, Herve, 226n1
passivity, 19, 33, 38n3, 188, 189, 191, 193, 216, 224, 230, 231, 234–237
pathos, 110, 150, 160n1, 162n24, 163n26
Paul (Pauline), 6, 7, 178–194, 231, 232, 238
Paul, David, 84, 100
Pausanias (Pausanian), 26–28
peace, 10, 29, 53, 127–142, 182, 183, 210; pre-political, 6; political, 129, 135–136
Peloponnesian War, 25
Peperzak, Adriaan, 50, 60n6, 78n9, 140, 165, 176n3
periphrasis, 182
Perl, Eric D., 227n12
Phaedrus, 26, 27, 29
phenomenology (phenomenological), 1, 3, 5, 78, 82, 97, 136, 144, 159, 174, 175, 182, 183, 187, 188, 215, 217
Philo, 39n12, 178
phonocentrism, 5, 81, 90
Photius, 167
phronesis, 116, 125n9, 134
phusis, xii, 12, 108, 119, 124, 125nn7,8, 146, 150
Plato (Platonic, Platonism, Platonist), xi, 4, 5, 7–10, 15–17, 20, 22, 23n8, 24, 26, 31, 33, 36, 38–74, 77–101, 104, 125n7, 147, 148, 161, 167, 197, 202, 209, 210, 215, 216, 218, 226n1, 227nn6,16, 237; works: *Gorgias,* 5, 26, 27, 37, 62, 63, 69, 70, 72–78, 83, 86, 93; *Parmenides,* 83, 215, 227n16; *Phaedo,* 39n7, 82, 88; *Phaedrus,* 5, 26, 35, 42, 43, 45, 55–57, 80–85, 87–91, 93–98, 100nn8,10,11, 101n18, 202; *Republic,* 25, 26, 36, 37, 41, 46, 51, 55, 63, 65, 69, 71, 77, 78, 82, 83, 87, 100, 101, 125, 147, 197, 215; *Sophist,* 41, 42, 59, 77, 101, 125, 220; *Symposium,* 24–31, 35, 48, 50, 51, 63, 83, 87; *Theaetetus,* 10, 54, 55; *Timaeus,* 24, 25, 36, 83
pleasure, 18, 29, 47, 52, 100, 161, 164
Plotinus (Plotinian), 4, 7, 83, 196–229
pneuma, 13–16, 19–22, 23n8
poetry, 30, 84, 86, 87, 96
poiesis, 12
polemos, 10
politics (political), 2, 6, 73, 78, 123, 125, 127–130, 133–136, 139–142, 152, 159–161, 178, 183, 184, 213, 217
poros and *penia,* 25, 26, 28, 29, 48, 51
Posidonius, 145, 161n10

possession, 18, 48, 49, 51, 88, 156, 197, 213; by a god, 132; by the One, 203, 204; divine, 202; of the same, 202, 203, 208, 217, 222
potential, 24
potentiality, 122, 125n16, 130–32, 192; and actuality, 120, 121, 133
power, 25, 28, 29, 32, 34–36, 47, 53, 65, 67, 70, 104, 109, 111, 117, 118, 122, 131, 134, 136, 141, 146, 150, 151, 154, 157, 161, 162, 172, 185, 186, 188, 200, 203, 214, 216
praxis, 46, 116, 183, 205, 212
predestination, 231, 232–237, 239, 241
pregnancy, 25, 30, 39n5, 75, 76
pre-originary, 7, 210
pre-primordial, 7, 230, 233, 236, 237, 241
Presocratic, 2, 4, 9–12, 18–22, 23n2, 227n13
pride, 238
privation, 208, 211, 220, 221–225, 233, 238
Protagoras, 54, 55
Proust, Marcel, 235
proximity, 3–8, 10, 20–23, 70, 71, 74, 81, 91, 93, 120, 139, 170, 196, 201, 202, 204, 208, 211, 213, 217, 219, 220, 226
psuche (psyche), 13–16, 19, 20, 68–70
psychism, 4, 16–22, 31, 34, 125, 212, 218
psychology (psychological), 14, 15, 66, 71, 120, 125n11, 134, 137, 161n7, 229n31, 238
Putnam, Hilary, 176n4
Pyrrho of Elis, 167, 175, 176
pyrrhonism, 6, 165, 167, 169–172, 174, 176

qoheleth, 182
quietism, 181, 183

rape, 26, 27
reason, 35, 45, 47, 49, 83, 88, 98, 106, 115, 118, 119, 122, 123, 128–132, 136, 137, 141, 146, 148, 149, 152, 160, 160n1, 161nn8,11, 165, 176n4, 190, 205, 216, 220, 224
recollection, 35, 47, 49, 50, 52, 56, 58
redemption, 178, 179, 183, 184, 232; in Benjamin (*Erlösung*), 186
religion, 2, 22, 97, 128, 180, 212, 215
remnant, 188
repetition, 40, 60n8, 186
responsibility, 2, 5, 7, 19, 53, 63, 64, 66, 69, 71, 74, 75, 77, 130, 137–141, 144–146, 150, 152–154, 156–160, 162, 181, 183–185, 190, 212, 214, 216, 223, 232–236, 240, 241
responsiveness, 4, 21, 25, 38, 110, 121
resurrection, 180, 185, 186, 193
return, 2, 24, 33, 213; to Platonism, xi, 40, 41, 45, 47, 60, 215; to a home, 178; to first things, 95; to Intellect, 203; to the One,

213, 220, 227n10; to origin, 211, 222, 226; to the self, 30, 31, 47–49, 52, 87, 90, 99
revelation, 32, 58, 66, 89, 95, 98, 101, 128, 129, 149, 214
rhetoric, 9, 83, 86, 101, 137, 146, 180
Rist, John M., 228nn22,26
Robin, Léon, 100
Romans (Letter to), 179
Rosenzweig, Franz, 191
Ross, W. D., 125n13
Russian Realists, 63

Sachs, D., 77n3
sacrifice, 175, 235, 240
Sallis, John, 78n9, 226n1
same, the, 7, 19, 30, 31, 36, 41, 42, 45–48, 50, 53, 55–60, 75, 77, 82, 83, 98, 101n15, 104, 119, 120, 131, 136, 139, 142n1, 144, 147, 156, 188, 190, 196–209, 211–218, 220, 222, 223, 226, 227n6, 228nn20,28,31, 240
Sanford, Stella, 8, 60nn2,6
Sartre, Jean-Paul, 240
savage, 26
Scholem, Gershom, 7, 195n9
Schroeder, Brian, 77n7
Schroeder, F. M., 228n16
Schürmann, Reiner, 198, 206, 209n3, 227n7
secularization, 186
seeing (sight), 48, 64, 66, 110, 204, 205, 207, 218; un-, 55
self, 24, 30, 31, 33, 34; without self, 203–206
self-same, 43, 47, 53, 56, 59, 120, 213
self-sufficiency, 12, 24, 25, 29, 30, 32, 48, 53, 55–57, 65, 67, 104, 108, 118, 132, 133
Seneca, 154, 155, 163n39
sensation, 54, 106, 109–113, 115–118, 121, 124n6, 147, 153, 189
sensibility, 5, 17–19, 21, 22, 32, 68, 103–105, 109, 110, 115, 117, 120, 160, 189, 193, 194
separation, 12, 13, 16–19, 28, 31, 36–38, 44, 47, 53–55, 58, 62, 64, 66, 68, 75, 98, 104, 120, 123, 125, 157, 198–200, 213, 214, 216–218
Septuagint, 182
sex, 27, 28, 133, 238, 239
Sextus Empiricus, 4, 161n6, 167–169, 171, 176
Sha'ul, 180
Shakespeare, 63
sick, 29, 70, 72, 153
sin, 223, 232, 235–241
singularity, 34, 36, 38, 68, 82, 135
skepticism, 165, 175, 176n10, 192, 193; Pyrrhonian, 6, 166–171, 173
skin, 20, 62, 69, 72–76, 188

slave (enslaved, slavery, slavish), 28, 35, 52, 135, 142, 143, 180, 181, 183, 232, 238, 239
sober, 26, 28
sociality, 31, 158, 217–219, 222
Socrates, 4, 24–30, 31–38, 39n7, 42–45, 47, 52, 54, 55, 60n8, 65, 69–73, 75, 82–90, 92, 93, 95–97, 100nn10,15, 144, 145, 154, 161nn2,3, 167, 170
soft, 26, 27
Solomon, 182
sophia, 118, 120
sophrosune, 8
soul, 4, 5, 13–17, 20–22, 33, 35, 48–50, 53–56, 59, 61, 62, 70–76, 78n12, 82, 86, 88, 90, 98, 101, 111–113, 119, 121, 123, 129, 132, 134, 141, 145–146, 148–151, 153, 162, 199, 200, 202–203, 207, 211, 213, 216–219, 221, 222, 228, 238
Sparta, 25
speech, 2, 5, 42, 60n4, 64, 66, 67, 74, 77, 80, 81, 84–87, 89–98, 100, 137, 158, 160, 189, 218, 219, 227
Spinoza, Baruch, 99, 196, 234, 236
Spirit, 4, 13–16, 21, 22, 50, 159, 183, 214, 228n28, 231, 238
spiritual (spirituality), 4, 13–18, 20–22, 54, 88, 136, 159, 211
Stamatellos, Giannis, 227n13
State, the, 2, 6, 70, 128, 133–135, 141–142; of Israel, 183
Stoic (stoicism), 6, 13, 15, 23n8, 144–163, 167
stranger, 24, 33, 41, 47, 59, 78, 95, 202, 204, 212
subject, the, 7, 10, 20, 34, 193, 212, 223, 233–235, 240; outside, 122, 212
subjectivity, 11–14, 21, 33, 34, 43, 101, 137, 139, 143, 187, 193, 214, 237; Abrahamic, 212; ethical, 12, 13, 21; modern, 171, 174, 177
substitution, 7, 19, 190
supplement, 183
surpassing, 37, 158, 203
surplus, 10, 32, 41, 43, 52, 58, 144, 156

Talmud, 83, 184, 215
Taminiaux, Jacques, 60n6
Tannaïm, 184
Taubes, Jacob, 179, 181, 194n1
techne (*tekhne*), 12, 51, 121, 125n14
telos, 129, 131, 151, 162, 212, 216
temporality, 6, 179, 181, 188, 192, 194
tense (tension), 28, 29
tensor, 182
Thales, 11
Theiler, Willy, 125n11
theology, 22, 94, 101, 120, 125, 146, 210, 215, 226, 231, 232
Theophrastus, 13, 23n3
theoria (*theorein*), 67, 110, 132

third, the, 74, 78n11, 155, 167, 219, 220
this, 37
time-image (Guillaume), 192
tode ti, 131
totality, 6, 10, 16, 18, 31–34, 41, 43, 44, 54,
    61n14, 63, 68, 87, 99, 104, 139, 144,
    147–149, 156, 196–200, 203–205, 208,
    209, 213, 215, 216, 222, 224, 229, 234,
    236
trace, 3, 7, 23, 61n15, 76, 94, 123, 182, 184, 211,
    213–215, 217–219, 223–225, 228n21
tragedy (tragic), 25, 29, 30, 228n27
transcategorial, 25, 36, 37
transcendence, 103, 104, 115, 120, 122, 123, 125,
    128, 138–141, 143, 156, 175, 177,
    196–198, 202, 211, 215–220, 222–226,
    228, 229
truth, 10, 43, 44, 49, 50, 54, 56, 57, 59, 61, 66,
    74, 78, 83, 85–88, 98, 100, 101, 113, 114,
    119–124, 128, 129, 137, 162, 163,
    166–168, 183, 214, 218

ugliness, 29, 46, 72
unity, 10, 11, 28, 31, 41, 76, 82, 117, 120, 135,
    139, 145, 151, 152, 188, 205, 210, 213,
    214, 216, 219, 220, 222
universal (universality), 2, 30, 38, 43, 99n5,
    130–133, 135, 136, 138, 139, 147, 157,
    159, 181, 236; face, 240; myth, 225; Soul,
    199, 200

universalism, 183–185
universals, 109–117, 124nn5,6, 139, 141,
    146–149, 162n17
upsurge, 24, 33; absolute, 24, 25, 35

Verbeke, Gerard, 23n9
victim, 71, 137, 240, 241
violence, 7, 33, 52, 53, 62, 101n18, 140, 141,
    172–174, 210, 211, 213, 216, 222
virtue, 27–29, 36, 42, 45, 87, 116–118, 123,
    125n9, 131–134, 138–139, 142, 144, 150,
    151, 155, 161n4, 162n23, 173, 221
vision, 45, 67, 74, 107, 118, 201, 204–207, 211,
    218, 224
vulnerable (vulnerability), 4, 21, 24–26, 28–32,
    38, 44, 62, 63, 75, 76

war, 6, 10, 61n14, 127–131, 133–137, 141–143,
    186
Weber, Max, 181–183
what, 37; versus who, 43
wholeness, 29, 30
will to power, 231, 234, 237
will, the, 33, 152, 213, 231, 232, 234, 235,
    237–240; willing, 28
woman, 2, 25, 27, 39n5
writing, 5, 6, 77n4, 80, 81, 84–98, 100

Zeno (of Citium), 150, 152, 161n3, 162n14, 167
Zeus, 72, 146